Although he regards himself primarily as a teacher of labor relations subjects, HAROLD W. DAVEY has been actively engaged in arbitration of union-management disputes since 1944 on a national basis. His extensive practical experience as an arbitrator contributes to the currency and authenticity of **Contemporary Collective Bargaining**. Davey has taught at Iowa State University of Science and Technology since 1948. His University honored him with an award as an "Outstanding Teacher" in 1970. Davey is a past president of the Midwest Economics Association and has been a member of the National Academy of Arbitrators since 1953. He has written numerous journal articles on the arbitration process and hopes to write a book on arbitration in the near future. The Iowa State University Library is making a special collection of Professor Davey's arbitration cases (approximately one thousand decisions).

Professor Davey is a **summa cum laude** graduate of Syracuse University. He received his Master's and Ph.D. degrees from Harvard University. He worked for the National War Labor Board, 1942-45, and taught at Illinois Institute of Technology and New York University before coming to Iowa State.

CONTEMPORARY

contemporary collective bargaining

HAROLD W. DAVEY

Iowa State University

THIRD EDITION

COLLECTIVE

BARGAINING

PRENTICE-HALL, INC., Englewood Cliffs, New Jersey

HAROLD W. DAVEY

contemporary collective bargaining

Third Edition

13-169607-6

Library of Congress Catalog Card Number: 74-152315

Printed in the United States of America

Current printing (last digit):
10   9   8   7   6   5   4   3   2   1

PRENTICE-HALL INTERNATIONAL, INC., *London*
PRENTICE-HALL OF AUSTRALIA, PTY. LTD., *Sydney*
PRENTICE-HALL OF CANADA, LTD., *Toronto*
PRENTICE-HALL OF INDIA PRIVATE LIMITED, *New Delhi*
PRENTICE-HALL OF JAPAN, INC., *Tokyo*

To

SEAN WILLIAM DAVEY and SHANNON ELIZABETH DAVEY
who may enjoy this book some years hence.

PREFACE

This is more a new book than a revision. Each chapter was written on a *de novo* basis. Although this approach resulted in a better quality product, it added considerably to the length of the gestation period.

The newness of the book can be illustrated in many ways. As one example, Chapter 13 on public sector labor relations is one of its lengthier chapters. Bargaining by government employees had not attained sufficient importance to merit attention in the second edition. Another example is the extensive discussion in Chapter 11 of the rise, fall and possible resurrection of the wage-price guideposts. This controversial public policy instrument was not "invented" until 1962. The table of contents indicates the treatment of many other new problem areas, including the adaptation of collective bargaining to the employment of disadvantaged persons, the special bargaining problems of teachers and nurses, novel approaches to the perennial challenge of job security and so on.

Collective bargaining as a process has been under intense critical fire for some time. Such criticism is mainly responsible for the adoption of a challenge-response theme in this edition. Particular attention is paid to the needs, achievements and failings of management and union practitioners of bargaining.

Few problem areas in collective bargaining yield final solutions. The most critical issues in labor relations are necessarily controversial. The field has an ample supply of conflicting value judgments as to appropriate policies. I have sought to treat each problem in a detached, objective way, distinguishing between hard evidence and opinion. At the same time I have felt free (in fact, obligated) to state my policy stance on controversial matters.

No single book can do justice to the rich variety and complexity of the collective bargaining scene. The chapter bibliographies have been thoroughly revised and updated. They should be of value to the reader who seeks more detailed analysis of particular problem areas.

As a writer I have always been what is termed "a loner." Therefore, I am solely responsible for any errors or shortcomings in the analysis. I am nevertheless indebted to many individuals for invaluable assistance.

My special thanks go to Professor Thomas J. McDermott, Professor of Economics, Duquesne University, Pittsburgh, Pennsylvania who reviewed the entire manuscript with painstaking care and critical candor. His pointed comments have served to improve both content and readability at many points. Words are imperfect instruments to express my debt to Tom McDermott for cheerfully performing this burdensome task.

An important obligation is acknowledged again to management and union representatives encountered in my grievance arbitration work. They have improved my understanding of important aspects of collective bargaining. I wish to thank in particular Robert S. Wolff, vice-president of industrial relations for the Louis Allis Company, for reviewing several chapters and contributing valuable comments.

I wish to thank also a number of colleagues and graduate students at Iowa State. Among those who helped me over some rough spots at various stages are Gary Abbott, Earl Baderschneider, Eugene A. Brady, Lou Cimmino, Randyl Elkin, David L. Maiers, and Jim Schepker. Once again Mrs. Gladys W. Gruenberg of St. Louis University gave me some valuable critical suggestions, as did James A. Socknat of the Ford Foundation.

My warm thanks are due for the third time to my wife, Mary, for putting up with the frustrations and difficulties associated with authorship on a moonlighting basis. I am also grateful beyond words to my arbitration secretary, Mrs. Dorothy B. Rust, for her invaluable cheerful cooperation in typing several drafts of the manuscript. For additional secretarial aid I indebted in particular to Mrs. Lynn Zwagerman and to Mrs. Charlene Carsrud, Mrs. Ellen Reynolds and Mrs. Vivian Trebbien.

Ames, Iowa   HAROLD W. DAVEY

CONTENTS

3 THE PUBLIC POLICY FRAMEWORK FOR COLLECTIVE BARGAINING   **51**

4 ALTERNATIVE VIEWS OF COLLECTIVE BARGAINING AS A PROCESS:
SOME OBSERVATIONS ON BARGAINING POWER THEORY
AND THE MANAGEMENT RIGHTS CONTROVERSY   **88**

summary form, 108; Limited government, administrative initiative and consultation, 110; Negotiation, consultation and joint study committees, 112.

5 CONTRACT NEGOTIATION: PRINCIPLES, PROBLEMS AND PROCEDURES   116

Procedural challenges in contract negotiation, 117; Achieving greater professionalism in collective bargaining, 118; Technical preparation for bargaining, 119; Management preparation for bargaining, 120; Union preparation for bargaining, 122; Internal pressures on union leadership in negotiation, 123; Internal pressures in 1967 bargaining: an illustration, 124; Experimentation in joint preparation for bargaining, 126; The prenegotiation conference, 127; Contract negotiation procedures, 128; Economic package bargaining, 130; The atmosphere of negotiation, 131; Personal requisites for negotiation, 133; Are negotiators improving their performance?, 134; Continuing problem areas for negotiators, 135; Coping with contract rejections, 136; The lengthy contract problem, 137; The problem of deleting outmoded provisions, 138; Special problems in first contract negotiations, 139; Conclusion, 140.

6 CONTRACT ADMINISTRATION: GRIEVANCE PROCEDURES   141

Management initiative in contract administration, 142; Defining the scope of the grievance procedure, 143; Combining the clinical and contractual approaches to grievance adjustment, 144; Basic principles of grievance adjustment, 146; The politics of grievance adjustment and "fair representation," 149; Improved procedures for effectuating contractual policies, 150; Promotional procedures, 151; Disciplinary action procedures, 151; A note on management grievances, 152; Penalties for failure to use contract grievance procedures, 153; A suggested solution to the wildcat strike problem, 155; Conclusion, 156.

7 GRIEVANCE ARBITRATION: PRINCIPLES AND PROCEDURES   158

An arbitration balance sheet, 159; Representative issues in grievance arbitration, 161; Proper phrasing of the arbitrable issue, 164; The grievance arbitrator and his function, 164; Strict versus liberal constructionists, 166; Judicial and problem-solving approaches: a comparison, 169; The federal judiciary and grievance arbitration, 170; Some continuing procedural problems in arbitration, 173; *Ad hoc* or permanent arbitrator machinery?, 173; Single arbitrator or tripartite board?, 175; Related problems of excessive arbitration, cost of arbitration and "brinkmanship," 176; The dangers in excessive arbitration, 177; The costs of grievance arbitration, 178; The "brinkmanship" problem as a threat to the arbitration process, 179; The supply of grievance arbitrators, 179; Restructuring of *ad hoc* grievance procedures, 182; Arbitration hearing "time-savers," 184; The expendability of transcripts and court reporters, 185; How can the arbitrator improve the arbitration process?, 187; The potential uses of "instant" arbitration, 187; Conclusion, 188.

11   Collective Bargaining and National Economic Policy   290

12   Negotiated Economic Security Packages and Other "Fringes"   316

COLLECTIVE BARGAINING TODAY
challenges and responses

CHAPTER ONE

Collective Bargaining and Its Critics

Collective bargaining is always under intense critical fire. This is as it should be for an institutional process whose practitioners are essentially pragmatic and opportunistic. Those engaged in collective bargaining think necessarily in terms of the short run, in nonideological terms and in a micro-economic frame of reference. Under these circumstances, it is natural for criticism to be continuous and varied in its nature. A pragmatic approach invariably disappoints the perfectionists.

Some critics contend that collective bargaining has not proved to be sufficiently adaptive and flexible to meet the needs of a dynamic economy. Others urge that in our present state of interdependence we cannot continue to tolerate a process that relies on economic force as the ultimate means of

1

producing agreement. It is also argued that collective bargaining, as traditionally practiced, cannot meet the requirements of the newer groups seeking
representation through unions, that is, such professionals as teachers and
nurses and government employees at all levels.

Also heard is the familiar refrain that collective bargaining has
proved unions are "too strong" and need further curbing through revised
antitrust legislation or some other form of public policy restraint. At the
same time we hear the voices of those who were crusading liberals in the
1930s. They deplore the allegedly narrow focus of bargaining today and
condemn the process for failure to meet the "real" problems of today's
economy[1].

The intensity and variety of recent criticism prompted me to adopt
the *framework of challenge and response* as the analytical spinal cord of this book.
We therefore begin with an inventory of the main challenges to management
and union practitioners of collective bargaining. Some challenges are comparatively new whereas others are of a continuing nature. Some suggest
problems likely to be encountered at the collective bargaining table in the
foreseeable future. The challenges are set forth in outline form. Analysis of
actual or possible responses will be found in the appropriate substantive
chapters.

The meaning and importance of these challenges to collective bargaining will be facilitated if we first define and describe collective bargaining
as a process.

WHAT IS COLLECTIVE BARGAINING?

A complex institutional process like collective bargaining is not
easily defined meaningfully in a single sentence, although custom appears to
demand an attempt. In our analysis collective bargaining is defined as a
continuing institutional relationship between an employer entity (governmental or private) and a labor organization (union or association) representing exclusively a defined group of employees of said employer (appropriate
bargaining unit) concerned with the negotiation, administration, interpretation and enforcement of written agreements covering joint understandings
as to wages or salaries, rates of pay, hours of work and other conditions of
employment.

The academic amenities having been satisfied by this one-sentence

---

[1] For a detailed rebuttal of the principal criticisms of collective bargaining as a
process, see Harold W. Davey, "The Continuing Viability of Collective Bargaining," *Labor
Law Journal*, XVI (February, 1965) 111–22. In the same vein, see Roger W. Walker, "Collective Bargaining and Its Critics: A Look at Some Selected Mythology," *Business Perspectives*,
V (Spring, 1969) 19–22.

definition, some elaboration is desirable in the interests of clarity. Of major importance is the fact that the collective bargaining relationship between employer and union is *a continuous one*, involving contract administration as well as contract negotiation.

Descriptions of collective bargaining that stress strategy and bluffing unfortunately convey the idea that negotiation of contracts is all there is to the process. Laymen envisage shirt-sleeved men in a smoke-filled room at midnight with a strike deadline staring them in the face. Such a melodramatic picture is, of course, a true one in particular cases at particular points in time. Yet it is never accurate as a portrayal of the *totality of the bargaining relationship*. Contract negotiation is vitally important but it is never the whole story.

When employer and union negotiate a contract, they are reaching a joint understanding on a written statement of policies and procedures under which they must live together for one to three years (perhaps longer in some cases). It is the process of *living together under the agreement* that gives meaning and significance to the written instrument. Experience in contract administration is the crucial factor in determining whether the collective bargaining relationship will be a constructive one. As Neil Chamberlain and the late Harry Shulman stressed in 1949, the negotiation of a contract is to labor relations what the wedding ceremony is to domestic relations. In their view, ". . . the heart of the collective agreement—indeed, of collective bargaining —is the process for continuous joint consideration and adjustment of plant problems."[2]

The term "collective bargaining" was reputedly coined by Sidney and Beatrice Webb, the famed historians of the British labor movement.[3] It was first given currency in the United States by Samuel Gompers and has long been an accepted phrase in our labor relations vocabulary. It has proved to be a useful shorthand term for describing a continuous, dynamic, institutional process for solving problems arising directly out of the employer-employee relationship.

Our definition of collective bargaining is deliberately elastic to cover the complete range of organized or institutional relationships between unions and employers. Although collective bargaining is a system or process of a *continuous* nature, it is customary and helpful to distinguish *negotiation* of contracts (the "legislative" phase of the union-employer relationship), *administration* of contracts (the "executive" phase) and *interpretation* or *application* of contracts (the "judicial" phase).

---

[2] Harry W. Shulman and Neil W. Chamberlain, *Cases on Labor Relations* (Brooklyn, N.Y.: The Foundation Press, Inc., 1949), p. 3.
[3] See Vernon H. Jensen, "Notes on the Beginnings of Collective Bargaining," *Industrial and Labor Relations Review*, IX (January, 1956), 225–34.

Some fundamental differences exist between the legislative phase and the executive and judicial phases. In contract negotiation the parties are creating an instrument to govern their relationship for a period of one to three years. If relations are to be stable and constructive, the legislative instrument (contract) must preclude the possibility of continuous bargaining for changes in its terms. Such "legislating" should be confined to specified contract negotiation periods, although the parties by mutual consent can modify an unworkable provision or meet an unanticipated problem through a "memorandom of understanding." The importance attached by the parties to the "statutory" nature of their negotiated agreement is often underlined by inclusion of a so-called "waiver" article, such as the provision cited below from the 1967–1970 John Deere-UAW contract:

> The parties acknowledge that during negotiations, which resulted in this Agreement, each had the unlimited right and opportunity to make demands and proposals with respect to any subject or matter not removed by law from the area of collective bargaining, and that the Understandings and Agreements arrived at by the parties after the exercise of that right and opportunity are set forth in this Agreement. Therefore, the Company and the Union, for the life of this Agreement, each voluntarily and unqualifiedly waives the right, and each agrees that the other shall not be obligated, to bargain collectively with respect to any subject or matter referred to or covered in this Agreement, or with respect to any subject or matter not specifically referred to or covered in this Agreement, even though such subjects or matters may not have been within the knowledge or contemplation of either or both of the parties at the time that they negotiated or signed this Agreement.[4]

Too rigid a separation between negotiation and administration can obscure the continuous nature of the organized relationship between the parties to the contract. A waiver article should not be a bar to vitally necessary change during a contract's span of life where both parties recognize the necessity for prompt action.

The Parties in Collective Bargaining

The chief participants in collective bargaining do not act for themselves. They are representatives of their respective institutions, the workers organized into a trade union and the collective entity of the corporation or business firm. Collective bargaining is always representative on the employees' side. The interests of nonsupervisory employees are represented to

---

[4] I served as permanent arbitrator under Deere-UAW contracts between 1952 and 1958. I have used Deere-UAW agreements over the years as teaching instruments at Iowa State because they are well-written and because their subject matter coverage is representative of agreements between manufacturing corporations and industrial unions.

employers by an institutional hierarchy ranging from shop stewards, committeemen and local union officers to the top officers and staff personnel of the national union. The bargaining is thus clearly "collective" on the union side. Union X is the *exclusive bargaining representative* of *all* employees in a defined unit for purposes of negotiating with their employer with respect to wages, hours and other terms or conditions of employment. The representative standing of Union X is frequently based on certification by the National Labor Relations Board after having won a secret ballot election conducted by an NLRB field examiner.

In most cases, bargaining is also "collective" on the employer's side. Those who negotiate and administer contracts for the corporate employer are acting in a representative capacity. Although there are still owner-managers who speak for themselves in collective bargaining, the corporation is the dominant form of business organization in the American economy. In any corporate enterprise, professional managers handle the employer's interests in labor relations. The managers of the enterprise speak in the name of the directors. The latter in turn represent the legal owners, the stockholders. The representative nature of the process on both sides of the bargaining table is most apparent in what is usually called multi-employer bargaining. In such a bargaining structure it is customary for an employers' labor relations association to speak for the member employers in negotiating with one or more unions representing the combined employees of the associated employers.

For these reasons collective bargaining typically involves organized group relationships rather than individual dealings between principals. It is an institutionalized representative process. The contract or agreement sets forth the procedures whereby the continuing relationship between management and union is carried forward.

Certain differences between the union as an institution and the corporation as an institution play an important role in shaping the nature and direction of the bargaining process and the respective goals of the parties.[5] Arthur M. Ross observed in 1948 that the trade union is a political agency operating in an economic environment.[6] This deceptively simple

---

[5] For informed, general analyses of contemporary unionism, see Jack Barbash, *American Unions: Structure, Government and Politics* (New York: Random House, Inc., 1967) and Martin Estey, *The Unions: Structure, Development and Management* (New York: Harcourt, Brace & World, Inc., 1967). For analysis of the corporation as an institution, see Earl F. Cheit, ed., *The Business Establishment* (New York: John Wiley & Sons, Inc., 1964). See also Edward S. Mason, ed., *The Corporation in Modern Society* (Cambridge, Mass.: Harvard University Press, 1959), particularly Chapter 7 on "The Corporation and the Trade Union" by Neil W. Chamberlain.

[6] Arthur M. Ross, *Trade Union Wage Policy* (Berkeley, Cal.: University of California Press, 1948), *passim*. The nature of the union as an institution has not changed appreciably since the late Dr. Ross first made his penetrating observations. His treatment remains fresh and directly pertinent for current understanding of why unions do not behave as "rationally" as some might wish. For more extensive development of this theme, see Chapter 10.

characterization emphasizes a fact of life about unions that many employers and students of labor relations still fail to comprehend. *Union leadership is elected at all levels.* Pressure is thus always operating on union leaders to prove that they are *doing something* for the represented employees. The union is in this sense a highly political agency, as is any other service organization whose leadership is elected. The ears of union leaders are constantly subjected to the haunting political refrain of their rank-and-file constituents, "What have you done for us *lately*?"[7]

This basic characteristic of unionism is helpful in explaining why union bargaining demands sometimes appear to be of a blue-sky nature to the detached observer or the cost-conscious employer. There should, however, be comfort in the knowledge that informed union leaders do realize they are operating in an economic environment. They know that the surging aspirations of the rank and file must, in the final analysis, be tempered by economic reality.

In short, the union is a body politic in which authority flows from the bottom up. This causes the dynamics of union policy determination to differ sharply from those of the corporation, where authority flows from the top down. On economic issues, for example, it is comparatively easy for management to formulate its policy in cost terms. The union approach on economic issues is necessarily conditioned by such "political" considerations as rank-and-file aspirations, gains made by other unions and the growth and survival requirements of the union as an institution.[8]

Reconciliation of the economic calculus of the employer with the union's "political" approach is often a difficult task. It serves to make collective bargaining as a process the despair of those "rational" observers who yearn for order and precision in determining the price of labor.

THE SUBJECT MATTER OF COLLECTIVE BARGAINING

In simple terms, collective bargaining covers two basic subject-matter categories: (1) *the price of labor*, broadly defined to include not only wages as such but any other working condition or term of employment involving direct monetary outlays, such as pension plans, group life insurance plans, paid vacations and so forth; (2) *a system of industrial jurisprudence*, that is, policies and procedures governing on-the-job relationships that apply to

---

[7] Joseph W. Garbarino is one of several scholars to note the importance of the "what have you done for me lately?" effect as related to collective bargaining. See his chapter on "The Economic Significance of Automatic Wage Adjustments" in Harold W. Davey, Howard S. Kaltenborn and Stanley H. Ruttenberg, eds., *New Dimensions in Collective Bargaining* (New York: Harper & Row, Publishers, 1959), p. 171ff.

[8] Arthur M. Ross, *op. cit., passim.*

all workers covered by the contract in like fashion in like circumstances. It embraces the vitally important function of collective bargaining in substituting a rule of law in shop relationships for the former arbitrary discretion of supervision.[9]

We can also define the subject matter of collective bargaining by utilizing statutory expressions of coverage as contained in Sections 9(a) and 8(d) of the National Labor Relations Act.

Section 9(a) covers the subject matter of collective bargaining by the now familiar phrase "rates of pay, wages, hours of employment, or other conditions of employment." Section 8(d), the first legislative attempt to define the obligation to bargain in good faith, describes the area covered by the duty to bargain as including "wages, hours, and other terms and conditions of employment. . ."[10]

The differences between 9(a) and 8(d) are not important for our present purpose. Both make clear that from a public policy standpoint the subject matter of collective bargaining remains essentially what it has always been, namely, the price of labor, the hours of work and policies and procedures relating to any phase of the employment relationship. Current contracts that run over 100 printed pages in length are *in essence* similar to the one-page documents negotiated by craft unions with employers in the 1890s. Whether the contract is 1 or 200 pages in length it is still dealing with wages, hours and other terms and conditions of employment. The range, diversity and complexity of issues treated in collective bargaining have expanded, but collective bargaining as a process and the essential nature of its coverage remain generically the same.

The length, complexity and wealth of detail in some recent contracts has prompted some critics to suggest moving toward simplified documents stating general principles. Some of this yearning for simplicity can be related to uncertainty over what are mandatory matters for bargaining under the national labor policy. The NLRB is a storm center in this controversy, as we shall see in Chapter 3. The problem of distinguishing between mandatory and voluntary subjects for bargaining is a difficult one, but it has an encouraging aspect as well. The encouraging factor is that the practi-

---

[9] Sumner H. Slichter, *Union Policies and Industrial Management* (Washington, D.C.: The Brookings Institution, 1941).

[10] Section 8(d) made its appearance as new language in the Taft-Hartley Act of 1947. When to provide footnote citations for statutory provisions can be troublesome. When using the term "National Labor Relations Act," I am generally referring to the federal law as it stands unless otherwise stated. The full statutory citation which embraces the original National Labor Relations Act of 1935 (Wagner Act), the Labor Management Relations Act of 1947 (Taft-Hartley Act) and the Labor Management Reporting and Disclosure Act of 1959 (Landrum-Griffin) is as follows: 49 *Stat.* 449 (1935), as amended by Pub. L. No. 101, 80th Cong., 1st Sess., 1947, and Pub. L. No. 257, 86th Cong., 1st Sess., 1959; 29 U.S.C. Sections 151–68, F. C. A. 29 Sections 151–68.

tioners of bargaining hold to the view that the process should still be principally concerned with bread-and-butter issues and on-the-job conditions. The parties may differ as to whether or not a particular proposal or demand falls under the conventional rubric. They do *not* disagree over the essential nature and purposes of bargaining. Nearly all management and union representatives hold firmly to the view that collective bargaining should be limited to negotiating and administering contracts that cover, in the late J. M. Clark's happily succinct phrase, "wages and human relations on the job."[11]

Are these self-imposed limitations too parochial for the modern age? Management and union leaders have been urged to undertake more imaginative joint efforts beyond their own enterprises. They are asked to address themselves to the social and economic problems of the community in which they operate. An example would be fostering the use of collective bargaining as a vehicle for institutional representation of slum tenants or the hard-core unemployed in urban ghetto areas.[12] We shall not be considering this particular challenge. Nor shall we attempt to evaluate another unusual effort at adaptation of collective bargaining—collective bargaining for farmers.[13] Instead we shall concentrate primarily on collective bargaining as a process to be described and analyzed in terms of the shared "conventional" views of those who participate in the process. In other words, the objective will be to analyze the effectiveness and shortcomings of collective bargaining as a process for determining the terms and conditions of employment. We shall not be primarily concerned with matters that go beyond collective bargaining or with problems that collective bargaining was not designed to handle.

CONTEMPORARY CHALLENGES TO COLLECTIVE BARGAINING

In the first two editions of this book,[14] attention was centered on three major problem areas defined in terms of goals or objectives as follows:

1. How to achieve full employment without inflation while maintaining "free" collective bargaining (that is, without direct control over wages and prices).
2. How to achieve effective democratization of industrial relations, although

---

[11] John Maurice Clark, *Guideposts in Time of Change* (New York: Harper & Row, Publishers, 1949), p. 148.

[12] For a recent appraisal of union successes and problems in the field of urban affairs, including landlord-tenant bargaining, see Derek C. Bok and John T. Dunlop, *Labor and the American Community* (New York: Simon and Schuster, Inc. 1970), Chapter 15, pp. 427–55.

[13] A cross-section of informed but conflicting views on the feasibility of collective bargaining for farmers will be found in National Farm Institute, *Bargaining Power for Farmers* (Ames, Ia.: Iowa State University Press, 1968).

[14] 1951 and 1959.

faced with an increased amount of centralization in bargaining structures and in decision-making in both union and management organizations.
3. How to achieve a stable, equitable condition of industrial peace while
avoiding undue governmental control.

These three challenges remain significant ones for now and the predictable future. Each challenge embraces a mixing of public interest goals
with private needs and requirements. Viable responses require achieving an
accommodation of public policy objectives with those of the private decision-
makers. How to dovetail private and public policy in ways that will maximize
the discretion remaining to the practitioners while insuring the attainment of
economy-wide goals continues to be *the* fundamental challenge.

Students of the collective bargaining process must look beyond the
specific requirements of particular union-management relationships. We
must be concerned with the macro-economic impact of thousands of micro-
economic bargains arrived at separately. However, the practitioners of bargaining focus naturally on the short run and on their particular needs as they
see them. The analysis must begin by acknowledging that *collective bargaining
must remain a micro-economic process if we are to continue stressing the values of private
decision-making.* Our inventory of challenges, however, *appropriately includes
macro-economic problems whose solution can be affected by the practitioners of bargaining.*

The inventory of challenges does not purport to be an exhaustive
one. The inventory is proof in itself of why this third edition is more new
than revised. Staying on top of the word "contemporary" requires many
important changes in content and approach. Writing three editions over a
twenty-year time span has confirmed the hypothesis that collective bargaining has continued to exhibit resiliency and the capacity to adjust to changing
needs and conditions. In many cases exercising this ability to adapt has been
done without fanfare. Creativity in solving new problems never seems to
receive the attention given to some conspicuous examples of failure to adapt.[15]

Job Security Problems: The Main Challenge to the Collective Bargaining Process

The principal challenge to bargainers concerns how to insure job
security without infringing upon management's right to innovate, to change
factor and job mixes and to relocate and restructure plants. This statement

---

[15] One effort to accentuate the positive was made in 1964 by a team of graduate
students from the Harvard Business School who did extensive field interviewing in a variety
of industries. Their findings and conclusions are reported in James J. Healy, ed., *Creative
Collective Bargaining* (Englewood Cliffs, N. J.: Prentice-Hall, Inc., 1965). See also Stanley
Young, *Innovation in Collective Bargaining* (Amherst, Mass.: University of Massachusetts Labor
Relations and Research Center, 1968).

should not be interpreted as minimizing the perennial importance of wages as a central issue. In 1968 and 1969, wage increases had top billing once again as prices rose rapidly.[16] Nevertheless, the complex of problems relating to job security has been and will remain of crucial significance to both management and union.

The conflict potential inherent in the job security problem can be illustrated by stating two propositions. The first conditions management thinking. The second is mandatory for union leadership to consider. These two propositions are as follows:

1. Management must retain freedom to innovate in terms of technology, structure of industrial operations and location of plants, involving the shutting down of obsolete installations and the construction of optimal size units.
2. Employees are entitled to contractual protection of bargaining unit work opportunities to the maximum extent consistent with point 1 above and to negotiated provisions for cushioning the impact of either technological displacement or loss of work occasioned by plant closures and/or removal to a different location.[17]

The 1967–1970 automobile contracts contain guaranteed annual income and guaranteed monthly income provisions for worker security, but industry retains freedom to innovate. This is one example of a practical accommodation of our twin propositions. The 1967–1970 contract between the major meatpacking firms and the two major unions in the industry could also be cited.[18] These contracts have special provisions on technological adjustment pay, liberalized transfer rights and increased notification time on plant closings.

Specific contract illustrations on job security issues will be given in Chapter 9. Since job security poses perhaps the most difficult problem area in contemporary bargaining, it has been accorded special mention in beginning this inventory. Other challenges are listed summarily, with editorial comment excluded at this stage. The ordering of these challenges has no particular significance.

---

[16] In calendar 1969, for example, many of the major craft unions in the building and construction field negotiated three-year agreements with contractors expected to yield rates for journeyman craftsmen as high as $8 to $10 per hour in calendar 1972.

[17] Harold W. Davey, "Current and Future Labor Relations Problems in the Meat Packing Industry," *Labor Law Journal*, XVIII (December, 1967), 746.

[18] The two unions in question, the Amalgamated Meat Cutters and Butcher Workmen of North America and the United Packinghouse, Food and Allied Workers of America, completed organic merger in July, 1968. The new union has assumed the name of the Amalgamated. Effective joint bargaining with the major packers in recent years was one of the positive factors making the 1968 merger a reality. An absorbing account of why an earlier effort at merger went on the rocks is provided by Joel Seidman's paper, "Unity in Meat Packing: Problems and Prospects," in *New Dimensions in Collective Bargaining, op. cit.*, pp. 29–43.

CHALLENGES TO THE PRACTITIONERS OF BARGAINING

1. How to negotiate master contracts and local supplemental agreements in such a fashion as to minimize the likelihood of strikes over the latter after the former have been peacefully negotiated.
2. How to achieve meaningful collective bargaining in the public sector, without the traditional private sector instrument of economic force as a means of producing agreement.
3. How to negotiate the conversion of blue-collar production and maintenance workers from the traditional hourly or incentive-pay basis to a salaried basis, including perhaps ultimately a guaranteed annual income plan.
4. How to achieve greater individual employee interest and participation in collective bargaining policies and procedures, including making the process more "relevant" in terms of the aspirations of the younger workers.
5. How to negotiate an appropriate wage differential for skilled employees in industrial bargaining units without alienating other production workers.
6. How to develop effective procedures for joint consideration of such long-range continuing problems as the impact of technological change and industrial relocation, outside the crisis atmosphere of regular contract negotiation periods.
7. How to achieve a sensible balance between wages on the one hand and monetary fringe benefits on the other.
8. How to negotiate mutually satisfactory provisions on the explosive issue of subcontracting of work.
9. How to negotiate the elimination of outmoded policies and procedures that are still regarded as sacrosanct (for example, outmoded working rules negotiated originally to cover a condition that no longer exists but whose continuance may benefit some incumbent employees).
10. How to improve grievance adjustment machinery to insure prompt settlement on the merits in the early steps.
11. How to make grievance arbitration procedures more effective and how to insure the utilization of large numbers of potentially qualified but untried neutrals.
12. How to prevent collective bargaining contracts from expanding into "Roman codes" that are too detailed and too technical for the average working mortal to comprehend.
13. How to develop a higher degree of professionalism and expertise in contract negotiation and contract administration.
14. How (and when) to make use of "informed neutrals" to facilitate negotiation and administration of collective agreements.
15. How to cope rationally with the enduring problem posed by the confrontation between management's cherished reserved rights and the union's penchant for enlarging the scope of collective bargaining.
16. How (or whether) to encourage the use of *joint* union-management committees in dealing with such matters as increasing productivity as well as with the more conventional areas of joint safety committees, joint job evaluation committees and so forth.

17. How to encourage creativity and innovation in collective bargaining, both procedurally and on substantive policy problems.
18. How to safeguard the procedural right of the individual worker to fair representation without sacrificing the institutional objectives of management and union aimed at stability in contract administration.
19. How to insure fair representation and due process in both contract negotiation and administration, for example, effective treatment of the job rights of blacks, who will always constitute a minority in many unions.

Some Macro-Oriented Problem Areas

The foregoing challenges are micro-oriented in the sense that the parties themselves have the capacity and the power to respond. The nature and adequacy of responses will be reviewed in subsequent chapters. It is apparent that how the parties solve (or fail to solve) them can have ramifications far beyond the purview of Company X and Union Y. It is also clear that some of these challenges cannot be met effectively by micro-economic decisions alone but require complementary and supportive public policy. The job security problem, for example, calls for a high degree of coordination between private and public policy.

Our inventory of challenges is concluded by noting some significant problems posed in macro-oriented terms, as follows:

1. How to inject macro-economic awareness into the consciousness of collective bargaining practitioners in a manner that will *effectively condition* their joint action on economic issues in bargaining.
2. How to minimize the possible use of economic force to resolve disputes over future contract terms in critical bargaining relationships while avoiding such extreme measures as compulsory arbitration or government seizure.
3. How to reformulate our national labor relations policy in ways that will strengthen the institutional processes of private collective bargaining and reverse the (seemingly) inexorable trend toward greater governmental control over labor relations.
4. How to coordinate national policy measures aimed at preventing inflation with related private approaches through collective bargaining.
5. How (or whether) to encourage those engaged in conventional collective bargaining to develop joint solutions to problems beyond or outside of the employment relationship.
6. How to improve our knowledge and understanding of the economic effects of collective bargaining on the economy as a whole as well as on particular industries and particular labor markets.
7. How to improve the general public's knowledge and understanding of what collective bargaining involves, what it can do and what it should not be expected to do.

In brief, these are some of the principal challenges faced by those engaged in collective bargaining. Listing challenges is less difficult than analyzing the nature and quality of the responses. The pattern of responses is one of astonishing variety. It is thus advisable to illustrate the diversity that characterizes collective bargaining in the United States.

ALTERNATIVE APPROACHES TO COLLECTIVE BARGAINING

Variety in contemporary bargaining can be shown in several ways. What collective bargaining looks like depends a great deal on what trade, industry, service or profession one is examining. *All* genuine collective bargaining deals in one fashion or another with the price of labor and human relations on the job. Beyond this it is hazardous to generalize. There is truly a protean diversity both in bargaining structures and in the treatment of substantive and procedural problems.

A natural way to begin an essay on variety is to contrast craft and industrial bargaining. Historically, skilled workers organized on a craft basis were the first to form stable, durable national unions. Their basic objectives have remained essentially the same over long periods of time. For example, building trades craft unions have sought to control employment opportunities exclusively for members in good standing, to increase steadily the monetary compensation for journeymen and to protect their carefully defined work jurisdictions against encroachment by other unions and against dilution of skills by the employer.

Such craft unions do not seek detailed contractual restriction of employer discretion in on-the-job situations. The business agent servicing a craft union in the construction field limits his attention to making sure that union wage scales are being observed and that no nonunion workers or itinerant journeymen without permits are employed on any project. Such a concentration on enforcing union-scale and closed-shop conditions makes for comparatively short written agreements between contractors and building trades unions. In bulky contrast are the contracts negotiated between manufacturing firms and industrial unions. The latter typically represent *all* nonsupervisory production and maintenance employees (skilled, semi-skilled and unskilled) in inclusive bargaining units.

Industrial union negotiators necessarily emphasize inclusion in *their* contracts of detailed statements of policy and procedure governing on-the-job rights and relationships because realistically they cannot control employer hiring or otherwise limit the supply of labor in a particular labor market. Membership in an industrial union is based on the industry in which the worker is employed rather than on the nature of the work he performs.

Industrial union leaders are, in their fashion, just as interested in job security for their membership as are the leaders of the highly skilled journeyman craft groups.

The industrial union leader must concentrate on *job security on the job*. He seeks to negotiate detailed rules and procedures governing layoffs, recalls to employment, promotions, transfers and the like, with seniority as the primary (if not sole) criterion whenever possible. Also, nearly all industrial contracts confine the employer's right to discipline to cases where he can prove "good and just cause." Finally, in an uncertain climate created by technological change, plant relocation and industrial structural change, union representatives in manufacturing are particularly concerned with negotiating provisions to reduce the adverse impact of any such changes on incumbent employees.

The contract between an employer and an industrial union is thus often a lengthy document that may run more than 100 closely printed pages. Contract administration in a large factory tends to be formalized, structured and institutionalized. Sheer numbers prevent the informal approach to grievance adjustment that is still possible in craft bargaining situations or in small manufacturing establishments.

This aspect of industrial union contracts helps to explain why the bulk of grievance arbitration in the United States appears to be generated from medium and large factory units rather than from small firms or craft units. Using an impartial arbitrator to make a final and binding decision as the last step in the contract's grievance machinery is regarded as standard operating procedure by most large manufacturing firms and the unions with which they bargain. Yet arbitration is seldom needed by employers and craft unions in building and construction or in small manufacturing establishments.

Variety in collective bargaining patterns can thus be shown by contrasting the different emphases of craft and industrial unions and also by differences deriving primarily from the size of the bargaining units in question. Diversity is also well illustrated by noting which bargaining issues are of central importance to the parties. The price of labor is a key issue in nearly every negotiation. Beyond this, it is difficult to generalize with safety. Unions in manufacturing stress seniority (length of service) as a primary criterion governing layoffs, recalls and promotions. Building trades unions do not concern themselves in the same fashion with seniority from a collective bargaining contract standpoint. They attempt to achieve security for members by controlling entrance to the trade. They function as an employment agency for the various contractors with whom they negotiate. The craft union's seniority system is internal to the union.

Unions in the hotel and restaurant field have a special interest in provisions governing split-shift employment. This is not even a problem for most other unions. Craft unions with closed-shop contracts do not stress contractual control of the employer's right to discipline. Industrial unions, however, invariably regard as a "must" a contract clause limiting the employer's exercise of the disciplinary prerogative to cases of "good and just cause."

Professional associations or unions representing teachers have a special concern over establishing through negotiation their voice in such matters as classroom size, curriculum, nonclass functions required of the teacher, credit for class preparation time and so forth. These are serious problems for *teachers as such*, but are not a concern of other unions. In any industry geared to assembly-line operations a critical problem area is likely to be the length and spacing of relief periods and coffee breaks. In other lines of work periodic rest may be less essential and thus of minor importance as a bargaining problem.

For those industries on continuous-shift operations (three shifts of eight hours each in a twenty-four-hour period) the paid lunch period while on the job is sometimes a critical issue. This problem can be even tougher when those on continuous shift with a paid lunch period are working side by side with other workers who are in the plant for eight and half hours with a thirty-minute *unpaid* lunch break.

Piece rates or incentive standards are serious bargaining problems in industries where labor cost is a substantial percentage of total cost (such as the garment and shoe industries). Employers who pay by the hour, however, are faced with difficulties in developing and maintaining performance standards for "measured day work."

Perhaps enough has been indicated on the variety-diversity theme to point up the fact that there is no such thing as a typical collective bargaining contract. The more contracts one studies the more one is impressed with the fascinating variety of policies and procedures developed by the parties in reaching a mutually satisfactory accommodation, contract after contract, on the deceptively simple problems of wages, hours and other conditions of employment.

BARGAINING RELATIONSHIPS CLASSIFIED BY DEGREE OF CONFLICT OR COOPERATION

The variety theme can also be illustrated by observing the broad continuum of union-management relationships, ranging from conflict and hostility on the one hand to constructive cooperation on the other. The late Benjamin M. Selekman's classification system remains useful for this purpose.[19] His eight structures are: (1) containment-aggression; (2) ideology; (3) conflict; (4) power bargaining; (5) deal bargaining; (6) collusion; (7) accommodation; and (8) cooperation.

These structures are not mutually exclusive. They shade into one another or overlap in particular cases. Union-management relationships based on collusion, ideology or cooperation are comparatively rare in the United States. Also, the disappearance of most of the unions expelled from the CIO in 1949 and 1950 has made the structure of ideology practically a dead letter.[20]

Unfortunately, examples of the structure of collusion are still extant. Collusion generally takes one of two forms. In one type union leaders and employers unblushingly combine to freeze out "unfriendly" or noncooperating employers and pass on the excessive costs of their collusive agreements to the consumer. In the second type, the unsuspecting union member is made the victim of contractual agreements providing wage scales and benefits that are below standard for the work in question. What Hoxie many years ago labeled predatory unionism can still be found. I refer to the taking over of a *bona fide* union by racketeers who proceed to exact tribute from both the employer and the union members. The usual technique is to sell "strike insurance" to the employer and to keep the rank and file terrorized by violence or the threat of violence while exacting kickbacks from those who wish to work.[21]

Collusive relationships are comparatively rare. They belong to the pathology of bargaining. Our analysis is concerned mainly with *bona fide* collective bargaining. We are thus principally concerned with the five most prevalent of Selekman's eight structures and also with the prospects for development of his structure of cooperation in more relationships.

Selekman's structure of cooperation contemplates going beyond the conventional framework of collective bargaining. The parties would be concerned on a *joint* basis with productive efficiency, the solvency of the business, improving technology and reducing economic waste. Such an orientation resembles the familiar model of union-management cooperation plans to increase productivity and reduce costs. These plans have found

---

[19] Benjamin M. Selekman, "Varieties of Labor Relations," *Harvard Business Reveiw*, XXVII (March, 1949), 175–99.

[20] Notwithstanding periodic critical outbursts from both the "old" and the "new" Left, the American labor movement continues to maintain its pragmatic, nonideological stance. This does not mean, however, that organized labor is not undergoing what Gus Tyler has termed "a deep and quiet revolution" whereby it is seeking to maintain its competence to deal with rapidly evolving changes in economic, political and community affairs. See Gus Tyler, *The Labor Revolution: Trade Unions in a New America* (New York: The Viking Press, Inc., 1967).

[21] See Chapter 51 of Philip Taft, *Organized Labor in American History* (New York: Harper & Row, Publishers, 1964), pp. 682–701. For earlier examples, see Malcolm Johnson, *Crime on the Labor Front* (New York: McGraw-Hill Book Company, Inc., 1950).

favor frequently with labor economists but seldom with the practitioners of bargaining except in time of war or when the company in question was in dire financial straits.[22]

Regrettably, many union-management relationships continue to fit the Selekman conflict model. The unfair practice caseload of the National Labor Relations Board has reached record heights in recent years. Many employers continue to deny rights to their workers that have been guaranteed by national labor policy since 1935. By the same token, some unions continue to interfere with the legislatively guaranteed (since 1947) rights of workers to refrain from unionizing if they so desire. Many of the NLRB's current cases are factually similar to the early Wagner Act (1935) or Taft-Hartley Act (1947) days.

Cases of open industrial warfare are perhaps on the wane. This does not mean that hard-nosed bargaining has declined. There are still many employers determined to be both "tough" in resisting union pressure and insistent on making their own negotiation demands instead of waiting to see what the unions propose. In fact, there would appear to be an increase in cases fitting Selekman's *containment-aggression* or *power bargaining* structures. Relationships fitting the *accommodation* type also are increasing, in my judgment.

A structure of accommodation is one where employer and union work cooperatively within the customary bounds of collective bargaining. The employer has accepted the union as an integral part of the industrial relations framework. However, he will negotiate only on the standard subjects of wages, hours and employment conditions. Neither the union nor the employer is interested in going beyond conventional bargaining to make an affirmative joint effort on such matters as increasing productivity and reducing costs, as contemplated by the structure of cooperation.[23]

STRUCTURAL VARIATIONS IN BARGAINING RELATIONSHIPS

Finally, the variety in United States labor relations patterns is shown by the many diverse structures for bargaining purposes. The most

---

[22] For some years I have been intrigued by the potential of union-management cooperation plans for making micro-economic decisions on wages and prices compatible with national policy efforts to maintain full employment and stable prices. See Harold W. Davey, "Union-Management Cooperation Revisited," *Business Perspectives*, IV (Winter, 1968), 4–10. I remain convinced that the basic idea has merit, subject to certain constraints discussed in the cited article and in Chapter 11 of this volume.

[23] See note 22 above. For analysis of specific examples of union-management cooperation plans, as first stressed by the late Sumner H. Slichter, see Slichter, J. J. Healy and E. R. Livernash, *The Impact of Collective Bargaining on Management* (Washington, D.C.: The Brookings Institution, 1960).

familiar bargaining structure involves a single employer negotiating with one or more unions. However, many important bargaining relationships involve an employer association and one or more unions negotiating a so-called multi-employer agreement.

Another structural arrangement is generally referred to as "coalition bargaining" or "coordinated bargaining." The structure applies to situations where several unions dealing with a large employer, such as General Electric or Westinghouse, combine forces for bargaining purposes and negotiate with the employer on a united-front basis. Coalition bargaining has been greatly facilitated by advice and stimulus from the Industrial Union Department of the AFL-CIO. In the long copper strike of 1967–1968 the United Steelworkers of America and some twenty other unions sought company-wide contracts. The major companies stood firm successfully on the old pattern of negotiating on a single plant basis.

An older version of coalition bargaining has been practiced for many years in some labor market areas by the principal craft unions in the building trades who negotiate on a joint basis with a contractors' association. In a limited number of industries we can observe what amounts to national bargaining between an employer association and one or more unions.

Generally speaking, however, the structure of bargaining in the United States can be described as decentralized or even "fractionalized" in character. The significance of fractionalization is diminished in some industries by the force of pattern bargaining. Without wishing to exaggerate the force of key settlements on other contracts, many negotiations today are clearly conducted in terms of both constraints and compulsions imposed by policies originally established in other negotiations.

Pattern bargaining involves, as the name suggests, a practice of following the lead on wages and/or some significant nonwage bargaining development established by a union and a major employer in a particular industry by other firms in that same industry or even in other and seemingly unrelated industries. In meatpacking, for example, it has been customary for the pattern to be established by initial negotiations with Armour, Swift or Wilson. The other national packers and many of the independent packers then follow suit in subsequent negotiations with the two principal unions (one since the 1968 merger) in the packinghouse field. This is what happened in negotiations culminating in the 1967–1970 and in the 1970–1973 contracts. The basic pattern on both wage increases and job security provisions set in the Armour negotiations was followed closely in negotiations with the other major packers and many of the principal independents.

Another variant of pattern bargaining occurs when the principal union involved has its roots in a number of industries. The United Automobile, Aerospace and Agricultural Implement Workers of America (UAW) has significant membership in the aircraft or aerospace field and in the farm equipment industry as well as in automobiles. Thus whatever the UAW regards as important gains made in negotiations with General Motors, Ford and Chrysler are likely to become priority (if not "must") demands when UAW negotiates with, for example, John Deere, International Harvester, Caterpillar and other farm equipment companies. Other multi-industrial unions, such as the International Association of Machinists and Aerospace Workers (IAM), the International Brotherhood of Teamsters, Warehousemen and Helpers (IBT) or the International Union of Electrical, Radio and Machine Workers of America (IUE), frequently seek to achieve a fairly homogeneous complex of bargaining demands in a variety of industrial settings. This strategy has important implications for the problem of centralized policy determination versus local union and local management autonomy, explored in some detail in the next chapter.

In this essay on variety, the diversity of collective bargaining relationships has been shown reflected in union structure and membership base (for example, craft or industrial), the range of issues stressed in bargaining from one economic context to another, different attitudes and approaches of the parties to one another and, finally, size and structure of bargaining units.

Such a discussion should serve to point up the danger in overgeneralizing about collective bargaining as a process. It is not difficult to find specific cases to support general statements in praise or condemnation of collective bargaining in practice. Although the field abounds in constructive examples, it is also easy to produce cases where collective bargaining has failed or worked imperfectly. In brief, there is no such thing as a typical bargaining relationship.

THE SEARCH FOR "FIRST PRINCIPLES" OF CONSTRUCTIVE COLLECTIVE BARGAINING

No social scientist worth his salt can resist the temptation to search for first principles and behavioral norms. Considerable scholarly effort has been devoted toward development of a "general theory" of industrial or labor relations.[24] Recent stress on comparative industrial relations is an example of this endeavor. Students of U.S. labor relations are no longer "isolationist" in their research emphasis.

It is generally recognized that the "one best way" to handle a variety of union-management problems may not necessarily be the American way.

---

[24] See Clark Kerr, John T. Dunlop, Frederick H. Harbison and Charles H. Myers, *Industrialism and Industrial Man* (Cambridge, Mass: Harvard University Press, 1960). See also John T. Dunlop, *Industrial Relations Systems* (New York: Henry Holt and Company, Inc., 1958).

Studies of the industrial relations systems of other countries can provide better insight into the workings of our own system. The search has begun for policies and ideas that may be transferable from other systems to our own as well to determine what U.S. collective bargaining procedures and policies may be of utility in other countries. The interest in comparative systems and the quest for a unitary theory of industrial relations are evidence of a compulsion to develop a body of "first principles."

We are some distance from this lofty objective. Pragmatism will continue to rear its earthy head. It reminds us forcibly that what works well for Company X and Union Y may not be feasible for Company A and Union B. On a broader scale, an industrial relations system viable in one country may, for many reasons, not be suitable to the legal, economic, social and institutional requirements of another country.

The present volume has a parochial and modest objective. We shall be concerned primarily with analysis of collective bargaining policies and procedures that fit the legal, economic, political and social milieu of the United States. Any discussion of "first principles" or norms is geared to U.S. experience and U.S. conditions.

VALUE JUDGMENTS OF THE AUTHOR

Collective bargaining constantly assumes new dimensions.[25] Since 1951 and 1959, when the first and second editions of this book appeared, new territory has been effectively opened for collective bargaining (for example, teachers, nurses and government employees at all levels). Also, some novel uses for variations of collective bargaining as a process have been urged and, in some cases, actually tried (such as collective bargaining for farmers, the "working poor," the urban unemployed, tenants in slum housing and in racial minority conflict situations).

These new dimensions and the dynamic potential of collective bargaining in established areas have contributed to the emphasis on challenges in the present volume. My basic value judgments have not changed appreciably. The old wine appears to go rather well in the new bottle.

In 1959 my value judgments were stated as follows:

> In the first place, a strong, independent, and responsible trade union movement is indispensable to a healthy, productive, private-enterprise economy and a vigorous political democracy. Secondly, excessive public control of labor relations tends to weaken or destroy private bargain-

---

[25] The validity of this observation can be demonstrated by comparing the problem areas stressed in this chapter with those regarded as "new dimensions" of collective bargaining in 1959 by the editors and authors of *New Dimensions in Collective Bargaining, op. cit.*, 1959.

ing relationships. The best interests of the community as well as of the parties themselves require that we work diligently toward a goal of what George Taylor has termed "free collective bargaining," wherein the scope of the relationship, the procedures for negotiation and joint dealing, and the substantive terms of employment are all private matters to be worked out by employers and the unions with whom they deal without government interference. In line with this thinking, the trend toward increased public regulation must be reversed if we are to make enduring progress in union-management relationships.

Finally, the public interest and the interests of both management and organized labor will be best insured by adoption of a positive, dynamic approach to collective bargaining. Such an approach requires unremitting effort to increase productivity, reduce costs, and effectively allocate and utilize available manpower. It involves a joint recognition of the perils of inflation and a realization of the need for responsibility and restraint in wage bargaining under full employment conditions. It involves full recognition of the crucial importance of solving the human equation by diligent attention to improve methods of living together under a contract. Finally, it involves a willingness to experiment and a receptiveness to innovation in order that collective bargaining may realize its full potential as a flexible instrumentality for intelligent accommodation to changing economic and industrial circumstances.[26]

COLLECTIVE BARGAINING AS A PROFESSIONAL TASK

The labor relations function demands trained professionals. Excluding a few "neanderthal" situations, collective bargaining is rarely performed any more by management representatives as a part-time chore or by union leaders without some training. The president of a very small firm may still handle collective bargaining along with numerous other responsibilities, but he needs specialized knowledge to cope effectively with his union counterpart.

Collective bargaining is a new venture for *both* parties in fields like nursing and education. Where this is the case, it has not taken the participants long to realize that intimate knowledge of their line of work is not enough. Both management and union organizations understand their need to develop specialized talent. The labor relations function is increasingly regarded by management as of primary importance. Unions are experiencing an acute need for more trained negotiators and "back-up" staff specialists to remain on a par with their management "rivals."

Developing professional expertise is easier for management. When management experiences a need, it can proceed to hire or develop the requisite professional talent. Unions are somewhat handicapped by their political

---

[26] Harold W. Davey, *Contemporary Collective Bargaining* (Englewood Cliffs, N. J.: Prentice-Hall, Inc., 1959), p. 19.

nature. The tradition still holds that collective bargaining should remain in the hands of elected leaders at both the local and national union level. Honoring this particular past practice has sometimes been done at the cost of inadequate representation of union interests.

The long-standing union distrust of "intellectuals" dates back to the time of Gompers. Although it has been overcome to a substantial extent, the fact is that even the more "advanced" unions seldom use appointed staff professionals directly on the collective bargaining firing line. Local unions are the logical source for career practitioners of collective bargaining, but the necessary steps to create a trained supply of such talent have not always been taken. The AFL-CIO's College of Labor Studies, authorized in 1969, constitutes a major move in meeting the urgent need for trained union practitioners.[27]

THE QUALITIES OF A MODEL PRACTITIONER OF COLLECTIVE BARGAINING

Today's practitioner of collective bargaining, whether union or management, needs more than a robust physical constitution, basic honesty and native intelligence. To be effective in today's collective bargaining, the union or management representative must be intelligent, resourceful and hard-working. He or she can be dedicated to the shorter work week only as a bargaining target for others, not as a personal goal.

Today's bargainer must be emotionally balanced and knowledgeable on the economics of the firm or industry in question, as well as on current practices in other fields. A true professional must have the talent to be flexible in one context and firm in another. The bargaining function requires a sense of humor and a sense of proportion. One must have the ability to "keep one's cool" in crisis stages of bargaining.

Perhaps most important of all, a competent union or management representative must be able *to see a problem whole*. An understanding of the compulsions and pressures operating on practitioners on the other side of the bargaining table is an indispensable requisite to intelligent bargaining.

Effective negotiators and contract administrators are mature realists who appreciate when it is desirable to compromise and when it would be fatal to concede. They must be capable of handling rather than hating difficult or unpleasant situations.[28]

---

[27] The first students began their labors in September, 1969, in Washington, D.C.

[28] The phrase is that of the late Benjamin M. Selekman. See his *Labor Relations and Human Relations* (New York: McGraw-Hill Book Company, Inc., 1947), Chapters 7 and 8.

The picture of today's model professional now emerges as a combination of diplomat, tactician, technical expert and psychologist. Such a "package" is obviously hard to come by. However, the professional nature of the task is generally appreciated in today's labor relations.

CONCLUSION

We are now in a position to begin the analysis of current and prospective problem areas, geared to the inventory of challenges presented earlier. Some topics selected for analysis are not new but have assumed new importance or have changed in qualitative ways in recent years. Several issues or problems to be analyzed are distinctively new. They were not even on the horizon in 1951 or 1959.

The new or comparatively new problem areas include the following:

1. Collective bargaining by nurses and public school teachers.
2. Coalition or multi-union bargaining with conglomerate employers.
3. Bargaining in the public sector at federal, state and municipal levels.
4. Collective bargaining as a vehicle for raising farm prices.
5. Use of collective bargaining as an instrument for improving the economic status of the "working poor" and for dealing with the problem of hard-core urban unemployment.
6. Alternatives to the use of economic force for resolution of disputes over future contract terms, particularly in the public sector but also in private bargaining relationships where technological developments and/or the "public interest" have contributed to making the strike and the lockout anachronistic.
7. The rise and fall of the wage-price guideposts policy of the Council of Economic Advisers as an effort to mesh micro-economic concerns with the needs of the economy as a whole.
8. New approaches to solution of problems associated with the impact of technological change and industrial relocation on income and employment security.
9. Impact of Title VII of the Civil Rights Act of 1964 on collective bargaining policies dealing with so-called male and female jobs and related matters.
10. NLRB policies defining the union "duty of fair representation" and their impact on contract grievance and arbitration procedures.
11. Procedural devices for avoiding crisis bargaining, such as joint study committees, prenegotiation sessions, employment of informed neutrals and so forth.
12. The developing federal law on arbitration stemming from Supreme Court decisions enforcing agreements to arbitrate under Section 301 of the Taft-Hartley Act.
13. Interrelationship between federal legislation to reduce "structural" unemployment (for example, the Manpower Development and Training Act of 1962, as amended) and private collective bargaining policies relating to manpower planning.

14. Analysis of new approaches to payment for work, together with recent thinking on income versus leisure preferences.
15. Reappraisal of collective bargaining as a process in terms of the probable requirements of the 1970s and 1980s.

Some of the problem areas just listed are adapted from the earlier inventory of challenges. The challenge list also includes old and continuing problem areas as well as the new. Our central theme, simply stated, is that the collective bargaining process continues to function reasonably well in most cases as an instrument for simultaneously preserving established standards and for introducing innovation in policies and procedures governing the work relationship.

SELECTED BIBLIOGRAPHY

Note: I have included after each chapter (except the last) a representative array of books and articles for the reader who wishes to probe more deeply. Many excellent references of an earlier vintage have been excluded, although a few classic references will be found.

Selection of articles has been influenced by availability to the reader. Many references were not used because the journals in which they appeared are not readily available to most readers. A few articles from major law school journals have been included.

Many references are taken from the *Industrial and Labor Relations Review* and *Labor Law Journal*. A reader who wishes to stay current in this field can do a reasonably good job by keeping track of these two journals. The book review and recent publications sections of the *Industrial and Labor Relations Review* are particularly helpful in this regard. The range of subjects covered by *Labor Law Journal* is much broader than its title suggests.

Among the other valuable sources of current analyses of problem areas in labor relations and collective bargaining are the following:

1. The proceedings volumes of the Industrial Relations Research Association and the National Academy of Arbitrators.

2. For more affluent readers, the labor relations reporting services of Prentice-Hall, Inc., The Bureau of National Affairs, Inc. or Commerce Clearing House, Inc.

3. An increasingly rich variety of articles, monographs and reliable statistical reports emerging from the Bureau of Labor Statistics (BLS) of the U.S. Department of Labor. The Department's *Monthly Labor Review* is a most useful journal.

References in all cases are listed alphabetically by author or editor. The painful task of attempting to rate in order of merit has been avoided.

BAKKE, E. WIGHT, CLARK KERR AND CHARLES W. ANROD, eds., *Unions, Management and the Public* (3rd ed.). New York: Harcourt, Brace & World, Inc., 1967.
DUNLOP, JOHN T., *Industrial Relations Systems*. New York: Henry Holt and Company, 1958.
————, and NEIL W. CHAMBERLAIN, eds., *Frontiers of Collective Bargaining*. New York: Harper & Row, Publishers, 1967.

25 *Collective bargaining today*

KERR, CLARK, *Labor and Management in Industrial Society.* New York: Doubleday & Company, Inc., 1964.

MACDONALD, ROBERT M., "Collective Bargaining in the Postwar Period," *Industrial and Labor Relations Review,* XX (July, 1967), 553–77.

PIERSON, FRANK C., *Unions in Postwar America; an Economic Assessment.* New York: Random House, Inc., 1967.

SAYLES, LEONARD R., AND GEORGE STRAUSS, *The Local Union* (rev. ed.). New York: Harcourt, Brace & World, Inc., 1967.

SHISTER, JOSEPH, "The Direction of Unionism, 1947–1967: Thrust or Drift?" *Industrial and Labor Relations Review,* XX (July, 1967), 578–601.

SLICHTER, SUMNER H., *Union Policies and Industrial Management.* Washington, D.C.: The Brookings Institution, 1941.

SULTAN, PAUL E., *The Disenchanted Unionist.* New York: Harper & Row, Publishers, 1963.

ULMAN, LLOYD, ed., *Challenges to Collective Bargaining.* Englewood Cliffs, N. J.: Prentice-Hall, Inc., 1967.

WORTMAN, MAX S., JR., *Critical Issues in Labor.* New York: The Macmillan Company, 1969.

STRUCTURAL PROBLEMS

in collective bargaining

CHAPTER TWO

Understanding the structure of collective bargaining relationships is essential to meaningful analysis of the problems faced by employers and unions in contemporary bargaining. This chapter is concentrated on recent developments in the structure of collective bargaining. The next chapter is concerned with another prerequisite for intelligent consideration of collective bargaining as a process, the framework of public policy within which employers and unions must operate.

THE EXCLUSIVE BARGAINING RIGHTS CONCEPT

A bargaining unit is an area of employee representation for purposes of collective bargaining. As a matter of law, a *bona fide* labor organization that can show that a majority of employees in a unit appropriate for collective bargaining desire it to represent them in collective dealings with their employer is entitled to *exclusive* representation rights. In other words, the union or association shown to have been designated by a majority of employees in an appropriate unit serves as and must be recognized as the *exclusive* bargaining agent for *all* employees in the unit, whether or not the employees are members of the union or association.

This concept of exclusive bargaining rights is a distinctive and important aspect of U.S. labor relations.[1] The *quid pro quo* for enjoying such rights is the employee organization's legal obligation to negotiate and administer agreements applying to all employees in the unit. Increasing emphasis has been given recently to the problem of giving meaning to the right of employees to be represented by "unions of their own choosing." This theme will be developed later in the chapter.

Variety in Bargaining Unit Structures

The nature and shape of the bargaining unit is frequently an issue of vital importance. How the unit is defined may be the determining factor in whether Union X is, in fact, entitled to representation rights. When an employer is first approached by a union with a demand that he bargain collectively, his initial response is often, "Which workers do you claim to represent?"

In most cases there is no dispute over the bargaining unit. A craft union will normally seek a unit consisting of employees performing the work covered by its jurisdiction as spelled out in its charter from the AFL-CIO and its own constitution. An industrial union typically will request that the bargaining unit consist of all nonsupervisory production and maintenance employees of Company X. In labor relations jargon this is called a "P & M" unit.

Sharp conflicts do develop in some cases over the appropriate structure for bargaining. Even where the general shape of the unit is agreed upon, differences may arise as to whether particular "grey zone" employees should be included or excluded (for example, should lead men or time study clerks in a factory be in or out?).

A more fundamental conflict can develop when an industrial union

---

[1] In many other countries worker representation is on a pluralistic basis. This is in part a function of unionism having a strong ideological orientation (such as democratic socialist, communist or Christian in both France and Italy). American unions are highly pragmatic and nonideological (for example, "business unions" in the Hoxie sense). The exclusive representation concept thus presents no problems of the type that would certainly be encountered in an ideologically split employee setting.

seeks exclusive bargaining rights for a "P & M" unit and one or more craft unions are at the same time petitioning for separate bargaining units. The craft-industrial unit issue has been a headache for the National Labor Relations Board ever since the split between the original American Federation of Labor and the rival Committee for Industrial Organization in November, 1935.[2] Although the two federations merged in December, 1955, after some twenty years of internecine warfare, the unit controversy still flares up periodically, as we shall see presently.

Among the newer types of unit controversies we should list problems arising from coalitions of unions seeking to bargain on a coordinated basis with an employer "conglomerate" (that is, a company with production operations in a variety of different fields). Coalition bargaining with conglomerate employers is discussed later in this chapter.[3]

Contemporary collective agreements reveal an astonishing variety of structural patterns. The usual bargaining structure throughout manufacturing and mining industries continues to be the "P & M" unit. Craft bargaining units prevail in such industries as printing, building and construction, railroads and airlines.

In some industries (such as coal mining) one union dominates the representational front and negotiates master contracts with employers. In others the pattern of bargaining units may be diverse and complex. Not infrequently one will find an industrial union, such as the UAW or the IAM, representing most of the nonsupervisory employees in a "P & M" unit, but the manufacturer in question may also be negotiating separately with one or more unions representing specific craft employee groups who have chosen to remain outside the "P & M" structure.

Multiple craft bargaining units remain characteristic in railroads, although this picture may be changed as the union merger movement develops. However, bargaining with the IAM for aircraft maintenance personnel is on an industrial unit basis.[4]

Modern metropolitan newspapers may bargain with a dozen or more labor organizations, including the International Typographical Union, the American Newspaper Guild, the Photoengravers and the Pressmen. The newspaper unit structure is a complex of craft and industrial groupings. A

---

[2] For an absorbing and exhaustive account of the twenty years of rivalry between AFL and CIO unions, see Walter Galenson, *The CIO Challenge to the AFL* (Cambridge, Mass.: Harvard University Press, 1960).

[3] For a brief, detached appraisal see Herbert J. Lahne, "Coalition Bargaining and the Future of Union Structure," *Labor Law Journal*, XIX (June, 1967), 353–59. See also a recent monograph by William L. Chernish, *Coalition Bargaining: A Study of Union Tactics and Public Policy* (Philadelphia, Pa.: University of Pennsylvania Press, 1969).

[4] For a thorough analysis of airline labor relations, mainly the "craft" or professional employee aspect, see John M. Baitsell, *Airline Industrial Relations: Pilots and Flight Engineers* (Boston, Mass.: Harvard Graduate School of Business Administration, 1966).

prime contractor in the construction field typically negotiates with seven basic craft unions, plus a number of "specialty" unions. In urban construction bargaining increasingly is on a multi-employer basis. The contractors negotiate through a labor relations association with a joint council made up of many but not always all of the craft unions concerned. When all building and construction unions are not parties to a master multi-employer agreement, problems can easily arise from differing contract expiration dates or from the unwillingness of a particular union to settle after all other labor organizations have agreed on future terms. This is also a major concern in the newspaper field.

We have no census of bargaining unit structures, but it is reasonably safe to conclude that the United States bargaining universe includes approximately 150,000 or more collective bargaining agreements.[5] The bargaining units can be enormous in their coverage (for example, the General Motors-UAW master agreement covering about 400,000 employees) or they can embrace a mere handful of employees.[6]

The bargaining unit universe is thus remarkably diverse and varied in its composition. The most common structure involves a particular grouping of employees represented by a labor organization negotiating with a single employer on a craft or industrial basis. Nevertheless, multi-employer bargaining, company-wide contracts and coalition or coordinated bargaining with conglomerate employers all appear to be on the increase.

Controversy over the most appropriate structures for collective bargaining will probably never disappear from the labor relations scene. There is no objective or scientifically decisive answer as to the one best way to establish the structure of bargaining. What appears to be appropriate in one case may not be acceptable in another seemingly identical situation. The decisive factor is usually the desires of the employees involved or the fortuitous circumstance of which labor organization first determined to unionize a given group of employees.

Scholars can expound readily on the superiority of one form of bargaining structure over another. It is not an easy matter to win adherents to such preferences in the real world of collective bargaining. History is hard to reverse. Short-run factors in particular labor markets are often decisive in determining whether a given group of employees is, for example, to be

---

[5] The basic picture has not changed substantially since Neil Chamberlain's comprehensive survey appeared in 1956, although the trend toward more centralized bargaining structures continues. See Neil W. Chamberlain, "The Structure of Bargaining Units in the United States," *Industrial and Labor Relations Review*, X (October, 1956), 3–25.

[6] In fact, under certain circumstances a bargaining unit of one employee can be held appropriate. The City of New York bargains collectively with a union representing an appropriate unit of two shoemakers. In 1968, I served as arbitrator in a dispute involving General Electric and the Teamsters, who were representing two employees. The latter constituted the entire appropriate unit in a GE warehouse in Indianapolis.

unionized by the Teamsters or by the UAW, by the Retail Clerks or by the Amalgamated Meat Cutters and Butcher Workmen, by the American Federation of Teachers or by a local unit of the National Education Association. Logic often plays a minor role.[7]

CRITERIA FOR DETERMINING THE APPROPRIATENESS OF PROPOSED BARGAINING UNITS

The National Labor Relations Board has always been on the hot seat in any case where the key issue was what constituted an appropriate unit for purposes of collective bargaining because the Board has the statutory duty to *decide* in each case what shall be the appropriate unit or units. In most cases, as already noted, all parties concerned agree on the delineation of the appropriate bargaining unit. When a unit dispute exists, however, either between Company X and Union Y or between two or more unions seeking certification for different units of representation, the Board has the unenviable task of deciding which unit (or units) is "appropriate" for assuring to employees "the fullest freedom" in exercising their guaranteed rights under the Act.

The national labor policy makes clear that it is the employees who should decide whether they wish to be represented by a union for purposes of collective bargaining or whether they wish to refrain from the exercise of their statutory right to self-organization.[8] In this context, therefore, it is

------

[7] To be candid, there are no purely objective criteria to determine the greater appropriateness of one bargaining structure over another. The writer has always found it necessary to acknowledge a built-in preference for "P & M" units, dating back to the early years of the CIO, when it was fashionable to regard the craft unionists as "archaic" or "hopelessly behind the times." Most employers in manufacturing share a preference for industrial units for simplifying their negotiation chores. Many contractors in the building trades and many newspaper owners doubtless wish that unionization in their fields had not taken the multiple craft approach. Craft unionism, is however, a durable phenomenon. There seems small likelihood that it will be completely (or even partially) replaced by another structural form in most of the areas where it is now dominant.

[8] It is desirable to quote Section 7 in its entirety at this point. The underlined words were added to the original Section 7 (Wagner Act) by the Taft-Hartley Act (1947). Section 7 reads as follows:

> Employees shall have the right to self-organization, to form, join, or assist labor organizations, to bargain collectively through representatives of their own choosing, and to engage in *other* concerted activities for the purpose of collective bargaining or other mutual aid or protection, *and shall also have the right to refrain from any or all of such activities except to the extent that such right may be affected by an agreement requiring membership in a labor organization as a condition of employment as authorized in section 8(a)(3).*

The last part of Section 7, quoted above, refers to a valid union-shop agreement.

logical that the *desires of the employees concerned* should be of paramount significance in determining the nature and shape of the bargaining unit.

The NLRB normally accords great weight to the desires of employees in unit cases. Where the unit question is in dispute, however, the Board's decision necessarily cannot honor the claims of all competing organizations. The NLRB generally gives short shrift to the employer's unit preference, no matter how logical it may be, if the pattern of unionization among his employees has taken a different course. When the employer and union agree on the structure of the bargaining unit, the Board will usually accept the joint determination of the parties.

The desires of the employees in particular cases will always be a factor of great importance, but many other factors or criteria are relevant to a decision of unit issues. These include the following:

1. Bargaining history in the plant or industry.
2. The membership eligibility requirements of the union or unions involved.
3. The presence of a "community of interest" among the employees in the unit sought as appropriate.
4. The similarity of wage scales, hours and working conditions among employees in the unit sought as appropriate.
5. The form or extent of present self-organization among employees.
6. The presence of a "functional coherence and interdependence" among the work operations covered in the unit sought as appropriate.
7. The organization of the employer's business and its relationship to the proposed bargaining unit, including geographical considerations if more than one plant is involved.

In cases of partial unionization, the NLRB is again considering the extent and manner of self-organization among employees. Formerly the Board had dismissed union petitions because organization had taken place only in one department of a multidepartment enterprise on the grounds that structural logic called for a bargaining unit embracing all nonsupervisory employees. Currently, in cases involving department stores, supermarkets and the like, the NLRB will recognize partial organization and establish units as appropriate that constitute only a part of the larger unit that might ultimately be deemed more logical.

OLD AND NEW STRUCTURAL PROBLEMS

Continuing structural problem areas for the NLRB and practitioners of bargaining include:

1. The craft versus industrial unit issue, with its companion problem of craft severance from an industrial unit.
2. Multi-employer bargaining structures and other forms of centralized

bargaining arrangements, with the variety of problems posed by increased policy-making authority in the hands of the international union.

Among the newer structural problems we may list:

1. The rise of coalition bargaining and increased interunion coordination in bargaining with employers.
2. Unit problems and related structural difficulties posed by the new laissez-faire, "first come, first served" organizational approach of unions attempting to reach the unorganized.

We shall first review the old or perennial structural problems and then take up some of the newer structural challenges.

THE CRAFT-INDUSTRIAL UNIT CONTROVERSY

The craft-industrial structural controversy is as old as the labor movement. Following the 1935 split between the AFL and the CIO the NLRB was frequently put on the spot in rival union disputes over representation rights. Section 9(b) imposed on the Board the duty to decide in each such case on the appropriate unit. There was no way to "duck" this responsibility. In 1937 the Board developed what I have always regarded as a sound pragmatic solution consistent with its statutory duty.

The Board's 1937 answer, known as the *Globe doctrine*, was also an ingenious approach to coping with the vexing political science problem of reconciling majority and minority rights. The Board applied it in cases where one or more AFL unions were petitioning for separate craft unit(s) as appropriate and an industrial union (CIO) was urging the appropriateness of a single plant-wide "P & M" unit. In such cases, the NLRB held that *when the considerations were evenly balanced*, it would allow the desires of employees in the minority craft group(s) to determine its decision.[9]

The ballots of employees in the disputed group(s) were segregated and counted separately. If a majority in a craft group voted for the petitioning AFL affiliate, the NLRB concluded that the employees desired a separate unit for purposes of collective bargaining. If a majority voted for the CIO union, this was interpreted by the NLRB as signifying a desire to be included in the broader industrial or "P & M" unit.

During the Wagner Act era the Board did not follow the *Globe* formula unless it found that the considerations were "evenly balanced" as between a separate craft unit(s) and an inclusive "P & M" unit. In 1947,

---

[9] *Globe Machine & Stemping Co.*, 3 *NLRB* 294 (1937), involved three AFL craft unions and the UAW. The Board held that in cases such as this, "where the considerations are so evenly balanced, the determining factor is the desire of the men themselves."

of course, Congress amended Section 9(b) in a way that was presumptively favorable to self-determination by minority craft groups. The NLRB's prior range of discretion was limited by precluding the Board from deciding that any craft unit is inappropriate on the ground that a different unit had been established by an earlier NLRB determination, unless a majority of employees in the proposed craft unit votes against separate representation. The amended 9(b) served to encourage craft separatism in a number of industries where industrial or "P & M" bargaining units had been operating for some time.

The best interests of free collective bargaining would not be served by freezing minority within an industrial unit against their will. It is questionable, however, whether statutory policy should openly favor any one type of bargaining-unit structure. The NLRB insisted that the amended language still left it enough discretion to determine under what conditions craft workers could vote for separate representation. The Board retained some low hurdles for any craft union seeking separate representation. These criteria were set forth in *American Potash*, which remained the leading case until 1967.[10] In *American Potash*, the Board set forth a basic requirement that the employees in the unit sought as appropriate must constitute a "true" craft grouping. Furthermore, the union seeking to represent these employees also needed to prove that historically it had represented workers in this craft. In simple terms, *American Potash* sought to distinguish between legitimate and illegitimate raiding of established bargaining units.

The NLRB's "New Look" (1967) at Craft Severance

In 1967 the Board chose *Mallinckrodt Chemical Works* as a vehicle for a re-examination of the issue as to the circumstances justifying craft severance.[11] In *Mallinckrodt* the Board put *American Potash* permanently to rest and also discarded an even older (1948) policy, represented by its *National Tube* doctrine, that had held certain industries to be so completely integrated functionally as to be exempt from organizing on a craft unit basis.[12]

Mallinckrodt appears at first to be more "liberal" from a craft unit standpoint than *American Potash* because the majority states that in determining craft severance issues the Board will consider *all* relevant factors, and not only the two prerequisites laid down in *American Potash*. Board member Fanning, however, was concerned over the prospect that *Mallinckrodt* in

---

[10] *American Potash & Chemical Corporation*, 107 *NLRB* 1418 (1954).

[11] *Mallinckrodt Chemical Works, Uranium Division*, 162 *NLRB* 387 (December 30, 1966).

[12] *National Tube Company*, 76 *NLRB* 1199 (1948).

application would rule out craft severance, thus negating the statutory presumption of Section 9(b)(2) in favor of craft units.

Under *Mallinckrodt* the Board considers *all* the following factors as relevant to a proper decision in any severance case:

1. Status of the employees as craftsmen working at their craft or of employees in a traditionally distinct department.
2. Existing patterns of bargaining relationships, their stabilizing effect and the possible effect of altering them.
3. Separate identity of the employees within the broader unit.
4. History and pattern of bargaining in the industry.
5. Degree of integration and interdependence of the production system.
6. Qualification and experience of the union seeking to represent the employees.

This sounds commendably thorough on the Board's part. However, Fanning predicted that consideration of *all* these factors "will inevitably make bargaining history the controlling consideration, and inasmuch as the issue cannot arise except where there is a bargaining history, the application of *Mallinckrodt* factors will effectively rule out craft severance."[13]

Enough time has passed since *Mallinckrodt* replaced *American Potash* as the ruling case to permit conclusions on its operational impact. Has *Mallinckrodt* made it easier (harder) for a craft group to split off from a "P & M" unit? This is the principal question.

Lawrence J. Cohen answers the above question in these terms:

> With respect to the severance cases as such, it has been noted that units have been severed in only two cases in the two years following *Mallinckrodt* and then only in circumstances which must be described as aberrational.
> . . . absent an abrupt change of direction, the future for separate craft or departmental units seems dim in general and positively bleak where severance is attempted. For one thing, the very application of the doctrine to date will tend to inhibit the filing of new petitions for severance. And, when such petitions are filed, the history of the *Mallinckrodt* doctrine to date affords little hope that those petitions will be granted.[14]

Cohen's conclusions were reached after a study of some fifty Board rulings in pertinent cases over about a two-year period since *Mallinckrodt*. Board member Fanning's views remained similar in April, 1969, to those he originally entertained.[15]

[13] The cold record since *Mallinckrodt* appears to bear out board member Fanning's forebodings. This at any rate is the conclusion of Lawrence J. Cohen in an April, 1969, *Labor Law Journal* article, cited in footnote 14 below.

[14] Lawrence J. Cohen, "Two Years under Mallinckrodt: A Review of the Board's Latest Craft Unit Policy," *Labor Law Journal*, XX (April, 1969), 195–215.

[15] John H. Fanning, "Representation Law: A Responsive Approach to the Exercise of Employee Rights" mimeographed (Address at the Pacific Coast Labor Law Conference, April 18, 1969), NLRB Release No. R-1139.

The temptation will be resisted here to take up the cudgels for or against *Mallinckrodt* as a way of handling the craft severance problem. It seems clear, however, that craft groups finding themselves unhappily locked into a "P & M" unit are not going to find the road out easy under *Mallinckrodt*. Perhaps the road should not be made easy for them. On the other hand, it goes against the grain to say that any group of employees should be constrained for any length of time to be represented in collective bargaining by a union or unions not of their own choosing.

I have already acknowledged my personal structural preferences. I believe these views are supportable on grounds of both logic and operational effectiveness in bargaining. At the same time it seems clear that congressional intent was to push the NLRB toward unit determinations presumptively favorable to craft groupings. If so, the Board has done a splendid job of bypassing such legislative strictures under both *American Potash* and *Mallinckrodt*.

There appears to be no completely effective or satisfying answer to the problem of craft severance. One can easily find fault with Congress for seeking to "move in" on the Board's discretion in determining units. One can also be critical of a sweeping policy that would sanction either automatic exit upon demand or the freezing of craft groups within "P & M" units against their manifest will.

The only effective approach seems to be a carefully eclectic one, weighing the special circumstances in each case as it arises. The long-run results of so doing may be inconsistent and will doubtless be unsatisfactory to any who seek a simplistic formula.

WILL CRAFT-INDUSTRIAL UNIT DISPUTES DECLINE?

Clashes between proponents of craft unionism and industrial unionism will probably never cease entirely, although the cost and futility of interunion raiding was demonstrated conclusively long ago.[16] In fact, the wastefulness of raiding was a key consideration leading to the merging of AFL and CIO in 1955.[17] Since the merger, craft-industrial unit conflicts have diminished considerably, although craft groups within "P & M" units

---

[16] The basic futility of raiding was conclusively demonstrated in the thorough statistical analysis made by Joseph Krislov, which showed that although particular affiliated unions might have gained by raiding, the net overall percentage change as between AFL and CIO unions was negligible. See Joseph Krislov, "Raiding Among the 'Legitimate' Unions," *Industrial and Labor Relations Review*, VIII (October, 1954), 19–29.

[17] See Mark L. Kahn, "Recent Jurisdictional Developments in Organized Labor," in Harold W. Davey, Howard S. Kaltenborn and Stanley H. Ruttenberg, eds., *New Dimensions in Collective Bargaining* (New York: Harper & Row, Publishers, 1959), pp. 3–28. Also Arthur J. Goldberg, *AFL-CIO: Labor United* (New York: McGraw-Hill Book Company, Inc., 1956).

frequently allege that their bargaining interests are being neglected as just noted. To cite just one of many examples, the UAW faced a delicate problem in satisfying the wage demands of its skilled trade components in both the 1967 and the 1970 negotiations in the automobile industry.

Craftsmen are customarily paid on an hourly basis, whether in manufacturing or elsewhere. Although their wages often seem attractive enough they often find that semi-skilled production workers (especially those on incentive payment plans) are "hot on their trail." The craft groups are thus always pushing to increase the interoccupational spread, not always successfully.[18]

The declining incidence of interunion warfare should probably be regarded on balance as a constructive development. We should acknowledge, however, that when rival union conflicts come to an end (through merger or otherwise) the cherished concept of "unions of their own choosing" loses much of its meaning. Employees currently seeking to unionize for the first time are often realistically limited to one union and to one form of bargaining unit structure.[19] They do not have the opportunity to shop around for the labor organizations competing for their allegiance.

The NLRB's Preference for Multi-Plant Units

Concerned about this lack of choice, George Brooks and Mark Thompson have been highly critical of the NLRB's strong predilection for multi-plant units with its consequent adverse effect on free choice of representation in particular plants.[20] The certified union on a multi-plant basis may not be serving the needs of employees in a particular plant, but the remedy of selecting another labor organization is difficult to achieve.

Brooks and Thompson contend that the NLRB has already made clear to the parties in multi-plant units how to continue living in their "carefully protected world," through avoiding such hazards as decertification, craft severance petitions, independent unionism or the nuisance of elections. They can do so, say Brooks and Thompson, by merely inserting in their contract a clear statement of intent to bargain on a multi-plant basis, carefully listing the plants covered thereby and always taking pains to use the words "agreement" and "unit" in the singular. In this way, it is asserted, the multi-plant unit becomes invulnerable to separatism by the dissatisfied at any one plant.

---

[18] For more complete discussion of this critical structural problem in wage determination see Chapter 10 of this volume.

[19] See George W. Brooks and Mark Thompson, "Multiplant Units: The NLRB's Withdrawal of Free Choice," *Industrial and Labor Relations Review* XX (April, 1967), 363–80.

[20] Brooks and Thompson would permit elections on a plant basis without regard to whether the plant in question is already a part of a multi-plant unit. *Ibid.*, p. 378.

The trend toward more inclusive bargaining units appears likely to continue, however. The requirements of bargaining will take priority over self-determination goals, particularly where the former accommodate the institutional security needs of the union involved and also make sense in terms of the structural development of the employer. The Brooks-Thompson critique is relevant, however, to the following discussion of multi-employer bargaining, centralized bargaining and multi-union, coalition or coordinated bargaining. Their indictment should not be casually dismissed.

THE LOGIC OF CENTRALIZED BARGAINING STRUCTURES AND MULTI-EMPLOYER BARGAINING

Structural forms of bargaining developed by both management and organized labor have been influenced by the apparent need for increasing centralization of authority over policy determination. There is a constant pressure to match organizational strength with co-extensive organizational strength wherever possible.

Centralization of bargaining structures has been in evidence for some time. It is a corollary of the increasing size of many business and labor organizations.[21] As a corporation or a labor organization expands, the possibility of effective local determination of basic policies (let alone conduct of actual negotiations in collective bargaining) diminishes accordingly.

This basic shift in the locus of power in bargaining relationships scarcely needs illustration. In many unions, particularly in manufacturing, there has been a steady accretion of power in the hands of the international union at the expense of its member locals. On the management side, the pattern of centralization is most clearly visible in the rapid development of employer associations for labor relations, chiefly when the key labor organization in the field is more powerful than individual employers in the industry affected.

Highly centralized bargaining characterizes such industries as automobiles, steel and rubber. Although contracts are still signed on a company-by-company basis, the negotiations themselves are hard to distinguish from formal multi-employer bargaining.

---

[21] According to BLS, reporting on membership for some 190 national unions, in 1966 the ten largest unions, each with membership over 400,000, accounted for 45 percent of total membership. At the other extreme, 91 unions, each with less than 25,000 members, represented less than 4 percent of total union membership. See U.S. Bureau of Labor Statistics, *Directory of National and International Labor Unions in the United States, 1967*, Bulletin No. 1596 (Washington D.C.: Government Printing Office, 1968), p. 59. These figures dramatize the extent to which there has developed a concentration within the labor movement not unlike the concentration of a more familiar nature in the big business category.

The UAW and the major auto companies still preserve the appearance of separate negotiations, but employers engage in constant communication and information-sharing as the nearly simultaneous negotiation sessions go forward. In steel, eleven major companies bargain on a united front basis with the Steelworkers' Union, although each company signs its own agreement. For some time, the major rubber companies have conducted virtually simultaneous negotiations with the United Rubber, Cork, Linoleum and Plastic Workers of America, AFL-CIO. Once again we can note a high degree of coordination on the management side, even though the bargaining remains technically on an individual company basis.

In the industries mentioned, it is most unlikely that the *de facto* centralization on the employer side will be transformed into *de jure* multi-employer structures and contracts. Information-sharing, coordination in strategy and constant communication are already well developed, but the technical bargaining structure in all probability will remain on a single company basis. An important consideration is the justifiable fear of running afoul of federal antitrust legislation.[22] Furthermore, steel, automobiles and rubber have been noted for the fierce individualistic autonomy displayed by the corporate giants involved.

Formal multi-employer bargaining has long been a popular bargaining structure when many small employers are confronted by a union that is far more powerful economically than any of them individually. When small employers must negotiate with a union representing all or nearly all the workers in the particular industry or labor market area, the pooling of management strength and know-how in a multi-employer organization for labor relations purposes makes complete sense from the employers' standpoint.

Employer labor relations associations developed first in highly competitive, small-firm industries such as men's and women's clothing, trucking and baking, rather than in oligopolistic industries such as automobiles, steel and meatpacking. The large and powerful firms in the latter case are reluctant to surrender any portion of their existing sovereignty to a central labor relations policy committee. They still consider their individual economic strength is sufficient to warrant effective separate negotiations with the chief labor organization involved, although "cooperation" among the corporate giants is visibly increasing.

The continued growth of multi-employer bargaining arrangements

---

[22] John Kenneth Galbraith argues persuasively that "the antitrust laws, in seeking to preserve the market, are an anachronism in the larger world of industrial planning." See his *The New Industrial State* (Boston: Houghton Mifflin Company, 1967), p. 197. However, in something as visible as the structure of collective bargaining relationships there would seem to remain some restraining impact.

is favored by both management and union needs for greater institutional security. Whether the industry be oligopolistic or competitive, the unions involved never feel entirely secure when employers are only partially organized. The economic power of an industrial union rests not on control of the labor supply but on control of the employer through negotiated job security provisions and union shop clauses. With some exceptions, such as longshoring, industrial unions do not concern themselves with the employer's hiring policies. Nor are they in a position to restrict entrance to the trade, as are many craft unions. The institutional security of an industrial union depends on consolidating its position in the industry by unionizing all employers if possible and certainly all the major ones. When an industry is only partially unionized, the unorganized segment represents a constant threat to (or restraint upon) standards negotiated with the union firms. Textiles and chemicals are two examples of partially unionized industries where the unions involved are always "insecure."

Such considerations are basic to union drives for full unionization of an industry in order to take wages out of competition and to insure effective similarity in basic employment conditions. Once these objectives have been achieved, the institutional security of the union (or unions) in question is assured. The union leadership can then become more "statesmanlike," particularly when industry coverage takes the structural form of a multi-employer bargaining unit. Associational bargaining sharply reduces the possibility of successful rival unionism and effectively narrows the options of the employees involved.

Where formal multi-employer bargaining arrangements are not feasible, as in the case of oligopolistic industries dominated by a few large firms, union emphasis will often be on pattern bargaining as the most effective instrumentality for achieving an approximation of uniformity on basic economic provisions, major fringes and key contract clauses governing on-the-job relationships. Again the underlying motivation is union institutional security flowing from the achievement and protection of desired standards.

A comparable logic often lies behind management support for multi-employer bargaining arrangements. Under an associational union agreement, an employer may actually be paying higher wages and benefits than would have been the case under single-company bargaining. However, if he knows that his principal competitors are operating under approximately the same conditions, he is freed from the fear of being "whipsawed" by the union or of being undersold in his market by other employers paying "substandard" wages.

The multi-employer agreement, by taking wages out of competition, removes important unknown factors in the employer's advance calculations. It reduces risk and uncertainty and promotes stability. In spite of the continued homage paid to the competitive ideal in our economy, most employers prudently seek to avoid the risks of competition when they can. Multi-employer bargaining arrangements are frequently a product of management desire to avoid the hazards of competition.

The necessity for equalizing bargaining strength has also been a powerful stimulus to multi-employer bargaining. A union organizing an industry with strong central employer control has to unionize the entire industry before it can achieve a power position equal to the employers' united front. Employers in an industry controlled by a single union have a similar incentive to combination. Such employers are individually incapable of negotiating effectively with a labor organization whose power is coextensive with the industry as a whole. It is in the self-interest of such employers to combine into a labor relations association under such circumstances.

MULTI-EMPLOYER BARGAINING STRUCTURES: BOON OR CURSE?

The arguments for and against multi-employer bargaining retain a lively interest for most observers of the collective bargaining process. The controversy illustrates a major finding in this analysis, as stressed in the preceding chapter, namely, the fascinating variety in bargaining arrangements.

There is no model structure in collective bargaining that can be scientifically approved as best for all concerned in all situations. How one views multi-employer bargaining as a structural form depends greatly on his expectations and assumptions. For example, multi-employer bargaining clearly promotes stability at the expense of some loss of discretion and flexibility in local union-management relationships. Whether this is viewed as a plus or a minus depends on the relative importance one attaches to stability on the one hand and local autonomy on the other.

To take one more illustration, multi-employer bargaining promotes wage uniformity for particular categories of labor. It insures similarity in the timing and amount of changes in wage levels and basic fringes in the entire unit covered by the master contract. Most parties to multi-employer arrangements, whether they be union or management, favor taking wages out of competition. Such a development will not be regarded favorably by those who prefer single-employer bargaining as a matter of principle or who fear that consumer costs will be higher when wages are not determined "competitively" through the market mechanism.

The arguments for and against multi-employer bargaining do not change appreciably over the years. We shall outline them at this point.

The Case for Multi-Employer Bargaining

The principal arguments in favor of multi-employer bargaining include the following:

1. Determination of wage policy on a multi-employer basis (particularly when the bargaining is genuinely industry-wide or area-wide) will effectively remove wages as a competitive element in cost. Such a stabilization through application of uniform standards enables employers to know where they stand on the vital element of labor cost in comparison with their competitors in the industry or in the area.

2. Removal of labor cost as a competitive item will intensify product and market competition in other areas such as managerial efficiency, worker productivity, quality of product and distributive efficiency. The consumer should actually benefit from this intensified nonwage competition.

3. Multi-employer bargaining is generally more mature and responsible than individual plant negotiations. The employers and the union may be expected to have an informed and far-sighted understanding of the future impact of their wage bargain.

4. Multi-employer bargaining is conducive to industrial peace. Fewer strikes will occur under multi-employer bargaining. The parties appreciate the external impact of a strike and its probable adverse effect on public opinion. Two common sources of strikes under individual plant bargaining are eliminated in a multi-employer bargaining structure. One is striking a particular employer as an industry target for gaining new objectives. The second is the strike to bring an erring employer into line.

5. Multi-employer bargaining permits effective joint efforts to withstand the ruinous competition from nonunion sectors of the same industry or from low-paying producers of substitutable products in other industries. As multi-employer bargaining approaches genuine industry-wide arrangements, the submarginal firm is either brought into line or frozen out.

6. The individual employer actually has more of a voice under multi-employer bargaining than he is likely to have under pattern bargaining. Also, multi-employer bargaining can be sufficiently flexible to permit special departures from the industry norm when this is necessary. Under pattern bargaining, on the other hand, the individual firm faced by a very powerful union may have to swallow the whole pattern on a take-it-or-else basis.

7. A multi-employer bargaining structure facilitates the possibility of reaching a mutually satisfactory and effective accord on such vital subjects as wage uniformity, standardization of job titles and job classifications

and interplant wage rationalization (that is, elimination of interplant occupational rate inequities).

8. Multi-employer bargaining should have greater beneficial effects in relation to general economic stability than bargaining on an individual employer basis for the following reasons:

a. In multi-employer bargaining serious consideration can be given to the relationship between increases or decreases in wage rates and the volume of employment opportunities. This is an unlikely possibility under a fractionalized bargaining structure.

b. General wage movements may be slower and less extreme under multi-employer bargaining arrangements than is frequently the case under individual plant bargaining. To the extent that this is the case, multi-employer bargaining may operate as a restraining influence in inflationary periods and as a cushioning or stabilizing force during deflationary periods.

9. Multi-employer bargaining arrangements permit workable accommodations between the simultaneous needs for uniformity and diversity. The interdependent structure of our economy increasingly requires central determination of major policy issues in the interest of uniformity. This can best be done through multi-employer bargaining. At the same time, the genuine values of democratic labor relations can be preserved by providing for a maximum of decentralization in administration and implementation of centrally negotiated collective agreements.

THE CASE AGAINST MULTI-EMPLOYER BARGAINING

The arguments generally raised against multi-employer bargaining include the following:

1. Multi-employer bargaining on wages and other economic demands will produce an undesirable uniformity rather than equitable stabilization of labor costs. The result will be joint collusion against consumer interests.

2. Instead of raising the intensity of nonwage competition, multi-employer bargaining will produce a cost structure so high that new firms will be unable to enter the industry. Undesirable economic concentration will occur at the consumer's expense.

3. Strikes may be fewer in number but their destructive potential, when they occur, is far greater than under individual plant bargaining. Strikes involving all or a large number of firms in an industry can have paralyzing effects on other sectors of the economy dependent on the struck industry.

4. Wage rigidities in a declining market will increase unemploy-

ment, reduce purchasing power and otherwise exacerbate the deflationary spiral.

5. Individual firms will be unable to achieve policies suited to their own needs. They will be bound by the terms of a master agreement in whose negotiation they had little chance to secure recognition for their particular problems and requirements.

6. Multi-employer bargaining destroys decision-making authority by local unions. Such a result completely negates the concept of the union as an instrument for democratization of industrial relations. The subordination of the local union to the international union is not limited to negotiation of major policy issues but takes place in contract administration as well.

7. Centralized bargaining structures, particularly when industry-wide in scope, are antagonistic to the principles of the competitive free-enterprise system. Monopoly power is strengthened on both sides of the bargaining table. It is unrealistic to assert that management and union "giants" will under organized bilateral monopoly be "responsible" and sensitive to consumer interests. As consumer frustration and anger increases, the demand for increased public intervention will lead eventually to wage-price-investment controls and the end of the private enterprise economy as we know it.

Detached analysis of multi-employer bargaining as a structural form requires the conclusion that a purely favorable or unfavorable verdict is not appropriate. The source and direction of the arguments listed must be carefully noted. In any event, academic controversy over the merits of multi-employer bargaining has not visibly affected the practitioners. Multi-employer bargaining structures have proven to be remarkably durable and seem to have been generally satisfactory to the parties.

My own evaluation of multi-employer bargaining has been on balance a favorable one over many years. These structural arrangements were developed in answer to legitimate needs of both employer and union forces. The advantages flowing from greater stability, more informed and professional bargaining and the incentive to employers to compete on bases other than labor cost to my mind outweigh the disadvantages of reduced local autonomy, somewhat greater rigidity in wage movements and perhaps, in some cases, increased product costs traceable to labor cost equalization at a higher level than under "competitive" conditions.

Perhaps the most publicized examples of multi-employer bargaining structures are those in trucking and construction. These are also industries where the tacit employer-union collusion against the best interests of the consumer is always a possibility. James R. Hoffa's amoral end-justifies-the-means approach in labor relations has caused him to be regarded as chief villain of the labor movement. His stormy career could form the basis for an interesting digression.[23] However, we shall simply note Hoffa's dedication to enlarging the coverage of multi-employer trucking contracts to approximate true national bargaining in this industry. Most trucking firms, understandably concerned about the economic strength of the Teamsters, appear to support multi-employer contracts just as vigorously as Hoffa himself. Only through such a structural form can trucking management hope to negotiate with the Teamsters on approximately equal terms. For economic power reasons, the Teamsters *and* the truckers *jointly favor joint bargaining.*

In the building and construction field, particularly in urban areas, the bargaining is often on a multi-employer basis between the basic craft unions and various employer construction associations. In construction labor cost represents a substantial portion of total cost. The wage bill is perhaps a bit stiffer than it might be if there were more complete multi-employer bargaining. Current practice generally involves separate negotiations at different times with several contractor associations. This suggests that management in the construction industry might improve their bargaining leverage through greater unity among contractors of all types.

TWO STRUCTURAL PROBLEMS WITH NEW DIMENSIONS— COALITION BARGAINING AND LAISSEZ-FAIRE UNIONIZATION

We have already noted the NLRB preference for multi-plant units and the Brooks-Thompson concern over the implications of this preference. Such discussion was couched in a framework of employer-union concurrence on the desirability of a multi-plant bargaining unit structure. Another important aspect of the centralized bargaining structure trend relates to what is termed "coalition bargaining" or "coordinated bargaining."[24] The structural phenomenon that has given prominence to coalition bargaining is the

---

[23] Much has been written about the Teamsters and James R. Hoffa. In my mind the most thorough and absorbing work is that of Ralph and Estelle James, *Hoffa and the Teamsters* (Princeton, N. J.: D. Van Nostrand Company, Inc., 1965).

[24] The terms "coalition bargaining" and "coordinated bargaining" are used interchangeably by some writers. Others seek to draw neat distinctions between the two. Management practitioners generally speak of "coalition bargaining" whereas union spokesmen clearly prefer the term "coordinated bargaining." Both are talking about what Lynn Wagner has termed "multi-union bargaining" in his analysis of the legal aspects of this structural phenomenon. See Lynn E. Wagner, "Multi-Union Bargaining: A Legal Analysis," *Labor Law Journal*, XIX, (December, 1968), 731–42. Wagner uses the term "coalition bargaining" to apply to situations where two or more unions bargain jointly for a common "master agreement" covering all the employees which they purport to represent. He applies the term "coordinated bargaining" to circumstances where two or more unions representing separate bargaining units are negotiating jointly for individual unit contracts containing common terms.

growth of "conglomerate" enterprises. Union efforts at coalition bargaining are not new.[25] However, the drive to achieve company-wide contracts with "conglomerates" is a new twist.

The term "conglomerate" has become a part of the living language so that we shall hereafter dispense with the quotation marks. A conglomerate enterprise is a large firm, well-known for one type of product(s) in a particular industry, that has expanded through purchase or merger into other industries or product lines.

The best-known example of union coalition bargaining with conglomerates involves the IUE (International Union of Electrical, Radio and Machine Workers, AFL-CIO) together with some eleven other AFL-CIO unions negotiating with General Electric and Westinghouse.[26] It is by no means the only one. The Industrial Union Department (IUD) of the AFL-CIO has established more than fifty interunion "coordinating committees." Most of these committees are set up on an employer basis and have been initiated with the hope that the interunion cooperation will be a continuing thing rather than just a contract-time association.

It is important to consider the possible impact on bargaining structures from such an intensified union emphasis on coalition or coordinated bargaining. The heart of the coalition bargaining matter is comparative economic strength. The unions' concern relates to the felt compulsion to match institutional management power. Which structural arrangement is the most logical and which bargaining unit is most appropriate are of secondary importance. The unions participating in coordinated bargaining efforts remain conscious of their traditional autonomy and organizational lines. However, they have a paramount interest in developing a united front in negotiating with conglomerate employers. The conglomerate illustrates an important structural change on the management side of the bargaining table. Whether it will be paralleled by organic structural changes on the union side is an intriguing question.

Herbert J. Lahne, a knowledgeable student of union structures, suggests that structural changes may involve consolidation of existing unions or the formation of new enterprise unions.[27] Lahne envisages the possible

---

[25] Multi-union bargaining in a more conventional sense is a familiar thing in building and construction and in the metal trades. In many cases the multiple craft unions involved maintain their craft identity while at the same time negotiating as a joint union council with either a common single employer or with a multi-employer association.

[26] For an optimistic union analysis of the 1966 bargaining with GE and Westinghouse, see David Lasser, "A Victory for Coordinated Bargaining," *AFL-CIO American Federationist* (April, 1967). For a less sympathetic analysis, see a recent monograph by William L. Chernish, *Coalition Bargaining: A Study of Union Tactics and Public Policy* (Philadelphia, Pa.: University of Pennsylvania Press, 1969). See also George H. Hildebrand, "Cloudy Future for Coalition Bargaining," *Harvard Business Review*, XLVI (November–December, 1968), 114–28.

[27] Herbert J. Lahne, *op. cit.*, footnote 3 above.

movement of the locals of all national unions dealing with a particular employer into the national union dominant with such employer. In the case of GE and Westinghouse, for example, this would be the IUE. In the copper industry, the flow would be toward the United Steelworkers of America (USA), the principal union in the unsuccessful 1967–1968 drive of twenty-five AFL-CIO affiliates to obtain company-wide agreements with common expiration dates from the major copper companies.[28]

Lahne has observed that there are many institutional barriers to any such consolidation of the coalition unions. There are also important legal problems relating to NLRB certifications, plus such problems as employer attitudes toward recognition of the new union consolidation as the bargaining representative. The ultimate structural logic, however, may well someday produce conglomerate unions facing conglomerate employers, with each union based on its employer identification regardless of what products he turns out. Such a development would approximate what Lahne terms "enterprise unionism."[29] Continued emphasis on annual (or even lifetime) guarantees in worker income and on welfare and pension security is a factor that might assist in ultimately bringing about enterprise unionism.

Multi-union coalition bargaining at contract time will continue in some areas and perhaps expand. Yet it seems unlikely that these efforts will produce structural union transformations of the type contemplated by Lahne in the near future, no matter how logical they may appear to be.

We now turn briefly to another recent development with significant structural implications—the laissez-faire approach to organizing the unorganized.

The Laissez-Faire Approach to Organizing the Unorganized— Its Impact on Bargaining Structures

In the days of Samuel Gompers great stress was laid on the importance of unique or exclusive jurisdiction. Each affiliated union had an assigned territory to which its organizational ambitions were to be confined. In a craft-dominated federation this principle of one union to a trade or

---

[28] The multi-union drive in 1967–68 against the major copper companies failed (after a long strike) to achieve the coalition's principal objective, company-wide agreements with common expiration dates. The unions also ran into NLRB unfair practice proceedings on the basis that they were insisting to the point of impasse on a nonmandatory demand.

[29] Herbert J. Lahne, *op. cit.*, footnote 3 above. Lahne engages in some intriguing speculation about the possibility of structural transformation into something akin to the Japanese form of unionism. The latter is geared to particular employers and employees who have a lifetime connection with the same employer. Anything of this nature strikes me as being a long way down the road, given the traditional American penchant for mobility.

craft made sense as a means of avoiding what Gompers regarded as a cardinal sin, that is, dual unionism.[30]

One reason why the CIO was anathema to old-line AFL craft unionists was because John L. Lewis took over the exclusive jurisdiction idea on behalf of industrial unions, thus seeking to foreclose any craft organizing within steel, automobiles and other basic manufacturing industries. Once the AFL recovered from the shock of early CIO success, many of its affiliated unions went into direct competition with the CIO by organizing on an industrial basis as well as seeking to maintain or create craft units within "P & M" domains. Twenty years of union organizational warfare had a shattering effect on the old concept of unique or exclusive jurisdiction. When the two rival federations were at last ready to merge there was a tacit recognition in both camps that merger was possible only through accepting the representational holdings of each AFL and CIO affiliate at the time as being appropriate, whatever they may have been, and then continuing to enforce the 1953 no-raiding agreement.[31]

In the years since the merger of AFL and CIO in 1955 there has not been any appreciable amount of tidying up of organizational status, either through organic merger of rival unions or through surrender by any union of membership territory already acquired. The voices of the structural purists have been muted. Furthermore, drives to organize the unorganized have been led mainly by unions such as the Teamsters who have displayed a thorough lack of concern over whether the employees they were signing up might not more logically have been unionized by another organization.

The enterprise shown by the Teamsters in recent years has made it our closest approximation to the British concept of a "general" union. The Teamsters have readily adapted their structural bargaining forms in custom-made fashion to the requirements and preferences of employee groups choosing them for representation purposes. In one case it may be a conventional "P & M" unit; in another, a strict craft unit or a multiple-craft structure. Among the more unusual categories currently represented by Teamster locals we can list the following: registered nurses, retail department store employees, soya bean processing mill employees, public school teachers, policemen and (unsuccessfully to date) professional athletes.[32]

If one starts from the premise that employees are better off being

---

[30] For a perceptive analysis of the erosion of the Gompers' unique jurisdiction concept, see Benjamin S. Stephansky, "The Structure of the American Labor Movement," in *Interpreting the Labor Movement*, ed. George W. Brooks, *et al.* (Madison, Wis,: Industrial Relations Research Association, 1952), pp. 39–69.

[31] See David L. Cole, "Jurisdictional Issues and the Promise of Merger," *Industrial and Labor Relations Review*, IX (April, 1956), 391–405.

[32] The Teamsters have made several well-publicized overtures offering to represent professional football players. The latter, however, appear to be doing rather well through their own brand of "independent" unionism.

bargained for by *some* union rather than *no* union, there is no cause to be concerned about the new approach to organizing the unorganized. If, however, one assumes that there should be *some* correlation between union specialization in employment categories and ability to provide effective representation, there is room to doubt whether the laissez-faire approach is likely to prove optimal from the standpoint of either the employees concerned or the labor movement as such. Whatever one's view may be, it is a fact that much organizing initiative has been successfully undertaken in recent years by the "wrong" unions.

Some intriguing examples of the new organizing approach can be found in the public sector. Although unions with traditional jurisdictional rights in government employment have shown substantial growth since January, 1962, considerable organizing initiative has also been displayed by some unions that are generally private-sector-oriented.[33] For example, the maintenance and custodial employees of the University of Northern Iowa in Cedar Falls, Iowa, sought to bargain with the university in 1968 through the United Packinghouse, Food and Allied Workers of America.[34] In 1969 the Communications Workers of America obligingly offered a union bargaining home to the employees of the Iowa Employment Security Commission.[35] These two illustrations are by no means unusual or atypical.

Perhaps it is appropriate that the drive toward unionization among public sector employees, whether on a logical or illogical basis judged by conventional jurisdictional norms, should have picked up steam in calendar 1969, the year in which the CIO's organizational genius, John L. Lewis, died peacefully at age eighty-nine.[36] Lewis made the slogan "organize the unorganized" the watchword of the CIO. It was he who created the controversial District 50 of the United Mine Workers as an organizational mechanism for unionizing any employees, regardless of their industry or occupation. Although some of District 50's more ambitious efforts must be

---

[33] Executive Order No. 10988, issued by President John F. Kennedy in January, 1962, had a pronounced catalytic effect on unionization among federal government employees, with strong side waves of enthusiasm extending to state and local government employees as well. For a concise review of the accelerated union push at all government levels, see Howard J. Anderson, ed., *Public Employee Organization and Bargaining* (Washington, D.C.: The Bureau of National Affairs, Inc., 1968). See also Everett M. Kassalow, "Trade Unionism Goes Public," *The Public Interest*, No. 14 (Winter, 1969), 118–30.

[34] The circumstances of this unusual bit of unionization and the subsequent court proceedings are related in Richard F. Dole, Jr., "State and Local Public Employee Collective Bargaining in the Absence of Explicit Legislative Authorization," *Iowa Law Review*, LIV (February, 1969), 539–59.

[35] *Des Moines Register*, August 6, 1969.

[36] John L. Lewis became something of a dog in the manger as far as the labor movement was concerned after resigning as head of the CIO in 1940. It seems certain, however, that by the year 2000 and thereafter his name will be among the few that are remembered in union history. Lewis' enduring contribution, in my judgment, was demonstrating conclusively the viability of industrial unionism in mass production industries.

labeled failures (for example, chemical workers and construction craftsmen), this Lewis brainchild continues to display considerable vitality in a rather startling variety of industrial and occupational lines.

The newer free-wheeling approaches to organization complicate the task of predicting the future of structural bargaining arrangements. To some they provide cause for grave concern, if not actual alarm. In the overall picture, however, the dominant structural patterns will not be greatly influenced by the more bizarre organizing efforts.

FUTURE STRUCTURAL DEVELOPMENTS

Union efforts to promote coalition bargaining will continue. Yet it seems unlikely that the conglomerate-wide master contract will become a reality in the near future (unless the target conglomerate firm should elect to go along on its own motion). An ironic sidelight is that many of the major conglomerates, notably GE, lay great store by their *decentralization* program to increase efficiency and promote more vigorous competition among units under the corporate umbrella. This management stress on decentralization has taken place at the same time the affected unions were stepping up their drive for company-wide agreements. Many of the major conglomerates are more effectively decentralized than ever before, for some purposes. It should be emphasized that the decentralized autonomy enjoyed by individual plants *does not extend to labor relations.* In this area policy control is centrally maintained in firm and undeviating fashion, thus lending support to the unions' repeated assertions that their only solution for effective bargaining is on a multi-union, conglomerate-wide basis.

In final summary on other structural problems treated in this chapter we can note as follows:

1. Single plant "P & M" units should continue to be the most prevalent in manufacturing. Multiple craft arrangements will remain dominant in building and construction and in many service industries such as airlines, railroads and newspapers.
2. The long-term trend toward centralized bargaining structures should continue, notwithstanding some resurgence of local union initiative. Structural logic and bargaining efforts to obtain company-wide contracts both will serve to promote greater centralization.
3. The craft-industrial controversy will remain with us, but its intensity should be reduced by the impact of technology (prefabricated construction, for example) and by the observed looser patterns of organizing the unorganized.
4. Craft severance from "P & M" units will be rare under the *Mallinckrodt* approach. The NLRB will continue to receive both deserved and unjust criticism for its decisional policies in this and other representation case matters.

In Chapter 3 we shall examine the impact of federal public policy on the collective bargaining process, stressing in particular legislative control over private discretion as to the subject matter and procedures of bargaining.

SELECTED BIBLIOGRAPHY

CHANDLER, MARGARET K., "Craft Bargaining," in *Frontiers of Collective Bargaining*, ed. John T. Dunlop and Neil W. Chamberlain, pp. 50–74. New York: Harper & Row, Publishers, 1967.

CHERNISH, WILLIAM L., *Coalition Bargaining: A Study of Union Tactics and Public Policy*. Philadelphia, Pa:. University of Pennsylvania Press, 1969.

COHEN, LAURENCE J., "Two Years under Mallinckrodt: A Review of the Board's Latest Craft Unit Policy," *Labor Law Journal*, XX (April, 1969), 195–215.

GALENSON, WALTER, *The CIO Challenge to the AFL*. Cambridge, Mass.: Harvard University Press, 1960.

GROSPIRON, ALVIN F., "Coordinated Bargaining—A Union View," in *Crisis in Bargaining?*, ed. Luke Power, Samuel H. Sackman and Eugene A. Walsh, pp. 33–41. Niagara Falls, N.Y.: Niagara University Press, 1969.

HILBERT, THOMAS F., Jr., "Coordinated Bargaining: A Management View," in *Crisis in Bargaining?*, Cited above, pp. 43–56.

HILDEBRAND, GEORGE H., "Cloudy Future for Coalition Bargaining," *Harvard Business Review*, XLVI (November–December, 1968), 114–28.

KLEINSORGE, PAUL L., AND WILLIAM C. KERBY, "The Pulp and Paper Rebellion: A New Pacific Coast Union," *Industrial Relations*, VI (October, 1966), 1–20.

LAHNE, HERBERT J., "Coalition Bargaining and the Future of Union Structure," *Labor Law Journal*, XVIII (June, 1967), 353–59.

ORR, JOHN A., "The Steelworker Bargaining Posture and the Future of Steel Collective Bargaining," *Labor Law Journal*, XIX (June, 1968), 352–57.

TAFT, PHILIP, *The Structure and Government of Labor Unions*. Cambridge, Mass.: Harvard University Press, 1954.

U.S. BUREAU OF LABOR STATISTICS, *Directory of National and International Unions, 1967*, Bulletin No. 1596. Washington, D.C.: Government Printing Office, 1968.

WAGNER, LYNN E., "Multi-Union Bargaining: A Legal Analysis," *Labor Law Journal*, XIX (December, 1968), 731–42.

WEBER, ARNOLD R., "Stability and Change in the Structure of Collective Bargaining," in *Challenges to Collective Bargaining*, ed. Lloyd Ulman, pp. 13–36. Englewood Cliffs, N.J.: Prentice-Hall, Inc., 1967.

THE PUBLIC POLICY FRAMEWORK
for collective bargaining

CHAPTER THREE

Public policy limits, conditions and controls relationships between unions and management in the United States in a more pervasive fashion than in any other country in the free world. Thus no realistic understanding of contemporary collective bargaining policies and procedures is possible without first considering the legal framework within which the practitioners of bargaining must operate, both as to contract negotiation and administration.

The cornerstone of federal policy in the field of labor relations law is the National Labor Relations Act of 1935 (Wagner Act), as amended substantially in 1947 by the Labor Management Relations Act of that year (Taft-Hartley Act) and again in 1959 by the Labor Management Reporting and Disclosure Act (Landrum-Griffin Act).[1] The national labor policy since 1935 has been to encourage the practice and procedure of collective bargaining and the freedom of employees to form and join unions of their own choosing. Since 1947, federal law has also sought to protect employees in their right to refrain from self-organization and collective bargaining if they so desire.

To effectuate such broad policy objectives, federal law prohibits as "unfair" certain specified employer and union practices that when committed interfere with or nullify the employee rights just mentioned. Federal law also establishes machinery for peaceful determination of questions in a variety of cases concerning employee choice as to representation or nonrepresentation.

ROLE OF THE NATIONAL LABOR RELATIONS BOARD

The federal administrative agency principally charged with administration of our national labor relations policy is the National Labor Relations Board. Throughout its lifetime since 1935 the NLRB has had two primary functions: (1) investigation and, where necessary, prosecution and adjudication of cases involving charges that unfair labor practices have been committed; and, (2) determination in particular cases, customarily by the technique of secret-ballot elections, as to whether workers desire to be represented by labor organizations for purposes of collective bargaining with their employers as to wages, hours of work and other conditions of employment.

The NLRB thus performs both *regulatory* functions (unfair practice cases) and *service* functions (representation cases) in the field of union-management relations. The Board has been a storm center of controversy over the years.[2] The critical attacks on the agency continue today.[3] Such criti-

---

[1] As indicated in Chapter 1, we are generally referring to the current federal law on labor relations as one statute—the National Labor Relations Act—except where otherwise indicated. Also, we are omitting the customary legal citations in referring to particular provisions of the law. For the initial (and sole) complete legal citation, refer back to footnote 10 in Chapter 1.

[2] In the late 1930s the NLRB was assailed as being, among other things "a drumhead court martial," "a Spanish inquisitory tribunal" and a "modern Judge Fury." This last characterization was applied to the Board by the famed *New York Times* correspondent, Arthur Krock. The torrent of criticism was so severe that *Fortune* magazine entitled a 1938 article on the Board and its operations, "The G—— D—— Labor Board." This was not, by the way, *Fortune*'s appraisal of the Board but a reflection of the tone of criticism that *Fortune* was investigating. See *Fortune*, VIII (October, 1938), 4. See also Harold W. Davey, "Separation of Functions and the National Labor Relations Board," *The University of Chicago Law Review*, VII (February, 1940), 328, 346.

[3] For a review of comparatively recent attacks, see Gene S. Booker and Alan Coe, "The NLRB and its Critics," *Labor Law Journal*, XVII (September, 1966), 522–31.

cism can be better understood if not justified when one remembers that the NLRB has always had the unenviable task of deciding cases in substantive problem areas where partisan convictions are strongly held and conflict of interests is both natural and unavoidable. At one time or another both employers and the unions have been extremely critical of particular Board decisions, policies and procedures. Furthermore, both management and organized labor in their political roles have sought to influence presidential appointments to the Board. They have tried to mold the agency to fit their conceptions of what should be by a variety of pressures. Both sides have appeared to prefer an NLRB that would be "impartially" in their own favor.

Attacks on the NLRB have marred its image and, in some cases, its performance. It is sometimes a far cry from the impartial, quasi-judicial administrative tribunal which Congress intended it to be. In retrospect it is also clear that many criticisms leveled at the Board should have been directed at the law the Board was administering.

The Wagner Act was *intentionally* one-sided in favor of unions in the sense that it prohibited employer practices and gave maximum encouragement to employees to unionize and to bargain collectively. Such a statutory bias was designed to redress a lack of balance heavily weighted in the employer's favor. The Taft-Hartley Act of 1947 was described by its supporters as an "equalizing" law because of its many specific restrictions and prohibitions of union conduct. The unions dubbed it a "slave labor law" at the time but have somehow managed to live with it. The federal law since 1947 has retained most of the strictures of Wagner Act days against employers while maintaining a batch of restraints on unions. It is scarcely to be wondered that the NLRB has been under a steady drum-fire of criticism through the years. It is charged with the unenviable task of administering a statute that is in a real sense schizophrenic.

SCOPE OF THE PRESENT ANALYSIS

No attempt is made here to evaluate all the criticisms that have at times nearly engulfed the Board and the legislation under which it operates. The focus is on selected statutory provisions and Board decisions whose impact has been on the private discretion of employers and unions engaged in collective bargaining. Anticipating no fundamental changes in federal labor relations law in the near future, I have elected not to comment on recurring proposals to deprive the Board of its unfair practice case jurisdiction and to turn such cases over to a system of federal labor courts.

In appraising the impact of federal law upon both procedural and substantive aspects of collective bargaining, the yardstick for evaluation will be whether, in my judgment, private collective bargaining institutions have been strengthened or weakened. This standard is concededly subjective. It incorporates my views on how collective bargaining should work and the appropriate role of public policy in furthering this objective.

Public Policy Problem Areas to Be Covered

Since it was not possible to cover the law relating to all important policy areas, the selection process, although somewhat painful, had to be undertaken.

The principal topics selected for analysis include the following:

1. NLRB policy on the scope of bargaining and the statutory duty to bargain.
2. A revisiting of public policy on union security provisions, state right-to-work legislation and Section 14(b).
3. Statutory restrictions on collective bargaining procedures, including limitations on the right to strike.
4. Brief examination of the controversy over the appropriate role of the NLRB, including analysis of both consensus and conflict areas on labor law revision.

We shall begin with a brief historical review and a summary description of the Board's function in representation and unfair practice cases.

State labor relations legislation is of vital importance to collective bargaining, but the analysis here is limited mainly to federal law.[4] Also, no detailed consideration can be given to such important matters as the state of the law relating to the weapons of economic conflict (for example, strikes, lockouts and boycotts); proposed legislation to bring union activity under the antitrust laws; and the impact of those sections of Landrum-Griffin that deal primarily with control of internal union affairs.

Whatever one may think of our national labor policy, one thing is certain: It is not the final word. In years past, for example, I was sufficiently optimistic (or, perhaps, naive) to hope that the incidence of employer and union unfair practices would decline over time to make legislation on these matters self-repealing. Reality made a mockery of such hopes. The

---

[4] Some knowledge of state labor relations law is essential to full understanding of the impact of public policy on collective bargaining. It is therefore excluded reluctantly from the scope of our analysis. For a comprehensive summary account of recent developments in the state labor legislation field, see Harold A. Katz and Bruce S. Feldacker, "The Decline and Fall of State Regulation of Labor Relations," *Labor Law Journal*, XX (June, 1969), 327–45. For historical comparison the reader should also consult an earlier survey by Katz, "Two Decades of State Labor Legislation: 1937–1957," *Labor Law Journal*, VIII (November, 1957), 747–58, 818. See also Katz's more comprehensive account covering the 1937–1947 decade, written with Harry A. Millis, in *The University of Chicago Law Review*, XV (1948), 282–310.

sober fact is that the NLRB's unfair practice case load has been running at record-high levels with no prospect of diminishing appreciably.[5]

By the same token, it was thought that the 1955 merger of the AFL and the CIO would remove some of the NLRB's problems in representation cases. This has not proved to be the case. The Board still must wrestle with some thorny bargaining unit questions.

Under President Eisenhower, the Board was charged by the unions with being pro-management in key decisional areas. Under Presidents Kennedy and Johnson, the Board was attacked by management for being pro-union. The criticism will doubtless never end. Some of it has been unfair, even vicious. Some has been healthy, constructive and probably deserved. We shall consider mainly the "responsible" criticism, adding some critical comments of our own.[6]

EVOLUTION OF PUBLIC POLICY

In general terms, public policy toward collective bargaining can be one of suppression, toleration, encouragement or regulation. All four governmental postures toward unionism and collective bargaining can be illustrated in U.S. experience.

Broadly speaking, public policy from the Revolutionary War period until 1842 was one of suppression. Union activity was stymied by the courts under English common law concepts of criminal conspiracy in restraint of trade. Following the famed 1842 decision, *Commonwealth of Massachusetts v. Hunt*,[7] unions were able to achieve some operational effectiveness, although they were still subject to severe judicial scrutiny as to whether their activities were for what the courts regarded as lawful purposes sought by lawful means.

From 1842 to World War I, public policy toward unions, as reflected in court decisions, followed an uncertain line between toleration and continued suppression. Whenever unions resorted to economic pressure from roughly 1900 on, they were likely to be blocked by court action through injunctions or antitrust prosecutions.

Federal recognition of union legitimacy and the legality of collective bargaining achieved no real momentum until the tight labor market period of U.S. participation in World War I. The anti-union policy syndrome

---

[5] In the last quarter of calendar 1968, a total of 2,819 charges of unfair labor practices were filed with the Board against employers and 1,491 charges of unfair labor practices against unions. NLRB Release No. S–121, February 13, 1969.

[6] As an illustration of responsible recent criticism, I refer the reader to Benjamin Aaron, "Labor Relations Law," in *Challenges to Collective Bargaining*, ed. Lloyd Ulman (Englewood Cliffs, N.J.: Prentice-Hall, Inc., 1967), pp. 113–33.

[7] 45 *Mass. 4 Met.* 111 (1842).

returned in force from 1918 until 1932. Passage of the Norris-LaGuardia Act[8] began a lengthy period of "encouragement" of unionism and collective bargaining, highlighted by the two years of Section 7(a) of the National Industrial Recovery Act (1933–1935) and ultimately the Wagner Act of 1935.

Prior to 1932 the public policy deck was stacked against unionism, with the exception of a brief period of emergency legitimacy during World War I and Railway Labor Act of 1926. At the bottom of the Great Depression, however, the pendulum swung toward a policy of "encouragement." Union needs and expectations were not met by the NIRA (1933–1935). Implementation of the fine-sounding language of Section 7(a) was partial and largely ineffectual.

The Wagner Act of 1935 was clearly the high point of unblushing *encouragement* of unionism and collective bargaining. It also marked the beginning of the *regulation* phase. Five employer practices were prohibited as unfair. Once the constitutionality of the Act was upheld in the Supreme Court's landmark decisions in April, 1937,[9] the National Labor Relations Board was able to move effectively to implement the national labor policy of encouraging the practice and procedure of collective bargaining.

It is difficult to exaggerate the importance of the Wagner Act and the Board as instrumentalities for facilitating the rapid growth of unionism.[10] Without wishing to deprecate the organizational genius of the late John L. Lewis and his fellow CIO leaders, we should recognize that unionization of steel, automobiles, rubber, electrical manufacturing and many other non-union industries would not have been possible without the psychological climate and the legal support that the Wagner Act and the NLRB supplied.

The Wagner Act period, 1935–1947, was basically one of governmental encouragement of collective bargaining. At the same time the specific prohibition of unfair practices for employers initiated the era of regulation in an inclusive and permanent sense. Also, the Board's representation case duties, notably its determination of appropriate units for bargaining in particular cases, demonstrated that performance of a service function can have important regulatory impact. The Board's unit decisions have vitally

---

[8] Act of March 23, 1932, 47 *Stat.* 70, 29 U.S.C. Secs. 101–15. The best comprehensive analysis of public policy prior to the Norris-LaGuardia Anti-Injunction Act of 1932 is that of Edwin E. Witte, *The Government in Labor Disputes* (New York: McGraw-Hill Book Company, Inc., 1932).

[9] The leading case of five decided by the Court on the same day was *National Labor Relations Board v. Jones and Laughlin Steel Corporation*, 301 *U.S.* 1 (1937).

[10] For the definitive study of the Wagner Act period (1935–1947), see Harry A. Millis and Emily C. Brown, *From the Wagner Act to Taft-Hartley* (Chicago, Ill.: University of Chicago Press, 1950). For an informed account of the antecedents and legislative history of the Wagner Act, see Irving Bernstein, *The New Deal Collective Bargaining Policy* (Berkeley, Cal.: University of California Press, 1950).

influenced the structure of unionism and the structure of bargaining relationships.

The successes of CIO unions in the late 1930s galvanized AFL-affiliated unions into action. Many of the latter amended their charters to permit unionizing on an industrial structural basis in direct competition with CIO affiliates. Between 1935 and the end of World War II, union membership grew from 3,728,000 to 14,796,000. In the war years, 1941–1945, AFL unions grew at a more rapid rate than did CIO unions. The AFL continued to gain comparatively in the postwar period. During wartime both employers and unions were operating under the constraints of National War Labor Board policy and the voluntary no strike–no lockout pledge taken by top management and union leaders shortly after Pearl Harbor. Joint concern for the effective prosecution of the war obscured the fact that tensions were building just below the surface.

As World War II drew to a close, a consensus of professional opinion urged a prompt return to "free" collective bargaining. Many management representatives, trade union leaders and top officials of the National War Labor Board expressed the hope that the government would be able to get out of industrial relations and stay out.[11]

Some dubious motives were at work in producing such a remarkable accord on the virtues of unregulated collective bargaining. Some companies and unions favored removing government from the bargaining table so that they could attack one another with no holds barred. Long restrained by wartime regulations, some unions were anxious to capitalize on their increased economic power. At the same time, there were some "unreconstructed" employers who looked upon a return to private bargaining as an opportunity to crush the unions with which they had been obliged to deal. Such confrontations made 1946 the most serious strike year in our history. One of the most important disputes was the 113-day strike of the UAW in 1945–1946 against General Motors.[12]

The positive side should not be overlooked, however. The values of free collective bargaining came to be appreciated by many employers and labor leaders as well as by government representatives. Wartime experience with extensive public control produced the knowledge that it is impossible to legislate industrial peace and that responsible relationships between labor and management develop from extensive experience in dealing with one another.

When both employer and union find that the true locus of power

---

[11] A classic statement of the case for "free" collective bargaining is that of George W. Taylor, formerly chairman of the National War Labor Board. See his *Government Regulation of Industrial Relations* (Englewood Cliffs, N.J.: Prentice-Hall, Inc., 1948).

[12] History did not repeat itself here until twenty-five years later in September, 1970, when the UAW "took on" GM instead of Ford or Chrysler.

lies outside their relationship, it is difficult for them to develop constructive private arrangements. Both parties are under pressure to shape their policies and strategies to persuade the governmental third force. Neither is required to face up to the necessity for establishing a satisfactory, enduring relationship with the other party.

THE LEGACY FROM THE NWLB

The National War Labor Board during its four years of operation constantly attempted to strengthen collective bargaining. Insofar as possible, the NWLB attempted to compensate for the fact of its own existence. It frequently returned cases to the parties for additional negotiation on unresolved issues.[13] It shunned the job of writing contracts whenever possible. When forced to do so, it generally avoided innovation.

Yet the NWLB could not avoid the consequences of its own position as *the* agency for final settlement of any labor dispute affecting the war effort. It made little difference that Board members ardently preached the virtues of private negotiation. Both labor and management knew that an unsettled dispute would wind up eventually in the lap of the Board. They shaped their strategies and policies accordingly.

All contracts were negotiated or renegotiated with a steady eye on War Labor Board policy. The parties were sometimes more intent upon winning their cases before the Board than in establishing good relationships with one another. Such attitudes did not help matters in the postwar period.

War Labor Board restraint in those decisions where it was in effect required to write terms for the parties resulted perhaps in "better" contracts than those the parties might have negotiated alone. Yet inadequate contracts, privately negotiated, may prove to be more effective in contract administration than those drafted in whole or in part by a third party. Management and unions made rapid strides toward "mature" collective bargaining (as far as subject matter is concerned) under War Labor Board direction or influence. They had less experience in the important business of learning to deal responsibly with one another.

Under NWLB nudging, employers and unions learned to appreciate for the first time the desirability of providing for final and binding arbitration of contract interpretation or application disputes. They also learned to

---

[13] Another practice was to assign a so-called "special representative" to meet with the parties in an effort to reduce the number of disputed issues prior to the appointment of a tripartite panel at the regional level. I recall vividly one assignment as special representative where the entire contract, including the preamble, was in dispute. This was a first contract case involving the Elizabeth, New Jersey, plant of the Singer Sewing Machine Company and the UE (United Electrical, Radio and Machine Workers of America).

appreciate the uses of rate ranges in wage administration. Some unions lost much of their traditional fear of job evaluation and wage incentive systems. Such matters as paid vacations, paid holidays not worked, sick leave and night-shift differentials also received a considerable impetus through decisions of the National War Labor Board.

In other words, the postwar contracts reflected a considerable legacy from NWLB policies. The resultant agreements were more complete and adequate instruments. Regrettably, the psychological maturity of the parties did not always measure up to the contents of their contracts. Responsibility and mutual confidence do not grow automatically from quality contract clauses. They are a product of experience in living together.

APPRAISING THE 1946 STRIKE RECORD

The industrial disputes record of 1946 can be better understood if we remember that collective bargaining was in its infancy in most key industries when World War II came upon us. At the time of Pearl Harbor (December 7, 1941), management and unions in many newly organized industries were still in the fighting stage. The war forced them into a shotgun marriage. Frictions, resentments and misunderstandings were concealed by the pressures for uninterrupted production. After V-J Day in August, 1945, the lid blew off.

The year 1946 did not prove that collective bargaining was a failure. It did reveal that bargaining in good faith had yet to be tried in many cases and in others was a long way from perfection. This was especially true in the newly unionized, critical mass-production industries like steel, automobile and electrical appliance manufacturing. The year 1946 was "abnormal" in several respects. The severe wave of major strikes was, in part at least, the explosive result of too rapid change in fundamental relationships and attitudes. Too much readjustment was needed in too short a time. The wartime necessity for self-restraint helped to conceal the fact that these adjustments had not been made.

FROM TAFT-HARTLEY (1947) THROUGH THE 1960s

When revising national labor policy in 1947, the Congress chose to ignore the exceptional aspects of 1946, looking only at the staggering total of man-hours lost due to strikes in 1946. This regrettable total, even though by far the most serious strike year in our history, nevertheless constituted only 1.43 percent of man-hours worked that year.

Employer and public pressure to "do something" about the situation proved to be overwhelming. Organized labor did not help its own cause.

Both the AFL and the CIO clung to the position that no amendments were needed to the Wagner Act. This stance proved to be a strategy of disaster for the unions. It cut the ground completely from under the "moderates" in both the House and the Senate. The end result was the Taft-Hartley Act, a law that contained nearly all the restrictions on unions then urged upon the Congress by the National Association of Manufacturers and the U.S. Chamber of Commerce.[14]

Technically, the 1947 law was "an act to amend the National Labor Relations Act and for other purposes." The "amendment" was roughly five times as long as the 1935 statute and contained many new provisions and concepts. Although properly rated as one of the most controversial laws in our history, experience under the 1947 law did not bear out either the extravagant hopes of its supporters or the worst fears of its opponents.

Capsule Summary of Selected Taft-Hartley Provisions

Most readers of this book are generally familiar with the contents of Taft-Hartley. Nevertheless, a brief review of some of the more important provisions of the Act may be helpful at this stage. Such a summary will permit more economical discussion of the specific problem areas selected for analysis.

Employers are prohibited by the Act from engaging in the following actions:

1. Interfering with, restraining or coercing employees in the exercise of their rights of self-organization and collective bargaining through representatives of the workers' own choosing.
2. Establishing and maintaining company-dominated labor organizations by financial assistance or in other ways.
3. Discharging or otherwise discriminating against their employees for joining a union or for being active in support of a labor organization.
4. Discharging or otherwise discriminating against their employees for testifying in an NLRB case.
5. Refusing to bargain collectively with a union designated by a majority of employees in a unit appropriate for collective bargaining purposes to represent said employees in collective bargaining.

The foregoing is a summary in the writer's words of Section 8(a) of the Act. With some changes in wording, these are the same five unfair prac-

---

[14] For a detailed legislative history of the Taft-Hartley Act, see the section by Harold A. Katz and Seymour Mann in Millis and Brown, *op. cit.*, pp. 271–392.

tices originally prohibited by the Wagner Act. Under Taft-Hartley, certain other aspects of employer conduct are prohibited in conjunction with certain of the prohibited unfair union practices.

Unfair union practices are not as easily summarized or counted. Therefore, a narrative form is used for describing prohibitions and controls of union activity under the Act.

Taft-Hartley imposes severe restrictions on the means that unions can use to induce workers to join. It prohibits labor organizations from restraining or coercing employees in the exercise of their rights under Section 7, one of which (as noted earlier) is the *right to refrain from* forming and joining unions and engaging in concerted activity. This limitation has had considerable impact on the means of conducting both organizing campaigns and strikes.

Unions are prohibited from coercing an employer in the selection of *his* representatives for purposes of collective bargaining or the adjustment of grievances. This provision is intended to leave the employer free to bargain through a multi-employer association for labor relations purposes *or* to stay out of such an association if he prefers to bargain on a single employer basis.

The Act prohibits unions from pressuring an employer to discriminate against one of his employees and thus commit an unfair practice himself. Unions cannot force an employer to discharge an employee who is in bad standing with the union in question, unless the reason for his bad standing is failure to tender periodic dues (or, originally, the initiation fee) required as a condition of employment under a legally valid union security provision of the contract.

Just as employers are prohibited from refusing to bargain in good faith with a labor organization lawfully entitled to exclusive representation rights under the Act, so also unions have been prohibited since 1947 from refusing to bargain collectively in good faith with employers. This provision is aimed at so-called "take-or-leave-it" bargaining on the union's part.

Unions are prohibited from charging initiation fees to prospective members that the NLRB may find to be "excessive or discriminatory under all the circumstances." Also, unions may not pressure employers into making money payments for services not performed or not to be performed where the payment is held to be "in the nature of an exaction."

THE SECONDARY BOYCOTT BAN

The most controversial, complex and publicized area of union unfair practices is found in Section 8(b)(4), which prohibits or restricts union use of economic pressure in a variety of ways.

Under Section 8(b)(4) unions are prohibited from:

1. Engaging in secondary boycotts.
2. Forcing an employer to bargain unless the union in question is the certified bargaining agent.
3. Forcing an employer to cease bargaining with a duly certified union.
4. Forcing an employer to assign particular work to employees of one union rather than another unless the employer is failing to comply with an NLRB order or certification.

The fourth prohibition declares the jurisdictional strike to be an unfair labor practice. In any such case the NLRB, by Section 10(k), is instructed to transform itself into what amounts to a compulsory arbitration board to make a final and binding determination of the work assignment issue if the matter is not resolved by the conflicting unions within ten days.

The ban on secondary boycotts is, clearly, the most important of the prohibitions. The term "secondary boycott" appears nowhere in the statute. This is a useful shorthand term for characterizing the type of indirect economic pressures prohibited by the Act. The most common form of secondary boycott involves the application of economic pressure against an employer with whom the union has no dispute in order to force him to cease doing business with an employer with whom the union *does* have a dispute or whose employees the union is seeking to organize.

Certain "loopholes" in the Taft-Hartley ban on secondary pressures were "plugged" by 1959 Landrum-Griffin amendments. For example, negotiation of "hot cargo" clauses is specifically banned as an unfair practice under Landrum-Griffin. A "hot cargo" clause is labor relations slang for a contract provision wherein the employer agrees that he will not discipline his employees for refusing to handle "struck work." Some were more broadly worded to extend to products made under "unfair" conditions. "Unfair" in such usage usually is equated with "nonunion" in the union's eyes.

Discussion of the law of secondary boycotts is specifically avoided here primarily because it lies outside the mainstream of our concentration on public policy as it affects ongoing bargaining relationships between Company X and Union Y.

Organized labor holds that federal law is too sweeping in its condemnation of secondary pressures. Union leaders distinguish between what they regard as legitimate uses of secondary pressures and those that they might tacitly concede to be out of bounds. The law, however, basically reflects the view of the late Senator Robert A. Taft that one cannot draw a meaningful legislative line between "good" and "bad" secondary boycotts.

Historically, the secondary boycott was often used to unionize the employees of Company X who could not be induced to join Union Y by direct approaches. Pressure was applied to other firms to cause them to cease doing business with nonunion Company X. The latter, upon feeling the economic pinch, would then urge its employees to sign up with Union Y.

Such indirect unionizing through the employer may have been defensible tactics when workers had no legislative or judicial protection of their rights, particularly when the target firm posed a genuine threat to wage and working standards that the union had established elsewhere in the industry or labor market area. Under modern conditions, however, it does not seem unreasonable to require that unions conduct their organizing campaigns in "front door" fashion.

Since 1935 the right of workers to form and join unions and to engage in concerted activities has been protected by law against employer interference, coercion and restraint. Since 1947 the workers' right to refrain from unionizing or concerted activity has been similarly protected. What is sauce for the goose should also be sauce for the gander. In the absence of unlawful employer coercion, if the employees of Company X have made clear that they do not wish to be represented by a labor organization their right to remain nonunion should be respected and protected.

REPRESENTATION CASES UNDER TAFT-HARTLEY

Having summarized some of the principal unfair practice provisions, it is essential to stress the importance of the NLRB's role in representation cases. As a matter of law, a so-called "R" case arises whenever the NLRB determines that "a question of representation exists." Such a case may arise in a variety of ways. The most common involves a labor organization petitioning for NLRB certification on the basis that a majority of employees in a unit appropriate for collective bargaining desire it to represent them for purposes of bargaining with their employer as to wages, hours and working conditions, and the employer in question doubts the majority status of the petitioning labor organization. Other common situations involve two or more labor organizations seeking to represent the same body of workers (no dispute on the appropriate unit) or different bargaining units being claimed as appropriate by the unions in question.

Another type of representation case concerns the reverse side of the coin wherein the Board receives a petition for *decertification* on the grounds that the incumbent union no longer represents a majority in the appropriate bargaining unit. "R" cases may also arise out of such technical issues as eligibility to vote, the appropriate payroll date for making up voter eligibility lists, alleged improper interference with elections and so forth.

From an administrative law standpoint, a representation case differs importantly from an unfair practice case. The latter becomes what the lawyers term an "adversary proceeding" from the moment the Board's general counsel determines that the charge has sufficient merit to issue a complaint against the union or employer in question. The matter then becomes NLRB *versus* Company X or Union Y. Both the prosecutory and adjudicatory sections of the agency swing into action.

A representation case, on the other hand, involves an investigation to determine whether a question of representation exists within the meaning of the Act. The most common factual matter is whether a particular petitioning union is entitled to be certified by the Board as exclusive bargaining representative. Such questions are typically resolved by conducting a secret-ballot election.

Each year since 1935 the NLRB has conducted several thousand elections in representation cases.[15] Every election held represents a civilized alternative to economic force. The Board's services in this area therefore make an incontestable contribution to the cause of peace and stability in labor relations.

Organized labor in particular and, on occasion, employers also have been critical from time to time of the Board's handling of its discretionary responsibilities in representation cases. Even the critics concede, however, that peaceful disposition of representation case issues has been an enduring accomplishment of federal labor policy. Union recognition was *the* major cause of strikes prior to 1935. Extensive use of the NLRB's election procedures has virtually eliminated recognition as a cause of strikes.

We now analyze selected statutory and NLRB policies with a direct impact on the subject matter and procedures of collective bargaining.

THE SCOPE OF COLLECTIVE BARGAINING AND THE STATUTORY DUTY TO BARGAIN

Philip Ross considers Section 8(a)(5) to be the "puissant heart" of the national labor policy.[16] Ross studied the aftermath of all cases where the NLRB had directed employers to cease and desist from refusing to bargain collectively in good faith with the certified representatives of their employees. He found that in the overwhelming majority of cases collective bargaining subsequently took place and contracts resulted. Ross firmly believes that our national labor policy of encouraging the practice and procedure of collective bargaining would be rendered virtually meaningless without an enforceable duty to bargain. Unions would need to enforce their demands on employers through economic power alone as in pre-1935 days.

---

[15] In recent years the total number of representation elections has been in the neighborhood of 8,000 per year.

[16] The quoted phrase is from a letter to the writer from Dr. Ross some years ago. The Ross study on the duty to bargain is, in my judgment, required reading. See Philip Ross, *The Government as a Source of Union Power: The Role of Public Policy in Collective Bargaining* (Providence, R.I.: Brown University Press, 1965).

I agree fully with Ross that historically the significance of the duty to bargain can scarcely be exaggerated. At the same time there is room to differ with him in friendly fashion on the question of whether the NLRB should continue to decide what are *mandatory* matters for bargaining and what demands or proposals are *lawful but nonmandatory*. In line with the Board's now famous *Borg-Warner* doctrine,[17] a nonmandatory demand cannot be pressed to the point of impasse without risking an unfair practice charge of bargaining in bad faith. The duty to bargain in good faith and how to determine presence or absence of good faith continue to be critically important and controversial policy issues.[18]

The situation in *Borg-Warner* should be reviewed briefly. In bargaining with the UAW, *Borg-Warner* had insisted on two proposals for inclusion in the contract: (1) a recognition clause that would have excluded the international union (certified) and acknowledged only the local union (uncertified); (2) a provision that would have required a secret-ballot election on the company's last offer in negotiations before a strike could be conducted. These twin proposals were made as a "condition precedent" to agreement on the rest of the contract. A strike ensued. The union ultimately yielded to the company's demands, but it then filed a charge with the NLRB against the company for violating Section 8(a)(5).

The Board (then chairman Guy Farmer dissenting) held that Borg-Warner had violated 8(a)(5) by insisting to the point of impasse on these two demands, even though it made no finding of bad faith on the company's part and conceded that the demands were lawful in nature. The Board's decision was based on a finding that neither demand fell within the mandate of the statute as to the subject matter of collective bargaining. The ballot clause on the employer's last offer was held by the Board to be an internal union matter, not related to any condition of employment. The proposed recognition clause was ruled nonmandatory on the basis that something won through NLRB processes (that is, certification) does not have to be rewon at the bargaining table.

Farmer's dissent was based strictly on the good faith concept. In his view, no violation of 8(a)(5) exists when the demands are lawful and bad faith bargaining is not an issue.

The controversy sparked by the *Borg-Warner* decision continues, with no visible consensus among the labor law experts. Some hold that the Board should stop trying to distinguish in particular cases between mandatory and nonmandatory proposals. The *Borg-Warner* approach, it is argued,

---

[17] Affirmed by the U. S. Supreme Court in *NLRB* v. *Wooster Division of Borg-Warner Corporation*, 356 *U. S.* 342 (1958).

[18] For a penetrating review of NLRB policy see James A. Gross, Donald E. Cullen and Kurt L. Hanslowe, "Good Faith in Labor Negotiations: Tests and Remedies," *Cornell Law Review*, LIII (September, 1968), 1009–35.

inevitably injects the Board into substantive and procedural areas of collective bargaining in a manner that is not healthy for the process and that was not contemplated by Congress either in the original Wagner Act or when Paragraph (d) was added to Section 8 in 1947.[19]

Defenders of the Board's approach (notably Dr. Ross) contend that the critics have consistently misinterpreted congressional intent over the years. The pro-NLRB scholars insist that the Board *must* continue to distinguish between mandatory and nonmandatory subject matters in particular cases *as a necessary aspect of defining and delimiting extreme behavior.*

I have always held that what the parties bargained about and what they chose to agree or disagree upon *should* remain their own business. At the same time I recognized that the Board had *necessarily* found itself "enmeshed in the difficult problems of determining what was bargainable and what was not."[20] I still find it difficult to envisage how the Board can avoid the *Borg-Warner* function. So apparently does the Board. It still determines as necessary on a case basis whether particular demands or proposals are mandatory or nonmandatory, following essentially the *Borg-Warner* rationale.

How (or whether) the Board should seek to extricate itself from the burden of this type of decision is a hard question. The difficulty can be highlighted through stating two propositions, each of which commands support, and then seeing where the logic of each proposition leads.

The first proposition is that an employer and a union should retain full private discretion on what matters to bargain about so long as neither seeks to compel the other to agree to something unlawful. This statement is consistent with the presumed consensus as to the virtues of "free" collective bargaining.

The second proposition holds that no party to collective bargaining should be permitted to frustrate the process by insisting to the point of impasse on a demand *outside the normal scope of collective bargaining,* even though such demand is not unlawful *per se.*

The logic of the first proposition requires that the NLRB stay out of any situation where an unlawful demand or proposal is not at issue. The logic of the second proposition encourages the NLRB to take hold in any

---

[19] In the original Act, Congress did not attempt to define the obligation or duty to bargain. Section 8(d) defines the phrase "to bargain collectively" in these terms—"the performance of the mutual obligation of the employer and the representative of the employees to meet at reasonable times and confer in good faith with respect to wages, hours, and other terms and conditions of employment, or the negotiation of an agreement, or any question arising thereunder, and the execution of a written contract incorporating any agreement reached if requested by either party, but such obligation does not compel either party to agree to a proposal or require the making of a concession. . ."

[20] Harold W. Davey, *Contemporary Collective Bargaining* (Englewood Cliffs, N.J.: Prentice-Hall, Inc., 2nd ed., 1959, p. 68; 1st ed., 1951, p. 399).

situation where an "unorthodox" proposal is being pressed by one party and complained about by the other.

Both supporters and critics of the Borg-Warner line can probably "buy" these two propositions in their abstract form. If the ultimate logic of each is pursued, however, there will doubtless be a tendency to back away from wholehearted acceptance and a felt need to qualify.

The sticking point in each case relates to the good faith concept. One can feel strongly about the desirability of the NLRB's staying out of the arena of collective bargaining and yet it is hard to object when the Board's help is sought in cases where stubborn adherence to a nonmandatory proposal appears to be in fact "bad faith bargaining." If the Board were suddenly to announce that it would no longer listen to unfair practice charges where the basis of the charge was insistence on a lawful but nonmandatory proposal as a condition precedent to agreement on all other phases of the contract, the probability is that such self-limitation of its discretion might open a Pandora's box of frivolous or malicious proposals as a guise for concealing refusal to bargain.

For such reasons I have concluded (with some reluctance) that there is no acceptable alternative to continuing the policy of drawing the line between mandatory and nonmandatory issues, *even where absence of good faith is not pressed as an issue.* This is essential to avoid the consequences that would almost certainly follow from a "hands-off" policy. It should be stressed, however, that the Board must stay attuned to changing requirements of the parties to collective bargaining if it is to be realistic in discretionary determinations as to which subjects are mandatory and which are nonmandatory. A proposal may properly be held to be nonmandatory today and yet take on a mandatory character in some future negotiation.

The NLRB guideline must be related to the same basic question in each case at all times: Does the demand or proposal fall within the statutory concept of "wages, rates of pay, hours of work, and other conditions of employment"? The guideline should be applied by the NLRB in a manner that will permit a maximum of discretion to the parties in determining the subject matter and procedures of collective bargaining.

THE NLRB'S "TOTALITY OF CONDUCT" DOCTRINE

Distinguishing between mandatory and nonmandatory bargaining proposals (demands) and relating this to the presence or absence of good faith is admittedly a sticky proposition. The task becomes stickier when the Board goes to the point of deciding that good faith is absent (or bad faith is present), even though no single act was illegal and where a contract resulted but where the course of bargaining conduct viewed in its entirety is held to constitute bad faith bargaining. This in summary was the Board's finding in the *General Electric* case.[21]

It is difficult to write detachedly about the Board's "totality of conduct" approach as applied in the *General Electric* case. The danger is real that one's views about "Boulwarism" as a negotiating strategy will affect critical judgment as to the wisdom of the Board's decision. To be specific, I do not believe Boulwarism is an approach calculated to yield durable and constructive employer-union relations. At the same time, I do not agree with the Board's finding that GE's use of this strategy of bargaining can properly be held to be a violation of the Act.

Good faith is a subjective thing. Overt behavior is not always a reliable index of its presence or absence. A "good" offer by management is not necessarily proof of "good faith," nor is a skimpy one necessarily proof of "bad faith."

As Gross, Cullen and Hanslowe have pointed out, it is interesting to speculate how the NLRB might have ruled on a case of what they term "union Boulwarism," that is, one where the union goes through the forms of bargaining, does not insist on any illegal or nonmandatory proposals and wants to sign an agreement, *but only one matching the terms of an existing area or industry pattern.*[22]

The futility of the Board's approach in the GE situation is underlined by considering the operational significance of the standard remedy of a directive to cease and desist in such a case. How can the Board through such a directive induce GE to change its frame of mind without necessarily changing any of its actions? Again, as Gross, Cullen and Hanslowe have suggested, the Board is in the anomalous position of finding GE guilty of everything in general and nothing in particular.[23]

If one is to be this critical of the Board, the obligation to offer constructive alternatives is a "mandatory" one. This is easier said than done. It seems clear that the Board should be more precise than it has been on what types of bargaining conduct it regards as illegal. Also, the Board could be clearer than in the past on evaluating the reasonableness or unreasonableness of particular bargaining proposals and perhaps more cautious on the matter of inferring bad faith. Finally, if we grant the deficiencies of a conventional cease and desist order as a means of correcting bad faith bargaining, it seems logical to move toward directing appropriate amounts of compensatory retroactive relief.[24]

---

[21] 150 *NLRB* 192 (1964).

[22] James A. Gross, Donald E. Cullen and Kurt L. Hanslowe, *op. cit.*, p. 1030, footnote 19.

[23] *Ibid.*, p. 1031.

[24] Philip Ross, in company with Gross, Cullen and Hanslowe, takes a strong position as to the need for adopting more adequate and realistic remedies, particularly in those cases where it is evident that the employer has a continuing intent to frustrate the objectives of the Act.

THE UNION SECURITY ISSUE REVISITED

Union members have always shown resentment at being required to work alongside employees who refuse to join the labor organization doing the bargaining with the employer. Ever since *Commonwealth v. Hunt* (1842),[25] feelings have run strong against these "free riders." At the same time, powerful sentiment has always existed against compelling workers to join unions against their will. Thus the union security issue is by no means a new one. It has always had an explosive character. Requiring by contract that a worker join a union before or at some point after his hiring has often been a source of bitter conflict and misunderstanding.

Membership requirement clauses have been constantly in the public eye through court decisions and legislative enactments. Federal and state legislation on this subject constitutes an important restriction on the discretion of employers and labor organizations in contract negotiation. The nature of these restrictions has not changed much in recent years, nor have the arguments for and against such public policy controls.

The struggle goes on at the legislative level with no end in sight. Unionists generally regard a state "right to work" law (one which bans any form of union security clause) as a prime target for elimination. Employer forces in "right to work" states generally strive to keep such laws on the books, even though some of them privately entertain doubts about the wisdom of devoting so much time, effort and money to this legislative hot potato. The legislative struggle probably has more symbolic than practical significance, although the presence or absence of a "right to work" law does affect the fortunes of the union movement in particular states.[26]

The pro and con arguments are usually couched in terms of high-sounding principles. Yet, the blunt fact is that proponents of "right to work" legislation hope that such a law will make it more difficult for unions to solidify their financial and organizational positions in particular bargaining relationships. Unions typically seek to repeal such legislation or to "modify" it where repeal is not feasible. Modification in this context means to legalize union-shop agreements and lesser forms of union security while retaining the ban on the closed shop. It then becomes easier for unions to consolidate their positions and improve their bargaining strength.

Professed concern for the rights of individual employees continues

---

[25] The dispute in the *Hunt* case, cited above in footnote 7, involved concerted refusal to work for any employer using a nonunion workman.

[26] The academic literature on "right to work" laws is staggering. Two sources from the many that might be cited is perhaps sufficient. See Joseph R. Grodin and Duane B. Beeson, "State Right-to-Work Laws and Federal Labor Policy," *California Law Review*, LII (March, 1964), 95–114. Also Thomas J. McDermott, "Union Security and Right-to-Work Laws," *Labor Law Journal*, XVI (November, 1965), 667–78.

to dominate discussion, but realistically this is rarely the true issue. It may even be completely beside the point. There are few, if any, unqualified or absolute rights in labor relations. No new employee has an inalienable right not to join the certified union if he elects to accept work with a company whose contract requires that he join the union at the end of his trial or probationary period. If the worker's religious or ethical principles prevent him from joining a labor organization, he must face up to the fact that his range of employment opportunities will be limited because more than three out of four collective agreements provide for some type of union membership qualification.

The term "right to work" is a misnomer. *There is no unqualified "right to work" anywhere, anytime, for whomever one chooses.* The right to work is a *qualified* right as are most other "rights" in labor relations (and in society). The right to strike and the right to lock out employees are qualified by a considerable body of federal and state legislation and court decisions. The right to bargain collectively is a conditioned right. Even First Amendment constitutional use of "free speech" by employers and union leaders is not unqualified in a labor relations context. Its constitutional force is subject to Taft-Hartley limitations. The Act prohibits both unions and employers from interfering with, restraining or coercing employees in the exercise of *their* rights.[27]

Looked at in this kind of perspective, a union security clause provides one more qualification on an always-qualified right to work as related to any particular employer. When the contract requires union membership, it is one more "condition of employment" the prospective employee must consider in deciding whether to accept a job with a particular concern.

Closed Shops and Closed Unions: Are They Special Cases?

Closed-shop contracts have been prohibited by federal law since 1947. I still hold to the view that this legislative ban was an unwise public policy control over private bargaining discretion. Under recent labor market conditions, however, it is harder to make a case for requiring that a prospective employee be a member of a labor organization before he can be hired, because technology and industrial restructuring have blurred or obliterated many former craft lines of demarcation and reduced or eliminated craft skills.

---

[27] The law's so-called "free speech proviso," Section 8(c), holds that the expression of any views, argument or opinion (and the dissemination thereof) shall not constitute or be evidence of an unfair labor practice, but this freedom is qualified by an important "if." Freedom of expression is endorsed in a labor relations context "*if* such expression contains no threat of reprisal or force or promise of benefit."

The original closed-shop rationale was directly related to a formal four- or five-year apprenticeship program leading to acquisition of journeyman status. For labor quality control it used to make sense to relate this training regimen to closed-shop provisions with the unions functioning as employment agencies. These arrangements have lost much of their validity under current labor market conditions. In any event, it is unlikely that closed-shop contracts will again become a valid form of union security under federal law.

The true problem still relates to *closed unions*, historically associated with craft unions in the building and construction field and the railroads. Although I have opposed outlawing closed-shop contracts *as such*, I have also urged firm governmental action to eliminate cases of *de facto* closed-shop arrangements being maintained by "closed" unions. The usual case was one where the local union members stubbornly refused to admit Negroes into apprenticeship programs. No defense is possible for a labor organization which discriminates against applicants on the basis of race, creed, color or sex. Unions in a democracy cannot be regarded as *bona fide* labor organizations if they are not in fact genuinely "open." The only legitimate restriction on union entry should be those relating to ability to learn the craft or trade in question.

Fortunately, the cancer of closed unions has been vigorously attacked both by governmental agencies and the AFL-CIO. All unions affiliated with the AFL-CIO and most of the major unaffiliated organizations have constitutional provisions on membership that are above reproach.[28] Serious pockets of discrimination remain, however, in some local unions in some areas, where the membership clings to a policy that should be labeled for what it is, *white racism*.

The Taft-Hartley approach to the closed union problem was oblique and generally unsatisfactory. Seemingly, unions were obliged to accept into membership anyone offering to pay the customary initiation fee and dues. Workers could be expelled from the union under the union's own rules, but employers could not be required to discharge employees for being in bad standing unless the reason for lack of good standing was nonpayment of dues.

The Act thus operated only to protect workers from the *employment consequences* of arbitrary restrictions on admission or undemocratic expulsions. It overlooked or disregarded the fact that arbitrary denial of admission to

---

[28] The Brotherhood of Locomotive Firemen removed its race bar in 1963. Since that date the AFL-CIO has been able to say that no affiliated union has racial restrictions in its constitution or ritual. Informal exclusion through local union departure from or defiance of national union policy is something else again. See Ray Marshall, *The Negro and Organized Labor* (New York: John Wiley & Sons, Inc., 1965), particularly Chapters 5 and 6. More recently, see Julius Jacobson, ed., *The Negro and the American Labor Movement* (New York: Doubleday & Company, Inc., 1968).

union membership can operate to the serious detriment of employees even if it does not actually cost them their jobs. Also, arbitrary expulsion from a union, even if it does not result in discharge from employment of the expelled member, can undermine the democratic structure of the union.

Taft-Hartley thus did not meet head-on the problem of undemocratic or discriminatory union admission and exclusion policies. In 1964, however, the National Labor Relations Board made a powerful contribution to the antidiscrimination drive in its *Hughes-Tool* decision.[29] In earlier cases the Board had taken such steps as refusing its services to unions found to be engaging in discrimination and revoking certification of unions found to be discriminating. In *Hughes-Tool*, however, the NLRB held that a union found to be violating its statutory duty of fair representation was also committing an unfair labor practice within the meaning of the Act.[30] The courts have also been instrumental in recent years in effectuating fair representation by forbidding a wide range of union discriminatory practices.

The Landrum-Griffin Act of 1959, with its much publicized "bill of rights" for individual union members, developed still another avenue to insuring *internalized fair treatment* for individual unionists. Landrum-Griffin as such, however, has no particular value as an instrument for eliminating discriminatory admission policies. In summary, there still appears to be a need for a comprehensive federal fair employment practices law. New York and a number of other states are far ahead of the federal government in this area.

Legislation and court decisions alone are not enough to wipe out the remaining bastions of union discriminatory conduct. More than legal remedies is called for to eliminate the racist attitudes of white trade unionists at the local union level. Employers can be of direct help by refusing to tolerate or condone existing discrimination by members of labor organizations with which they have contractual relationships. There is some evidence that concerned unions will crack down harder on local unions that persist in flouting the clear mandate of the national union's constitution. The trusteeship device is one mechanism to achieve this purpose. Strong worker educa-

---

[29] *Hughes Tool Co.*, 147 *NLRB* 1573 (1964).

[30] The NLRB majority in *Hughes Tool* found that the union, by refusing to process a grievance of a Negro bargaining unit employee, Ivory Davis, violated Sections 8(b)(1)(A), 8(b)(2) and 8(b)(3). Davis was not a member of the union. Chairman McCulloch and Member Fanning, concurring in part and dissenting in part, agreed with the majority on the 8(b)(1)(A) count (although for a different reason) but dissented from the conclusion that the union's actions were violations of 8(b)(2) and 8(b)(3). The *Hughes Tool* thesis remains a highly controversial one. There is a strongly held view that the Board majority is "legislating" in this decision. The dissenting NLRB members note that if Congress had really intended that violation of the duty of fair representation was to be treated as an unfair labor practice it had ample opportunity to clear up any uncertainty in the 1959 revisions of the law.

tion programs of an "out-reach" type are urgently needed in many cases.[31]

This discussion of closed shop–closed union can be concluded on the encouraging note that the incidence of union member discrimination against nonwhites is declining. Public pressure, legislation, the courts, increased activity of the AFL-CIO itself—all are contributing to progress toward genuine internal equality. But much remains to be done.

SECTION 14(b), TAFT-HARTLEY AND STATE "RIGHT TO WORK" LAWS

To a professional trade unionist perhaps the most irritating provision in the Taft-Hartley Act is one small innocent-appearing sentence, Section 14(b), which reads as follows:

> Nothing in this Act shall be construed as authorizing the execution or application of agreements requiring membership in a labor organization as a condition of employment in any State or Territory in which such execution or application is prohibited by State or Territorial law.

In layman's terms Congress is saying: "On the subject of union security clauses in collective bargaining agreements, a state law that is more restrictive than ours will prevail over the federal statute." Thus 14(b) reverses the usual constitutional presumption by making state law superior to federal. It does so in an area of extreme sensitivity.

Repeal of 14(b) has always been a major AFL-CIO goal. The federation made an all-out lobbying effort against 14(b) in both the 1965 and 1966 congressional sessions. The repeal bill actually passed the House of Representatives but was filibustered to death in the Senate. At its 1967 biennial convention the AFL-CIO was apparently so discouraged that it did not even make 14(b) the subject of a resolution. In the 1969 convention 14(b) once again was made a target for a repeal effort, but the provision remains intact.[32]

---

[31] The 1969 demonstrations against construction unions and contractors in Chicago and Pittsburgh constitute eloquent testimony to the fact that a serious and explosively dangerous gap in thinking between white and black workers exists in these and other metropolitan areas. Intensive education is needed. The situation is now such that open unions alone will not be sufficient.

[32] Repeal of 14(b) *could* become likely in the new Congress following the November, 1970, election, but this prospect seems doubtful at this writing (September, 1970). If Congress ever gets around to full-scale reexamination of our federal labor relations law, perhaps the detrimental (to my mind) aspects of 14(b) could be better appreciated. Regrettably, such a prospect also seems doubtful.

The AFL-CIO has more to cope with than its frustration over the failure to persuade Congress to repeal 14(b). It must also be continuously on guard to defeat the vigorous lobbying efforts of a national right-to-work law committee which would amend Taft-Hartley to outlaw all union security provisions. At the state level, the situation has been "stable" for some years with the count remaining at nineteen with right-to-work laws (or constitutional provisions). Most of these are in the South and Midwest.[33]

A Note on the Agency Shop

State right-to-work laws typically ban any contractual provision requiring union membership as a condition of employment at any time before or after hiring. Such legislation thus invalidates not only closed-shop contracts but also union-shop provisions and maintenance of union membership clauses. One strategem designed to circumvent these prohibitions is the agency-shop provision. Under an agency-shop arrangement the union certified as the bargaining agent receives dues money from the new employee as though he were a member, but he is not obligated to join the union.

The agency shop has appealed to some unions as a practical solution to the "free rider" problem. In my personal view, the agency shop has more disadvantages than advantages. For one thing, it furnishes live ammunition for opponents of unions. The latter are always saying that unions are not interested in workers as people but only in their dues money. The agency shop lends the ring of truth to such arguments. Furthermore, the device has not worked in most cases as a means of getting around right-to-work legislation.

Summary Statement on Union Security Provisions

The union security issue should be resolved at the bargaining table rather than by legislation. Even in right-to-work states many employers and unions have written union-shop provisions into their contracts. These are to go into formal effect if and when state law permits or if Congress should repeal Section 14(b). These "if and when" union shops are properly regarded as evidence of employer agreement with the labor organizations involved that the union shop is a sound contractual requirement.[34]

---

[33] The listing of "right to work" states is as follows: Alabama, Arizona, Arkansas, Florida, Georgia, Iowa, Kansas, Mississippi, Nebraska, Nevada, North Carolina, North Dakota, South Carolina, South Dakota, Tennessee, Texas, Utah, Virginia and Wyoming.

[34] John Deere and UAW have included standard union-shop and checkoff clauses in their contract for many years. However, in deference to the Iowa law, the agreement carries the caveat that "certain provisions of this Article XIII are in conflict with Iowa laws. These provisions will not be placed into effect until it is legally possible to do so under Iowa and Federal laws." 1967–1970 Agreement between Deere & Company and UAW, p. 79.

Requiring membership in a labor organization as a condition of employment nevertheless continues to be an explosive issue in some sectors. No knowledgeable person is neutral on right-to-work legislation. One's viewpoint is conditioned principally by his value judgments as to unionism and as to the proper role of public policy in relation to collective bargaining as a process. There can be no scientific position for or against right-to-work legislation.

The Taft-Hartley Act
and the Appropriate Bargaining Unit

We need not repeat the discussion in Chapter 2 as to the importance of key NLRB decisions for the structure of bargaining relationships. The Board's function in deciding unit cases will continue to be a critical one. Although one may quarrel with the logic of particular Board decisions, in my view it is essential that the NLRB continue to perform this function. The Board is better able to make such discretionary judgments than the Congress. For this reason I have always thought it unwise to build into the statute any legislative presumptions on the unit question.

To remain consistent, it is necessary to state that the Board itself should be careful not to adopt unit policies that are presumptively favorable to one form of unit structure or another. The fluidity of both union structure and organizational patterns in today's economy suggests the wisdom of maintaining discretionary freedom in particular cases. The uncertainties caused by flexibility on a case-by-case basis would appear to present less of a problem than would an effort to freeze the pattern of bargaining units into molds of the Board's choosing rather than the choice of employees.

Statutory Restrictions
on Collective Bargaining Procedures

The framers of the Taft-Hartley Act paid considerable attention to procedures for renegotiation or termination of existing collective agreements. The Act specifies directly certain procedural requirements that must be adhered to by management and the union.

The party wishing to terminate or to make changes in an existing contract must serve notice of such intention on the other party not less than sixty days prior to the expiration date of the current contract. Negotiations therefore presumably begin at least sixty days before the "old" contract is due to expire. If agreement has not been reached within thirty days prior to the expiration date, the Act imposes a further obligation to notify the Federal

Mediation and Conciliation Service of the existence of the unresolved dispute. Resort to economic force during the sixty days prior to the expiration of an agreement is for all practical purposes prohibited by a stringent provision that makes strikers subject to discharge without recourse.

The legislative intent is clear. Congress wished to insure sufficient time for full bargaining over any proposed contract changes. It is hard to quarrel with such an objective. The point may be urged, however, that the parties are in the best position to work out suitable renegotiation procedures. The law nevertheless casts all contract renegotiations into one inflexible procedural mold.

Although there is nothing intrinsically unreasonable in the procedural regulations of the Taft-Hartley Act described above, these objections should be noted:

1. The law allows no room for negotiation of alternative procedures to suit special situations.
2. The penalties for violation of the sixty-day "freeze" are exceptionally severe upon employees.
3. The law in practice may encourage evasion of fundamental responsibilities on a legal technicality. If one party fails to live up to the precise letter of the law, the other party may contend that he is thereby relieved from further bargaining obligations. This tactic could increase rather than reduce industrial strife.

Collective bargaining procedures ideally should be left to the private discretion of unions and management. The Congress, however, insists on having some say in such matters. It is important, therefore, to make sure that public policy is consistent with the need for flexibility in private arrangements. Public policy could lay down a general proposition that the party intending to renegotiate or terminate a contract should give "reasonable" notice to the other party and thus provide an "adequate" opportunity for conferring on its proposals prior to the contract expiration date. This would leave determination as to what is reasonable and adequate for the National Labor Relations Board to determine in disputed cases.

The sixty-day compulsory negotiation period precludes surprise strikes. The average layman would probably say "fine" to this. When the element of timing its strike is denied to a union, however, the effectiveness of its legal right to resort to the strike weapon is materially reduced. In contrast, the employer has a known amount of time to prepare his defenses. Further, the employer can use his liberalized rights of free speech under the Act during this sixty-day period to communicate directly with his employees in an effort to undercut union contract demands with arguments just short of crossing the dividing line between free speech and coercive conduct. The union is, of course, equally free to use this period to stir up strike sentiment in the event negotiations prove unsuccessful. The sixty-day period thus offers no assurance that negotiations will be on a mature and constructive basis. It can develop into a "heating-up" period.

We need not dwell longer on the law's procedural restrictions. In many relationships the negotiation machinery is set in motion well in advance of the sixty-day statutory requirement.[35] Considerable experimentation is going on with approaches for handling problems of a continuing nature that carry over from one contract to the next, such as shifting manpower requirements in a technologically dynamic situation. There is also renewed interest in the utility of prenegotiation exchanges of viewpoints on probable "tough" issues well in advance of either statutory or contractual deadlines. There is increasing joint concern over how to minimize the incidence of crisis bargaining. The now widespread use of FMCS's highly publicized "preventive mediation" services bears witness to this fact. Joint study committees operating between contracts in many relationships are still another indication of increasing private concern and responsibility.[36]

STATUTORY RESTRICTIONS ON THE RIGHT TO STRIKE

The right of the union to strike and the right of the employer to lock out his employees are essential concomitants of the free collective bargaining process. The will to agree in collective bargaining is conditioned by the presence of the ultimate sanction of resort to economic force.

The Wagner Act placed no statutory restrictions on the right to strike. The Taft-Hartley Act specifically outlaws several types of strikes, including the following:

1. Any strike by federal government employees.
2. Any strike to achieve an objective that is unlawful under the Act (such as a strike to secure a closed-shop contract).
3. Any strike to force an employer to violate the Act (for example, one to compel him to cease bargaining with a duly certified union).
4. Any general or sympathetic strike (outlawed by clear implication by the complete legislative ban on secondary boycotts).
5. Any jurisdictional strike.

These are the principal outright prohibitions of strike action. Severe limitations on the right to strike also are provided in sections dealing with contract renewal procedures, as just noted, and in connection with any

---

[35] Some employers and unions have developed the practice of "exploratory" bargaining conferences as much as one year ahead of the date for initiating formal negotiations.

[36] For a knowledgeable but not particularly sanguine view of such committees, written from a historical perspective standpoint, see William Gomberg, "Special Study Committees," in *Frontiers of Collective Bargaining*, ed. John T. Dunlop and Neil W. Chamberlain (New York: Harper & Row, Publishers, 1967), pp. 235–51.

labor dispute that may be designated by the president as of a "national emergency" character. Such designation calls into play a special chain of procedures under Title II of the Act. These restrictions are discussed in Chapter 8. The restrictions or prohibitions would appear to be of sufficient scope to make the phrase "except as provided herein nothing shall be construed as abridging the right to strike. . . " sound a bit hollow.

Many state legislatures have been active in placing their own prohibitions and limitations on the right to strike. The variety in state patterns is so great that no summary analysis can do it justice. Some states require a majority vote by affected employees before any strike can be called. Mandatory cooling-off periods are called for in other state statutes. Strikes in violation of collective agreements, strikes by government employees or public utility workers, strikes in the nature of a secondary boycott or a jurisdictional strike—these and many others are often outlawed at the state level.[37]

Most students of union-management relations agree that the number and duration of work stoppages has been encouragingly low in most years since 1946. To some extent this is attributable to the impact of federal or state legislation. However, the comparatively low number of man-hours lost as a result of strikes is also due in some measure to the growing maturity of the parties in labor relations.

The reduced incidence of economic force in labor disputes can be attributed to a combination or "mix" of the following elements:

1. The increasing maturity, self-restraint and economic sophistication of the parties in bargaining.
2. The declining practical value of economic force as a means of inducing agreement in highly mechanized operations that can be run for lengthy periods of time by supervisory employees.
3. The increasing impatience of the *general public* and also of *particular publics* adversely affected by the operational impact of strikes, such as airline and subway passengers or newspaper readers and advertisers.
4. Recent growth of collective bargaining in the public sector where the right to strike is not generally recognized and where alternative procedures must therefore be used in most instances.
5. Recognition by many employers and unions in key bargaining relationships that their decision-making, including the decision to use economic force, is no longer (if it ever was) a purely private affair and an appreciation of the necessity of considering the public interest.

The complex of statutory and practical limitations on economic force and the decline in its use should not obscure the continuing validity of

---

[37] As we shall see in Chapters 8 and 13, only two states, Hawaii and Pennsylvania, have legalized the right to strike by government employees, although there appears to be some increased understanding that flat prohibitions with harsh sanctions are unlikely to achieve public sector labor peace.

the proposition that the *right* of employees to strike and the *right* of employers to lock out employees or to "take" a strike are *essential elements of free collective bargaining* as we have always understood it in the United States. The knowledge that economic force *may* and *can* be used as a last resort is a powerful factor in keeping the parties at the negotiating table.

Under contemporary conditions of economic interdependence, the strike is rarely used. It has become literally a last resort device where negotiation, mediation and other efforts to reach a peaceful solution have failed. The meaningfulness of bargaining, however, is still directly related to preserving the right to use economic force. If this most powerful of incentives to reach agreement should be eliminated by law, collective bargaining would cease to be either free or productive. Viable alternative procedures are constantly being sought after, as we shall note in Chapter 8, but no magic formula to insure meaningful negotiation has yet been developed.

SUMMARY OF THE IMPACT OF FEDERAL LAW ON COLLECTIVE BARGAINING RELATIONSHIPS

Evaluation of public policy necessarily depends on the value judgments of the beholder. Whether extensive governmental regulation is viewed as a blessing or a curse depends on whether one is favorable to collective bargaining as a process and, beyond this, how one considers the process should operate. It has always been my view that public policy should aim to strengthen and encourage the practice and procedure of collective bargaining. Holding such a view, I regard much federal labor relations law as unduly restrictive of private discretion, although in certain respects the law has strengthened the institutional processes of collective bargaining.

Some critics would advocate repeal of all federal law, leaving nothing in its place. Others urge that current legislation does not go far enough in the direction of control and advocate more sweeping regulation of private discretion.

The reader must make his own evaluation in terms of his views as to the proper role for public policy. I shall not attempt a brief either for those who would abolish controls altogether or who would increase the quantum of current regulation.

FAVORABLE EFFECTS OF FEDERAL LAW ON COLLECTIVE BARGAINING

On the favorable side, the first thing that needs emphasis is that the National Labor Relations Act as amended is so complex, sweeping, inconsistent and pervasive in its impact that it has been a potent instrument for encouraging employers and unions to "do their own thing," thus avoiding NLRB entanglement wherever possible. This is a rather unusual route to achieving a favorable effect. Yet, it is a fact that many employers and unions have found it preferable to develop responsible relationships with one another on their own after observing the "troubles" of other employers and unions who have relied extensively on using the NLRB and the Act to hit one another over the head.

Those employers and unions who are going it alone in a constructive manner find that there is seldom any compelling need to concern themselves with the NLRB because the requirements of our national labor policy *for the most part* do not interfere seriously with the even tenor of "normal" bargaining relationships. Of course, compliance must be achieved with the controls on the subject matter and procedures of bargaining we have noted earlier. Generally speaking, however, Company X and Union Y can deal with one another over a considerable period of time without feeling excessively impinged upon by the law.

Another favorable effect would be the reduced incidence of both employer and union practices which formerly interfered with development of stable bargaining relationships. Elimination of strikes to force an employer to bargain with a union other than the certified union would be one illustration in this category. We can conclude also that the Act has had some influence in reducing the amount of take-it-or-leave-it bargaining by some powerful unions dealing with small employers and by some employers practicing crude versions of GE's Boulwarism strategy.

The law's sixty-day-notice requirement on intention to terminate or to seek changes in existing contracts has doubtless encouraged more timely and thorough consideration of proposed contract changes. It may also have reduced the number of strikes after contract expirations, although such a conclusion is necessarily speculative.

Section 301's provision for damage suits by employers and unions against each other for breach of contract and its designation of the federal courts to enforce both agreements to arbitrate and arbitration awards have contributed without doubt in some degree to improving both the quality and stability of contract administration. Also, the law's stricter conception of agency since 1947 has caused many national unions to exercise tighter control over their locals to curb wildcat strikes.

When wildcats do occur, there is a visible need either for instant arbitration or injunctive relief if the significance of the contractual no-strike pledge is not to be rendered a nullity. The matter of timing makes the damage suit approach under Section 301 an unsatisfactory one from the employer's viewpoint. It is likely therefore that we shall see increased usage of expedited arbitration for wildcat situations, with the arbitrator being granted the power to assess damages as the situation may dictate.

The cause of greater stability in administration of collective bargaining agreements received a substantial boost in June, 1970 when the U.S. Supreme Court took the bit in its teeth and specifically overruled the much-criticized *Sinclair* case (370 U.S. 195 (1962)) which had held that a wildcat in defiance of a contractual no-strike pledge was unenjoinable as a "labor dispute" under Norris-LaGuardia. The high court's new stance[38] should help in reducing the magnitude of the wildcat stoppage problem, although this is by no means a certainty.

The various limitations and prohibitions on the right to strike can probably be credited with the declining union use of economic force in recent years, although this is difficult to pinpoint, as noted earlier in this analysis.

The complexity and comprehensiveness of present federal labor relations law may be said to have had a favorable effect in that employers and unions have been compelled not only to improve their conduct and performance (that is, compliance) but also to improve the quality and knowledgeability of their representatives. No one can do a competent job these days for either an employer or a union unless he is up to date on the do's and don'ts of federal labor relations law. Amateurs have no place in today's labor relations.

Under the law a special burden has rested on union leaders and staff people since 1947 to do a competent and fair job of representing their constituents, the rank and file. There is always the possibility of a decertification proceeding when employees feel their interests are not being properly served by the incumbent bargaining agent. Although decertification procedure has not been used extensively, the infrequency of its use may be in some measure a mute tribute to improved quality of union representation.

Prohibition of coercive union practices in organizing employees has to be counted as a plus for sound collective bargaining. "Indirect" unionizing through the employer via secondary boycott is unlawful. The easy road to organizing the unorganized is thus no longer available. The required direct and democratic approach to union qualification for exclusive bargaining rights may have limited the number of new certifications. However, it is more likely to be productive of constructive union-employer relations.

---

[38] The case in question is *The Boys Markets, Inc.* v. *Retail Clerk's Union, Local 770*, 90 *S. Ct.* 1583 (1970). I am sure that the death of *Sinclair* will not be a cause for grief. However, the future is not trouble-free. Employers, with their new freedom to seek injunctions in wildcat situations, may elect to go the court route rather than revamping grievance arbitration procedures to handle wildcats through instant arbitration with fine-assessing powers in the arbitrator's discretion. The first appraisal of *Boys Markets* to come to my attention is a rather bearish analysis by Martin Markson, "The End of an Experiment in Arbitral Supremacy: The Death of *Sinclair*," *Labor Law Journal*, XXI (October, 1970), 645–53.

Finally, the law's emphasis on individual rights in grievance presentation and in internal union affairs has contributed to greater union leadership awareness of the need to do a complete representation job.[39] The NLRB's stress on the duty of fair representation is an important manifestation of the intensified concern for individual rights in today's highly institutionalized framework of union-employer relations. This emphasis has to be counted as a plus factor, although it must be said that overzealous concern for the individual can result in an unstabilizing, even chaotic, environment which militates against effective collective bargaining.

Unfavorable Effects of Federal Law on Collective Bargaining

An unfavorable effect is defined in the present context as one which tends to discourage the practice and procedure of collective bargaining. The law's stress on the right of employees to refrain from forming and joining unions and from concerted activity can be said to have had an "unfavorable" impact in terms of some dampening of enthusiasm for new organizational activity. I do not favor pressure methods of unionization, now prohibited by law. I do believe, however, that the schizophrenic character of the law since 1947 (simultaneously encouraging collective bargaining and protecting employees who wish to refrain from unionization and bargaining) has had a negative or blunting effect on the growth of collective bargaining as well as having the salutary result of prohibiting coercive methods.

To put this another way, the revised Section 7 (quoted earlier) has provided an excuse for those unions who preferred to "consolidate gains" rather than to work hard at organizing the unorganized. At the same time, employers achieved a new measure of freedom to structure the choices of their employees between staying nonunion and electing to be represented. The NLRB, for example, still adheres to the *Blue Flash* doctrine that employer interrogation of employees individually as to their position on unionization is not coercive *per se*.[40] The *Blue Flash* view does not to my mind take proper account of the realities of labor relations. Furthermore, employer exercise of liberalized speech prerogatives and other forms of communication under Section 8(c) has been developed into a fine art, notably by some southern employers, with visibly adverse effects on union organizing efforts.

---

[39] For a comprehensive discussion of the individual employee in relation to the collective structure, see Harry H. Wellington, *Labor and the Legal Process* (New Haven, Conn.: Yale University Press, 1968), pp. 127–213.

[40] *Blue Flash Express, Inc.*, 109 *NLRB* 591 (1954).

In 1959, along with Bernard Samoff, I deplored the paucity of empirical studies of the operational impact of federal labor relations law.[41] Relatively few studies have been made. The most notable is the work of Philip Ross, cited earlier, on what happens following a Board order to cease and desist from refusing to bargain collectively in good faith.[42] The need is still urgent for sound empirical research. In its absence, the view still appears to be warranted that the law's adverse effects on collective bargaining as a process have been largely on new or developing relationships rather than on the established ones. The latter have in many cases learned to operate on their own, as noted in the preceding section on "favorable" effects.

From my standpoint, the law's various controls and limitations on the discretion of the parties as to both the subject matter and the procedures of collective bargaining should be listed on the negative side of the ledger. A related point is the uncertainty and confusion introduced by the NLRB's decisions in the *Borg-Warner* vein that serve to make the parties aware that they are not the last word on what is bargainable and what is not. Continuing uncertainty as to how the Board majority may view a particular bargaining demand or proposal is in itself a constant invitation to litigate instead of bargaining out the disputed matter. In its *General Electric* decision the Board has come virtually full circle. Its totality-of-conduct thesis now adds up to a finding of bad faith bargaining where the "whole" is declared to be more than the sum of its individually legal parts.

The Act's underlying assumption that a gulf exists between unions and its members, with the latter in need of protection against the former, is in my view, incorrect. Furthermore, it has on balance had an unstabilizing effect on collective bargaining relationships. Particularly when we add some of Landrum-Griffin's "bill of rights" provisions to our spectrum, there are numerous invitations to employers under present law to attempt to drive a wedge between union leadership and rank-and-file. Most employers who accept the legitimacy of unionism and collective bargaining have not taken advantage of such invitations and continue to regard the union as an integral part of their industrial relations picture. Others have sought to undercut and undermine unions in a variety of ways, thus making stable bargaining relationships an impossibility.

In the foregoing remarks I do not seek to sanctify the union as an institution that can do no wrong. On the contrary, as previously indicated,

---

[41] See Harold W. Davey, "The Operational Impact of the Taft-Hartley Act Upon Collective Bargaining Relationships," in *New Dimensions in Collective Bargaining*, ed. Harold W. Davey, Howard S. Kaltenborn and Stanley H. Ruttenberg (New York: Harper & Row, Publishers, 1959), pp. 179–99. My 1959 paper was a response to a 1956 challenge by Bernard Samoff. See Bernard Samoff, "Research on National Labor Relations Board Decisions," *Industrial and Labor Relations Review*, X (October, 1956), 108–17.

[42] See footnote 16 above.

I believe that the current emphasis on rights of individual employees in relation to their unions as well as to employers is eminently sound. In many cases, such an emphasis is long overdue. The duty of fair representation, properly carried through, can be the means of genuine democratization of labor relations. However, it must be stated also that in the name of such noble concepts serious damage can be done to the effectiveness of unionism as an operating institution and to collective bargaining as a vehicle for effectuating the dignity and status of the individual employee.

Concluding Comments: Consensus and Conflict

The net impact of current federal law must be held to be negative rather than affirmative in terms of the goal of encouraging the practice and procedure of collective bargaining. The law is complex, inconsistent, schizophrenic and burdensome in the weight of its pattern of limitations and prohibitions on the discretion of employers and unions. It is thus impossible to say that we enjoy a system of free collective bargaining in the United States in any true sense of the word "free."

At the same time, it should be emphasized that *most* employers and *most* unions engaged in good faith bargaining do so year after year with minimal contact with the NLRB. Also, with some exceptions, such employers and unions do not regard themselves as oppressively hampered by the law's provisions. The "good faith" employer does not need to worry about unfair practice charges. Neither does the "good faith" labor organization. For the most part such parties need only the *service* aspects of the Board's functions, such as resolving questions of representation under Section 9. The NLRB's *regulatory* functions have application only to employers and unions still chargeable with having committed actions denominated as being unfair practices under Section 8.

Nearly universal expert consensus can be reported on the value and utility of the Board's representation case service functions. Few would dispute the superiority of a secret ballot election to use of economic force as a means of resolving a dispute as to whether Union X is entitled to certification as exclusive bargaining representative of a defined unit of employees. Thus Section 9 is not a matter for fundamental controversy, although specific differences will perhaps always exist as to what constitutes sound policy on appropriate unit questions, on contract bar rules, on certification based on card checks only and on other everyday types of representation case rulings that the Board necessarily must make.

It is also true that under current economic conditions there are few unfair practice bans that genuinely disturb what I have termed the good faith employers and unions. Such parties desire to get on with the business of collective bargaining and to make it work in the best way they can. They are not, therefore, among those who account for the NLRB's staggering unfair practice caseload. The Board still confronts the necessity of dealing with thousands of unfair practice charges each year. The prospects are not bright for this enormous caseload withering away.

Most of the unfair practice caseload can be termed conventional. That is, it is not attributable to inconsistencies, ambiguities or defects in the law as such. Some part of the caseload, however, is attributable to the urge to litigate in an effort to bend or reverse earlier Board interpretations.

The "political" nature of presidential appointments to the NLRB for many years through several presidents must be held to be a responsible cause of such probings and searches for new directions in Board policy. Some of this may be inevitable, but much of it could be avoided if employers and unions who seek to politicize the NLRB could be made to appreciate the long-run wisdom of emphasizing the Board's quasi-judicial role. The one best way to accomplish this latter objective is to make Board member and key staff appointments solely on the basis of labor relations expertise and demonstrated capacity to function in a judicially detached manner.

Quality appointments in the manner suggested are not enough, however. The time is long overdue for a complete re-examination and over-hauling of our present federal complex of labor relations law. Nearly every-one agrees that "something should be done" to change the content of our national labor relations law policies, but the consensus does not extend to what needs to be done. Each year numerous proposals for "liberalizing" or "toughening" various sections of the law find their way into the congres-sional hopper. Many of these proposals are not objective, to put it mildly. Fortunately, the highly partisan proposals have tended to cancel each other out up to now with the law remaining unchanged. A clear need exists for an objective job of statutory revision, but it is unlikely that Congress will settle down to this task in the near future.

The temptation is strong to conclude this chapter with a personal statement as to what needs to be done. However, I am not that confident of my own objectivity. Furthermore, some important areas of suggested revision fall outside the scope of this chapter's analysis. One of these is the Railway Labor Act. It has been suggested that the Act be repealed and railroad and airline labor relations placed under the same law as all other industries. This suggestion has intrinsic appeal on grounds of consistency and predict-ability, but it would be inappropriate to urge it without laying a proper foundation for the recommendation.

Within the chapter enough has been said on a variety of specific policies and procedures to suggest that basic statutory revision is urgently needed. We shall not repeat the discussion in the body of the chapter. At some future point it can be anticipated that Congress will attempt a "restatement" of our national labor policy. Hopefully, when this occurs, the voices of responsible scholars will be listened to with greater attention than has been true in past years.[43]

It is asking too much to expect an objective consensus on all essentials in a thoroughgoing revision, but this consideration is not a valid argument against making the effort. Perhaps the best way to get the job done would be through the medium of a tripartite presidental task force, consisting of respected management and union leaders, NLRB personnel and academic specialists. The findings and recommendations of a high-level group of this type might serve as a catalyst to stir Congress to positive action.

SELECTED BIBLIOGRAPHY

Note: No other chapter presents as difficult a problem of selectivity. Year after year, articles and books pour forth on labor relations law. It is a full-time task simply to keep up with NLRB and court decisions and commentary thereon.

Legal periodical references alone could easily run longer than the text of this chapter. If one were to consider the polemical and ax-grinding articles as well, the bibliography would dwarf the text.

My final choice of references has been guided by considerations of recency, quality and objectivity, but I am sensible of the fact that many good references may well have been excluded.

The bibliography offered here has the merit of being sufficient to permit the curious reader to become engulfed in well-documented sources on those phases of public policy that have principally occupied our attention in the present chapter.

BOND, DEBORAH T., "1967 Changes in State Labor Laws," *Monthly Labor Review*, XC (December, 1967), 21–28.

BOOKER, GENE S., AND ALAN C. COE, "The Labor Board and Its Reformers," *Labor Law Journal*, XVIII (February, 1967), 67–78.

BUREAU OF NATIONAL AFFAIRS, *Major Labor-Law Principles Established by the NLRB and the Courts, December 1963-February 1968*. Washington, D.C.: The Bureau of National Affairs, Inc., 1968.

DAVIN, R. P., "Duty to Bargain: Law in Search of Policy," *Columbia Law Review*, LXIV (February, 1964), 248–92.

ESTEY, MARTEN S., PHILIP TAFT AND MARTIN WAGNER, eds., *Regulating Union Government*. New York: Harper & Row, Publishers, 1964.

EVANS, ROBERT, JR., *Public Policy Toward Labor*. New York: Harper & Row, Publishers, 1965.

FANNING, JOHN H., "Individual Rights in the Negotiation and Administration of

---

[43] Illustrative of what I have in mind by "responsible" scholarly proposals for basic changes in our national labor policy would be the writings of Benjamin Aaron, Philip Ross, Russell Smith and Harry Wellington, to name a few. See references in the selected bibliography at the end of this chapter.

Collective Bargaining Agreements," *Labor Law Journal*, XIX (April, 1968), 224–29.

GRODIN, JOSEPH, "The Kennedy Labor Board," *Industrial Relations*, III (February, 1964), 33–45.

———, AND DUANE B. BEESON, "State Right-to-Work Laws and Federal Labor Policy," *California Law Review*, LII (March, 1964), 95–114.

GROSS, JAMES A., DONALD E. CULLEN AND KURT L. HANSLOWE, "Good Faith in Labor Negotiations: Tests and Remedies," *Cornell Law Review*, LIII (September, 1968), 1009–35.

LAW NOTE, "Agency Shop, Federal Law and the Right to Work States," *Yale Law Journal*, LXXI (December, 1961), 330–43.

———, "Developments in the Law-Injunctions," *Harvard Law Review*, LXXVIII (March, 1965), 994–1093.

———, "Primary Picketing at a 'Movable Situs' as a Test for Secondary Boycotts," *Columbia Law Review*, LXVII (December, 1967), 1535–45.

———, "Successor Employer's Obligation to Remedy Unfair Labor Practices," *Columbia Law Review*, LXVIII (December, 1968), 1602–17.

MuCULLOCH, FRANK W., "Past, Present and Future Remedies Under Section 8(a)(5) of the NLRA," *Labor Law Journal*, XIX (March, 1968), 131–42.

MCDERMOTT, THOMAS J., "Union Security and Right-to-Work Laws," *Labor Law Journal*, XVI (November, 1965), 667–78.

MILLIS, HARRY A., AND EMILY CLARK BROWN, *From the Wagner Act to Taft-Hartley*. Chicago: University of Chicago Press, 1950.

MOORE, JOSEPH E., "The NLRB and the Supreme Court," *Labor Law Journal*, XX (April, 1969), 216–38.

PLATT, ELIHU, "The Duty to Bargain as Applied to Management Decisions," *Labor Law Journal*, XIX (March, 1968), 143–59.

ROSS, PHILIP, *The Government as a Source of Union Power: The Role of Public Policy in Collective Bargaining*. Providence, R. I.: Brown University Press, 1965.

SCHLOSSBERG, STEPHEN I., *Organizing and the Law*. Washington, D.C.: The Bureau of National Affairs, Inc., 1967.

SHISTER, JOSEPH, BENJAMIN AARON AND CLYDE W. SUMMERS, eds., *Public Policy and Collective Bargaining*. New York: Harper & Row, Publishers, 1962.

SMITH, RUSSELL A., LEROY S. MERRIFIELD AND THEODORE J. ST. ANTOINE, *Labor Relations Law: Cases and Materials* (3rd ed.). Indianapolis, Ind.: The Bobbs-Merrrill Company, Inc., 1968.

WELLINGTON, HARRY H., *Labor and the Legal Process*. New Haven, Conn.: Yale University Press, 1968.

WINTER, RALPH K., JR., "Collective Bargaining and Competition: The Application of Antitrust Standards to Union Activities," *Yale Law Journal*, LXXIII (November, 1963), 14–73.

ALTERNATIVE VIEWS OF COLLECTIVE BARGAINING AS A PROCESS

some observations on bargaining power theory and the management rights controversy

CHAPTER FOUR

The many-sided nature of collective bargaining as a process is shown by reviewing three familiar theories of bargaining. In Neil Chamberlain's 1951 nomenclature, these are the marketing theory, the governmental theory and the managerial theory.[1] Economists understandably lean toward the market explanation whereas lawyers and political scientists favor the governmental theory. Most practitioners of bargaining (management *and* union) generally prefer the managerial theory.

Realistically, each theoretical explanation contains some important ingredients essential to a complete understanding of what collective bargaining is all about. Collective bargaining as an interdisciplinary process is a

---

[1] See Neil W. Chamberlain, *Collective Bargaining* (New York: McGraw-Hill Book Company, Inc., 1951), Chapter 6.

multifaceted elephant. One who generalizes on the basis of viewing or touching only a part of the elephant can achieve only a partial understanding.

THE SOCIAL SCIENTISTS LOOK AT COLLECTIVE BARGAINING

Social scientists study collective bargaining in terms of the special assumptions and concerns of their particular academic disciplines. Total understanding is an impossibility but this should not be a source of discouragement. Awareness of imitations in knowledge and insight is essential, however, if we are to avoid overgeneralizing.

Many economists, naturally enough, consider the marketing theory of collective bargaining to be the most meaningful explanation of behavior. Unless interdisciplinary seasoning has been acquired through direct involvement in labor relations, such economists may be inclined to shrug off collective bargaining as merely a puzzling example of bilateral monopoly intruding in the price theorist's world. Collective bargaining is viewed as an institutionalized process with negotiation leading to an indeterminate solution for the price of labor. Negotiated wages or salaries are viewed as being similar to "administered prices" or to prices negotiated by a "monopolist" (Union X) and a "monopsonist" (Company Y). Usually, however, there is recognition that such a picture is oversimplified.

No union in the real world fits the economist's monopolist concept unless it would be that increasingly rare species, the pure craft union, closed to additional entrants and controlling the total supply of said craft in a particular labor market. By the same token, no employer fits the monopsonist prototype with precision. More importantly, in "real world" situations management and union practitioners do not bargain purely in economic terms.

Collective bargaining is more than an exercise in economic calculus. This fact tends to discourage many economists who are unable to cope satisfactorily with this "uncertain" process in their analytical framework of price determination. The easy way out is to dismiss collective bargaining as an "aberration" or "special case" while continuing to develop price theory models that are more easily manipulable, predictable and satisfying.

In spite of the difficulties, the effort continues among the less easily daunted economists to develop a theory of collective wage determination that can encompass satisfactorily the impact of the union.[2]

When collective bargaining is viewed by social psychologists or sociologists, we see another side of the process entirely. Social psychologists

---

[2] To my mind, an excellent example of improved theory based on solid empirical evidence is Harold M. Levinson, *Determining Forces in Collective Wage Bargaining* (New York: John Wiley & Sons, Inc., 1966).

and sociologists are concerned primarily with group or organizational behavior.

In their eyes collective bargaining presents another intriguing medium for studying the institutionalizing of conflict relationships between groups or organizations. They are also interested in problems such as:

1. The reconciliation of conflicting interests within the union as an institution.
2. The phenomenon of "dual loyalty" of the worker to his union *and* to his employer.
3. The accommodation of conflicting demands within the management hierarchy essential to presenting a "united front" toward the union at the bargaining table.

All students of conflict resolution are (or should be) fascinated by collective bargaining. Those with a behavioralist tendency are determined to quantify somehow the bargaining power of the parties and then to make estimates of the probability of industrial conflict or peaceful dispute resolution in such terms. Game theory thus has an undeniable appeal, although the assumptions of most game theory applications to bargaining are still so oversimplified as to be of little practical value in predicting actual behavior and results in specific collective bargaining relationships.[3]

Lawyers and political scientists are disposed to view collective bargaining as a method of private government. They are also particularly interested in the impact of public policy on union-management relations. Thus their concern over collective bargaining as a mechanism for determining the price of labor is a secondary matter. They are more concerned with how contract negotiation and contract administration procedures can be fashioned to optimize the functioning of the process as a system of industrial government.

The managerial theory has intrinsic interest for both union representatives and their management counterparts because it stresses the role of collective bargaining as a *mechanism for joint decision-making* on matters directly affecting the employee on the job, such as wages, hours and other conditions of employment. The enduring controversy over alleged union "encroachment" on management rights finds its fullest expression in terms of the managerial theory.

Significantly, Professor Chamberlain no longer employs the term "managerial theory." He now favors the concept of *joint industrial governance,*

---

[3] This does not mean, however, that game theory may not be of value in terms of achieving analytical insight into aspects of the negotiation process. See Carl M. Stevens, *Strategy and Collective Bargaining Negotiations* (New York: McGraw-Hill Book Company, Inc., 1963).

thereby stressing both the continuity of the relationship and the important consideration that union representatives are *joining with* employer representatives in reaching decisions on matters of vital concern to both.[4] Chamberlain's change of terminology is more than a semantic one. It underlines the closeness and, in fact, the partial overlapping of the "governmental" theory with the former "managerial" theory.

We still lack a fully integrated theory of collective bargaining as an interdisciplinary phenomenon. We have not moved appreciably beyond the stage where what collective bargaining looks like rests in the eye of the beholder. Notable progress is achieved, however, when we recognize that *any* theory of collective bargaining *geared exclusively to economic, legal or sociological criteria alone* will be necessarily inadequate to the task of explaining and predicting the behavior of the participants in collective bargaining.

Toward an Integrated Theory of Collective Bargaining

Serious efforts have been directed toward constructing "general theories" of industrial relations. These studies have deepened understanding of the U.S. system, mainly through systematic comparative analysis of the industrial relations systems of other countries, both "mature" and "developing" in nature.[5] We know a good deal more today about the transferability and nontransferability of industrial relations policies and procedures between countries. Some of our favorite procedures (for example, grievance arbitration) appear unsalable as "exports" to most other countries. We have learned that many types of employee benefits handled strictly by collective bargaining in the United States, (such as vacations) are provided for by law in other countries. We have a better understanding of why our policy of exclusive bargaining rights within a particular unit for one labor organization is incomprehensible to unions and employers in many other countries that are

---

[4] See Neil W. Chamberlain and James W. Kuhn, *Collective Bargaining* (2nd ed.), (New York: McGraw-Hill Book Company, Inc., 1965), Chapter 5.

[5] See, for example, John T. Dunlop, *Industrial Relations Systems* (New York: Henry Holt and Company, Inc., 1958); and Clark Kerr, John T. Dunlop, Frederick H. Harbison and Charles A. Myers, *Industrialism and Industrial Man* (Cambridge, Mass.,: Harvard University Press, 1960). In a related though strictly empirical vein, six comparative studies are completed or nearing completion which contrast the U.S. system of industrial relations and labor relations law with that of the United Kingdom, Belgium, West Germany, France, Italy and Spain. Volumes 1 and 2, dealing with the United Kingdom and Belgium, were published in 1968 and 1969 respectively by the Bureau of Business Research of the Graduate School of Business Administration, University of Michigan. All studies are conducted by the Chicago management law firm of Seyfarth, Shaw, Fairweather and Geraldson.

accustomed to pluralistic union representation. We realize that in countries where unionism is associated with divergent political ideologies (Communist, Democratic Socialist and Christian, in most cases), our American brand of nonideological unionism is regarded as strange and peculiar.

These brief insights from the new comparative wisdom bring a sharper appreciation of the difficulties facing those who are striving to develop a viable general theory of industrial relations or collective bargaining. *The striving itself is important.* The insights obtained can be used to improve our industrial relations policies and procedures.

Collective bargaining in the United States offers enough problem areas to challenge nearly all the social science disciplines. The dynamics of labor relations insure the continuing emergence of new problems as some of the older ones are solved or disappear. Furthermore, there will always be hardy perennials such as the wage issue and the conflict between management's cherished right to manage and the union's concern to cover by contract a broader spectrum of on-the-job conditions.

The economists outnumber their fellow social scientists engaged in studying collective bargaining. Such numerical superiority is not proof of the economists' superior insights. It could be due to nothing more startling than the historical consideration that economists were among the first to stake a study claim in the field. More realistically, it can be related to the fact that employers and unions assign a high priority to economic issues. Finally, there has been a visibly growing interest in, and concern over, the impact of key bargains upon the economy as a whole. Nearly all economists, whatever their area of specialization, are interested in the economic effects of unionism and collective bargaining.

In recognizing both the pragmatic and theoretical concerns of the economist we should not overlook the possibilities for improved understanding of collective bargaining that can be derived from the studies of the political scientists, the industrial sociologists, the social psychologists, the labor relations lawyers, the organizational behavioralists and all students of conflict resolution, including game theorists. Worthwhile contributions to an integrated theory of collective bargaining can emerge at any time from any and all of the disciplines listed.

An integrated theory of collective bargaining is an ambitious goal in itself. It is related to the even more ambitious one of an integrated theory of human behavior. The latter, presumably, is *the* ultimate goal of *all* social science research. Viewed in such a broad frame of reference, collective bargaining stands as only one of many manifestations of institutionalized human behavior. It is, however, a critically important one. More than enough challenges are available for testing the mettle and ability of all students and practitioners.

THE KNOWLEDGE GAP BETWEEN PRACTITIONERS AND STUDENTS

Improved understanding as to how collective bargaining works (or fails to work) is hampered to a degree by the failure of the bargainers themselves to contribute a great deal to the literature on the process. Some plead lack of time. Some lack the capacity to write with detachment and objectivity. Others have no particular desire to quench the academic thirst for greater knowledge. Most management and union representatives regularly engaged in contract negotiation and administration are pragmatic activists rather than scholars, although there are a few exceptions.[6] Therefore, the journal articles and books on the process come mainly from academicians who "never met a payroll" or walked a picket line. To put it another way, much that is written about the labor relations scene, including this book, is based on "hearsay" evidence.

Few scholars engage in collective bargaining in the bilateral sense, although many have derived some expertise from trilateral participation. The most common way of acquiring trilateral wisdom is through serving as an arbitrator of grievances under existing contracts. Also, a considerable number of lawyers and academicians are getting a new type of trilateral experience by serving as members of contractually established joint study committees (such as the Armour Automation Fund Committee) or as "informed neutrals" serving as private mediators, fact finders or advisory arbitrators on "future terms" cases.

Many arbitrators learn a good deal about collective bargaining from systematic (or even casual) "interviewing" of practitioners during recesses and luncheon breaks in arbitration hearings. This is not, however, an ideal way to discover objective truth about conflict relationships. No outsider can develop internalized insights into the dynamics of collective bargaining as a process. These can come only from the practitioners themselves. It is difficult, of course, for contract negotiators and administrators to engage in completely objective appraisal while actually practicing their profession.

Perhaps a "sabbatical leave" program is in order for an elite task force of practitioners who could then be commissioned to engage in a rigorous taping, recording and writing program in cloistered surroundings. Their

---

[6] In reflecting upon these "exceptions" one realizes they fall into such categories as management or union lawyers, research economists for unions or recent converts from the "firing line" to the supposedly less hectic pursuits of academic life. Perhaps it is mainly to this last category that we must look for meaningful insights.

charge could be to describe how collective bargaining actually works and to propose how to make it work better. The resultant breakthroughs in knowledge should be worth the time, expense and effort.

As matters stand, the analytical chasm is regrettably wide between those who practice bargaining and students of the process. The need for continuing dialogue is better understood today by both practitioners and academicians. However, no systematic continuing effort has been made to insure communication and exchange of insights and ideas.

The limitations imposed by this communication gap are serious. Scholarly writing on collective bargaining may be read by other scholars and by long-suffering university students, but it is known to only a fractional minority of those who engage in collective bargaining for a living. Many of the scholars have no direct contact with the "real world" of collective bargaining. Consequently, much of what they write is not especially meaningful or helpful to the practitioners.

The writer has no pat answer to the communication problem. No individual can achieve totality of experience in the relatively short span of effective years available to him as academician or practitioner. However, a better job of communication between the "two cultures" should be attempted. A systematic effort to bridge the communication gap is surely preferable to blithe disregard for the "other culture's" activities and ideas.

These considerations have moved me to place greater emphasis on analysis that will be meaningful to participants in the collective bargaining process. The purely academic orientation and jargon have been intentionally soft-pedaled.

It is logical to focus on the practitioners. They are the ones who must carry the main burden of improving the bargaining process. It is their responsibility to keep collective bargaining meaningful and viable in a highly dynamic environment.[7] The familiar witticism about the problems and questions remaining essentially the same with the answers being different is more true than humorous in labor relations.

As a first step toward improved communication and understanding, we shall next consider two problem areas favored by the academic theoreticians and explore their relevance to the "real world" of bargaining. The first of these is bargaining power theory. The second is the always troublesome question of the relationship between managerial authority and the scope of collective bargaining.

---

[7] A serious difficulty facing nearly all practitioners is that they must concentrate their abilities and energies on the particular labor-management relationship(s) with which they are involved. Precious little time or energy is left for communication of any generally useful insights either to the academic community or their fellow practitioners. Somehow time *must* be made available for reflection, communication and meaningful integration of knowledge.

BARGAINING POWER THEORY:
WHAT DOES IT OFFER TO THE PRACTITIONERS?

Economists and game theorists are perhaps the principal contributors to bargaining power theory, but the Congress of the United States and the U.S. Supreme Court may be said to have done their bit at a much earlier date. The game theorists are a recent entry, historically speaking.

The legislative and judicial approaches both start from the proposition that the individual worker is relatively powerless to negotiate with his employer. He thus needs to join forces with his fellow employees in a collective entity to "equalize" bargaining strength in the labor market. To put it another way, both the Supreme Court and the Congress have repeatedly espoused the view that inequality of bargaining power is not only unfair but is also a source of labor unrest and conflict.

The statutory foundation of the National Labor Relations Act of 1935 is the proposition that workers must be guaranteed the rights of self-organization and collective bargaining and must be protected against employer interference, restraint or coercion in the exercise of these rights. The reasoning is that over time such a policy will contribute to reducing a serious cause of labor conflict, namely, inequality of bargaining power.[8] Since 1947, as noted in the preceding chapter, employees have been protected also in their right to *refrain from* unionizing or bargaining collectively if that is their desire. Unions are prohibited from interfering with such a negative choice.

The emphasis in our national labor policy on "restoring equality of bargaining power" (positive statement) is a hard one with which to quarrel. It is essential to keep in mind, however, that there is no such animal as general equality or inequality of bargaining power. Bargaining power is not an economy-wide concept, congruent with the scope and coverage of our federal law. It is necessarily a particularized rather than a general entity. Meaningful analysis of bargaining power therefore can only be undertaken in the context of particular union-management relationships rather than in a generalized sense. Objective understanding requires that we avoid such glib generalizations as "the unions are too powerful," or "employers are running roughshod over their workers," or "Hoffa is so strong he can do anything he wishes to" or "no matter how affluent unions appear to be

---

[8] It is of interest to recall that the original "Findings and Policies" statement of the Congress (as contained in Section 1 of the 1935 Wagner Act) remains in full force and effect, with the addition of one paragraph in the 1947 Taft-Hartley amendments. Thus the thesis remains the same: inequality of bargaining power is a source of labor relations strife whereas, conversely, restoring equality of bargaining power between employers and employees will contribute to removing certain recognized sources of industrial strife and unrest.

they are still no match for the giant corporations." This type of remark impedes rather than facilitates understanding. The generalized connotation upon close analysis turns out to have little if any operational value.

Analysis of bargaining power or economic strength in meaningful terms must be done in terms of comparative evaluation of Company X and Union Y in their contractual relationship with each other at a particular point in time. Such analysis of bargaining power (economic strength) or lack of bargaining power (economic weakness) does not have to be quantified precisely to be of value. We need to be well enough informed about the economic and institutional realities in a particular bargaining situation to state that the "bargaining power" of Company X and Union Y appears to be "about equal" at present, or that Company X appears to be in a stronger bargaining position than Union Y or vice versa. We do not need mathematical values for such informed comparisons to enable us to make reliable judgments as to the probable outcome of particular negotiations.

In fact, a mathematical approach to estimating relative bargaining strength can be misleading if weights are assigned only to those elements in the complex entity of "bargaining power" that appear to be quantifiable. There are, of course, some important components of bargaining power that do not lend themselves to quantification, such as the talent and experience of Negotiator X when compared with his opposite number who may be less gifted in the art of negotiation and/or lacking in X's depth of experience.

The widespread desire to quantify is probably not unrelated to certain assumptions common in bargaining power analysis that may not correspond to reality. For example, it is often assumed that in any particular negotiation the party with greater bargaining power will necessarily prevail or "win." A related conception is that "better" bargains are reached when the bargaining power of the parties is "relatively equal." Conversely, we are led to believe that "poor," "unfair" or "unstable" bargains will be the result whenever there is a clear disparity in the bargaining strength of the negotiation parties.

Such reasoning contains a tacit assumption that the stronger party will always in some fashion take advantage of the weaker. Achievement of relative equality in bargaining power thus becomes a *sine qua non* of a fair, stable and constructive agreement. Such assumptions and conclusions, however, are not invariably applicable in the real world of bargaining. They may be a reliable guide in many cases, but not in all.

Might does not always make right in labor relations. The parties themselves realize this better than the theorists. In particular situations the party with the greater bargaining strength will often take pains not to "rub it in." He will refrain because of the realization that in a continuing management-union relationship such tactics could easily boomerang. The stronger party today realizes that his bargaining power may be greatly reduced in the future by circumstances he cannot control. He is also aware that the other party's strength may increase substantially two or three contracts down the road. Therefore, sophisticated bargainers seldom thump their chests and say "take it or leave it." Nor will the presumed weaker party meekly accept whatever the stronger party may be prepared to concede.

THE DEGREE OF BARGAINING STRENGTH AS A DETERMINANT OF STRATEGY IN NEGOTIATIONS

Management and union practitioners are, to be sure, keenly aware of the importance of "bargaining power" (defined here as "strength" in both economic and noneconomic aspects). They appreciate fully that its presence (absence) can be an aid (limitation) to their effectiveness in negotiation. As pragmatists they can be expected to make use of bargaining power when they have it and to try to minimize its relevance when they don't have it.

Knowledgeable practitioners do not experience a burning need or desire to measure or weigh their own or their "opponent's" bargaining power in precise fashion as a requisite for shaping and structuring their strategies and policies for any particular negotiation. Their operational knowledge and estimation are regarded as sufficient for all practical purposes. The negotiators do not need to have bargaining power defined in ratios or percentages to know where they stand.

To the management or union negotiator, bargaining power as a quality or attribute may be akin to sex appeal. Most individuals have a talent for knowing whether a member of the opposite sex has sex appeal. If the other party has *any* sex appeal, judgments will be made with some confidence that he or she has this indefinable characteristic in abundance or has "some, but not a great deal."

Similarly, for operational purposes, practitioners usually know a great deal about each other's bargaining strength or weakness without refining such knowledge into mathematical equivalents. It must be conceded that such subjective estimations of the other party's capacity to resist or to concede may prove to have been rather far off the mark when put to the ultimate test of a strike or a lockout. The best-informed professionals can, on occasion, overestimate or underestimate the other party's "staying power" in particular situations. In the main, however, experienced negotiators have a firm understanding of the many ingredients that blended together compose each party's bargaining power in specific short-run situations.

The short-run aspect is stressed because of the fluidity and changeability of bargaining power in a short span of time. The negotiators know that Company X may be in a "strong" bargaining position today but that entry of new and more efficient firms may reduce its comparative strength by the time of the next contract negotiation. They know that Union Y appears to be comparatively "weak" in today's negotiations, but they may also know that the federation with which Union Y is affiliated has earmarked substantial funds for the next few years to assist Union Y in new organizing drives which, if successful, will improve its bargaining power considerably.

Many unions that enjoyed strong bargaining positions in former years because of strike effectiveness and complete membership commitment have seen their bargaining power drastically reduced by technological changes that have made the industries in which these unions operate virtually strike-proof. The conventional strike, for example, is no longer an effective power instrument for the Communications Workers of America in the telephone industry or for the Oil, Chemical and Atomic Workers in the petroleum refining industry.

Finally, and perhaps most important of all, the men and women directly involved in collective bargaining as a process know that what we gliby refer to as "bargaining power" is in fact a many-faceted entity embracing much more than economic strength or, as the economists often put it, the capacity or power to reach an agreement *on one's own terms*. The latter conception overemphasizes the economic strength component of bargaining power.

Preoccupation with the word "power" causes a tendency to forget or minimize the word "bargaining." There is also an implication that in any negotiation one party necessarily "wins" something and the other party "loses" something. This kind of reasoning rejects the view that the ultimate goal of management and union is the development of a *mutually satisfactory* contractual relationship.

The preceding discussion is not merely playing with words. In sophisticated collective bargaining relationships there is a joint understanding that bargaining power is a composite of economic and noneconomic factors. The latter include:

1. The knowledge, skill and experience of the principal negotiators and their back-up men.
2. The historical pattern of the particular union-management relationships.
3. The impact on the bargaining table of *external forces and conditions*, economic *and* political, which at one time may strengthen the management hand and at another the union's.
4. *Internal* pressures operating on both negotiating parties, such as friction or conflict within the union or within the management hierarchy which may have an eroding impact on their position at the bargaining table.

Such factors are essential parts of the full picture that the responsible negotiator must take into account. None of the factors just listed lends itself presently to meaningful quantification, in my judgment.

The Values in Realistic Use
of Bargaining Power Analysis

In noting some of the pitfalls and shortcomings in analysis of bargaining power as a concept, we should not fail to stress the positive contribution that can be made by realistic analysis. A major aid to better understanding can come from remembering the continuing nature of the union-management relationship and the critical role of contract administration. Bargaining power analysis has tended to concentrate on the negotiation phase of collective bargaining, couched in gain-loss, pleasure-pain or cost-benefit terms. The clear inference that a "gain" to X must be a corresponding "loss" to Y is neither sound nor accurate. It overlooks the salient point that *living together under a written three-year contract* (the customary length of major contracts currently) requires that the agreement be *mutually acceptable*. The contract is the end product of *joint decision-making*. When emphasis is placed on "bargaining" rather than on "power" the final agreement is more likely to contain *something of value for both contracting parties*.

Such an emphasis in thinking is of crucial importance. Effective contract administration depends upon considerations not always appreciated by bargaining power theorists. Arbitrators who make final and binding decisions on the merits of grievances under existing contracts do not decide cases on the basis of which party has the greater bargaining power. They make an impartial determination as to whether particular grievances have merit under the contract as written. To put the matter more forcefully, when the parties agree to final and binding determination of disputes over contract interpretation or application they are *signifying their joint willingness to abandon relative bargaining strength as a means of resolving grievances which they could not dispose of short of arbitration*. In about 94 percent of all collective labor agreements, management and union are saying in effect the following:

> We hereby jointly agree to give up the right to use economic force as the ultimate arbiter of disputes arising under our contract. Instead we choose to accept as final and binding upon us the decision of an arbitrator as to what our contract means and as to how or whether it applies to specific factual circumstances in unresolved disputes that may arise between us.

The true meaning and utility of bargaining power as a concept and as a force can be appreciated only when, as Neil Chamberlain has emphasized, it is viewed as "an effective force behind the whole collective bargaining relationship and the process of intergroup agreement. . ."[9] Chamberlain

---

[9] Neil W. Chamberlain and James W. Kuhn, *Collective Bargaining* (2nd ed.), *op. cit.*, p. 170.

does not make the mistake of analyzing bargaining power in strictly economic terms. He notes that bargaining power must be viewed as relevant to fixing all the conditions under which the cooperation of the economic partners takes place, with the costs of agreement considered relative to the costs of disagreement (using "costs" here in the broadest possible sense rather than in the purely economic or pecuniary sense). Bargaining power also must be viewed not only in relative terms but as a dynamic, shifting phenomenon depending on the objectives sought.

Meaningful bargaining power analysis must also consider the capacity of the parties to secure specific objectives. Chamberlain underlines that bargaining power is *relative* to what is being bargained for in these words:

> A group's bargaining power may be weak relative to one set of demands, whereas the *same group's* bargaining power may be strong relative to a different set of demands. Since the different demands affect the costs of disagreement and agreement to the other party differently, bargaining power varies with the demands.[10]

Whenever Company X and Union Y enter into negotiations for a new contract, they are engaged in the process of evaluating the costs of disagreeing relative to the costs of agreeing. They are doing so in terms of their respective specific objectives. This cost-balancing operation, however, is not entirely or even primarily a pecuniary one. Rather it is an effort to appraise relative advantage and disadvantage when viewing a range of issues. Some factors lend themselves to quantitative appraisal, but many clearly do not.

The very process of appraising *nonmeasurable* costs of agreement and disagreement is what lends value and importance to negotiation. It is through this process that the employer and the union search for feasible combinations that can lead to joint agreement for the next contract period. If their search fails, a strike or lockout results.

The basic function of a strike or a lockout is to produce an agreement. Excluding the extreme case of one party seeking to smash or obliterate the other, the objective of economic force is the same as the goal of negotiations, that is, the reaching of a mutually acceptable agreement on wages, rates of pay, hours of work and other conditions of employment for a future period of time.

Put in the simplest possible terms, agreement between the parties occurs when the costs of agreement are judged to be equal to or less than the costs of disagreement. In the overwhelming majority of cases, this end is reached without the use of economic force to produce the agreement.

Realistically, bargaining power must be considered as a relative,

---

[10] *Ibid.*, p. 182.

dynamic and complex kind of thing. The employer's and the union's bargaining power in a particular relationship are subject to variation over time, affected by a complex of factors beyond the economic calculus such as the nature of the objectives sought by each, the respective skills and experience of the negotiators and contract administrators and the impact of *external* considerations on the parties and their objectives. Bargaining power calculated solely in economic strength terms is incomplete. Meaningful estimation of relative bargaining power in particular employer-union relationships requires considering the totality of the relationship.

SUMMARY STATEMENT ON BARGAINING POWER

In summary, productive analysis of bargaining power requires the following:

1. Bargaining power analysis must consider the total situation—not only the striking or resistance capacities of the parties but the entire range of economic, political and social circumstances that may have a bearing upon the costs of agreement or disagreement.
2. Bargaining power must be realistically treated as a shifting matter where, even in a fairly brief period of time, substantial changes may occur in relative positions, for example, as a result of political pressures.
3. For agreement to be reached, terms must be negotiated that for all parties concerned represent a cost of agreement equal to or less than a cost of disagreement. Disagreement may persist where the parties find that the terms under discussion constitute a cost of disagreement equal to or less than a cost of agreement.
4. Bargaining power for any party may be increased by any variable or any proposal or any contemplated consequence that contributes to lowering the relative cost of agreement to the other party or to raising to the other party the relative cost of disagreement.

BRIDGING THE GAP BETWEEN THEORY AND PRACTICE: THE MANAGEMENT RIGHTS CONTROVERSY REVISITED

The conflict over managerial authority in relation to the scope of collective bargaining is of perennial interest and continuing importance. In each of the first two editions a full chapter was devoted to this problem area. Its "demotion" to a section of this chapter should not be interpreted as evidence of a decline in either interest or importance. It is true, however, that many employer-union relationships have been successful in achieving a long-run *modus vivendi* on what was formerly a bitter issue over alleged union encroachment on the managerial domain. In others, the controversy continues, but with a defined focus that permits more economical analysis.

The management prerogative controversy is an ideal medium for demonstrating the communication and understanding gap between the academicians and the practitioners of bargaining.

Discussing management rights just ahead of the chapters on contract negotiation and administration has a plausible logic of its own because of the pivotal role still played by issues relating to bargaining scope as this affects the breadth of management discretion.

THE RIGHT TO MANAGE
AND THE SCOPE OF COLLECTIVE BARGAINING

Since 1952 I have used John Deere-UAW contracts as teaching instruments. The current "edition" (1967–1970) runs to 238 closely printed pages. For dramatic contrast I use an 1893 collective labor agreement between Chicago contractors and the Lathers' union. This early contract runs slightly more than one typed page. *Both the 1893 contract and the Deere-UAW agreement cover the same basic trinity of wages, hours and other conditions of employment.* The substantive content of matters bargained about has clearly expanded over the years. It will continue to do so. The steady growth in the number and variety of items that unions seek to bargain over has proved to be a source of grave concern to many management representatives. Accustomed in pre-union days to having 100 percent of the authority to decide unilaterally upon the terms and conditions of employment, these management representatives have understandable fears over the contractual impact of union demands on management's right to direct the enterprise in question.

CONTROVERSY ON TWO LEVELS

The first level of the debate over managerial authority and the scope of collective bargaining takes place at the negotiation table. It finds expression customarily in a firm refusal by management to deal with any union demand that it deems to be beyond the scope of its legal duty to bargain.

The second level of controversy takes place during contract administration whenever a union seeks to obtain through the grievance and arbitration machinery of the contract something that management believes the union failed to obtain at the bargaining table. Management in some cases is also concerned over the possible "erosion" of its proper authority through union success in persuasion of arbitrators to chip away at basic management rights.

The dispute over what is bargainable and what is not bargainable may reflect genuine disagreement in principle over which matters should be subject to joint decision making or the dispute may reflect a power conflict where the ultimate outcome is determined by the comparative economic strength of the parties. In some cases, both principle and bargaining power as such are involved.

Management frequently seeks to define and limit the scope of collective bargaining in concrete terms. Employers wish to draw a clear line between management functions immune to contractual rule-making and those properly amenable to joint decision-making. Union representatives typically urge that collective bargaining remain fluid and dynamic. They contend that it is unwise (or even impossible) to limit the scope of collective bargaining. Management and union representatives often agree *in principle* that collective bargaining should be concerned only with *matters directly relating to wages, hours and other conditions of employment*. In specific cases, however, they can and do differ sharply over whether certain subjects are *directly related* to wages, hours and working conditions.

When management and union disagree basically on the scope of collective bargaining, a constructive relationship is unlikely to be achieved. Difficulties are enhanced by the disposition of *some* employers and *some* unions to use the scope of bargaining controversy as a vehicle for waging a struggle for ultimate supremacy. The sovereign status of competing institutional entities is then at stake. When the issue is joined in terms of management prerogatives versus union rights, the basic will to agree, essential to a constructive relationship, may be dissolved in the ensuing power struggle.

The constant increase in the number of items on which bargaining takes place should not be the source of worry to management representatives that it appears to be. The expanded scope of bargaining does not necessarily involve encroachment upon essential management functions *outside* the employment relationship. It is rather a reflection of today's affluent society. Our economic health now makes it possible to bargain over many employee conditions and benefits that were not even under contemplation twenty years or even a few years ago.

To be more specific, negotiated vacation and pension plans are taken for granted today in most unionized firms. Both were a rarity prior to World War II. Periodic "sweetening" of such benefits in no way impairs the essential nature of managerial authority. Current contracts generally spell out policies and procedures governing layoffs, recalls, transfers, promotions, handling of discipline and many other matters. Such practices account for the swollen size of many current agreements, but they do not constitute evidence of erosion of essential managerial authority. They are clearly embraced within the conventional trinity of wages, hours and other conditions of employment.

Such negotiating about more and more subjects as the years go by reflects the expanding desires of employees. This expanding subject coverage does not connote a union "takeover" of managerial decision-making authority. Negotiating over more employment conditions may leave fewer matters for management to decide upon unilaterally. Yet the essential quality of management's freedom need not be impaired thereby.[11] Management is still controlling and directing the working force. The writer can find no persuasive evidence of a concerted drive on the part of unions to bargain on matters traditionally regarded as exclusively within management's bailiwick. Most unions do not seek to bargain on matters that do not directly concern the employment relationship. There is, for example, no American union movement in the direction of codetermination following the West German pattern, or even of joint consultation following the British pattern, let alone any drive toward worker control of industry.[12] Management concern along these lines is simply not supported by the record.

Employers are alleged to have said in mock or real despair to the unions with whom they negotiate that they wanted the unions "to take over our businesses and see what you can do with them." Should such an offer be made by an employer in a serious vein, the union would probably turn it down. American unions do not wish the responsibility of running businesses. Union leadership in most cases lacks both the interest and the know-how to perform the full range of managerial functions needed for successful conduct of a business enterprise. Furthermore, the rank-and-file union members have expressed little interest in having their leadership participating in the managerial function. In short, American unions want management to continue to manage. They insist only on bargaining with management over any policies that, *in their view*, directly affect the economic well-being and the on-the-job conditions of the employees whom they represent.

ALTERNATIVE THEORIES
ABOUT THE NATURE OF MANAGERIAL AUTHORITY

Of the two principal theories on the nature of managerial authority in labor relations, the one clearly preferred in management circles is the *residual rights* theory. The second theory, the *trusteeship* theory, plays down

---

[11] This vitally important consideration was underlined many years ago by Rev. Leo C. Brown in a thoughtful paper presented at the first annual meeting of the Industrial Relations Research Association. It remains a significant (and perhaps comforting) insight for contemporary management practitioners. See Leo C. Brown, S.J., "The Shifting Distribution of the Rights to Manage," IRRA First Annual Meeting *Proceedings* (Champaign, Ill.: Industrial Relations Research Association, 1949), pp. 132–44.

[12] Perhaps ironically, the one place where an approximation of "codetermination" may be sought in U.S. labor relations is among professional employees such as teachers and nurses. The bargaining horizons of both teachers and nurses extend beyond "bread and butter" to a number of "professional" subjects where a joint voice with management is sought. Thus, the prerogative controversy is taking on special dimensions in professional employee bargaining. For additional discussion see Chapter 13.

the sovereignty rationale of management rights and stresses the *multiple obligations* of modern management.[13] It emphasizes that management has responsibilities toward its employees, the community in which it functions and the consumers of its product(s) or service(s). Many residualists do not dispute the fact that management has multiple obligations. However, they are generally more concerned to maintain functions as exclusively management's than are those in the trusteeship school.

The nature and tone of the collective bargaining relationship between a particular company and union are conditioned by management philosophy. The residualists generally seek to draw a firm line of demarcation between what *they* regard as bargainable and what *they* think of as being *unchallengeably* within their decision-making authority. Adherents of the trusteeship school are not usually preoccupied with sovereign prerogatives. They are more concerned with achieving a rational allocation of functions, which, in their eyes, should be pragmatically determined. That is, the division of functions should be made on the basis of "comparative advantage" rather than in terms of which party was there first. Residualists appear to be preoccupied with historical primacy. They espouse what can be termed the Book of Genesis approach (that is, *in the beginning there was management*). In such a context, the union as a "late arrival" can claim only those controls over a previously unlimited management authority that it can negotiate into the contract.

THE RESIDUAL RIGHTS THESIS IN SUMMARY FORM

Residualists tend to view unionism and collective bargaining as a vehicle for progressive encroachment on a formerly exclusive management domain. The contract is viewed as an instrument that may condition or limit previously complete managerial authority. Should the contract be silent on any subject, residualists maintain with vigor (and considerable logic) that management retains 100 percent discretion. In everyday language, residualists are saying, "If we haven't given it away or agreed to limit ourselves, we've still got it completely."

In pre-union days management did have sole say-so as to what wages to pay and what type of working conditions to provide for its employ-

---

[13] The literature on the nature of managerial authority and the impact of the union thereon continues to be extensive. The pioneer analysis, still useful, is Neil W. Chamberlain, *The Union Challenge to Management Control* (New York: Harper & Row, Publishers, 1948). An excellent treatment of more recent vintage is Margaret K. Chandler, *Management Rights and Union Interests* (New York: McGraw-Hill Book Company, Inc., 1964). Empirical evidence on the explosive subcontracting issue is of prime importance in Professor Chandler's interdisciplinary, cross-cultural treatment. A perceptive early analysis of managerial authority is that of Florence Peterson, "Management Efficiency and Collective Bargaining," *Industrial and Labor Relations Review*, I (October, 1947), 29–49.

ees. Many employers voluntarily paid good wages and provided satisfactory working conditions. Some even established grievance procedures or fostered and supported what were usually called "employee representation plans." The latter functioned in a limited sense as a voice or channel for worker complaints. However, even under the most benevolent of managerial regimes any rights and privileges that employees might have enjoyed were a function of *unilateral management acts rather than joint decision-making.*

Whether employers were militantly anti-union or benevolently paternalistic (or both), they tended to regard union entry as an intrusion on provinces assigned by natural law to management. When employers found themselves under a legal duty to bargain in good faith with unions certified as the exclusive representatives of their employees, their attitudes were often defensive and negative in nature. Few employers welcomed the coming of unions. Instead, collective bargaining was looked upon as an instrument to limit management's essential discretionary activity. When management holds such a psychological view it is easy to adopt a "they shall not pass" approach. Few employers of such a persuasion had the vision to anticipate the positive uses of collective bargaining for improving relationships with their employees.

Most proponents of the residual rights theory have not shirked their legal obligations to bargain, once their employees chose to be represented by labor organizations. In many cases, however, they did not go beyond satisfying the minimum legislative standards of required performance in bargaining. Residualists nearly always seek to separate out exclusive management functions from those subject to negotiation.

Perhaps the most comprehensive formulation of *proposed exclusive management functions* was made by the management members of a joint union-management committee at President Truman's Labor Management Conference held in November, 1945. The passage of years has not diminished appreciably the basic enthusiasm in management circles for this 1945 listing. It is therefore reproduced below:

> The determination of products to be manufactured or services to be rendered to customers by the enterprise; and the location of the business, including the establishment of new units and the relocation or closing of old units. (When it becomes necessary to relocate a unit, or close an old unit, or transfer major operations between plants, management should give careful consideration to the impact of such moves on the employees involved, and discuss with them or their accredited representatives possible solutions for the resulting problems.)
> The determination of the lay-out and equipment to be used in the business; the processes, techniques, methods, and means of manufacture and distribution; the materials to be used (subject to proper health and safety measures where dangerous materials are utilized) and the size and character of inventories.

The determination of financial policies; general accounting procedures—particularly the internal accounting necessary to make reports to the owners of the business and to government bodies requiring financial reports; prices of goods sold or services rendered to customers; and customer relations.

The determination of the management organization of each producing or distributing unit; and the selection of employees for promotion to supervisory and other managerial positions.

The determination of job content (this refers to establishing the duties required in the performance of any given job and not to wages); the determination of the size of the work force; the allocation and assignment of work to workers; determination of policies affecting the selection of employees; establishment of quality standards and judgment of workmanship required; and the maintenance of discipline and control and use of the plant property; the scheduling of operations and the number of shifts.

The determination of safety, health, and property protection measures, where legal responsibility of the employer is involved.[14]

Each of these functions is undeniably appropriate for managerial action. The crucial question is which should be regarded as so exclusively management's as to be declared "off limits" at the bargaining table. As might have been expected, the union appointees to the 1945 presidential committee took a dim view of *any* statement that might have implied waiving the right to negotiate on *any* function whose exercise could have a direct impact on the employees represented. They thus argued against building a fence around any specific list of management functions. The management committee members regarded the stance of the unionists as confirmation of their fears about union penetration. Assurance that such fears were groundless was treated by management with a healthy amount of scepticism.

Since this 1945 confrontation many employers have retained their residualist assumptions, seeking to maintain exclusive performance rights to many of the functions in the 1945 list. The method is usually to insist on a management rights clause. A representative example of such a provision is the following taken from the 1965–1968 agreement between Fairbanks Morse, Inc., and the United Steelworkers of America:

The Management of the Company and the direction of the working forces, including the products to be manufactured, the schedules of production, the methods, processes and means of manufacturing, the establishment and maintenance of reasonable production standards based upon the principle of a fair day's work, the right to hire, promote, demote, transfer, establish reasonable rules of plant conduct, discharge or discipline for just cause, and to maintain discipline and efficiency of employees are the sole and

---

[14] U.S., Department of Labor, Division of Labor Standards, Bulletin No. 77, *The President's National Labor-Management Conference*, November 5–30, 1945, Summary and Committee Reports (Washington, D.C.: Government Printing Office, 1946), p. 58.

exclusive rights and responsibilities of the Company, except as limited by the expressed provisions of this Agreement. It is understood that this section will not be used for the purpose of discriminating against members for activities in the Union. The Company, in the exercise of its rights, shall observe the provisions of this Agreement.[15]

Most employers prefer to include a management clause in union agreements. A significant minority of residualists, however, maintains that logic suggests omitting any such clause. The point is stressed that such a clause is unnecessary when management has unchallengeable authority to act on anything that is not limited or conditioned by contract. In this view, a management rights clause may in fact be dangerous because it can lead to erosion of managerial rights by interpretation in contract administration. If there is no management rights clause, there can be no limitation of authority by shortsighted grievance settlements or ambitious arbitration decisions. Its omission from the contract removes an important source of friction in cases where management is firm about its prerogatives and is dealing with a militant, aggressive union. A management clause sets up one more target for the union to shoot at, with the constant possibility of further circumscribing of managerial authority through interpretation.

To summarize, the residualist position can be stated as follows:

1. Prior to unionism, management possessed full power over all phases of employee relations.
2. Collective bargaining introduces certain specific restrictions on managerial authority and discretion.
3. Management retains all powers, rights and privileges not specifically given away or restricted by the collective agreement. Any subject not covered by the agreement remains under exclusive, unilateral management control.
4. Management has an obligation to contain unionism and to preserve intact the essential functions of management. Supporters of the prerogative approach vary considerably in their views as to which functions are so essential as to require their remaining exclusively in management's hands.

THE TRUSTEESHIP THEORY OF MANAGEMENT RIGHTS IN SUMMARY FORM

In emphasizing the multiple obligations of management, the trusteeship theory envisages the manager as a highly skilled employee hired for these specific purposes: (1) to make a profit, to satisfy stockholders; (2) to

---

[15] The reader will note the similarity between the list of functions in the quoted contract provision and those listed by the management members of President Truman's 1945 committee. The "melody" remains the same, although the "lyrics" may vary slightly from one contract clause to another.

sell a quality product at a just price, to satisfy customers; and (3) to ensure sound industrial relations policies, to satisfy employees.[16] A rational or pragmatic allocation of functions is stressed rather than a defense of absolute rights or prerogatives. The expanding scope of collective bargaining is not regarded as a threat to effective managerial performance.

According to the trusteeship view, unilateral management control may remain as the preferred method of running an enterprise, but such a preference does not preclude a willingness to experiment with collective bargaining as a method of management. There is a recognition that collective bargaining can be the means for deciding upon the allocation of the fruits of enterprise among the various interested groups.

Once an employer has become reconciled to a long-run relationship with a union representing his employees, we can assume that he will seek to achieve maximum value from this relationship. Optimization is difficult to achieve if one is constantly saying that certain management functions are taboo for negotiation (or even for consultation). It is hard for the union leadership to take a positive line when management asserts that certain functions are exclusively and irrevocably its sole concern.

A main asset of nonresidualist or trusteeship thinking on the nature of managerial authority is that it sees no pressing need to claim authority in terms that are absolute, unlimited, indivisible or unchallengeable. There is instead a healthy understanding that long-run constructive relationships with unions and employees are determined through recognition of the concepts of limited government and, in the final analysis, on the consent of the governed. Viewing collective bargaining as a method of industrial government precludes regarding either managerial or union authority as inherently unlimited or unchallengeable.

Even after old-fashioned sovereignty notions have been discarded, *management will continue to perform alone* most of the functions required in the running of any enterprise. Management will be managing, however, *because it is pragmatically wise to do so and not because such functions are eternally management's by divine right.* Management will be performing alone, without union hindrance or encroachment, because it makes good common sense that management do so. Furthermore, most American union leaders have neither the interest nor the competence to perform in these areas, even if their raw economic strength could be used to "take over."

---

[16] Although I continue to use the term "trusteeship theory," essentially similar views are widely referred to in the literature as the "implied obligations" concept of managerial authority. The "implied obligations" thesis will be found frequently in discussions within the arbitration fraternity and between management and union practitioners. See, for example, the presidential address of Charles C. Killingsworth, entitled "Management Rights Revisited," at the twenty-second annual meeting of the National Academy of Arbitrators, published in late 1969 by the Bureau of National Affairs, Inc., Washington, D.C.

In American collective bargaining, generally speaking, joint administration is a rare phenomenon. The only examples that come readily to mind include joint time study where incentive systems continue to operate, joint job evaluation and joint administration of plant safety programs. This is not impressive support for a thesis that unions are determined to share in managerial authority.[17]

Management remains in the hands of management unless there are special reasons for the union to perform what is customarily a management function as, for example, in women's clothing. In this industry with such a large number of small firms, the International Ladies' Garment Workers Union (ILGWU) must function as a stabilizing force. This involves decisions by the union relating to introduction or discontinuance of dress lines, advertising and pricing, matters that are never performed by unions in most other industries. The ILGWU also serves as "policeman" of the industry's incentive system through its own industrial engineering department.[18]

LIMITED GOVERNMENT, ADMINISTRATIVE INITIATIVE, AND CONSULTATION

Most employers, including many residualists, recognize that the essence of authority resides not in the power to give orders but in the degree to which such orders or directives are accepted and carried out. Consent thus forms the basis of sound administration in labor relations as it does in our system of constitutional government. Unlimited sovereign authority is regarded as an unrealistic, outmoded notion under such a view of effective administration.

Endorsing a limited government thesis as a foundation for employer-union relations logically requires the conclusion that *the scope of collective bargaining must itself remain subject to negotiation.* The residualist has difficulty accepting this dictum because of his conviction that a permanent line must be drawn between matters that are bargainable and those that are not. The fact is that in any dynamic situation such a rigid view is neither realistic nor practical.

The scope of bargaining over time depends upon and is influenced by: (1) the policies and attitudes of management and the union; (2) the power relationships between the parties; (3) economic conditions in the industry and (4) the general economic situation. A generalized formula

---

[17] By the same token, I do not regard the recent usage of joint study committees for continuing examination of long-run problems as a "threat" to the conventional scope of managerial authority.

[18] The ILGWU role in the women's clothing industry continues to be the exception that proves the rule, in my judgment.

defining tightly sovereign management (or union) prerogatives cannot prove effective over time in a dynamic relationship.

In most union-management relationships some differences will surface at contract negotiation time as to whether a particular union (or management) demand is properly bargainable. Abstract principles should not count heavily in resolving such disputes, in my judgment. The decisive consideration should be whether Demand X relates directly to the employer-employee or employer-union relationship.

The dividing line between what is bargainable and what is not has meaning only in terms of specific cases and circumstances. Employers who consider collective bargaining to be a method of management are inclined to a practical view as to what may be functionally most effective under the particular circumstances. They appreciate that the line may be drawn at a certain point at one time and at a different point when the contract next comes up for negotiation. Concern for protection of management (or union) prerogatives *as such* is likely to be of secondary importance.

In former years, many employers refused to yield discretion on how vacancies should be filled. They were especially opposed to giving decisive weight to length of service as a criterion. For these reasons, many contracts contained detailed provisions on layoff and recall procedure, but were completely silent on promotional policy. In current contracts, however, it is common to find completely articulated policies and procedures on the posting of vacancies, receiving of bids, determination of qualifications and selection of those qualified and the criteria governing promotion.

This constitutes an "encroachment" on management's former domain to the extent that management's free hand has been limited by jointly determined contractual policy. Yet it can scarcely be argued that promotional policy is outside *the mandatory bargaining category*.

Other examples of evolving bargaining scope can be found in provisions designed to cushion the impact of technological change on bargaining unit employees. In former years many contracts were silent on employer obligations relating to structural unemployment. Currently we can observe an astonishing range of contract approaches designed to ease the burdens of employee adjustment. These include: (1) technological severance pay related to years of service; (2) mandatory reassignment to other jobs, with retraining provided wherever necessary; (3) interplant transfers; (4) early retirement plans and (5) gearing the introduction of labor-saving method or equipment changes to the normal attrition rate caused by voluntary quits, retirements or deaths, thereby eliminating layoffs for structural reasons.[19]

Some employers consider job security provisions to be an unwarranted intrusion on managerial freedom to dispense with labor as they would

---

[19] These matters are treated in more detail in Chapter 9 of this volume.

discard and replace machines, holding themselves opposed to "buying" their right to introduce technological change. Such comments do not alter the fact that the subject matter is clearly within the scope of the employer's legal duty to bargain. Avoidance of or minimizing the burdens of technological unemployment is clearly a legitimate aim of unions in negotiations.

Vacancy filling and adjusting to technological change are two common examples of problem areas *always subject to the duty to bargain* that currently are bargained over as a matter of course although formerly decided upon solely by management. It is certain that illustrations of this type will multiply in the years to come. Yet it seems highly unlikely that American unions will ever seek to control *any* management functions that are not tied pretty directly to the employment relationship.

Finally, unions seek only the role of challenger in administration of contract provisions. There is a tacit but general recognition that on purely practical grounds management must assume the administrative initiative by taking the actions required to make the contract a living force.

It is management that promotes; management that decides when discipline is called for; management that decides who to call in on overtime; management that decides which employees to retain and which to lay off during a reduction in force; management that decides on the staggering of vacation periods—these and a host of other actions on matters covered by the terms of the contract are taken by management acting alone.

These acts of administrative initiative may be challenged through the contract's grievance and arbitration machinery whenever an employee or the union believes that management has violated the contract. We need not plow here ground to be covered in Chapters 6 and 7. The intention at this point is to stress once more the fact that management continues to retain and exercise the authority needed to operate efficiently and profitably. Employers and unions in established bargaining relationships have generally achieved a stable allocation of functional responsibilities. Each party has a pretty clear idea of where the dividing line is drawn. Neither is wasting time and energy in trying to achieve either permanent immutability or major breakthroughs in established functional patterns.

NEGOTIATION, CONSULTATION, AND JOINT STUDY COMMITTEES

Some employers seek to benefit from *consultation* with employees and union leaders as a matter of administrative common sense. An employer's use of the consultative approach generally indicates that he is free from irrational concern over guarding his prerogatives. He is institutionally and contractually secure and therefore has no fear that an invitation to consult will be used as a wedge for intruding on sacred managerial ground. Employers practice consultation on a wide range of problems, including some that will be recognized as traditionally exclusive with management. Others are clearly subject to the duty to bargain if and when the union elects to do so. A selective listing of consultation subjects follows:

1. Establishment of a new plant or relocation of an existing plant.
2. Determination of layout and equipment to be used.
3. Processes, techniques and especially methods of manufacture.
4. Services rendered to customers and customer relations.
5. Selection of employees for promotion to supervisory positions.
6. Determination of job content.
7. Allocation and assignment of work.
8. Selection of new employees.
9. Establishment of quality and performance standards.
10. Discipline.
11. Scheduling of operations and number of shifts.

Companies and unions with well-established union-management cooperation plans regularly confer about items 2, 3 and 6. Craft unions frequently bargain with management on items 5, 7, 8 and 9. In short, the nature of the labor-management relationship in particular cases determines the subject matter or scope of collective bargaining.

Some employers continue to be rather "sticky" about consulting with union representatives or seeking the latter's advice on any matter considered to be outside the statutory duty to bargain. Other employers do not indulge in contractual hair-splitting over whether to include the union on discussion of problem areas where consultation makes good practical sense and appears to be sound personnel procedure.

An "outsider" perhaps should not be advising management as to how much informal consulting it should do with the union, particularly on matters exclusively within management's discretionary authority. I suggest nevertheless an informal psychological principle, as follows:

> The secure employer does not hesitate to consult anybody on anything. The insecure employer will be fearful about going outside the ranks of his own hierarchy on any matter.

The secure employer can gain a real practical advantage over his less confident and venturesome competitors if he will put his prerogatives temporarily in his pocket and take full advantage of union expertise wherever and whenever he can.

Although the future is difficult to read, the newer procedural devices such as joint study committees on long-range problems and renewed interest in profit-sharing and productivity-gains sharing programs are hopeful signs of growing reciprocal confidence between employers and unions.

This does not mean that the management prerogative controversy has become "old hat." Hard-nosed bargaining for the preservation of exclusive managerial authority on many matters will almost certainly continue, principally among small firms and in newly unionized establishments.[20]

Union entry as a joint decision-maker is nearly always an upsetting experience for *any* employer, whether he be large or small, private or public. The novel necessities of bargaining on the terms of the employment relationship generally appears to take on the aspect of undesirable penetration into hitherto unilateral managerial precincts.

The shock effect is perhaps greater on the smaller firm, frequently owner-managed, because of the sudden substitution of written policies and procedures for the former highly personalized discretion.[21] The larger firm, even in nonunion days, was often forced by sheer size to develop personnel rules and procedures. The conversion to joint decision-making is thus seldom as strange for the larger firm as it is for the small employer.

The prerogative controversy usually diminishes as employers come to realize that their initial fears are not justified by experience. Furthermore, current pressures are severe enough to make it both practical and necessary for employer and union to do more together on a continuing basis than they have ever done before. They must face up to such urgent problems as continuous training and retraining needs; insuring greater vertical and horizontal mobility for both blue-collar and white-collar employees; developing greater opportunity channels for nonwhites; and the like. Coping with these challenges in adjusting manpower requirements smoothly to changing technology and industrial relocation inevitably will probably leave employers and unions less time to worry about their respective prerogatives.

Selected Bibliography

Ashenfelter, Orey, and George E. Johnson, "Bargaining Theory, Trade Unions and Industrial Strike Activity," *American Economic Review*, LIX (March, 1969), 35–48.

Bishop, R. L., "Game-Theoretic Analyses of Bargaining," *Quarterly Journal of Economics*, LXXVII (November, 1963), 559–602.

Brandt, Floyd S., "Unions, Management and Maintenance Subcontracting—An Industry Experience," *Labor Law Journal*, XIV (July, 1963), 601–13.

Brown, Leo C., S. J., "The Shifting Distribution of the Rights to Manage," In-

---

[20] Also, as noted in footnote 12 above, the scope of bargaining in relation to managerial authority will be a matter of prime concern in the public sector (education) and to a degree in bargaining with professional employees generally.

[21] I have found this to be true in my arbitration experience. I also found evidence to support this generalization when interviewing small plant managers in the Midwest as part of a research study on the labor relations problems of small firms by virtue of their being small. See Harold W. Davey, "Labor Relations Problems of Small Firms and Their Solution," in *Studies in the Factor Markets for Small Business Firms*, ed. Dudley G. Luckett, (Ames, Ia: Iowa State University for the Small Business Administration, 1964), pp. 199–222.

dustrial Relations Research Association First Annual Meeting *Proceedings.*
Champaign, Ill.: Industrial Relations Research Association, 1949.
pp. 132–44.

CHAMBERLAIN, NEIL W., *The Union Challenge to Management Control.* New York: Harper
& Row, Publishers, 1948.

CHANDLER, MARGARET K., *Management Rights and Union Interests.* New York: Mc-
Graw-Hill Book Company, Inc., 1964.

CHRISTENSEN, THOMAS G. S., *et al.*, Papers on "Management Rights and Prerogatives
in Union Relations," New York University Annual Conference on Labor,
Proceedings, pp. 141–228. Washington, D.C.: The Bureau of National
Affairs, Inc., 1964.

CODDINGTON, ALAN, "A Theory of the Bargaining Process: Comment" (and Reply
by John G. Cross), *American Economic Review*, LVI (June, 1966), 522–33.

CONTINI, BRUNO, "The Value of Time in Bargaining Negotiations: Some Experi-
mental Evidence," *American Economic Review*, LVIII (June, 1968), 374–93.

CROSS, J. G., "A Theory of the Bargaining Process," *American Economic Review*, LV
(March, 1965), 67–95.

CULLEN, DONALD E., AND MARCIA L. GREENBAUM, *Management Rights and Collective
Bargaining: Can Both Survive?* Bulletin 58. Ithaca, N.Y.: Cornell University,
New York State School of Industrial and Labor Relations, 1966.

FELDESMAN, WILLIAM, "How Issues of Subcontracting and Plant Removal Are
Handled by the National Labor Relations Board," *Industrial and Labor
Relations Review*, XIX (January, 1966), 253–64.

KORETZ, ROBERT F., "How Issues of Subcontracting and Plant Removal Are Handled
by the Courts," *Industrial and Labor Relations Review*, XIX (January, 1966),
239–52.

MABRY, BEVARS DUPRE, "The Pure Theory of Bargaining," *Industrial and Labor
Relations Review*, XVIII (July, 1965), 479–502.

MCKERSIE, ROBERT B., AND RICHARD E. WALTON, "The Theory of Bargaining"
(Comment on Febars D. Mabry, "The Pure Theory of Bargaining"), *Industrial and Labor Relations Review*, XIX (April, 1966), 414–35.

NORTHRUP, HERBERT R., *Boulwarism.* Ann Arbor, Mich.: Bureau of Industrial Relations, Graduate School of Business Administration, 1964.

PETERSON, FLORENCE, "Management Efficiency and Collective Bargaining," *Industrial
and Labor Relations Review*, I (October, 1947), 29–49.

PRASOW, PAUL, AND EDWARD PETERS, "New Perspectives on Management's Reserved
Rights," *Labor Law Journal*, XVIII (January, 1967), 3–14.

SCHELLING, THOMAS C., *The Strategy of Conflict.* Cambridge, Mass.: Harvard University Press, 1960.

SIEGEL, SIDNEY, AND LAURENCE C. FOURAKER, *Bargaining Behavior.* New York:
McGraw-Hill Book Company, Inc., 1963.

SLICHTER, SUMNER H., JAMES J. HEALY AND E. ROBERT LIVERNASH, *The Impact of Collective Bargaining upon Management.* Washington, D.C.: The Brookings Institution, 1960.

STEVENS, CARL M., *Strategy and Collective Bargaining Negotiation.* New York: McGraw-
Hill Book Company, Inc., 1963.

TORRENCE, GEORGE W., *Management's Right to Manage.* Washington, D.C.: The
Bureau of National Affairs, Inc., 1959.

WALLEN, SAUL, "How Issues of Subcontracting and Plant Removal Are Handled
by Arbitrators," *Industrial and Labor Relations Review*, XIX (January, 1966),
265–72.

WALTON, RICHARD E., AND ROBERT B. MCKERSIE, *A Behavioral Theory of Labor Negotiations.* New York: McGraw-Hill Book Company, Inc., 1965.

CONTRACT NEGOTIATION

principles, problems, and procedures

CHAPTER FIVE

The importance of the negotiation phase of the collective bargaining process is underlined by the blunt fact that if negotiation fails, for whatever reason, there is no contract and thus no viable bargaining relationship. In the drama of collective bargaining as a continuous process, therefore, nearly all actions over time by management and union representatives are geared, consciously or unconsciously, to the period of actual contract negotiation. This usually takes place in contemporary bargaining every two or three years, although many contracts are still negotiated annually and some for longer than three years.

Nearly all the micro-economic challenges to collective bargaining inventoried in Chapter 1 *could* logically be considered in this chapter, because these challenges are met first by the negotiators. However, if we divide the challenges into *substantive* and *procedural* problems it makes sense to consider only the latter here.

PROCEDURAL CHALLENGES IN CONTRACT NEGOTIATION

Among the procedural challenges we may list the following:

1. How to achieve a greater degree of professionalism in contract negotiation and contract administration (that is, greater reliance on objective economic data in formulating and evaluating bargaining proposals).
2. How to develop genuinely new approaches in collective bargaining.
3. How to "sell" a new policy or approach developed by management or union leadership to the constituents of both.
4. How to prevent collective bargaining contracts from expanding into "Roman codes" that are too detailed and technical for the average working mortal to comprehend.
5. How to negotiate out of a contract policies and procedures that are no longer pertinent or essential but that may be regarded as sacrosanct by one party or the other (such as outmoded working rules negotiated originally to cover a condition that no longer exists, but whose continuance may benefit some incumbent employees).
6. How to develop effective procedures for joint consideration of such long-range continuing problems as the impact of technological change and industrial relocation, outside the crisis atmosphere of contract negotiation periods.
7. How to negotiate master contracts and local supplemental agreements to reduce the likelihood of strikes on local issues after the master contract has been agreed upon.
8. How to improve grievance adjustment machinery to insure prompt handling on the merits at the lower levels by line foremen and union stewards.
9. How to restructure grievance arbitration procedures to make more effective use of the limited supply of experienced, competent and acceptable arbitrators without sacrificing fair representation and due process rights.
10. How to insure the procedural rights of the individual worker, thereby complying with the statutory requirement of fair representation, without sacrificing institutional objectives of stability in contract administration.

The last three problems are reserved for the subsequent discussion of contract administration. The others are considered briefly in the present chapter.[1]

---

[1] Worthwhile academic writing on the negotiation phase of collective bargaining is in comparatively short supply, although there is a considerable amount of "how to" literature. To my mind, the most perceptive of the academic treatments is Carl M. Stevens, *Strategy and Collective Bargaining Negotiations* (New York: McGraw-Hill Book Company, Inc., 1963). In a more popular but authentic vein, see Edward Peters, *Strategy and Tactics in Labor Negotiations* (New London, Conn.: National Foremen's Institute, 1955).

ACHIEVING GREATER PROFESSIONALISM
IN COLLECTIVE BARGAINING

Collective bargaining is better understood if we remember that negotiation is more an art than a science. There is no one best way to negotiate, no one procedure preferable in any and all situations. The requisite personality attributes of good negotiators cannot be learned. In this sense negotiators are born, not made. This is not to say that the negotiation process is intuitive, mystical or impossible to learn. On the contrary, the job of a negotiator is a professional one that demands a high order of specialized knowledge and skill. Most experienced union and management negotiators agree that the time to begin preparing for the next contract negotiation is immediately after the current agreement has been signed and put into effect. In a constructive relationship, both parties are constantly looking ahead. They do not take pride in recent accomplishments, nor lick their wounds after a real or fancied defeat in negotiations just concluded.

The nature of advance preparation for negotiations will vary considerably in terms of the size and importance of the bargaining relationship. If the company and local union in question are part of a multi-employer bargaining set-up, their roles may be limited. If it is customary in a particular relationship to use a pattern set by an industry leader as a policy guide in negotiations, a great deal of advance preparation may not be necessary. Many bargaining relationships do not differ greatly from what they were fifteen or twenty years ago and involve comparatively uncomplicated bargaining issues.

As a general proposition, however, most employers and unions do a great deal of factual spade-work and opinion-seeking in preparation for negotiations. The larger industrial unions have a rather elaborate apparatus for obtaining accurate information on rank-and-file demands and pressures. They are also adept in the use of modern public relations techniques for "creating" membership enthusiasm for future contract demands regarded as critical by the leadership.

The UAW over the years has placed special emphasis on developing membership (and public) support for its key bargaining demands well in advance of the actual negotiation period. Its publicity campaigns on the Guaranteed Annual Wage prior to the 1955 negotiations and on a thirty-hour week as a 1958 bargaining aim may be recalled in this connection. In 1967, the UAW's publicized targets were guaranteed annual and monthly income plans and conversion to a salaried method of payment for blue-collar workers. In 1970, the major publicized items were an unlimited escalator clause and retirement at not less than $500 per month after thirty years of service, regardless of age. In 1973, one can be sure that the UAW will somehow key its negotiating demands to the environmental pollution crisis and the ultimate rejection of the combustion engine.[2]

The employer is not usually as publicity-minded in advance of negotiations as his union counterpart. Many companies, however, are skilled in anticipating critical union demands and in mounting effective communication campaigns to pave the way for their ultimate rejection at the bargaining table. No prudent management, whether the enterprise be small, medium or large, can afford not to anticipate and prepare for negotiations. It is now standard practice to schedule conferences between line supervision and industrial relations personnel to discuss contractual changes desirable from management's standpoint at the next negotiation. The ink is scarcely dry on a new contract before it is carefully examined by both the employer and the union for flaws, policy "booby-traps" or troublesome ambiguities requiring clarification. This assumes that errors are not so serious as to require an immediate mutual consent adjustment.

In medium to large enterprises it is also customary for both parties to analyze the nature and sources of grievances as a guide to contract trouble spots. When contract language proves to be either ambiguous or unworkable, the grievance procedure usually reveals the fact in short order. Daily contract administration thus provides much of the raw material for future demands and counterproposals at the bargaining table.

TECHNICAL PREPARATION FOR BARGAINING

The increasingly technical nature of certain problem areas in contemporary collective bargaining makes it mandatory that the parties prepare thoroughly well in advance of actual negotiation time. The truly professional touch is essential when it is clear that a complicated new proposal will be a crucial negotiation item.

For example, the employer may know he will be required to bargain on a union demand to scrap his incentive system and convert all bargaining unit personnel to payment on the basis of weekly or monthly salaries. A great deal of study and data preparation are needed for intelligent discussion of such a demand. To take another example, bargaining on health and welfare plans has become so technical and specialized in recent years that both management and union often need to bring in "hired mercenaries"

---

[2] When the automobile industry finds the answer to producing cars that will meet antipollution requirements, one consequence will almost certainly be substantial changes in job content and manning requirements. Any such changes will be critically relevant to the 1973 negotiations.

to work out the substantive and procedural content of the package of benefits.[3]

Other "technical" issues requiring considerable advance preparation include the following:

1. A revision of the existing pension plan to provide for increased benefits, the option of early retirement and an "escalator" clause.
2. A proposal by management for elimination of written (or customary) work rules rendered obsolete by changed technology and work methods.
3. A proposal to write a clause into a previously silent contract on management's right to subcontract work under certain conditions.
4. Revision of contract seniority language to provide for interplant transfers of employees displaced by the closing of a plant.
5. Incorporation into the contract of a profit-sharing plan or a productivity-gains-sharing plan.
6. Establishment of a special joint committee for consideration of basic problems of a continuing nature to avoid crisis bargaining.
7. Changing the basic work week from, for example, forty hours down to thirty-five or less, involving some difficult scheduling problems.

Nearly all issues in bargaining demand more thorough preparation than was formerly the case. Fortunately, the number and quality of data sources continue to improve, particularly on wage problems. The parties are inclined to rely increasingly on such data to support their respective positions on the basic wage issue. Many major unions and large companies have their own economic research units to supply factual ammunition on wages and other collective bargaining issues. Exhibits tailored for particular negotiations may contain data prepared by staff economists. The substantial improvement in "official" data has reduced the need for self-help in this area.[4] The bargaining can be more objective when both parties are agreeable to arguing their cases in terms of data published by the Bureau of Labor Statistics, the Federal Reserve Board or a state agency whose information is jointly regarded as reliable.

MANAGEMENT PREPARATION FOR BARGAINING

It is easy to stress the importance of careful preparation for bargaining but somewhat more difficult to lay down a meaningful prescription as

---

[3] One of the most experienced and objective of the consultants on employee benefit plans is Robert E. Tilove. For a summary overview of developments in this area, see his chapter, "Pensions, Health and Welfare Plans," in *Challenges to Collective Bargaining*, ed. Lloyd Ulman, (Englewood Cliffs, N.J.: Prentice-Hall, Inc., 1967), pp. 37–64.

[4] BLS in recent years has expanded greatly its wage data series. Especially helpful to negotiators are rates on selected occupations and wage information for particular labor markets, for example, community wage surveys.

to how to do it. The scale of preparation will depend both on the bargaining requirements of the parties and their economic resources. There will be a difference between the preparations by General Motors and the UAW on the one hand and those of a small machine shop and a local lodge of the IAM.

Some preparation techniques or procedures used by major companies are summarized below. The small firm may utilize some of these, but will not have the resources or the need to use others. The listing includes:

1. Thorough study of the current contract with a view to discovering any sections or language which may call for modification at the upcoming negotiations.
2. Systematic analysis of prior grievances for clues to defective or unworkable contract language or as an indicator of probable union demands.
3. Frequent conferences with line supervision for the dual purpose of better training of supervision in contract administration and receipt of intelligence as to how the contract is working out in practice.
4. Conferences with other employers in the same industry or area who deal with the same union to exchange viewpoints and anticipate the union's demands.
5. Use of attitude surveys to test the reactions of employees to various sections of the contract that management may feel require change or modification.
6. Informal conferences with local union leaders (stewards, shop committeemen or business agents, as the case may be) to discuss the operational effectiveness of the contract and to send up trial balloons on management ideas for change at the next negotiations.
7. Systematic use of a commercial reporting service on labor relations for the purpose of keeping abreast of developments that may affect forthcoming contract negotiations.
8. Collection and analysis of economic data on matters of importance in the next negotiations.
9. Review of any arbitration decisions under the current contract as an aid in proposing changed contract language during negotiations.
10. Participation with the union(s) in prenegotiation conferences to agree on ground rules and sources of data for upcoming negotiations.
11. Participation with the union(s) in informal but scheduled "talks," starting perhaps as much as one year prior to actual negotiation time to consider probable problem areas.

Few empirical studies of how employers and unions prepare for bargaining are available. Improved understanding of the process on the management side can be achieved by study of a monograph by three "informed neutrals," Meyer S. Ryder, Charles M. Rehmus and Sanford Cohen, whose findings confirm that management is attaching greater importance to the task of intelligent, thorough preparation for bargaining.[5] Most

---

[5] Meyer S. Ryder, Charles M. Rehmus and Sanford Cohen, *Management Preparation for Collective Bargaining* (Homewood, Ill.: Dow Jones-Irwin, Inc., 1966).

of the techniques and procedures found by management to be workable and helpful are clearly usable by union representatives as well.

The Ryder-Rehmus-Cohen research team reports that most companies in their sample made effective use of "bargaining books." The nature and shape of such books can be basic or elaborate, depending on the requirements and choice of the user. The utility of such a book lies in its breaking down of the contract on a clause-by-clause basis, with notations on past management and union proposals and their fate in prior negotiations. In ongoing negotiations this organized reference makes it easier "to cope with the disorder of bargaining." Such bargaining books would also be of value to union negotiators.

Union Preparation for Bargaining

Unions vary considerably in the manner and extent of their advance preparation for negotiations. A building trades craft union business agent will discuss future demands with his executive board. He may sound out craftsmen informally as he makes his rounds of various construction projects. He will probably confer with other business agents servicing related crafts and attend meetings of the joint bodies in his area. From this combination of meetings and interviews the business agent will develop an idea of what to shoot for at contract time. He will then formulate his own union's demands as he participates in coordinated bargaining with the other construction unions and an association of the major contractors in the area.

In a large industrial union major negotiation objectives are determined by the top international officers. A lengthy and complex procedure of gathering and sifting opinions usually precedes the reopening of any major contract. All local unions affected will hold special meetings to bring out matters that the rank and file feel require action. Demands emerging from these local meetings will be discussed and separated into local issues and those relating to international union policy. District or regional meetings attended by local officers follow a similar procedure. There is usually a candid interchange of views between local union officers and international representatives. If the top international officers have decided that a particular contract demand is a "must" in the next negotiations and no substantial grass-roots sentiment for it has emerged, an effort to build support is made through the union newspaper and by international representatives. Public media of communication may also be used. The larger unions can assign their full-time economic research units the task of developing the factual underpinnings for key demands decided upon by the policy-making officers.

In all unions, large or small, regardless of the structure and degree of internal democracy, there is considerable "communication" between membership and leadership. To take one illustration, the United Mine-workers was never a shining example of internal democracy during the hey-day of John L. Lewis, but few questioned Lewis' ability to remain sensitive to the economic goals and aspirations of the great majority of UMWA members.[6]

The task of union preparation for bargaining—certainly for the major industrial unions, if not for the relatively homogeneous craft unions—is complicated by the constant necessity for reconciling a variety of internal pressures before and during contract negotiation.

INTERNAL PRESSURES ON UNION LEADERSHIP IN NEGOTIATION

The life of an industrial union leader is not an easy one. Industrial unions are not homogeneous entities. The typical industrial union has a variety of conflicting interests and pressures that need to be welded together in cohesive fashion at negotiation time, particularly when a strike appears likely.[7] In many industrial unions there is a built-in conflict between a skilled trades minority and the preponderant majority of semi-skilled production workers. The craft worker invariably holds that the current wage schedule, whatever it may be, does not reflect a suitable differential in his favor. By the same token, the typical production worker's thinking is likely to be that his job demands greater effort than the craftsman's and also calls for considerable skill and know-how. He is likely to think that the craftsman is overpaid by comparison.

Another source of internal conflict that sometimes plagues industrial union leadership relates to the different goals of the low-seniority and high-seniority members. The former is frequently concerned about being laid off. He may thus give a high priority to contract demands for job security provisions. The high-seniority worker is less concerned because he knows his

---

[6] For a thorough analysis of the Lewis strike strategy and its economic impact on coal production and consumption during his "hey-day," see two articles by C. Lawrence Christenson: "The Theory of the Offset Factor: The Impact of Labor Disputes Upon Coal Production," *American Economic Review*, XLII (September, 1953), pp. 513–47; and, in the same journal, "The Impact of Labor Disputes upon Coal Consumption," XLV (March, 1955), pp. 79–112.

[7] The structural problem of maintaining an "appropriate" differential between occupational rates for the skilled trades and production workers is one that faces most industrial unions each time a contract comes up for renegotiation. To cite just one example, the 1969–1972 agreement between the Bendix Corporation, Kansas City Division, and District Lodge No. 71, Machinists, provided in its first year (effective May 5, 1969) for a general increase of twenty cents per hour to "all employees coming under the scope of this Agreement" and, *in addition*, a thirty-cent "wage adjustment" was "granted" to specified seniority groupings, all in the skilled trades category (1969–1972 Agreement, p. 83).

length of service will protect him in most layoff situations short of plant closure.

The battle of the sexes is also a matter of concern for some industrial union leaders. Problems may arise as to alleged discriminatory treatment in distinguishing between so-called male jobs and female jobs. When both men and women are employed in the same job categories, a different set of problems may arise. The traditional equal-pay-for-equal-work mandate has had greater operational significance in many plants through the impact of Title VII of the Civil Rights Act of 1964 and the Equal Pay for Women Act of the same year.

Another facet of expanded job horizons for female workers is reflected in demands for inclusion in the contract of a no-discrimination-against-spouses policy on hiring. Employers are being asked to abandon historic policies against hiring spouses of incumbent employees into bargaining unit jobs. Management, understandably enough, may have mixed feelings on this matter. So also may union leaders in a previously male-dominated union. Yet the handwriting is on the wall. There will be an increase of contract clauses adding "marital status" to the customary list of race, creed, color, religion and so forth as still another factor that an employer may *not* consider either in hiring or in on-the-job treatment of employees.[8]

Craft unions ordinarily do not encounter the above problems because of their more uniform composition and interests. However, when several craft unions bargain either jointly or separately with the same employer(s) they confront a variation of the industrial union leader's dilemma. A necessity arises for accommodation of conflicting pressures among the separate craft groupings, each of which is likely to regard itself still as a sovereign state.

Internal Pressures in 1967 Bargaining: An Illustration

A dramatic instance of the problems associated with reconciling internal pressures occurred during the 1967 negotiations between the UAW and the major automobile firms. The UAW has been plagued for years by friction relating to the differential between its so-called "skilled trades" group and the great bulk of semi-skilled production workers that man Detroit's giant assembly lines. The skilled trades group is in fact a miscellaneous collection of various occupations, some of a pure craft nature and others that would not be definable as skilled in the usual sense of the term. However, those in this group have always regarded themselves as a breed

---

[8] There is no compelling evidence as yet to support the validity of this prediction. Nevertheless, I shall disregard sound advice by letting it stand.

apart. They have complained constantly that their wage needs were not being properly taken care of by the UAW leadership. At various times the skilled trades have threatened to pull out of the UAW. The UAW amended its constitution some years ago to guarantee representation to the skilled trades and has taken other steps to assure adequate consideration of their demands, without conspicuous success.

As the 1967 negotiations began, it was clear that Reuther needed to achieve an impressive wage increase for *all* workers and also a substantial additional increase for the skilled trades group. When Ford was struck, some observers predicted the strike would be a lengthy one because of the political divisions within the UAW. The reasoning of these observers was that nothing Ford could have offered Reuther would have prevented a strike or could have been accepted by him in the early stages of the strike, no matter how intrinsically attractive such an offer might have been. To satisfy UAW internal needs, Reuther had to strike Ford for a long enough time to make the ultimate settlement one that would satisfy the skilled trades group and not alienate the production workers. The strike lasted about two months. I understand that the skilled trades group had in fact been given veto power by Reuther. The wage settlement called for a first-year increase of twenty cents per hour for all workers and an extra thirty cents per hour increase on top of this for the skilled trades group. There was no particular magic in these figures other than that they were the figures agreed upon.

The differential between the skilled trades group and the production workers had been widened enough to satisfy the complaining craftsmen for another three years. The 1970 negotiation answer to this sticky problem is unknown at this writing. It is a type of problem that is never solved in any complete sense.

Unions are not alone in facing the problem of reconciling internal pressures. Ryder, Rehmus and Cohen found that the concept of a consensus within management ranks is frequently an illusion. The "management position" at any one time often reflects the dominance of one viewpoint over other conflicting views rather than a true consensus.

In any enterprise there is always a potential for conflict between production-minded "line" management and contract-oriented "staff" personnel from industrial relations. The latter at times have more in common with their union counterparts than with their management peers or superiors.[9] In other words, it is dangerous to visualize the internal profile of management in unitary terms.

---

[9] Top management in any enterprise must make clear that *on matters relating to the union contract* the word of the industrial relations department is to be regarded as "gospel" by production and all other departments. It is discouraging to report that I still encounter dramatic instances where production has either ignored or overridden industrial relations personnel on contract matters, with the predictable disastrous results. It is sad but nevertheless true that labor relations people must still "sell" the importance of their function to production people in some enterprises.

EXPERIMENTATION IN JOINT PREPARATION
FOR BARGAINING

The discussion to this point may have left an impression that since preparation precedes bargaining it is not a part of the negotiation phase. This is true only in a literal chronological sense. *The main reason for thorough preparation is to facilitate the agreement-making process.*

Establishment of joint study committees on special problems of a continuing nature (for example, relating manpower adjustments over time in terms of technological changes or locational shifts) offers recent evidence of intelligent preparation for negotiation. We would be wrong in assuming that management and union negotiators are in contact only at contract negotiation time. In all relationships there is continuous interaction of some type during the life of the contract, even though not of a formalized character. Regular sessions for grievance adjustment under an existing contract, for example, may be devoted in part to a discussion of extracontractual problems that have arisen or are anticipated. Any discussion of this nature can properly be regarded as preparation for bargaining at contract renewal time.

A joint study committee has no special magic.[10] However, the use of such committees is encouraging evidence that some employers and unions appreciate the need for continuing rather than intermittent attention to key problem areas. The findings and conclusions of such joint study committees are not binding upon negotiators at contract time. However, the net impact in most cases has been to facilitate the agreement-making process.

Logic would suggest continued growth of joint study committees and related procedural devices. One pressure comes from the increasingly complex and technical character of many bargaining subjects. Another is the growing impatience of the public at large with "conventional" bargaining methods. Any new procedure that gives promise of enhancing the prospects for industrial peace is likely to find favor in the public's eyes. A third reason to develop continuing joint approaches to problem-solving is recognition that it is *to the mutual advantage of the parties* to consider long-run problems in a calm context divorced from the immediate pressures of the bargaining table.

The casualty rate has been high among these new joint approaches outside the bargaining table. One observed difficulty has been the suspicion of the rank and file as to what is going on behind closed doors between

---

[10] Miracles should not be expected from such committees. Some of the pitfalls are candidly discussed by William Gomberg in "Special Study Committees," in *Frontiers of Collective Bargaining*, ed. John T. Dunlop and Neil W. Chamberlain (New York: Harper & Row, Publishers, 1967), pp. 235–51.

contracts.[11] Valid findings may be rejected if the joint committee operations
have been clothed with secrecy. Communication channels need to be kept
open. One answer to suspicion is to broaden the base of participation,
although this may reduce the operating efficiency of such committees.

Granting setbacks here and there, a trend toward professionalization in attitudes and methods relating to the bargaining task is clearly
visible. Results achieved at the bargaining table can often be directly related
to the nature and quality of advance preparation. Clearly, the better part
of wisdom is to prepare as thoroughly as possible for negotiations and to
explore jointly how areas of probable disagreement can be eliminated or
at least reduced. In this latter connection the prenegotiation conference can
be useful. This is a comparatively simple procedural device, usable by any
company and union, large or small, who are sufficiently mature to appreciate
the desirability of negotiating on a factual rather than an emotional basis.

THE PRENEGOTIATION CONFERENCE

George W. Taylor pioneered in the usage of a prenegotiation conference while serving as impartial chairman in the full-fashioned hosiery
industry in the years before World War II. This procedure could grow and
flourish under current conditions, although it is not widely used.[12]

A prenegotiation conference has the following advantages:

1. It enables management and the union to explore jointly in
informal fashion the relevant economic facts about the plant or industry in
question before either party crystallizes its negotiation demands in final
form.

2. Such advance discovery of the relevant facts serves to prevent
extremism in formulating demands or the publicizing of insupportable
demands in advance of negotiations.

3. Ideally, a prenegotiation conference can produce advance agreement on pertinent factual data. This can serve to eliminate or narrow the
subsequent area of conflict in negotiations.

Serious attention to preparation is warranted if only because success

---

[11] For example, the steel industry's Human Relations Committee became a victim
in 1968 of rank-and-file suspicion that the Steelworkers' international union officials were too
close to management.

[12] The prenegotiation conference idea never really caught on in the private sector.
Perhaps its value will be better appreciated in the public sector, where the need to resolve
future terms disputes without a strike is particularly compelling. The prenegotiation conference has high potential in state and municipal labor relations, where its intelligent use by
the parties might frequently eliminate the need to use formal fact-finding procedures with
outside neutrals. Properly instructed, the parties can become experienced in doing their own
fact-finding as an integral part of the prenegotiation conference.

or failure at the bargaining table is closely related to the nature and quality of such preparation. Some important problems relating to conduct of negotiations will now be considered.

CONTRACT NEGOTIATION PROCEDURES

Success in bargaining requires a combination of factors including the following: (1) knowledgeability of one's own case and the other party's case as a result of careful preparation for bargaining; (2) contract proposals that are both attainable and workable; (3) an economically strong position from which to negotiate; (4) personal skill and experience in negotiations and (5) a positive approach to the bargaining function based on good faith and a willingness to reach agreement.

The mutual purpose of negotiation should be achievement of a collective agreement that will work. The attitude of the parties in negotiation and the procedures they employ should be governed by a continuing joint awareness of this fundamental objective. *Workability is the test of an agreement.*

The goal of negotiation is an instrument that can serve as the "statutory law" governing the parties' relationships over a period of usually three years. The contract will be good private law only if it permits smooth administration of its provisions for its duration. A contract that avoids or straddles fundamental conflicts of interest will produce, at best, an armed truce. A contract that attempts to conceal or gloss over actual differences of intent will be productive of continuing friction and disagreement in subsequent attempts at application. These are considerations that the able negotiator keeps constantly in mind.

Which negotiation procedures are best suited to achieve a workable collective agreement? Experienced negotiators hold that sound procedures can be of great value in facilitating agreement on substantive issues. Advance accord on negotiation procedures can be an excellent medium for establishing a constructive relationship between the parties. The bitterness on such explosive substantive issues as union security, wages, seniority and management rights can frequently be alleviated by intelligent initial attention to desirable and efficient negotiation procedure.

The actual procedures employed will vary considerably from one case to another. Much depends on whether the bargaining is between one company and a local union, between one company and the international union or between a multi-employer group and a local or international union.

In multi-employer bargaining, even in a first contract experience, the parties have developed a degree of sophistication through individual plant negotiations that should minimize difficulties over bargaining procedures. But when single employers are bargaining with a local union or with the union's international representatives, prior agreement on procedures to be followed in negotiation is particularly helpful.

No one procedure can be put forward as suitable to the requirements of all parties in all situations. It is nevertheless possible to list some common sense guidelines that appear to have general utility:

1. Both the union and management negotiating committees should be reasonably small. If the union or company committee is too large and everyone insists on participating, much time will be consumed, tempers will become frayed and much irrelevant material may be introduced.
2. One person must be in charge of conducting the negotiations for each side. Division of authority in negotiation is fatal to orderly procedure and usually impedes the agreement-making process.
3. The parties should agree in advance on the time of day and desired length of bargaining sessions. Each side can then make its plans accordingly.
4. Careful preparation for negotiations should include exchange of demands or proposals for study before actual bargaining begins. A frequent source of trouble is the springing of a complicated new proposal during negotiations.
5. Advance agreement on procedures will eliminate such unnecessary arguments as whether subject X is "in order at this time."
6. Negotiators should have authority to make decisive commitments in the course of negotiations. Company negotiators generally have the power to bind their principals. In most unions the negotiated terms are subject to ratification or rejection by the membership. Membership rejection can be a serious problem.
7. Negotiations should begin with a well-planned agenda that includes a complete statement of all disputed issues together with a listing of proposals and counterproposals on the disputed points.
8. If possible, an agreed statement of relevant economic data should be employed. This can be done when the parties have made effective use of the prenegotiation conference.
9. The negotiators should first resolve the less controversial issues and reduce their agreement to writing before proceeding to the tougher issues.
10. The difficult issues can be divided into those that involve money outlays and noneconomic demands.
11. Many noneconomic issues can be negotiated individually in terms of their intrinsic merit rather than in terms of the bargaining strength of the principals. This generalization would clearly not apply, however, to union demands relating to such "noneconomic" matters as union security or seniority.
12. Finally, and of critical importance in most negotiations, a decision must be made as to whether to bargain out the demands involving money outlays one by one or to negotiate on an economic package basis.

Economic Package Bargaining

Nearly all management negotiators and most union negotiators favor disposing of all labor cost items on a unified and related basis rather than separately. The key decision is generally over how much money may be available *in total* for allocation between wage or salary increases as such and a miscellany of money fringe proposals.

Management may be comparatively indifferent as to the "mix" between wage increases and fringe benefits. Yet no prudent employer can commit himself to an increased outlay for specific fringes without a clear idea of what the total "tab" is going to be. Most union negotiators arrive at the bargaining table with a mandate to achieve more than is realistically attainable. They know that at some point they will have to cut and trim their proposals involving labor cost in some fashion. It thus becomes important to the union to know how much total money may be extractable in any particular negotiation before deciding how much emphasis to place on wage increases as such and how much on new or expanded fringes.

Package bargaining is therefore the rule and likely to remain so. Both management and union practitioners are becoming skilled in the art of "translating" the cost of a particular fringe item into *x* cents per hour if given out in the form of an across-the-board wage or salary adjustment. The particular "mix" between wages and fringes is usually of greater concern to the union than to management, but not necessarily so. Management recognizes that introduction of a new fringe item into its complex of labor costs may prove burdensome in the future, even though not seemingly significant at the time of its negotiation. Fringes are readily institutionalized and not easily retractable. The problem of being saddled with an excessive fixed-cost fringe complex is one of special concern to smaller firms.[13]

Management is always concerned over labor cost increases, whether in the form of wage increases or new or expanded fringes. Unions at all times strive to negotiate visible gains that can be publicized as bargaining victories, whether they be wage increases as such or a much sought-after fringe benefit. Thus for different but equally compelling reasons, both management and union prefer to know the overall dimensions of the economic package before either is willing to forego any one economic demand or to make a particular economic concession.

To be specific, we refer again to the negotiating of a suitable "special" increase for skilled trades that was a UAW must item in 1967. This

---

[13] Generally speaking, the smaller employer prefers to negotiate mainly in terms of wages as such, understandably enough. He may, however be confronting a union with an established fringe policy from which it is reluctant to deviate.

problem could not be handled by either side in a vacuum. Various alternatives had to be costed out by the parties. The UAW had a balancing task to perform between the skilled trades and the great majority of production workers. Automobile management, on the other hand, could not commit itself to a specific differential increase until it knew the probable total dimensions of increased labor cost over the future three-year period.

Some economic package items are difficult to cost out. It is hard to know, for example, what the net increase in labor cost will be from adopting a guaranteed annual or monthly income security plan for production workers, or to estimate the cost of converting blue-collar workers from an hourly method of payment to a weekly or monthly salaried basis.

Package bargaining is more complex when the give and take at the bargaining table involves a trade-off at some point between a key noneconomic demand and a money issue. Circumstances can arise when it makes sense to the union leadership to forego a substantial potential gain on a money demand in return for an important noneconomic concession such as, for example, a union-shop clause or an improved understanding on subcontracting.

In summary, in any negotiation today there are likely to be several disputed issues involving increased money costs to the employer as well as a number of noneconomic issues to which the parties attach varying degrees of importance. The consensus among practitioners on both sides of the bargaining table clearly favors deferring formal commitment on *any one* economic issue until tentative agreement has been reached on *all* such issues. Such an approach is the one sure way for each party ultimately to determine the true bargaining priorities of the other party and what the probable requirements for a mutually acceptable package will be. The most common method appears to be the reaching of a preliminary understanding as to how much additional labor cost (if any) the employer is willing to accept for the coming contract period and then to engage in the requisite bargaining for allocating this estimated overall sum among the various competing economic demands.

THE ATMOSPHERE OF NEGOTIATION

The atmosphere of contract negotiations will vary from one relationship to another depending on such factors as (1) prior relations between the parties, (2) the basic attitude of the employer toward unionism, (3) the economic circumstances of the employer and (4) the compulsions operating upon union leadership, which may or may not be related to the specific situation in which the union is negotiating. Each of these factors deserves brief attention.

If the parties have a past history of conflict, or if tensions have built up during the administration of the contract about to expire, the bargaining is likely to be tough, long drawn out and perhaps unsuccessful. On the other hand, many employers and unions renegotiate contracts with a bare minimum of friction time after time.

When past relations have been unsatisfactory, negotiations may be conducted on a "goldfish bowl" basis, with a maximum of partisan communication designed to impress constituents.[14] If conditions have been stable and peaceful, negotiations may involve only the principals directly concerned (the firm's industrial relations director and the union's business agent or international representative). Membership ratification of the agreement in such circumstances is often merely a formality.

The pattern of negotiations may be affected by the economic circumstances of the employer. The union must always seek "improvements" in the new contract. A company that accepts the union will not begrudge such political compulsions operating upon union leadership. In a situation where the company in question cannot grant any contract changes involving added labor cost (or may even require a decrease in labor costs), however, a realistic union will recognize the requirements of a hard-pressed firm. In one such case, when asked what he obtained from the negotiations, the union representative replied cryptically, "We couldn't get any money, but we got a lot of language." This statement acknowledged the straitened economic condition of the employer, but stressed the presumed "gains" to the membership from a firming-up of contract language on various noneconomic issues.

The pattern and atmosphere of negotiations can also be affected by conditions external to the company or union. A particular employer may be under pressure from other employers to resist a particular union demand. On the union side the policy of the international may involve pressing hard for a certain demand (such as an income security plan) that the local union(s) may not be particularly enthusiastic about. In such cases the external pressures on one or both participants may be strong enough to convert the negotiations into an endurance contest that is desired by neither.

The lay observer is often puzzled by the apparent ferocity with which negotiators attack one another during the early stages of bargaining. He is disturbed by the extremity of the union's initial demands and the niggardliness of the employer's original counteroffers. What is not appreciated is that collective bargaining has many attributes common to other types of bargaining in human society.

To abstain entirely from a certain amount of melodramatic build-

---

[14] A good illustration of this would be several highly publicized negotiations in the 1950s and 1960s between General Electric and the IUE (International Union of Electrical, Radio and Machine Workers of America) that made the term "Boulwarism" part of our labor relations language. In 1969 there was evidence that both GE and the IUE had "cooled it," at least in comparison with former years. They began their negotiations well in advance of the formal deadline without the former fanfare and mutual recrimination.

up by approaching the matter coldly and logically would "take all the fun" out of bargaining. It would also destroy the maneuverability and flexibility that each party needs to maintain until reasonably sure in his estimates of the relative strength or weakness of the other party and also of what the other party's true minimum demands or real offers are likely to be.

I do not mean to suggest that negotiators should not endeavor to rely more on objective facts. Nor am I suggesting that all negotiations proceed until the participants are physically and emotionally exhausted with a strike deadline staring them in the face before concluding an agreement. No harm is done, however, by judicious respect for the dramatic unities in the negotiation process. Considerable harm to union-management relationships can come from such approaches as "Boulwarism" that intentionally circumvent bargaining conventions by stressing a "first and last offer."

Contract negotiation is the most dramatic part of the collective bargaining process. There is a constant awareness that if agreement is not reached, a strike or a lockout can result. *The possibility of economic force is the chief sanction that keeps the parties at the table in search of an agreement.* Each party has a minimum position from which he will not retreat. In the great majority of cases an accommodation of conflicting demands is found through negotiation. Resort to economic force is thereby avoided. The union's minimum requirements and the employer's final ability to grant improvements can generally be made to overlap or dovetail in such a way as to make agreement possible. Where this is not possible, collective bargaining is continued by harsher methods of producing agreement, such as a strike or a lockout.

PERSONAL REQUISITES FOR NEGOTIATION

The most skilled negotiator is not likely to be successful at the bargaining table if the party he represents lacks "bargaining power," as this term was used in Chapter 4, or if the positions he is required to support lack merit or feasibility. The reverse is also true. A party bringing impressive economic strength and intrinsically meritorious proposals to the bargaining table can be poorly served by an inept negotiator or a badly designed strategy of negotiation. It is thus important to have a well-thought-out approach to bargaining and to place its execution in the hands of the most skilled personnel available. Carl Stevens has properly stressed that there is such a thing as "negotiation power," which, along with other kinds of power, determines the final result.[15] What are some of the personal requisites needed for success in negotiation?

---

[15] In Stevens' frame of reference, negotiation power comes from such attributes as "facility and shrewdness in the execution of negotiation tactics such as manipulation of the communications structure of the situation to achieve commitment of a threat, use of rationalization of a position to win allies. . ." Carl M. Stevens, *Strategy and Collective Bargaining Negotiation, op. cit.,* p. 3.

First, there can be no substitute for personal integrity and courage. Second, a negotiator must have an intimate knowledge of the essential facts relevant to the positions of his own party and those of the other party. Third, he must have a highly developed understanding of the pressures and compulsions that condition the conduct of the other party's negotiator.

A knowledgeable management negotiator, for example, will not become disturbed when his union opposite number begins negotiations with a flaming speech about the callous, hard-hearted, stingy company whose profits are enormous but whose offers are meager. Nor will an adept union leader become incensed when the management negotiator launches into a prolonged dissertation on the inviolability of certain managerial prerogatives. In each case, other things being equal, there is an awareness of the need for a certain amount of speech-making for the benefit of constituents. Such conduct in negotiations is not deliberately deceitful or harmful, provided it is not carried to extremes. No poised negotiator will be thrown off balance by such tactics.

Fourth and finally, a successful negotiator (management or union) must believe in collective bargaining as a viable method of joint decision-making and accommodating conflicts of interest. A negotiator with a cynical or a "take-it-or-leave-it" approach, no matter how personally intelligent or experienced he may be, cannot be successful in achieving constructive union-management relationships.

Negotiating is a demanding, wearing kind of business. It requires a rather unusual personal chemistry, an abundance of physical and mental vigor and specialized know-how. The model negotiator lives only on the printed page. Few, if any, mortals satisfy all criteria in the required amounts.

We shall consider next the available evidence on whether the practitioners of bargaining are facing up successfully to the various procedural challenges posed earlier in the chapter.

ARE NEGOTIATORS IMPROVING THEIR PERFORMANCE?

Negotiation performance in general has been improving by whatever standard one chooses. Work stoppage data for recent years indicate the overall record on industrial peace to be an excellent one. Another index of improvement would be sequential analysis of contract language. Most experienced arbitrators would, I think, agree that many employers and unions have improved the clarity of their contracts, if not their brevity. Negotiators are becoming more skilled at saying what they actually intended. They are thus avoiding disputes caused by poor draftsmanship or unintentionally fuzzy language.

Another index of maturity and stability is the apparent consensus among experienced negotiators that three years is an optimal duration for a contract. The five-year contracts of the 1950s were demonstrably too long to satisfy the "living document" concept. On the other hand, most management and union negotiators join in the view that it is neither necessary nor economical to negotiate once a year or every two years.

Additional evidence of improved negotiation performance can be found in such developments as: (1) creation of joint study committees to give systematic, continuing attention to long-range problems outside the framework of contract deadlines; (2) use of various prenegotiation procedures to facilitate the agreement-making process; (3) instances of renegotiating new contracts well in advance of expiration deadlines; (4) evidence of a disposition to consider the public stake in private bargains, for example, the willingness in some cases to consider utilizing binding arbitration for resolution of disputes over future contract terms and (5) evidence of a declining propensity to strike in some key bargaining relationships, including a willingness to operate without a contract if necessary in marked contrast to the previously rigid "no contract—no work" stance.

Such developments illustrate the professionalization that marks negotiation in many bargaining relationships. Although there is a darker side of the picture, it is simply not accurate to say that collective bargaining as a process has remained procedurally static and unreceptive to new ideas.

Continuing Problem Areas for Negotiators

Negotiators are concerned about their inability to cope effectively with a number of procedural problems. Perhaps the most disturbing problem is the one posed by the sharp increase in the rate of membership rejection of negotiated settlements. A recent report on cases in which FMCS mediators were involved shows an increase in the percentage of settlements rejected from 8.7 percent in fiscal 1963 to 14.1 percent in fiscal 1967. The cases covered by the FMCS survey were presumably among the more difficult since they required the services of a mediator. Even so, the sharp upward trend of rejections is enough to give pause.[16]

What factors lie behind this contract rejection phenomenon? In some cases rejection is clearly a consequence of overselling of the membership on management's ability to pay. When union leaders prior to negotiations promise more than they can conceivably deliver the membership, in reviewing the ultimate settlement, may suspect that they have been "sold out" by their representatives. Although this is seldom the true explanation,

---

[16] See William E. Simkin, "Refusals to Ratify Contracts," *Industrial and Labor Relations Review*, XXI (July, 1968), 518–40.

union leaders can justly be blamed when they themselves create a gap between expectations and reality.

Some rejections are due to rank-and-file conviction that the settlement can be "sweetened" (improved) following failure to ratify. This has happened often enough to lend credence to such beliefs. A well-known case of this type concerned membership rejection of a settlement that triggered New York City's garbage strike in the winter of 1968. The initial contract terms agreed upon by union and city negotiators were voted down by the sanitation workers. The resultant strike created a potentially explosive crisis for our largest city. The ultimate settlement was in fact "sweeter" than the initial terms. It thereby created headaches for the city's negotiators in subsequent bargaining with other municipal unions.[17]

COPING WITH CONTRACT REJECTIONS

What is the best way of dealing with the rejection phenomenon? As long as union constitutions require membership ratification, the most direct way to improve matters is for the unions to do a far better job of educating the membership toward greater realism in their expectations from negotiations. Experienced union representatives usually know what is attainable and what is feasible in a forthcoming negotiation. They have a responsibility to themselves and to the membership, as well as to the employer with whom they are dealing, to avoid creating either false or excessive expectations.

One approach would be to eliminate the membership ratification requirement. Management negotiators have the authority to bind their principals in most cases. Should not union negotiators be armed with the same authority? Union leaders are accountable to their members and must bear the burden of showing that they did the best they could in any negotiation. In today's economy, however, it is difficult to defend the kind of direct democracy required by the ratification process. It does not make sense to have the work of "professionals" subject to veto by "amateurs." The normal union electoral processes should suffice to replace incompetent or complacent leaders.

Moving to eliminate membership ratification would require amending many union constitutions and would provoke formidable resistance. Yet if we are to insure the continuing viability of collective bargaining as a

---

[17] The City of New York negotiates with some 70 unions representing employees in about 200 bargaining units. One can thus imagine the burdens imposed on the Office of Collective Bargaining (OCB), the City's official labor relations agency established in 1967.

process for resolving increasingly complex economic and noneconomic issues we must think in terms of more representative government rather than more direct democracy.

The probability of contract rejection by the membership can be reduced in specific negotiations in two related ways. One calls for a firm, unambiguous management statement that a negotiated settlement will not subsequently be improved upon should ratification be withheld. Another is to insist on provision that the effective date of any monetary benefits, whether in the form of wage increases or new or improved fringes, will be the date on which management is officially notified of membership ratification rather than going back to the expiration date of the prior agreement. Such an approach has the merit of underlining the importance of the negotiations and the status of the negotiators. It also makes clear that no retroactivity windfalls or better terms will be gained by a settlement rejection strategy.

The Kennecott Copper Company and the coalition of unions headed by the United Steelworkers of America used such an effective date definition in their March, 1968, settlement agreement following an eight-month strike. The pertinent sentence reads as follows:

> For purposes of this Agreement, date of settlement shall be the date on which the appropriate Company Director of Industrial Relations is notified by Union that the settlement has been approved as the result of Union-required approval or ratification procedures.

The Lengthy Contract Problem

Another challenge that negotiators have not met effectively is how to prevent contracts from becoming elephantine in length and size. Some variant of Parkinson's law seems to be causing an alarming growth in the size of contracts. The range and number of issues bargained over are steadily increasing. Furthermore, deletion of anything that has once found its way into contractual writ is exceptional.

Industrial unions and large manufacturing firms are particularly susceptible to this curse of bigness (if it is in fact a curse). Defenders of marathon contracts urge that the detail and length are worthwhile as a means of eliminating sources of dispute in contract administration. Proponents of shorter contracts generally counter by asserting that there is frequently a direct relationship between the length of a contract and the grievance case load. Neither school is in a position to prove its thesis to the other's satisfaction. In the meantime, contracts grow longer.

The prevalence of lengthy contracts perhaps reflects the American passion for the written word. British employers and unions, in sharp contrast, follow their country's dedication to an unwritten constitution by not reducing to writing most of the shop rules and customs under which British unionized firms operate on a day-to-day basis.

I suggest that written contracts, no matter how lengthy, are not a serious problem if they include arbitration for final and binding disposition of interpretation disputes arising under the contract. About 94 percent of all agreements in the United States so provide. The salutary result has been that few work stoppages occur in this country under contracts already in effect. In Great Britain, on the other hand, such work stoppages are numerous and are directly traceable in many cases to conflict over the meaning or application of the unwritten industrial contract (constitution).

To be realistic, no serious moves in the direction of contract shrinkage and/or simplification appear to be likely. We should probably abandon efforts to use the entire contract as an instrument for worker and line foreman education. What seems to be needed in many cases are authorized contract abridgements, written in readable shop English with the essential meaning retained. Such synopses could be approved for informal use by those who formally negotiated the contract itself. They could be extremely useful in broadening the understanding of all workers (and foremen) operating under the contract. The official contract would, of course, remain the sole guide in any formal dispute over its meaning and application.

The Problem of Deleting Outmoded Provisions

Another formidable task is that of removing from a contract a provision that no longer has any reason for being there, particularly if such a provision gives a real or fancied advantage of some sort to a few incumbent employees. Many work rules fit this category.

An effort to eliminate an obsolete contractual provision can be successful only through a convincing demonstration that the provision no longer serves a useful purpose. Realistically, there must also be assurance that no incumbent will be adversely affected. This latter point has been the rock on which many well-intentioned management efforts have foundered through suspicion or misunderstanding. If a group of employees continues to benefit from an obsolete working rule, they must usually be offered some kind of a *quid pro quo* if the rule is to be eliminated.

In this connection, use of a joint committee to develop ways and means of increasing productivity and reducing costs logically comes to mind. Properly handled and publicized, the findings of such a joint committee that certain provisions or rules are obsolete or vestigial could facilitate their elimination from the contract at negotiation time. Such surgery will not work, however, unless provision is made to insure that no present employee or group of employees will be disadvantaged thereby.[18]

Companies and unions plagued with elephantine contracts could charge a special joint committee to recommend ways of simplifying the contract without loss of essential meaning and to identify portions of the contract suitable for deletion. Such a committee could also be given the task of preparing an informal contract synopsis in layman's language, as recommended earlier.

Special Problems in First Contract Negotiations

Most of the discussion has contemplated parties that have been bargaining collectively over a considerable period of time. We now consider briefly some difficulties encountered when a newly certified union is bargaining with an employer for the first time.

The atmosphere in negotiation of a first contract generally ranges from uncertainty to outright hostility. A strike or a lockout may be imminent or actually in progress. Negotiations are often being held following certification of the union as exclusive bargaining agent by the National Labor Relations Board.

Most first contract cases generally have the following features:

1. The union has to make a good showing. This is a political necessity in dealing with a recently unionized employer.
2. Management generally is determined to give as little as possible.
3. The negotiators probably do not know one another. They do not know each other's strengths and weaknesses. Suspicion, if not outright distrust of the other party, is usually present.
4. The parties often lack experience in negotiation.
5. The local union committee may attempt to convert the negotiations into a complaint session over an accumulation of past grievances. Such a tactic can hamper negotiation of the basic contract.
6. When the company is one of the last to be organized in its industry or area, the pressure to achieve at one stroke the gains accrued in years of bargaining with other firms may seriously complicate the agreement-making process.

---

[18] I have always been intrigued by the potential of this form of union-management cooperation and therefore distressed at the comparative scarcity of such efforts over the years. My most recent "pitch" for such a procedure involves picturing it as a private policy at the micro-economic level that could be complementary to national economic policies to maintain stable prices. See Harold W. Davey, "Union Management Cooperation Revisited," *Business Perspectives*, IV (Winter, 1968), 4–10. See also Chapter 11 of this volume.

Such difficulties common to first contract negotiations will not be overcome by procedures alone, but knowledge and use of effective methods can help. With the possible exception of the prenegotiation conference, the procedural suggestions outlined earlier can be utilized effectively in first contract cases. The prenegotiation conference requires stability and mutual understanding in the relationship. These qualities are not usually present in first contract situations.

CONCLUSION

Management and union practitioners are generally doing a better job of preparing for and conducting negotiations than was formerly the case. Innovation and experimentation can be observed in a variety of bargaining situations. Worthy of special mention is the device of the joint study committee: Both formal and informal use of "informed neutrals" as aids to negotiation are no longer unusual. In many instances, the procedures have not changed, but the practitioners have improved. Negotiators are better informed and more skilled in human relations than their predecessors.

We turn next to analysis of how collective bargaining contracts are administered. I have intentionally omitted consideration of problems arising when negotiation has failed and a strike or lockout ensues. These matters are held for consideration in Chapter 8.

Selected Bibliographies for Chapter Five and Chapter Six are combined at the end of Chapter Six, page 156.

CONTRACT ADMINISTRATION
grievance procedures

CHAPTER SIX

Contract negotiation is the part of the collective bargaining iceberg that shows above the surface. The larger and more important part of the iceberg, seldom seen, is the administration of collective agreements. *A contract is no better than its administration.* The test of the soundness of a union-management relationship lies in how effectively the parties implement their contract in the troublesome process of living together under the agreement.

Just as contracts vary in subject matter, so also does experience vary in the matter of contract administration, making generalization hazardous. In some hostile and undisciplined relationships, the union enforces (or ignores) the contract through slowdowns, wildcats or chronic absenteeism. In other similarly unsatisfactory relationships, management enforces (or ignores) the contract in an arbitrary and inequitable manner, knowing that the union with which it is dealing is too weak to challenge effectively such an approach to contract administration. We are not concerned here with these undesirable extremes, but rather with the great majority of management-union relationships where the parties have a shared desire to administer the agreement equitably in accordance with their understanding of its meaning.

The collective agreement is properly regarded as *the statutory law* of the union-management relationship for its effective length, which is increasingly a three-year period. Usually no contract language changes can be made until the expiration date except by mutual consent. Under these circumstances, the importance of developing sound policies and procedures for smooth administration of contractual provisions can hardly be exaggerated.

MANAGEMENT INITIATIVE IN CONTRACT ADMINISTRATION

Contracts do not administer themselves. The initiative for putting contract terms into effect rests with management in nearly all cases. It is management who hires, management who disciplines employees in varying degrees from verbal or written warnings to discharge in serious cases, management who initiates action on transfer and promotion of employees, management who decides on the layoff and recall of workers in response to changing production requirements and management who introduces new jobs and abolishes existing jobs in response to technological change or other requirements. The list could be enlarged, but perhaps enough examples have been given.

Few provisions are self-administering or jointly administered. The primary responsibility for giving operational meaning to the written contractual provisions governing the employment relationship is that of management as the agent for direction and control of the work force. Whenever management moves (or fails to move) on any matter covered by contract, its action must be in accord with the contract. For this reason, most employers go to considerable pains to insure that supervisors are thoroughly informed as to how their operating responsibilities are affected and conditioned by the contract.

In small firms the production manager is usually his own labor relations man. Having negotiated the contract himself or through an attorney representing him, the small employer in theory should know the contract well enough to insure proper contract observance when he and his subordinates are performing their roles as production supervisors. In medium to large firms, the significance of the contract must be communicated to all supervisors in meaningful fashion. My field research indicates that contract administration is not a particularly serious problem for the small employer—

certainly not as troublesome as contract negotiation.[1] Small employers have a clear comparative advantage in contract administration. This is reflected in the low incidence of formal grievances and the rare use of arbitration even though provided for by most contracts. I arbitrated a case in 1968 involving a small Iowa firm that has had contractual relations with the UAW since 1946. It was the first case requiring arbitration in the twenty-two years of the relationship. The arbitrated case was also the first time it had been found necessary to reduce a grievance to writing. Such informality is not at all unusual in small-firm labor relations.

Defining the Scope of the Grievance Procedure

We have stressed the need to regard the collective agreement as the law of the relationship. This necessitates distinguishing clearly between those grievances that relate to the contract and those relating to problems not treated by contract or outside the employment relationship.

Intelligent contract administration should encompass consideration of *any* grievance relating in any fashion to the employment relationship in the early steps of the grievance procedure. The contract should be clear, however, that *only* grievances raising an issue of contract interpretation and application can be appealed to the arbitration step.[2]

If final and binding arbitration is available on grievances raising issues outside the statutory law of the relationship (that is, the contract), stability and consistency in contract administration will be hard to achieve. Under such wide-open arbitration the contract may become merely a point of departure instead of settling the rules of the game for the life of the agreement.[3]

Most employers presumably wish to run efficient, orderly enterprises with a minimum of friction and resentment on the part of employees. Management is therefore interested (or should be) in resolving any individual

---

[1] Harold W. Davey, "Labor Relations Problems of Small Firms and Their Solution," in *Studies in the Factor Markets for Small Business Firms*, ed. Dudley G. Luckett (Ames, Iowa: Iowa State University for the Small Business Administration, 1964), pp. 199–222.

[2] This view is held by most practitioners and arbitrators. Under some contracts, however, virtually anything can be appealed to arbitration. Defining the limits of the arbitrator's authority and jurisdiction is a critically important policy decision that the parties themselves must make.

[3] If the grievance raises a matter on which the contract is silent, under most contracts such a grievance would be held to be nonarbitrable. An important exception to this generalization relates to past practice issues where it is contended that the practice is in fact a part of the contract by custom and usage. To put it another way, arbitrable grievances can and do arise as to the contractual significance of contractual silence. Such grievances usually concern past practice.

or group dissatisfaction that may threaten the achievement of these objectives. Similarly, the union's principal role in contract administration is to function as an agent or representative of employees in handling individual or group complaints that may arise. The union wishes to check independently on the way in which management is exercising administrative initiative in effectuating contract terms and conditions.

Taking this broad view of their respective functions, all employers and unions should endorse the psychological proposition that *a grievance exists whenever an employee feels aggrieved*, whether or not the source of his grievance is contractual. If an employee or some employees feel, rightly or wrongly, that they are being unjustly treated, a human relations problem exists that merits the attention of both management and the union.

The goal of intelligent and orderly administration of contracts, however, requires that a distinction be made and clearly understood by all parties between those grievances which raise a question of contract interpretation or application and those grievances that, no matter how intrinsically sincere or meritorious they may be, are outside the scope of the collective agreement. Some highly prerogative-conscious managements will refuse even to discuss with union representatives any grievance that does not relate directly to the contract. Such an approach may succeed in "putting the union in its place," but it is not conducive to constructive labor relations. From a realistic standpoint, a grievance procedure should be designed to carry all grievances in its early steps.

At some point in the grievance procedure, however, a line must be drawn. If a collective labor agreement is to mean anything, its provisions must be adhered to by both parties for its duration. It would be inviting chaos to say that all grievances must be resolved whether or not they bear any relationship to a contractual provision. At the same time, genuine grievances will arise over problems not covered or contemplated by the contract. These grievances are no less real because the contract may happen to be silent on the matter. Some procedural outlet should therefore be provided.

Combining the Clinical and Contractual Approaches to Grievance Adjustment

Opening the early steps of the grievance procedure to *any* grievance concerning the employment relationship permits effective use of the machinery for both communication and catharsis. It permits the so-called clinical approach to grievance handling, as advocated by the late Benjamin Selekman more than twenty years ago.[4] Selekman favored seeking out the root causes

---

[4] Benjamin M. Selekman, *Labor Relations and Human Relations* (New York: McGraw-Hill Book Company, Inc., 1947), pp. 75–110.

of grievances rather than accepting their surface rationale. Many grievances *as filed* do not reveal the true basis for the grievant's antagonism or sense of injury. The written allegation in the grievance may relate to a trivial surface complaint. The truth may be that the grievant is convinced in his own mind that his foreman has been systematically discriminating or otherwise administering a number of contract provisions unfairly over a considerable period of time.

The clinical approach stresses thorough investigation and treatment of the problems that may underlie the grievances rather than mechanistic handling according to whether or not they lie within the contractual frame of reference. Depth investigation of all but obviously frivolous grievances should be worth the time and effort expended. Frequently a grievance on a noncontract matter enables management to resolve it to the satisfaction of all concerned while this potential oak of a problem is still in the acorn stage. Most employers appreciate the logic and economy of practicing preventive labor relations.

The Selekman method is in no sense inconsistent with recognizing the primacy of the contract. Grievances which do *not* raise an issue of contract interpretation and application can be received, investigated and, where found to be meritorious, adjusted by management. At the same time management can and should make clear that it is practicing prudent personnel administration above and beyond its contractual obligation. The contractual obligation is limited to effectuating the terms and conditions of the agreement. Only when a grievance alleges that management has failed to observe the contract should there be the opportunity to appeal the complaint for final and binding determination by an impartial outsider.

The wisdom of limiting the authority and jurisdiction of the arbitrator to grievances of this type is still questioned by some management and union practitioners who consider arbitration to be an extension of the collective bargaining process and use it for handling extracontractual disputes as well as straight contract interpretation cases. The great majority of practitioners and arbitrators, however, favor confining grievance arbitration to cases involving issues of contract interpretation and application.[5]

The needs of the clinical approach can be accommodated by a

---

[5] A typical clause circumscribing the arbitrator's authority and jurisdiction is the following, taken from the 1969–1972 contract between the Bendix Corporation, Kansas City Division, and District Lodge No. 71 of the International Association of Machinists and Aerospace Workers, p. 21: "The arbitrator shall have no power to add to, subtract from or modify any of the terms of this Agreement, or any other terms made supplemental hereto, or to arbitrate any matter not specifically provided for by this Agreement or to arbitrate any new provision into this Agreement. The arbitrator's authority is to interpret and apply provisions of the Agreement. The arbitrator shall have no power to establish new or change the existing wage rate structure or establish new or change existing job content or to decide any matter pertaining to production standards."

simple declaration that the grievance procedure is available to any employee or to the union desiring to present a grievance concerning any matter involving rates of pay, wages, hours of employment or any other condition of employment. At the same time the contract can make clear that grievances involving interpretation and application of the provisions of the contract *and only such grievances* can be appealed to arbitration.

Basic Principles of Grievance Adjustment

Certain general principles should govern the handling and adjustment of grievances. One is that grievances should be adjusted *promptly*, preferably at the first step in the grievance procedure, and that such adjustments of grievances should be *on their merits*. Few would dispute this principle, but there are cases in which the principle is ignored. In some relationships there is an inclination to by-pass the departmental foreman and the union steward in grievance adjustment, although the great majority of grievances can and should be finally adjusted at the foreman-steward level. When the foreman's discretion to adjust is denied, the authority of the steward correspondingly declines. He is the foreman's opposite number. Some employers and union representatives are determined to achieve uniformity and avoid embarrassing precedents. In so doing they destroy democratic decision-making at the shop level.

The sounder approach is not to take away discretion from foremen and stewards but to do a thorough job of training both in contract administration. Training sessions for small groups of fifteen or twenty foremen and stewards at a time should be conducted shortly after a contract is negotiated. These programs are admittedly difficult to plan and administer, but the time and effort spent should be worth the trouble. Properly trained foremen and stewards can then be encouraged and trusted to adjust grievances instead of passing them up the line.

My view is that such training programs should be conducted on a joint basis wherever possible. Some years ago Charles J. Cranny, an industrial psychologist, and I surveyed a substantial sampling of management and union practitioners to ascertain their preferences as to joint versus separate training programs for foremen and stewards. We found that most respondents favored separately conducted programs on new contracts. We found, however, that those companies and unions *who had actually tried joint training* were satisfied and even enthusiastic. Employers and unions who had not tried joint training invariably held the view that it either would accomplish little or would not be feasible.[6] Whatever form the training in contract

---

[6] The research findings just summarized did not make their way into print because the co-investigators became too involved in other pursuits. Our intent was to do additional interviewing and corresponding to "enrich" the original sampling.

provisions may take, its value and utility in encouraging the prompt and contractually correct disposition of grievances at an early stage cannot be doubted.

A second principle of effective grievance adjustment is that the procedure and forms for grieving must be easy to utilize and well understood by employees and their supervisors. The functional relationship involving the employee, his union steward and the foreman needs to be clearly established. The employee should understand, for example, that as a matter of law he can discuss conditions and circumstances involving his work with his supervisor without his union steward being present. Also as a matter of law, of course, no adjustment of an employee complaint or grievance can be made by management that is not consistent with the provisions of the collective agreement. Whenever an employee elects to present his own grievance individually, exercising his option to do so under Taft-Hartley, the law provides that a union representative has the right to be present at such individual adjustment sessions.

A third basic principle calls for a direct and timely avenue of appeal from the rulings of line supervision. The number of steps in the grievance procedure will vary in terms of the size of the bargaining unit and the needs of the parties, but in all cases the appeal ladder from one level of supervision to another must be clear and direct.

Finally, effective grievance adjustment machinery should provide for appeal to arbitration by an impartial outside party whose decision shall be final and binding upon the company, the union and the aggrieved employee(s).

The spirit and substance of grievance handling are of the greatest importance. Sound contract administration requires that grievances be handled in an equitable, nondiscriminatory and reasonably uniform manner in conformity with the contract provision(s) involved. At the same time there should be a joint awareness of the need for *some* flexibility in the practical solution of problems. A good illustration of the need on occasion to depart from the letter of the contract can be found in the customary contract prohibition against supervisors doing any production work, except as instructors or in starting new jobs.[7] The historic reason for such a policy is the conservation of job opportunities for employees in the bargaining unit. Yet in daily business it may make sense occasionally for the foreman to lend a hand

---

[7] A typical provision of this type is Article II, Section 3 of the Deere-UAW 1967–1970 agreement, which reads as follows (p. 4): "*Section 3.* Management employees shall not perform work covered by the terms of this Agreement, except in the following types of situations: A. In the instruction or training of employees, B. In the performance of necessary supervisory work when production difficulties are encountered on the job, or in starting new jobs."

on a particular production job. Should the union *always* grieve in such situations, or should it occasionally look the other way? A policy of always grieving, regardless of the realities of the situation, might well cause management to take an extremely strict or literal approach to contract interpretation in other types of cases where a more realistic approach might be to the employee's advantage.

In a large plant many grievances may be filed due to misunderstanding of contractual provisions. Since they lack contractual merit, such grievances must be dismissed, if not withdrawn. Similarly, in any large plant foremen will make mistakes in contract application, because of either ignorance or misunderstanding of the contract. Grievances can be pushed in such cases as technically sound on a strict contractual basis. Yet the interests of the parties often may be better served through a disposition to stretch a point on occasion in adjusting a grievance or to refrain from exacting literal enforcement, particularly if no one has been injured by the contractual mistake.

In each bargaining relationship there should be a joint effort at achieving a pattern of fair-minded common sense in grievance filing and grievance handling. Such a pattern would avoid the extremes of both laxity and rigidity in applying contract language.

I dwell on this theme because, like most arbitrators, I have heard my share of cases over the years where going strictly by the contract (as the arbitrator must do) has produced a Pyrrhic victory for one party and has probably increased the friction rather than reducing mistrust or clarifying a misunderstanding. The union view in such cases is "we can't let management get away with this inch or they'll take a mile next time." Management lyrics for the same melody run as follows: "We can't grant this grievance on an equity basis when the contract does not require it. If we do, we will open a Pandora's box of similar cases lacking contractual merit."

Clearly it is hard to generalize on when to press and when to bend in grievance handling. There must be an intuitive wisdom guiding the parties to enable them to preserve the essential meaning and force of contract provisions without ignoring the tangible values of recognizing the equities and practicalities of particular situations.

Management ordinarily takes a stricter view of the contract than the union, perhaps because of concern over the union's desire to expand the agreement's applicability. I do not say that there is not a basis for management to be cautious in this regard. However, in special circumstances where denial of a technically weak grievance would be "unjust," the employer can always win points for being fair while at the same time stressing that the settlement shall not be regarded as having any precedential value.

THE POLITICS OF GRIEVANCE ADJUSTMENT
AND "FAIR REPRESENTATION"

Industrial unions in particular are not characterized by a homogenous membership with common problems and a community of interest deriving from a common background of training and experience. With the exception of the longshoring and coal mining unions and perhaps a few others, conflicting pressures and interests are at work, complicating the task of union leadership in contract administration as well as in negotiation. In processing grievances relating to promotions, layoffs and transfers, for example, the union leader is often in the unenviable position of making one employee or group of employees happy while incurring the displeasure of any workers who may be adversely affected by the "winning" of the grievance. Another sensitive area in contract administration concerns allocation of available overtime work. The grievance procedure may also serve as an arena for conflicts of interest between skilled and unskilled, between hourly paid and incentive paid or between male and female employees.

The accommodation of these conflicting interests can be a source of real difficulty for union leadership in grievance handling. This political burden is not always well understood by management. An employer who is interested in building durable relationships with a responsible union, however, usually understands the multiple pressures operating upon local union leaders. He will try to avoid actions or policies that embarrass or undercut such leadership. Much of the formalism in contract administration is due not so much to management's initiative as to the union leadership's need to insulate itself from rank-and-file pressures.

Sayles and Strauss in 1953 noted five ways in which local leaders can maintain their freedom to choose the grievances they want to push while at the same time avoiding identification with defeats: (1) requiring members to sign grievances; (2) careful screening of grievances before negotiating with management; (3) never negotiating without another officer being present; (4) relying on precedents and legalistic interpretations and (5) "passing the buck" to the arbitrator.[8] In revising their 1953 study, Sayles and Strauss added one more technique, that of involving the international union.[9] This is nearly universal practice today prior to the arbitration step.

The current stress on individual rights has made even more difficult

---

[8] Leonard R. Sayles and George Strauss, *The Local Union* (1st ed.), (New York: Harcourt, Brace & World, Inc., 1953), p. 74.
[9] —— and ——, *The Local Union* (rev. ed.), (New York: Harcourt, Brace & World, Inc., 1967), p. 44.

the unpleasant duty of screening out grievances that lack contractual merit. Every employee believes that his grievance has merit. If his leadership fails to process the grievance, the employee may conclude that he is being ignored or sold out. Although this is rarely the case, the employee may nevertheless become convinced in his own mind that he is not getting his money's worth from his dues and is not being fairly represented.

The NLRB's *Hughes Tool* decision and other "duty of fair representation" cases appear to have contributed to some exaggerated ideas as to what kind of service by the union is required under a contract. The right to fair representation does not, for example, include a right to have one's grievance go all the way to arbitration, regardless of its contractual merit. By the time the international union representative enters the grievance picture, if not before, it is the contract that must become the decisive consideration in further processing of a grievance, rather than the personal whims of an individual worker or the factional operations of a discontented minority.

The current emphasis on individual rights is a healthy development, generally speaking. Such an emphasis can serve as an effective deterrent to the dubious practice of trading off legitimate grievances in the game of union or management politics. *Grievances should stand or fall on their contractual merit.* Their political weight should not be the relevant variable.

Individual rights can be critical in bargaining units where the certified union does not have a union-shop contract. When employees who do not belong to the union file grievances, the union leadership understandably may be tempted at times to give poor service or no service to these "free riders." Yet the only sound policy is to give good service to membership holdouts to prove to them that the union as bargaining agent for all employees takes its responsibilities seriously. It is also the union's legal obligation to represent all employees in the unit, without regard to whether they are members.

IMPROVED PROCEDURES FOR EFFECTUATING CONTRACTUAL POLICIES

In sizable bargaining units with a considerable number of grievances filed regularly there is a continuing need to improve the functioning of the machinery and also to control (and if possible to reduce) the volume of cases. What constitutes an "excessive" number of grievances and what is an optimal grievance procedure are questions that each union-management relationship must answer for itself. There is no model of universal utility. Some suggestions can be offered, however, that should contribute to improved contract administration.

We can begin by restating the conventional wisdom on the grievance procedure as such. First, the contract sections on grievance procedure should be written with special attention to clarity and directness. The task of contract administration is facilitated when the procedural guidelines in the contract are easy to follow.

Second, the contract should make clear that *any* grievance relating to the employment relationship will be processed in the early steps but that *only grievances raising an issue of contract interpretation or application are appealable to arbitration.*

Third, the contract must treat clearly such matters as the time and manner of reducing a grievance to writing; the time limits for filing, appealing and answering at the various steps; penalties for failure to use the grievance machinery and procedures for cases where employees elect to process their grievances independently of the union.

Many grievances can be avoided when the parties take pains to spell out in their contracts procedures for implementing substantive policies on such matters as transfers, promotions, layoffs, recalls from layoff, discipline, merit increases and allocation of overtime opportunities. In these and other matters there is a need for clearly defined procedures. When this has been done in clear and even-handed fashion, much misunderstanding and confusion can be avoided.

The logic of industrial jurisprudence demands uniform, acceptable and understandable procedures relating to on-the-job activities. If the contract is clear on the rules of the game and also on how to play the game procedurally, there will be less friction and fewer grievances. Some examples may help to underline the importance of these considerations.

PROMOTIONAL PROCEDURES

On promotions some contracts state a policy without a procedure. The policy may be barely stated as one of filling vacancies wherever possible by promotion from within. If the contract stops here, however, many unanswered questions arise, such as: (1) Must vacancies be posted—if so, for how long? (2) If several applicants are qualified, does the vacancy go to the senior among them or to the most qualified among them? (3) If no applicant appears to be qualified, how shall the vacancy be filled? (4) Is management obligated to give a trial on the job to any applicant who insists he is qualified to perform it? If so, how much of a trial?

DISCIPLINARY ACTION PROCEDURES

Another example of the importance of defined procedures concerns management's exercise of the discipline function. Most contracts state the policy that employees shall be disciplined only for "just cause." Such contractual protection against arbitrary or ill-founded disciplinary action is properly regarded as perhaps the most important single contribution to the meaningful democratization of industrial relations.

The "just cause" principle is easy to state in one sentence. However, some contracts are silent or unsatisfactory on procedures to be followed when disciplinary action is taken. A uniform procedure in all discipline cases is of great value to all parties in contract administration. Disciplinary action cases frequently result in conflicting versions of what happened and often involve serious emotional reactions. Such factors make it important to spell out in the contract the "due process of law" available to any employee charged with conduct meriting discipline.

The procedure used in administering discipline, whatever its particular form, should satisfy the following requirements:

1. The employee should be advised by management of the charges against him. He should have the right to have his union representative hear such charges and the employee's statement of *his* position.

2. Before *formal* discipline is assessed, management should conduct a hearing within a reasonable period of time after the determination that disciplinary action is required. The charged employee should be present with appropriate union representation at such a hearing. Both parties should be allowed to call witnesses in order to ascertain all the facts and circumstances of the case. Formal disciplinary action should be taken only after the completion of such a hearing.

3. Written minutes of the disciplinary action hearing should be furnished to the employee's union representative.

The objective is to assure a full review of the circumstances while they are fresh in the minds of all concerned. The testimony at the disciplinary action hearing may show that the foreman had called for discipline on the basis of erroneous or incomplete information, or the statements may make clear to the union representative that "just cause" for discipline has been proved. The disciplinary action will therefore not be grieved.

In serious discipline cases (discharge) it may be prudent to require the employee to leave the plant upon notification that disciplinary action is contemplated. In other situations, such as discipline for garnishment, tardiness or absenteeism, such a precaution is probably unnecessary.

A Note on Management Grievances

The grievance machinery of the contract is not necessarily a one-way street for employees and the union only. Some contracts provide for management filing of grievances, although use of such a contractual option appears to be comparatively rare.

Realistically, management does not find the grievance procedure a suitable instrument for initiating complaints against its employees or against the union as their institutional representative. One logical situation for management to use the grievance procedure would be to process a charge that employees and/or union officials had violated a union responsibility clause. Another might involve charges that the union was seeking to discredit management in the eyes of the employees.

A union responsibility clause is one stating an affirmative commitment by the union to police its membership in the interests of stable contract administration. The union agrees, for example, to condemn and discourage absenteeism, wildcat strikes and other employee actions designed to interfere with production or to short-circuit the grievance procedure.

In any such cases, management usually will exercise its disciplinary prerogatives directly against offending employees or take formal action against the union through a civil damage suit under Section 301 of Taft-Hartley. The damage suit option has little appeal for most employers.

Even though it may rarely be used, there is some virtue in making the grievance procedure available to management. Such an option supports the idea of the *joint* commitment to achieve stability, consistency and equity in administration of contract terms. The document then becomes something more than a cataloging of policies and procedures for the effectuation of which management assumes virtually the whole burden. The joint aspect of the undertaking can be underscored by the management option to use the grievance procedure against employees or the union leadership through a "general" or "policy" grievance of its own.

This line of thinking brings us logically to the final topic on contract administration prior to discussing the uses of grievance arbitration—namely, the problem of how to prevent going outside the contract's grievance and arbitration machinery.

Penalties for Failure to Use Contract Grievance Procedures

BLS data for calendar 1968 reveal an alarming number of work stoppages under existing agreements.[10] In most contracts, walkouts of this nature are specifically prohibited by the agreement itself. Such "wildcat"

---

[10] The BLS Summary Report, *Work Stoppages in 1968*, mimeographed (Washington, D.C., Bureau of Labor Statistics, 1969), indicated that almost one-third of all stoppages arose during the term of agreements and did not involve negotiations of new contract terms. Some of these would be for contractually agreed-upon purposes. Some took place under contracts that do not provide for arbitration as the last step in the grievance procedure. However, it is probable that the greater number were of the unauthorized or wildcat variety.

154 Contract administration

stoppages are a critically serious problem whose solution is not an easy one. The grim irony is that most wildcats occur under contracts with a suitable grievance and arbitration mechanism specified as a *quid pro quo* for a sweeping no-strike clause.

Many unions have done a good job of educating the rank and file to utilize the grievance procedure instead of resorting to "direct action." In some cases, however, employers are unable to plan on uninterrupted production during the life of the contract. They are plagued intermittently (and, in some cases, with alarming frequency) by walkouts of particular departments or possibly of the entire work force. Sometimes these wildcats may have been engineered behind the scenes by the union leadership. More usually, however, the union leadership is just as interested as management in eliminating this flouting of contract obligations.

In any valid contractual situation there can be no excuse for a group of employees taking the law into their own hands by walking off the job, deliberately slowing down their work pace, becoming collectively "sick" or otherwise breaking their commitment to use the contract's grievance and arbitration machinery. The alleged intrinsic merit of the employees' complaint is not a valid excuse for using economic force instead of the procedures jointly agreed upon as the sole method for handling allegations of contract violation. Employees on many occasions may be restless and understandably impatient over the delays in a clogged or overloaded grievance procedure. The remedy, however, is not to go outside the contract but rather to press hard for speeding up the grievance procedure through their authorized union representatives. Unfortunately, employees do not always appreciate that they themselves are the principal beneficiaries of scrupulous adherence to the prescribed contract method for adjustment of complaints.

Many wildcats are triggered by the discharge of a single employee. His fellow employees then walk off the job in protest in an effort to pressure management into reinstating him on the spot. This is perhaps the least excusable basis for direct action, if one concedes (which I am not prepared to do) that some wildcats have a better rationale than others.

Perhaps the most plausible circumstance for unauthorized direct action would be in any case where workers are told to do a job that they believe is dangerous to their health or safety. Even here the remedy is not to risk discharge for insubordination or a wildcat. The remedy is not a walkout or a refusal to perform, but rather an immediate union steward appeal to top supervision over the foreman's head.

The writer has heard discipline cases involving wildcats where the defense was that the workers were contractually correct in their position and the foreman's order was wrong. In such cases, the discipline was sustained, even where the foreman's order was contractually in error. In labor relations, as in other phases of interpersonal relations, *two wrongs do not make a right.*

Some contracts do not provide for arbitration as the terminal step in the grievance procedure. In such cases management always has the last word unless the union resorts to direct action. In a contract with a clear channel of grievance adjustment steps culminating in arbitration, however, there is no excuse for resort to economic force.

Under most contracts the scope of the arbitrator's authority is congruent with the coverage of the contract's no strike–no lockout clause. If under the contract a grievance is arbitrable, the union is estopped from strike action during the life of the agreement. In some contracts certain issues are reserved for strike action during the life of the contract by excluding them from the scope of the arbitrator's authority.[11] However, most contracts provide that any grievance relating to contract interpretation and application may go to arbitration. In these cases there can be no lawful strike during the life of the agreement.

A SUGGESTED SOLUTION
TO THE WILDCAT STRIKE PROBLEM

For management the problem of periodic wildcat interruptions of production is a troublesome one, particularly during periods of full employment when all employees are needed to maintain production in a race with the firm's competitors. Under such circumstances, management is frequently tempted to take precisely the wrong approach, that is, to be lenient in discipline for instigating or participating in a wildcat. If a disposition to direct action is already present and the employees sense management's vulnerability and consequent willingness to appease in order to keep production going, the wildcat problem may become much more serious. Union leaders cannot fulfill their contractual obligation to discourage and prevent direct action because the employees will be unmoved by warnings that the union cannot protect or defend them if they practice illegal stoppages.

The conclusion must be that management needs to make clear to both employees and the union leadership that swift, certain discipline will be meted out to all employees, no matter how many are involved, who violate their contractual commitment not to bypass the grievance procedure. *This is the only logical, effective route to elimination of wildcats.* A management that somehow conveys the impression it will be tough if only a few employees are involved, but soft if the illegal stoppage involves large numbers will

---

[11] Deere and UAW provide for "legal" strikes during the life of the contract on certain types of grievances, for example, the rate range for new hourly classifications or the occupational rate on new incentive standards.

reap the whirlwind. Stable contract administration will become virtually impossible.

Some employers continue to yearn for built-in, self-executing penalty systems that will be operational automatically in case of illegal work stoppages. This is a vain hope. There is no adequate substitute for a policy of firmness, clearly enunciated in advance and then put into effect if and when the occasion arises.

CONCLUSION

Such sobering thoughts on the wildcat strike problem should not be permitted to cloud over much encouraging evidence of progress in contract administration. Most employers and union leaders agree that the heart of collective bargaining lies in the (sometimes) mundane task of contract administration. Contract negotiation is a "some time thing." It occurs usually once every three years. *Contract administration requires daily initiative by management in effectuation of terms.* The contract's grievance machinery is of crucial importance in giving operational significance to the written word. It provides a peaceful way of resolving *any* dispute that may arise concerning interpretation and application.

Orderly and efficient operation of any enterprise and the logic of employee democracy require that a mechanism be available for fair disposition of any case where an employee feels aggrieved. This machinery should also be available to management for registering complaints about union or employee violation of contract.

If procedures and principles of grievance adjustment are clearly understood both by line supervision and by union officials and employees, most problems in contract administration can be resolved in the early steps of the machinery. Much needless friction can thereby be completely avoided. *Perhaps most important, an effective arbitration procedure eliminates any necessity for interruption of production during the life of a contract.*

Arbitration has become such an important aspect of contract administration that we consider the process separately in the following chapter.

SELECTED BIBLIOGRAPHY

AARON, BENJAMIN, "Strikes in Breach of Collective Agreements: Some Unanswered Questions," *Columbia Law Review*, LXIII (June, 1963), 1026–52.

CORZINE, JAMES E., "Structure and Utilization of a Grievance Procedure," Personnel Journal, XLVI (September, 1967), 484–89.

CULLEN, DONALD E., *Negotiating Labor-Management Contracts*. Bulletin 56, 56 pages.

Ithaca, N.Y.: Cornell University, New York State School of Industrial and Labor Relations, 1965.

DROUGHT, NEAL E., "Grievances in the Non-Union Situation," *Personnel Journal*, XLVI (June, 1967), 331–36.

FELDACKER, BRUCE S., "Processing Grievances When Bargaining Units are Combined: Conflict with the Doctrine of Exclusive Representation?" *Labor Law Journal*, XVIII (November, 1967), 649–64.

FORKOSCH, MORRIS D., " 'Take It or Leave It' as a Bargaining Technique," *Labor Law Journal*, XVII (November, 1967), 676–98.

GOLDSMITH, FREDERICK M., AND NINO E. GREEN, "Union Settlement of Disputes, the Rights of Members, and the Role of Doctrine of Exhaustion of Remedies," *Wayne Law Review*, IX (Winter, 1963), 360–68.

GOULD, WILLIAM B., "The Status of Unauthorized and 'Wildcat' Strikes under the National Labor Relations Act," *Cornell Law Quarterly*, LII (Spring 2, 1967), 672–704.

HAMPTON, DAVID R., "Fractional Bargaining Patterns and Wildcat Strikes," *Human Organization*, XXVI (Fall, 1967), 100–109.

HELMES, ROBERT H., ed., *Handling Employee Grievances*. 74 pages. Chicago: Public Personnel Association, 1968.

JAMES, RALPH, AND ESTELLE JAMES, "Hoffa's Leverage Techniques in Bargaining," *Industrial Relations*, III (October, 1963), 73–93.

KUHN, JAMES W., *Bargaining in Grievance Settlement*. New York: Columbia University Press, 1961.

LAHNE, HERBERT J., "Contract Negotiation: Who Speaks for the Union?" *Labor Law Journal*, XX (May, 1969), 259–63.

LAW NOTE, "Boulwarism and Good Faith Collective Bargaining," *Michigan Law Review*, LXIII (June, 1965), 1473–81.

LEAHY, W. H., "Arbitration Union Stewards, and Wildcat Strikes," *Arbitration Journal*, XXIV (1969), 50.

LOVE, T. M., "Joint Committees: Their Role in the Development of Teacher Bargaining," *Labor Law Journal*, XX (March, 1969), 174.

MCKERSIE, ROBERT B., AND WILLIAM W. SHROPSHIRE, "Avoiding Written Grievances: A Successful Program," *Journal of Business of University of Chicago*, XXXV (April, 1962), 135–52.

PETERS, EDWARD, *Strategy and Tactics in Labor Negotiations*. New London, Conn.: National Foremen's Institute, 1955.

REPAS, BOB, "Grievance Procedures Without Arbitration," *Industrial and Labor Relations Review*, XX (April, 1967), 381–90.

ROGOW, ROBERT, "Membership Participation and Centralized Control," *Industrial Relations*, VII (February, 1968), 132–45.

SIMKIN, WILLIAM E., "Refusals to Ratify Contracts," *Industrial and Labor Relations Review*, XXI (July, 1968), 518–40.

STERN, IRVING, AND ROBERT F. PEARSE, "Collective Bargaining: A Union's Program for Reducing Conflict," *Personnel*, XLV (May–June, 1968), 61–72.

STEVENS, CARL M., *Strategy and Collective Bargaining Negotiation*. New York: McGraw-Hill Book Company, Inc., 1963.

SWERDLOFF, SOL, "Manpower Facts in Labor-Management Negotiations," *Monthly Labor Review*, XC (January, 1967), 9–14.

WAGNER, LYNN E., "Multi-Union Bargaining: A Legal Analysis," *Labor Law Journal*, XIX (December, 1968), 731–42.

GRIEVANCE ARBITRATION
principles and procedures

CHAPTER SEVEN

Arbitration for final resolution of disputes under an existing contract is provided for in about 94 percent of all collective agreements.[1] To my knowledge there are no significant instances of grievance arbitration having been abandoned in favor of a return to economic force as a means of ultimately settling grievances under existing contracts.

In this chapter I have drawn freely on five of my journal articles on the arbitration process, two published in 1969, two in 1961, and one in 1962 as follows: "Restructuring Grievance Arbitration Procedures: Some Modest Proposals," *Iowa Law Review,* LIV (February, 1969), 560–78; "The Use of Neutrals in the Public Sector," *Labor Law Journal,* XX (August, 1969), 529–38; "The Supreme Court and Arbitration: The Musings of an Arbitrator," *Notre Dame Lawyer,* XXXVI (March, 1961), 138–45; "The Arbitrator Views the Agreement," *Labor Law Journal,* XII (December, 1961), 1161–76; and "The Arbitrator Speaks on Discharge and Discipline," *Arbitration Journal,* XVII, No. 2 (1962), 97–102.

[1] U.S. Bureau of Labor Statistics, Department of Labor, Bulletin No. 1425–6, *Arbitration Procedures* (Washington, D.C.: Government Printing Office, 1966), p. 5.

The nearly universal acceptance of arbitration as the terminal step in contract grievance machinery is remarkable when one recalls that the process was comparatively rare prior to World War II. Increasing utilization of the procedure dates from the years 1942–1945 when the National War Labor Board in a sense imposed the process on many employers and unions by writing it into their contracts through directive orders. Its value as an instrument of contract administration is conclusively demonstrated by the joint willingness to continue and expand its utilization after 1945 when employers and unions resumed "private" collective bargaining.[2]

Referring back to our list of challenges in Chapter 1, the key challenge for consideration in this chapter is how to cope effectively with the problem of a short supply of competent, experienced and acceptable arbitrators in the face of an increasing demand for the services of "informed neutrals," not only as arbitrators in conventional contract administration but also as mediators, fact-finders and advisory arbitrators in public sector labor relations.

We shall begin the analysis of the grievance arbitration process with a summary listing of pluses and minuses, followed by an outlining of the arbitrator's function and a representative listing of issues he is called upon to decide. Next in order is a re-examination of the perennial controversy over whether arbitrators should function strictly as interpreters of contract language or as "problem-solvers" for employers and unions. This discussion will be related to a brief consideration of the role of the federal courts under Section 301 of the National Labor Relations Act, as amended, in enforcing agreements to arbitrate and arbitrators' decisions. We shall then briefly review some common procedural problems in arbitration. In the concluding sections of the chapter we shall consider how to reform or restructure grievance arbitration procedures with the dual purpose of improving the process and of making more effective use of the limited supply of arbitrators.

AN ARBITRATION BALANCE SHEET

On the affirmative side, we can list the following:

1. Continued acceptance of arbitration as the terminal step in the contract's grievance procedure, combined with more intelligent and sparing use of arbitration as an integral element in contract administration.

---

[2] The literature on the grievance arbitration process is so extensive that a single bibliographical footnote cannot possibly do justice to the many excellent contributions in this area. The best single source of authentic critical treatment on an annually recurring basis is the published proceedings of the National Academy of Arbitrators. These are published by the Bureau of National Affairs, Inc., Washington, D.C. An excellent analytical treatment is that of Robben W. Fleming, *The Labor Arbitration Process* (Urbana, Ill.: University of Illinois Press, 1965.)

2. Improved contract language for defining grievance and arbitration procedures and stating the limits of the arbitrator's authority and jurisdiction.
3. Growth of the practice of naming a permanent arbitrator or a panel of arbitrators in the contract to minimize the delays and uncertainties that often occur in *ad hoc* selection procedures.
4. Visible improvement (in many relationships) in reducing the arbitration case load to manageable proportions by more rigorous screening on the part of both management and union.
5. Growing sophistication in treating the problem of acceptability of arbitrators, that is, an apparent decline in "blacklisting" and the related practice of "shopping around" for new arbitrators.
6. Improved understanding of the need for firm agreement between the parties as to the proper function of arbitration under the contract.
7. A clear majority preference for the "judicial" conception of the arbitrator's task and a corresponding decline in the use of arbitration for additional bargaining or problem-solving.
8. Increasing competence of management and union representatives in case preparation and presentation.

Most of these "assets" have a distaff side, presented as "liabilities" in the following listing:

1. Some relationships continue to be marred by "excessive" arbitration for a variety of reasons, including poor screening, friction between the parties and inability or unwillingness on the union's part to educate its membership on the point that everyone with a grievance does not have a constitutional right to arbitration.
2. Continuing "immaturity" in some relationships, as evidenced by unjustified blacklisting of arbitrators on such sophomoric bases as "box scores."
3. A continuing failure in some relationships to recognize the economies to be achieved by careful preparation and presentation of cases.
4. The continued resort to "brinkmanship" in contract administration (that is, failing to adjust or withdraw the case until just before the hearing).
5. A tendency in many relationships to make too much of a production out of arbitration by insisting on posthearing briefs, transcripts, citations of decisions by other arbitrators under the contracts and so forth. Such practices increase the delays, costs and formalism of arbitration. They are contrary to the spirit and rationale of the process as originally conceived.
6. Reluctance to make use of qualified new arbitrators for either or both of two reasons: (a) the new arbitrator has had a prior professional affiliation solely with management or union; or (b) the new arbitrator has no direct case experience. He is therefore rejected, no matter how good he may look on paper.

These pluses and minuses are set forth with no elaboration at this point. In subsequent analysis of how to make optimal use of grievance arbitration procedures the conversion of liabilities into assets may become more readily visible.

REPRESENTATIVE ISSUES IN GRIEVANCE ARBITRATION

Still the most common of all cases in grievance arbitration concerns employee discipline or discharge.[3] An issue involving discharge is usually phrased in the following manner: "Did the Company have just cause under the contract to discharge Richard Roe?"

Many cases involve disciplinary penalties less severe than discharge. Most unionized employers have developed formal systems of corrective or progressive discipline for a variety of rules infractions by employees. Such offenses as tardiness, absenteeism or smoking in the washroom generally call for a written warning on first offense and for a three-day disciplinary layoff for the second. A third offense may result in discharge. Such employer discipline may be challenged through arbitration when the union and the employee do not think that "just cause" existed and wish to clear the employee's personnel file.

For arbitration of discipline cases other than discharge, the issue may be phrased: "Did the Company have just cause under the contract to discipline John Doe by a three-day layoff in March, 1971, for excessive absenteeism?"

One of the most troublesome problems in contract administration is posed by wildcat strikes, that is, unauthorized walkouts by a group of employees (or, in some cases, *all* employees in the bargaining unit) in violation of the union's contract pledge not to strike during the life of the agreement. The employer's dilemma on discipline in these cases is a real one, as we noted in the preceding chapter. Wildcat discipline cases are among the most difficult that an arbitrator can be called upon to decide. Many involve situations where the employer has discharged those he believes were responsible for triggering or leading the wildcat and has meted out lesser penalties to employees who walked off or stayed off the job in response to such leadership. These cases are often "tough" for arbitrators because difficult issues as to the nature and quality of proof of cause for discipline may be involved.

In any discipline case the arbitrator sits as both judge and jury. He decides both the "law" and the "facts." He must decide in each case *on the basis of the record made before him* whether the employer has proved "just cause" for discipline under the contract.

Many grievance arbitration cases concern disputes over the meaning

---

[3] Taking the thousands of cases arbitrated nationally each year, the customary estimate is that more than one out of every four involves a discipline issue. For a careful and illuminating study of the impact of arbitrators' decisions in discipline cases, see Dallas L. Jones, *Arbitration and Industrial Discipline* (Ann Arbor, Mich.: Bureau of Industrial Relations, University of Michigan, 1961). See also a useful earlier study by Orme W. Phelps, *Discipline and Discharge in the Unionized Firm* (Berkeley: University of California Press, 1959).

and application of the contract's language as to the role of seniority in connection with layoffs, transfers, recalls to work, super-seniority for union officials, promotions to higher job classifications, interplant moves and the like. In many industrial contracts the seniority article is the longest. For example, the seniority provisions of the John Deere-UAW 1967–1970 master contract cover twenty-two closely printed pages. This is not unusual. On the other hand, some contracts are very brief on this issue. They may be limited to a general statement of policy that in layoffs from and recalls to employment length of service will be the controlling factor, that is, a "straight" seniority clause. In many contracts, however, ability to perform the available work is required before seniority takes on decisive importance.

A brief policy statement often reflects confidence on the part of the employer and the union in their ability to resolve disputes that may arise without spelling everything out in detail. In large bargaining units, however, the joint preference is usually for a detailed treatment. The parties must decide through experience what is the preferable approach for facilitating contract administration.

In spite of apparent clarity of contract language, seniority issues are often hard to decide. Recent seniority arbitration issues I have heard have included disputes over: (1) denial of posted vacancies to senior applicants; (2) transfer of supervisory employees back into the bargaining unit in connection with reductions in force and (3) how to merge or integrate seniority rosters when company facilities are combined or shut down. Disputes are less frequent these days on straight layoffs or recalls. Contract language on these matters has been satisfactorily clarified in most relationships over the years in earlier arbitration cases or by negotiation.

Changing technology frequently requires changes in seniority policies. The impact of technology in the years ahead is likely to be substantial. One major contract innovation that required reworking of conventional seniority concepts is the guaranteed income security plan incorporated in 1967–1970 agreements in the rubber, automobile, farm equipment and other industries.

Management's right to subcontract work has often been a source of arbitration cases. Subcontracting issues can be explosive in nature when the exercise of one of the employer's most cherished managerial prerogatives poses an apparent (or real) threat to the job security of bargaining unit employees. The sensitivity of this issue can be illustrated by the 1967 discharge of Ford-UAW umpire Harry Platt by the UAW. Platt had served as permanent umpire in the Ford-UAW system for many years. He is nationally known and respected as a fair and knowledgeable arbitrator with a wealth of experience. The "heat" following an adverse decision on subcontracting was so great that the UAW terminated Platt's services.

We should note that arbitrators differ in their philosophies on subcontracting issues, particularly as to how to decide such cases when the contract is silent or vague.

A typical subcontracting issue might be phrased in these words: "Did Company X violate the contract by assigning the work of collecting unpaid accounts to an outside collection agency?"[4]

Other issues commonly faced by grievance arbitrators include the following:

1. Did the Company violate the contract by failing to call in Employee X for overtime work on Saturday, May 11, 1968?
2. Did the refusal of John Zilch to work overtime on Saturday, February 17, 1968, constitute a violation of the agreement and render Zilch subject to discipline by the Company?
3. Did the Company violate the contract when it assigned hourly operating employees to clean and wax the ammonia production control room floor?
4. Was the Company's action in assigning four bus drivers to work out of a garage other than their "home" garage on a particular Saturday a "transfer" within the meaning of the contract or was it a "temporary assignment" that the Company was privileged to make under the agreement?
5. Was the Company's revision of its operating methods in Department 13 and establishing of the B-20 job classification privileged or prohibited under the contract?
6. Does the Company policy of refusing to hire spouses of bargaining unit employees violate the contract's no-discrimination clause?
7. Under the pertinent provisions of the contract did John Doe receive the proper amount of vacation pay for 1967?
8. Does Appendix A of the contract require automatic progression within rate ranges?
9. Is the grievance of Sam Blotto arbitrable under the contract? If so, did the Company violate the contract by failing to offer grievant overtime on October 25, 1967?
10. Did the change in method instituted on Job X on June 7, 1968, constitute a "substantial" change within the meaning of Section 2 of Article XVI of the contract between the parties?

Issue listing could be continued for many pages. Those already noted should suffice to illustrate the range and variety of issues coming before an arbitrator. The last issue listed is representative of many issues that arise in administration of a contract's job evaluation or wage incentive system. Such "technical" cases are common today, particularly with frequent changes in "job mix" being made because of technological developments.

Finally, we should note that use of psychological tests as an employer

---

[4] The phrasing of this arbitrable issue and those to follow are taken from actual cases heard and decided by me in calendar 1967, 1968 and 1969. Changes in wording have been made only to avoid identification of companies, unions and individuals.

instrument in administering recruitment, promotion and transfer policies has produced a considerable volume of arbitration cases. Unions are concerned about adverse effects of tests on employee job security under the contract. The psychological test issue is likely to be a troublesome one for arbitrators in the years ahead.

Proper Phrasing of the Arbitrable Issue

The reader will note that nearly all issues listed above were worded to call for a yes or no answer. The words "under the contract" can frequently be found in the statement of the issue to be decided. Most union and management representatives regard their contracts as private statutory law, binding upon the arbitrator as well as upon themselves. When they go before an arbitrator they have agreed to disagree. They do not want the arbitrator to function as a "philosopher king," resolving their dispute in terms of how *he* personally thinks it should be resolved. Nor do they want a compromise decision. They want the arbitrator to stick with the contract and decide cases in no-nonsense terms such as "under the contract, Grievance No. 99 should be and is hereby denied." If the award calls for a denial, that ends the matter. An award sustaining Grievance No. 99 would generally embrace the remedial relief sought.

If John Doe has been discharged, for example, his grievance usually contains a demand for reinstatement with all contractual rights restored and full back pay. Under most contracts the arbitrator has authority to modify penalties if his finding is that discharge was too severe under the circumstances but that the record establishes proof of cause for *some* discipline. In such cases, the award may direct reinstatement but deny some or all of the back pay that might be involved.[5]

Whatever may be the issue, arbitrators have a common concern to achieve a precise understanding at the hearing as to what they are being asked to decide. This can be done through a submission agreement drawn up by the parties in advance or through a stipulation arrived at during the hearing. The parties may prefer to leave the phrasing of the issue to the arbitrator's discretion.

The Grievance Arbitrator and His Function

Arbitrators owe allegiance to the contract under which they are operating. Even when the contract is clear as to the nature of the arbitrator's

---

[5] There are still contracts, however, that limit the arbitrator to a finding of whether the company has proved cause for discipline. Such contracts provide no discretion to modify penalties deemed to be excessive.

authority and jurisdiction, one of the parties may encourage an arbitrator to pursue a different course. If this occurs, the arbitrator must follow the contract from which his authority flows. He must not permit himself to extend or to exceed his authority.

Employers and unions can make optimal use of arbitration as an instrument for improved contract administration only when they agree on the type of arbitration they want. If one party seeks a "judicial" approach to arbitration and the other wants the arbitrator to function as a mediator, the process will not work very well.

If the parties prefer an arbitrator to function as a "problem-solver," they should select an arbitrator who can do so competently by mediating a solution. If they prefer the arbitrator to adhere to the judicial approach, such preference must be made clear.

Most practitioners and arbitrators hold that the arbitrator's function is essentially judicial in nature. Most arbitrations are handled on an *ad hoc* basis, notwithstanding the rapid growth in permanent umpire machinery. In *ad hoc* arbitration the judicial approach is clearly the more appropriate. In most permanent arbitration systems as well the arbitrator is expected to function in a judicial manner.[6]

Only a gifted minority of arbitrators can handle the delicate dual assignment of mediator-arbitrator. Comparatively few employers and unions wish the arbitrator to depart from straight adjudication. The arbitrator is the employee of the company and the union jointly. If they wish to utilize him in a consultative capacity during negotiations or to initiate proposals for settling grievances formally submitted to him for arbitration, their wishes should be respected. The fact remains that there are few arbitrators who can function effectively in the Harry Shulman, George Taylor, Dave Cole, Saul Wallen manner.

Whatever their individual beliefs may be as to the arbitrator's proper function, experienced professional arbitrators will find no quarrel with the following basic propositions:

1. The arbitrator's authority is determined and governed by the contract. His duty is to the contract.
2. The parties are entitled to the type of arbitration they want, which should be clearly expressed in their contract.
3. The parties must share the same basic expectations from the arbitration process if maximum value is to be achieved.

---

[6] Some permanent arbitration systems have evolved from a problem-solving type into a judicial type. The evolution has never gone the other way, to my knowledge. For an excellent comparative review of permanent arbitration systems, see Charles C. Killingsworth and Saul Wallen, "Constraint and Variety in Arbitration Systems," in *Labor Arbitration: Perspectives and Problems*, ed. Mark L. Kahn. (Washington, D.C.: Bureau of National Affairs, 1964), pp. 56–81.

STRICT VERSUS LIBERAL CONSTRUCTIONISTS

Notwithstanding the apparent consensus on the three propositions, professional arbitrators will differ in evaluating their interpretive functions under the contract. Some regard their role as a negative, self-limiting one. Others take an expansive view of the breadth of their discretion. This distinction in attitudes is a little difficult to pin down, but it is real. At some risk of oversimplification, it can be described as one between "strict" and "liberal" construction of contract language.

Let us take Arbitrator X and Arbitrator Y, each of whom is operating under typical contract language limiting arbitration to grievances concerning contract interpretation and application and prohibiting the arbitrator from adding to, subtracting from or otherwise modifying the language of the contract. Arbitrator X is a "strict" constructionist with a self-limiting view of the nature of his arbitral authority. Arbitrator Y is a "liberal" constructionist who believes that his responsibilities under the contract allow for imagination and perhaps "innovation" in the interest of stable and progressive industrial relations.

Both Arbitrator X and Arbitrator Y may classify themselves as belonging to the "judicial" school of arbitration. Yet their different mental sets on the task of contract construction could lead to different decisions on identical cases. One area where such a difference might show up is in cases involving arbitrability. Arbitrator X, operating as a strict constructionist, might rule certain grievances to be not arbitrable, whereas Arbitrator Y might not hesitate to assume jurisdiction.

Another category of cases where strict or liberal construction can be of critical significance might be grievances challenging managerial discretion in discipline, promotion and job classification cases. Arbitrator X, a strict constructionist, may show greater respect for the finality of managerial discretion (unless he finds it to have been exercised in an arbitrary or discriminatory fashion). Arbitrator Y, reviewing the same factual situation, might not hesitate to modify or reverse an exercise of managerial discretion.

The distinction between strict and liberal constructionist approaches reveals itself also in the significance attributed to past practice where the contract language and the practice appear to differ. A strict constructionist inclines to the view that the contract governs when past practice and the contract are in conflict, notwithstanding the duration and uniformity of the practice in question. A liberal constructionist may hold that the parties have determined the "true meaning" of the contract language by their past practice. He may thus conform his decision to the past practice, even if this requires some "torturing" of the contract's actual wording.

Being human, arbitrators are not completely consistent or predicable. One who regards himself as a strict constructionist may be unable to resist the temptation to adopt a "liberal" interpretation of contract language in a particular case if he finds the equitable considerations to be compelling. On the other hand, a liberal constructionist may decide that a particular case calls for a strict or rigorous interpretation.

Few practicing arbitrators engage in introspection as to their proper function in contract interpretation, although this is necessary for accurate self-classification. The arbitrator's concept of his contract construction duty is thus usually an unarticulated one.[7] Some clues to an arbitrator's philosophical orientation can be gleaned perhaps from a careful study of an extensive sampling of his decisions.[8] Also a considerable number of arbitrators, myself included, cannot resist the impulse to write about their profession. Journal articles are likely to be revealing as to the arbitrator's conception of his function.[9]

Differences in approaches to the task of contract construction can produce significant differences in substantive decisions. Knowledgeable employer and union representatives are therefore alert to these differences in how arbitrators look upon their duty to the contract. The selection of arbitrators on particular cases is often made with such differences in mind.

The best evidence that such games of point-counterpoint do take place can perhaps be found in selection of arbitrators for discipline cases. Experienced arbitrators acquire reputations for being "tough" or "soft" on discipline issues. In this context, "tough" can have two different connotations. An arbitrator can be regarded as "tough" because he is exacting as to the amount of proof of "just cause" he requires of management in disciplinary action cases. One who is "tough" on proof may be sought after by unions and shunned by management in discipline cases. However, "tough" can also be a fitting label for an arbitrator with strong convictions about not modifying the penalty where cause for discipline has been proved. Any

---

[7] I have a lively curiosity as to how my fellow arbitrators perform their decision-making function. Since late 1967 I have been engaged intermittently in research on this aspect of the arbitration process through the medium of lengthy (two to three hours) interviews with experienced arbitrators. My ultimate goal is to compare findings based on some fifty interviews and to relate these findings to the literature on the nature of the judicial process. At this writing (1970) I have completed about half of the projected fifty interviews. Those interviewed to date differ greatly in their study and writing habits, but all reveal one important attribute—they worry a great deal before actually deciding the difficult cases.

[8] James A. Gross, for example, found (to *his* satisfaction) a common denominator among arbitrators deciding issues relating to subcontracting and out-of-unit transfers of work. He reports evidence of "a dominant value theme-efficiency, as the *summum bonum.*" See James A. Gross, "Value Judgments in the Decisions of Labor Arbitrators," *Industrial and Labor Relations Review*, XXI (October, 1967), 55–72.

[9] Many management and union practitioners, particularly in the more sophisticated relationships, will "research" arbitrators by reading published decisions and journal articles as background for deciding on an arbitrator's acceptability, either generally or on particular types of cases.

union arbitrating a discipline case for the purpose of tempering justice with mercy will seek to avoid arbitrators who are reluctant to modify penalties.

Arbitrators also differ in their views as to the relative seriousness of different types of rule violations. All might agree in the abstract that insubordination, fighting on the job, reporting drunk on the job, stealing company property and other serious offenses merit discharge the first time they occur. Arbitrators will differ, however, as to how much weight, if any, should be accorded to evidence of mitigating circumstances.

Let us suppose two employees, X and Y, are shown to have stolen equivalent amounts of company property. X has been with the company twenty years. This is his first offense of any nature. Y has been with the company only two years and already has a poor disciplinary "record." Both are discharged. The proof of guilt is convincing in each case. Should the discharge be sustained in both cases or should a requested "second chance" be given to X? Many arbitrators would not support a differential in penalty when theft is the basis for discharge. Others would regard the employee's entire record as proper for consideration and would review the propriety of the penalty.

Reasonable men in management and union circles can and do differ in specific situations, even though sharing similar views on the proper uses of arbitration in contract administration. So also do arbitrators differ in their views as to the proper disposition of basically similar cases and in their philosophical approaches to the task of contract construction.

Employers and unions have a right to know how the arbitrator views his task of contract construction. By the same token, the arbitrator has a right to know what the parties expect from their arbitration system. This can be made clear both in the contract language describing grievance and arbitration procedure and also by the method of case presentation and argument.

Arbitrators are frequently urged to be "consistent" in performing their interpretive duties. The parties themselves, however, are not always models of consistency. They sometimes depart from *their* customary positions in particular cases. Most experienced arbitrators can recall instances where Company X, usually a bear for strict construction of contract language, has urged in a particular case that strict application of the contract will bring "deplorable" results unintended by the parties. Union Y, normally an apostle of equity, reasonableness and "flexibility" in contract interpretation, may nevertheless demand its pound of flesh in strict accordance with the letter of the contract in a particular case.

In my judgment, most experienced arbitrators are more likely to have an internally consistent (even if not articulated) conception of their duty to the contract than are the parties. Much of the difficulty in arbitration continues to be caused by inability of the parties to reach a true meeting of the minds as to the proper uses of arbitration and a consequent tendency to shift position in terms of the nature of the case being arbitrated.

JUDICIAL AND PROBLEM-SOLVING APPROACHES: A COMPARISON

In discussing strict and liberal contract construction, an effort has been made to avoid up to this point a final and binding decision as to which approach is more likely to produce better long-run results. Which approach is favored depends on how the parties and the arbitrators regard the collective bargaining contract. Do they see it as an instrument setting forth the "law of the plant" or as a set of flexible guidelines for a continuous process of mutual accommodation? In the former view, the contract becomes a binding statement of rights, obligations and responsibilities, applicable to the company, the union and bargaining unit employees covered by the instrument. Contract terms are assumed to stand as written for the duration of the agreement. No modification is possible save in the rare situation of mutually acknowledged necessity for change as a result of unanticipated contingencies or the intrusion of external variables that neither party can control. If, however, the parties (and the arbitrator) regard the arbitration step as an extension (or continuation) of the bargaining process, such views will encourage a "liberal" approach on the arbitrator's part to his contract interpretation role. He may also he urged by the parties to *mediate solutions* of grievances appealed to the arbitration step rather than to decide such cases on a grievance-denied or grievance-sustained basis, as outlined earlier in the discussion of typical issues in grievance arbitration.

One question has haunted me since I began arbitrating in 1944—is there a real philosophical gulf between the judicial and problem-solving approaches to the task of contract construction? My reasons for preferring the judicial approach have been stated and restated many times in journal articles. Some of my earlier efforts must have conveyed the impression that if an arbitrator is "judicial" (that is, if he decides by the book in an essentially strict constructionist fashion), he is somehow not engaged in problem-solving. Any such simplistic view is certainly misleading because *both* conceptions of the arbitrator's task involve solving problems by providing a means of finally and peacefully disposing of unresolved grievances under an existing contract.

The essence of the judicial approach is that it reasserts constantly *the primacy of the contract as the governing instrument for both the parties and the arbitrator*. This is my basic reason for favoring the judicial approach. It forces the employer and union to do their own work on perfecting their contract at negotiation time by requiring them to live together under the same contractual instrument between negotiation periods.

At the same time, considerations of both candor and realism require the admission that arbitrators of the judicial persuasion *do change the unchanging contracts* by their decisions no matter how strictly they construe the language. Each arbitration decision by an unmeasurable but nonetheless real amount in some sense and to some degree adds to, subtracts from or otherwise alters the contract, notwithstanding contract prohibitions to the contrary. The contract language being interpreted and applied in a particular case *necessarily has a subtly different meaning or connotation after a particular decision than it had before.* Therefore, no arbitrator of the judicial school should delude himself or the parties into believing that his decisions do not have *some* qualitative impact on the contract being construed.

Having said this, it remains true that there *is* a difference of importance between the two conceptions of the arbitrator's task under consideration here. In judicial arbitration, *the primary responsibility for the contract always remains with the parties.* It is the employer and the union who must live with particular decisions or take on the job of changing the contract language themselves whenever particular decisions may reveal that certain provisions are administratively impracticable or even unworkable as written, or whenever decisions enforce a significance to particular contract language that calls for a revision of such language.

On the other hand, devotees of the problem-solving type of arbitration assign a more free-wheeling role to their arbitrators. The latter are expected (in fact, encouraged) to mediate solutions in some (although not all) situations. They are not constantly reminded by their parties that they are operating under the contract as it is written. Such attitudes toward the arbitrator's task can result in excessive dependence on the outside neutral. This can result in the arbitrator actually doing what amounts to a contract-writing job through the decisional process. I do not believe that this is the way to achieve optimal results in contract administration. It permits the parties to evade their own primary responsibilities. Using arbitration for extending the negotiation aspect of collective bargaining invites both excessive arbitration and excessive dependence on the arbitrator.

The preceding discussion leads logically into the next section on the role of the federal judiciary in connection with grievance arbitration. Some landmark decisions of our highest court have played a vital role in determining the place of arbitration in contract administration.

The Federal Judiciary and Grievance Arbitration

In the great majority of cases contractual agreements to arbitrate are honored and enforcement of arbitration decisions presents no problem. In some instances, however, it is necessary to go into court to compel enforcement of an agreement to arbitrate or to obtain a decree enforcing an arbitrator's award. This can be accomplished through the federal district court system under Section 301 of the National Labor Relations Act, as amended, pursuant to criteria laid down by the U.S. Supreme Court in the famous *Lincoln Mills* case (1957)[10] and elaborated upon in a number of important subsequent decisions, most notably those that have come to be known in the literature as the *Warrior* trilogy.[11]

Through such decisions as *Lincoln Mills*, the *Warrier* trio and their lineal descendants the United States Supreme Court has unquestionably strengthened the institutional process of grievance arbitration in the following two respects:

1. The Court has made clear that issues over arbitrability are for arbitrators to decide unless the contract in question assigns the arbitrability issue to the courts or contains *positive assurance* that a particular issue is *not* arbitrable.

2. The Court has also made clear that in enforcement proceedings federal judges should not, under any circumstances, substitute their judgment for that of the arbitrator either as to his findings of fact or conclusions of law, even if the latter might be erroneous. Judicial enforcement of an award can be denied only if the court should find that the arbitrator exceeded his jurisdiction by failing to base his award on the "essence of the agreement" between the parties.

From a practical standpoint, most employers and unions regard arbitration as a preferable alternative to court proceedings or economic force. Even Judge Paul Hays entitled his controversial polemic against arbitrators "a dissenting view."[12] Judicial enforcement of awards and agree-

---

[10] *Textile Workers* v. *Lincoln Mills*, 353 *U.S.* 448 (1957).

[11] *United Steelworkers of America* v. *American Manufacturing Co.*, 363 *U.S.* 564 (1960); *United Steelworkers of America* v. *Warrior and Gulf Navigation Co.*, 363 *U.S.* 574 (1960); and *United Steelworkers of America* v. *Enterprise Wheel and Car Corp.*, 363 *U.S.* 593 (1960).

[12] See Paul R. Hays, *Labor Arbitration: A Dissenting View* (New Haven, Conn.: Yale University Press, 1966). Before going on the federal circuit court bench in 1961, Judge Hays had an extensive career (twenty-three years) as a professional arbitrator while a member of the law faculty at Columbia University. His monograph is a scathing indictment of arbitration as a system of private adjudication and of arbitrators as a class. The system he describes as having "fatal shortcomings" and the arbitrators he regards generally as incompetent and venal.

Based on my experience as an arbitrator, most of what Judge Hays writes about sounds like melodramatic fiction. I know *some* incompetent arbitrators and a very few that I suspect may be venal. Most of the experienced professionals, many of whom I have known and respected since 1942, are competent, dedicated and incorruptible men. The arbitration process has its faults, but none can fairly be described as "fatal" in nature. Arbitrators have faults, obviously, but they do not merit the undocumented assault of Judge Hays.

Judge Hays cites me with approval as an "authority" on the proper function of an arbitrator, quoting extensively from my 1961 *Notre Dame Lawyer* article (cited *above*, footnote 1). It is clear that Judge Hays and I agree that the arbitrator is performing a "judicial function" and that Mr. Justice Douglas' conception of the arbitrator's task is erroneous. It is therefore deeply disturbing to me to find that the arbitrators Judge Hays and I know are apparently so different in character and ability. I am glad I do not know those he has in mind. My years as an arbitrator have been happily free from the disillusioning encounters that Judge Hays must have had as an arbitrator.

ments to arbitrate is now firmly entrenched in our system. We are developing a federal body of substantive law on labor dispute arbitration that must be held on balance to be favorable for improved contract administration.

It seems a bit ironic to the writer to note that the U.S. Supreme Court (speaking through Mr. Justice Douglas in the *Warrior* trilogy) is willing to grant arbitrators a much more expansive range of decision-making authority than most practitioners and arbitrators believe the arbitrator should enjoy. In *Warrior*, for example, Mr. Justice Douglas refers to the arbitrator as being "usually chosen because of the parties' confidence in his knowledge of the *common law of the shop* and their trust in his personal judgment to bring to bear *considerations which are not expressed in the contract* as criteria for judgment (emphasis supplied).[13]

These gracious words are enough to make a strict constructionist's hair stand on end. But Mr. Justice Douglas goes on beyond this, seemingly determined to grant arbitrators a virtually unlimited charter of authority. He states: "The parties expect that his judgment of a particular grievance will reflect not only what the contract says but, insofar as the collective bargaining agreement permits, such factors as the effect upon productivity of a particular result, its consequence to the morale of the shop, his judgment whether tensions will be heightened or diminished."[14]

Candor requires an admission that even the most experienced of arbitrators are not as sage and omniscient as Mr. Justice Douglas may think. Nor are they as incompetent as the diatribe of former arbitrator (now judge) Hays would have one believe. In the great majority of cases they are journeyman professionals doing a task of contract interpretation under agreements that state categorically that they have no power to add to, subtract from or otherwise modify the terms of the agreements under which they are operating.

The net result of U.S. Supreme Court action has been to strengthen both the arbitration process and the hands of arbitrators. Since the *Warrior* trilogy challenges on arbitrability grounds are not likely to be successful unless the parties have provided positive assurance of their intent to exclude certain types of cases from the arbitrator's jurisdiction. This being true, there is a considerably reduced need for any further displays of "judicial inventiveness" on the Supreme Court's part.

One dark cloud on the grievance arbitration horizon (at least from the arbitrator's standpoint) deserves comment in concluding this brief section on the courts and arbitration. The "cloud" consists of evidence that some state courts and lower federal courts are not limiting their review of arbitrators' awards in the manner so clearly spelled out for them by the U.S. Supreme Court.

[13] 363 *U.S.* 574, 582.
[14] 363 *U.S.* 574, 582.

In his 1968 report to the National Academy of Arbitrators as chairman of the Academy's committee on law and legislation, Professor Edgar A. Jones, Jr., notes a "trend beginning to take shape—that of courts assessing the 'authority' of the arbitrator to act as he did."[15] This is the very thing that received the high court's express disapproval in the *American Manufacturing* case. In Jones's view, this new trend, unless checked by the Supreme Court, could "gain a momentum which could return labor arbitration to the pre-trilogy days of judicial interposition in the merits of disputes more properly resolvable by an arbitrator."[16] Such interposition is taking the form of vacating, modifying or refusing to enforce an award because, in the court's opinion, the arbitrator lacked the authority to issue it.[17]

SOME CONTINUING PROCEDURAL PROBLEMS IN ARBITRATION

Grievance arbitration has achieved such widespread endorsement as a procedure that it is surprising that some significant differences remain as to optimal procedures and best usage of arbitrators. We shall consider briefly the following:

1. The respective merits of *ad hoc* and permanent arbitration systems.

2. The respective merits of single arbitrators and tripartite boards.

3. The related problems of excessive use of arbitration, costs of arbitration and "brinkmanship" as a strategy.

The concluding section of this chapter will be concerned with what I regard as the most critical problem area—the scarce supply of competent, experienced and acceptable arbitrators and the difficulties associated with increasing the supply.

Ad Hoc OR PERMANENT ARBITRATOR MACHINERY?

Medium-sized to large employers and the unions with whom they deal can usually benefit greatly from using a permanent arbitrator to serve on all cases appealed to arbitration under the contract. Permanent arbitration systems are now firmly institutionalized in steel, automobiles, rubber,

---

[15] 1968 *Proceedings* of National Academy of Arbitrators (Washington, D.C.: Bureau of National Affairs, Inc., 1968), pp. 223–24.

[16] *Ibid.*, p. 224.

[17] I may be overly sensitive on this point, having been "burned" by the Iowa Supreme Court in the only arbitration award I have ever issued that was contested in court. On the basis of a misreading of my opinion the court proceeded to the conclusion that I had not drawn my award from the essence of the contract and then vacated it in the name of the U.S. Supreme Court's guidelines.

men's and women's clothing, farm equipment, hotels and restaurants (in multi-employer urban contracts) and in many other fields. Selection of arbitrators on an *ad hoc* basis as cases arise is, however, still the most common procedure in grievance arbitration. *Ad hoc* arbitration was formerly the rule for smaller employers and small local unions. Many large firms and their unions also retain a preference for the *ad hoc* method.

Many employers and unions who operate with *ad hoc* arbitration are finding it increasingly difficult to obtain experienced, competent and acceptable arbitrators, particularly on short notice. The delay on scheduling hearings and in getting out decisions are related matters for concern.

Some employers and unions are showing ingenuity in meeting the arbitrator shortage. One technique is to write jointly to Arbitrator X, advising him that he has been named as permanent arbitrator in the enclosed copy of their new contract. In the same letter, X is asked when he can hear Grievance No. 99 which has just been appealed to the arbitration step. Arbitrators are susceptible to flattery just like other mortals. Confronted with the "honor," the chances are they will accept the designation even though miffed at not being consulted beforehand. Six small Iowa firms and their unions "honored" me in this fashion in 1967 and 1968. The aim of such a procedure is to insure availability and, presumably, priority treatment on scheduling. Another approach to the shortage is to name a panel of three to five arbitrators in the contract and use them in rotation.[18]

The permanent arbitrator system has advantages over *ad hoc* selection, both for the parties and for the arbitrator, particularly when there is a reasonably predictable arbitration caseload (such as ten or more cases per year). The parties can insure the availability of a competent professional through a suitable combination of annual retainer fee and per diem fee for cases heard and decided. An arbitrator working on such a basis can and should give priority in scheduling and deciding cases. He can also in many cases continue to handle some *ad hoc* work and perhaps even other umpireships. This would, of course, depend on the demands on his time and the need to avoid overcommitment.

The word "permanent" can be a misleading one. Contracts formerly provided that the appointee's services could be dispensed with by either party *at any time* through a "Dear John" letter to the arbitrator with a copy to the other party. This has been "softened" in many cases to provide tenure for the life of the agreement. The best arbitrators in the United States have

---

[18] The Bendix Corporation and the Machinists used the panel device for many years, principally because any arbitrator in this relationship must have Atomic Energy Commission "Q" clearance, thus not being readily replaceable in case of death, resignation or discharge. Under the 1969–1972 contract, however, Bendix and IAM have moved to a single permanent arbitrator with a designated alternate, perhaps because of a reduced volume of cases.

been gently (or harshly) relieved of their duties in one or more permanent arbitration systems over the years. The life span of the permanent arbitrator is usually long enough to permit him to develop an informed understanding of the contract and the industry involved. His availability and understanding are important advantages to the parties. In marked contrast, under an *ad hoc* system the arbitrator hits the hearing "cold." Even experienced arbitrators need some briefing in any case. Yet under prevailing practice the arbitrator arrives at the hearing knowing only the names of the parties and (perhaps) the bare statement of the issue(s) involved in the grievance(s) he is expected to hear and decide. He starts from ground zero.

I know of no instance where a permanent arbitration system has been abandoned in favor of a return to an *ad hoc* basis. Experience clearly favors further growth of permanent arbitrator systems. The shortage of arbitrators should accelerate such a development as more employers and unions experience difficulties in arbitrator selection and wish to secure priority treatment for *their* cases.

The stability of a permanent arbitrator system is the best procedural insurance of receiving informed, impartial decisions in reasonably expeditious fashion, in my judgment. There are those who believe that arbitrators selected on an *ad hoc* basis are somehow more free to decide cases impartially. My comment on this view is that *impartiality, knowledgeability and personal integrity attach to the arbitrator rather than to the procedural system.* Arbitration may well be suspect in *some* relationships where it is apparently not unusual for the arbitrator to hand down "rigged awards" on a prearranged basis. This can occur also under an *ad hoc* set-up if the arbitrator is willing to accommodate the parties. In my judgment there are very few arbitrators or management and union representatives who use such an approach to dispute settlement.

Single Arbitrator or Tripartite Board?

Grievance arbitration in the United States is usually handled by single impartial arbitrators, selected directly by the parties or from panels of five, seven or nine names, submitted upon request by the Federal Mediation and Conciliation Service or the American Arbitration Association. The single arbitrator concept is consistent with the judicial approach to arbitration, although there is, of course, nothing to preclude a single arbitrator using the problem-solving (mediatory) method if the parties wish him to do so.

A vigorous minority of employers and unions retain their preference for tripartite boards (usually consisting of one management-designated arbitrator, one union-appointed arbitrator and a third impartial arbitrator who serves as chairman). The use of tripartite boards is frequently (but not always) indicative of a union-management preference for the problem-solving approach. Some parties retain the tripartite mechanism in their contracts as "extra insurance" for the crucial case when they wish to make certain that the impartial chairman fully understands the import of the evidence and argumentation. Customarily, however, the parties stipulate that the third man shall act in fact as though he is the sole arbitrator.

In 1955 I was a bit hasty in predicting that tripartite boards would soon become vestigial in grievance arbitration. The tripartite mechanism is still far from being defunct. Strong minority support remains, although use of the single arbitrator is steadily gaining ground.

The logic of tripartite boards for grievance arbitration of the judicial type is open to question. However, the device has merit whenever final and binding arbitration is to be used for resolving disputes over future contract terms. In these cases, the decision frequently may require a "political" or "mediatory" approach. The presence of management and union-appointed arbitrators at the decision stage can thus be helpful in arriving at a solution (decision) that satisfies the needs, expectations and capabilities of the parties.[19]

Related Problems of Excessive Arbitration, Cost of Arbitration, and "Brinkmanship"

Experienced arbitrators can still report that they hear much too high a percentage of cases that should probably not have been appealed to arbitration. This excessive resort to arbitration is one of the more serious ways of "wasteful" utilization of a critically short supply of experienced, competent and acceptable arbitrators. It is also obviously related to the growing costs of arbitration as an instrument of contract administration. Frequently, the excess or surplus of cases appealed to arbitration is related to the strategy of "brinkmanship," a term used here to describe the contract administration equivalent of the dragsters' game known as "chicken." Some brief comments on these three interrelated phenomena will be followed by analysis of the arbitrator shortage and suggestions for increasing the supply as well as improving arbitration procedures to insure more effective utilization of the scarce supply of qualified neutrals.

---

[19] For a full examination of the pros and cons of tripartite boards in grievance arbitration, see Harold W. Davey, "The Uses and Misuses of Tripartite Boards in Grievance Arbitration," in *Developments in American and Foreign Arbitration*, ed., Charles M. Rehmus (Washington, D.C.: Bureau of National Affairs, Inc., 1968), pp. 152–79.

THE DANGERS IN EXCESSIVE ARBITRATION

Most arbitrators are (or should be) professionally concerned to make arbitration more efficient, swifter and less costly. There is also an obligation to encourage parties to utilize arbitration as infrequently as possible. One way to cut down on arbitration is to price it out of existence. This is clearly not a salutary way of reducing the caseload. The logical approach is to do a far better job in earlier steps of the grievance procedure, along lines suggested in the preceding chapter. An "excessive" arbitration caseload is usually a sign of a "distressed" grievance procedure. Some excellent practical suggestions as to how to relieve such distress will be found in a paper by Arthur Ross delivered at the sixteenth annual meeting of the National Academy of Arbitrators.[20] It would be most helpful if more arbitrators would follow the Ross lead of encouraging the parties to remedy their procedures at a stage early enough to preclude the need to go to arbitration as often as many do. Arbitration is a desirable ultimate procedure. It should not become a way of life in any relationship.

One friendly management critic of my views in this section urges high costs as a desirable deterrent to excessive arbitration. He favors making arbitration relatively expensive in order to increase pressure for screening out those grievances that are lacking in contractual merit or are being appealed for "political" reasons.

This view assumes that the union will go to arbitration frequently if the financial burden of doing so is not too great. Perhaps this is the case in some relationships, but there is another side to the matter. I refer to situations where an employer is stubbornly refusing to observe certain provisions of the agreement and is denying grievances in wholesale lots. The union in such circumstances can quickly go broke through taking all such cases to arbitration. Its other alternative is to abandon arbitration and return to economic force. Both are undesirable routes to effective contract observance.

Clearly there is no way to generalize as to what is an "excessive" amount of arbitration. Optimal frequency in usage will vary markedly from one situation to another. Frequency and cost will depend on such factors as the size of the company and union, tradition as to the sparing or frequent use of arbitration and the availability of acceptable arbitrators. Optimal usage is not a matter on which generalization is easy.

---

[20] Arthur M. Ross, "Distressed Grievance Procedures and Their Rehabilitation," in *Labor Arbitration and Industrial Change*, ed., Mark L. Kahn (Washington, D.C.: Bureau of National Affairs, Inc., 1963), pp. 104–45.

My view is that the appeal to arbitration should always be available as needed. Considerations of cost or delay should never have to be the decisive reasons for causing a union to drop grievances that in its view are valid under the contract.

Courts of law (in theory at least) are available on the same basis to rich and poor alike. The judicial appeal channel in administration of collective agreements should somehow be available if and when necessary to the less affluent unions as well as to those whose dues income can sustain a considerable arbitration caseload. When arbitration is available only on an ability to pay basis, there is a constant temptation, in the face of accumulation of unresolved grievances, to resort to wildcat stoppages instead of following contract procedures.

It must be conceded that if arbitration is made "too easy," political or face-saving cases may be brought so that the arbitrator can absorb the heat for denial of grievances that are known to lack contractual merit. Some of these cases are doubtless unavoidable. The fact remains that arbitration should be reserved for the really tough cases where the parties have exhausted all possibilities of informal adjustment. Neither management nor the union should be encouraged to use arbitration as a crutch. Nor should arbitration serve as a means of escaping the consequences of sloppy or inefficient performance by either management or union representatives at earlier stages in the grievance procedure.

THE COSTS OF GRIEVANCE ARBITRATION

Rising costs are a favorite allegation of those who are critical of arbitration and arbitrators. In some cases the criticism is justified. In general, however, careful review by both FMCS and AAA indicates that at least the blame for increasing costs of arbitration does not properly attach to the arbitrators.[21] The villains in the picture are actually costs assumed by the parties themselves—needlessly in many cases—such as using court reporters, retaining outside counsel for case presentation and filing of posthearing briefs. All these are in the category of expensive luxuries in most situations. This theme is developed more fully in the concluding sections of this chapter.

The arbitrator's fee is usually *not* the major cost item in grievance arbitration if the parties do a candid job of counting all the other cost factors properly attributable to appealing any case to arbitration.

It goes without saying that the surest method of reducing costs of arbitration is to resolve grievances. In a good faith relationship it is a reason-

---

[21] See Robben W. Fleming, *The Labor Arbitration Process, op. cit.*, Chapter 2, "The Cost Problem," pp. 31–56.

able expectation that only rarely will it be necessary to go to arbitration. The right to arbitrate is as indispensable to good contract administration as the right to strike is to productive negotiation of future contract terms. Actual use in either case can and should be minimal. This is a particularly important consideration when one fully appreciates the fact that good arbitrators are in critically short supply. This is also a reason for abandoning the strategy of "brinkmanship."

THE "BRINKMANSHIP" PROBLEM AS A THREAT TO THE ARBITRATION PROCESS

"Brinkmanship" is defined here as the practice of selecting an arbitrator, fixing a hearing date and then at the last minute adjusting or withdrawing the appealed grievance. FMCS and AAA, the principal designating agencies, are concerned about this practice. So are those arbitrators who are plagued by late cancellations of this type.

The brinkmanship approach is a particular problem of the full-time *ad hoc* arbitrator. He blocks off a hearing date several weeks ahead that he obviously cannot use if he is cancelled out just before the hearing. Often he has turned down other cases to avoid overcommitment. Should several untimely cancellations occur, the arbitrator will be left with considerable unutilizable time on his hands. Furthermore, by reserving hearing dates in advance, the arbitrator has caused frustrating delays for other parties waiting to use him on their own cases.

We are not "bleeding" for the *ad hoc* arbitrator just described. He is probably too busy anyway. Perhaps he should welcome two or three unexpected days of freedom to catch up on his backlog or even to rest and reinvigorate himself. We *are* saying that such brinkmanship by the parties is *wasteful* because it is often the busier, more experienced arbitrators who find themselves with these unutilized blocks of time. If the practice is to continue, as it doubtless will, *proper* notice of hearing cancellation must be defined as at least *two weeks* prior to the scheduled date. This would not preclude selection of an arbitrator and setting a hearing date as instruments of brinkmanship in contract administration. It would serve to reduce the present waste of a scarce resource—the time and availability of experienced arbitrators.

THE SUPPLY OF GRIEVANCE ARBITRATORS

The total volume of grievance arbitration cases heard and decided in the United States each year is hard to estimate accurately. Conservatively speaking, it runs annually in the neighborhood of ten to fifteen thousand cases. We also have a special type of "concentration" problem. The bulk of the national arbitration caseload is handled by a comparatively small number of overworked arbitrators, numbering not more than 250 to 300. Only a small percentage of these (perhaps 30 to 50 in number) are full-time arbitrators, not counting those on the staff of state agencies such as those in New York and Massachusetts.

Some full-time arbitrators handle two to three hundred disputes per year or even more. Most active arbitrators, however, are lawyers or university professors (principally in law or economics) with a full-time academic connection. Their arbitration work is in the nature of moonlighting. Some overdo it. Most part-timers, however, try to avoid over-commitment and do not usually take more than perhaps twenty to forty cases per year. This is an estimate. It should not be taken too literally. Some who arbitrate part-time handle very few cases each year. Others let their law practice or university duties take a back seat while striving to handle a large volume of arbitration cases.

The demand for arbitrators' services continues strong and is certain to increase as public sector bargaining expands. Whether the supply side will prove adequate is problematical.

Those administering some of our permanent arbitration systems have prudently insured their future supply by financing internships. In basic steel, for example, promising young lawyers with the requisite education, personality and temperament are "recruited" by the contract permanent arbitrator with the knowledge, consent and financial help of the parties. The intern works with the senior man on a continuous, daily basis over a period of twelve to eighteen months. He is expected to immerse himself totally in the process of learning the whys and wherefores of effective arbitration through intensive on-the-job training. This includes attending hearings, writing draft opinions which are then torn apart by the senior man and doing extensive reading of decisions by experienced arbitrators as a guide to improved opinion-writing and understanding of the range and variety of issues. In the later stages of his training the "apprentice" arbitrator may handle some cases with the advance consent of the parties. At first his opinions and awards will be reviewed by the senior umpire before they are issued.

Such a regimen is essential before it can be said that the prospective new arbitrator is prepared to enter the labor market on his own. Rome was not built in a day. Competent new arbitrators cannot be produced by short institutes in metropolitan areas, supplemented by accompanying experienced arbitrators on an unspecified number of hearings in intermittent and discontinuous fashion. Much more is required. The intern system should be encouraged, strengthened and introduced wherever it can feasibly be undertaken. It can also serve as a model for individualized training of younger academic staff members by senior academician-arbitrators.[22]

Solving the arbitrator supply problem is complicated by the fact that most arbitration is of an *ad hoc* variety. No internship program has yet been devised to meet the needs of the *ad hoc* market. This can be done only through foundation financing or perhaps by joint funding by the AFL-CIO and the top management organizations such as the NAM or the U.S. Chamber of Commerce. The academic phase of such a program should not be a problem. It can be devised by management and union representatives in a cooperative undertaking with FMCS, AAA and the National Academy of Arbitrators. Financing the field training for "students" in such a program would be costly but a substantial amount of it is clearly essential. It is to be hoped that some progress will be made by two special committees of the National Academy of Arbitrators, one on public employment disputes settlement and the other on development of new arbitrators.[23]

The supply shortage will be a problem for employers and unions for some time to come. The parties are always looking for new faces—or say they are—but they exhibit uniform reluctance to pioneer in the trial use of comparatively young and inexperienced arbitrators. They also rarely accept experienced labor relations prospects as arbitrators if the experience of the would-be arbitrator was gained on either the management or the union side of the bargaining table.

This is understandable, regrettable and, in my view, short-sighted. There are many highly capable former "advocates" who would be better arbitrators than some of the academic "virgins" who have avoided any work experience with a management or union organization.

Both FMCS and AAA have placed considerable numbers of former management and union representatives on their panels for selection as impartial arbitrators after careful evaluation of their capacities for judicial detachment. Yet former management practitioners are struck off by the unions and former union representatives are vetoed by management. Such out-of-hand rejection is especially to be regretted when so few acceptable arbitrators are available for service. Many hold umpireships that make them unavailable for *ad hoc* work. If operating *ad hoc*, they are often so busy

---

[22] One should not be too optimistic about this source, however. With the best intentions in the world, I have been able to train and introduce only one promising new arbitrator into the ranks. Others have done better than this, but it is still not a very certain way of increasing the quality supply.

[23] The public sector committee has concentrated since 1969 on training experienced private neutrals in handling public sector disputes. The second committee, chaired by Thomas J. McDermott, is analyzing feasible approaches to improving both the quantity and quality of new arbitrators.

that they advise FMCS and AAA periodically not to send their names out on panels for months at a time to prevent themselves from becoming seriously overcommitted.

The supply crisis is serious enough to merit detailed consideration of ways to make grievance arbitration more "efficient," thereby contributing to both better contract administration and more discriminating usage of arbitrators.

The focus will be on *ad hoc* arbitration. It is assumed that those who utilize permanent arbitrators can solve their problems in mutually agreeable fashion.

Restructuring of *Ad Hoc* Grievance Procedures

We shall begin by a summary restatement of what I choose to call *The Problem* in the following fashion:

1. Competent, experienced and acceptable arbitrators are in critically short supply in relation to the increasing demand for their professional services in *ad hoc* arbitration where the problem of everybody's business being nobody's finds its most conspicuous demonstration.

2. Many of our best arbitrators are continuously busy hearing and deciding what can fairly be described as routine or run-of-the-mill grievances that *could* have been handled effectively by a prospective new arbitrator working as a hearing officer under a senior arbitrator's review and supervision.

3. Experienced arbitrators are frequently "sinners" in at least two respects: (a) they allow themselves to become overcommitted, thus contributing to the delay factor and (b) they often appear to feel obligated by some undiscoverable tablet custom to write lengthy opinions—even on mundane, routine cases.

4. Experienced arbitrators are, by hypothesis, in the greatest demand. They are thus overworked much of the time. This chronic condition cannot help but impair their professional efficiency. It may even lead in some instances to an inability to retain the required judicial perspective, detachment and calm called for by the contract interpretation function.

5. Many nationally known arbitrators in great demand are frequently unavailable for assignment in critical labor disputes, either because they are tied up (or down) by full-time permanent umpireships or because they are already loaded up with crisis or emergency disputes. This factor correlates with the reluctance of practitioners to use many experienced and competent arbitrators in their own crisis situations because they are held to be lacking in the "big name" attribute.

6. Finally, *The Problem's* inherent difficulties are being compounded by the intense demand for arbitration expertise in the newly unionizing

sectors of our economy—public employees at all levels of government, professional employee groups such as nurses and new uses for arbitration in the resolution of such tense conflict situations as those involving racial minorities and collective bargaining between landlords and tenants in ghetto areas.

In my judgment, substantial improvement in arbitration can be achieved by adoption of any or all of the following suggestions:

1. Switching from *ad hoc* selection on each case to regular usage of the same individual as arbitrator over a considerable period of time for any cases that may arise.
2. Regular use of either "dry-run" arbitration or formal development of prehearing statements and submission agreements.
3. Avoidance of the "brinkmanship" strategy discussed earlier in this chapter.
4. More effective use of factual stipulations and consequent reduced use of witnesses.
5. Elimination of transcripts, except under special circumstances.
6. Elimination of posthearing briefs in most cases.
7. Drastic shortening of arbitration opinions.
8. Early issuance of Award with brief statement of reasoning, followed later by full Opinion.
9. Greater use of memorandum opinions or even the equivalent of bench rulings.
10. Use of "instant" arbitration where feasible.
11. Expanded use of the hearing officer technique for routine cases under guidance of senior arbitrators.

Many of the foregoing suggestions explain themselves and need not be commented on in detail. The reader who wishes the full treatment might find two of my articles in this area to be of interest.[24]

The idea of "dry-run" arbitration appeals to me, but most of my practitioner friends do not regard it as feasible or desirable. I have in mind a pre-arbitration hearing with all parties present except the arbitrator.

Actually conducting a dry-run hearing of the appealed case *without the arbitrator being present* has several advantages. First, it would call for more thorough investigation and preparation than is customary in many employer-union relationships. If instituted with appropriate time limits, the investigation and preparation would be conducted with reasonable promptness. This should result in adjustment, settlement or withdrawal of many grievances at this procedural stage. Participation in a dry run of a case will show up weaknesses to the employer or union that may bring about an informal solution and thus obviate the need to proceed with the mechanics of selecting an

[24] See Harold W. Davey, "Restructuring Grievance Arbitration Procedures," *Iowa Law Review*, LIV, (February, 1969), 560–78; and "The Use of Neutrals in the Public Sector," *Labor Law Journal*, XX (August, 1969), 521–38.

arbitrator and going forward with the actual hearing. On the other hand, if the parties do decide to go forward to arbitration, their "homework" has already been done. They would be prepared and their experience in the trial arbitration should enable them to do a more effective presentation job at the hearing. The possibilities should thus be enhanced for reaching agreement on the arbitrable issue, on fact stipulations and on other time-savers in the formal proceeding.

The most serious objection to dry-run arbitration is likely to come from already overburdened union international representatives or business agents. It is an open secret that management, generally speaking, is in a better position than the union to do a complete grievance investigation job and to prepare thoroughly for arbitration. Unions are often understaffed in contract administration at the arbitration level. International representatives have too many local unions and/or too much geographical territory to handle effectively.

This is not a new problem nor will it disappear overnight. If we assume that unions cannot increase their service personnel budgets to the degree necessary, the only possible way to insure better preparation and presentation must be to give increased training and responsibility to local union officers. This prescription is easier to write out than to put into effect. However, restructuring of procedure to utilize the dry-run or trial arbitration technique would actually save man-hours and money for both parties in the long run. The arbitration caseload would certainly be reduced. Efficiency and effectiveness of presentation would be increased for those cases that did have to be arbitrated.

Arbitration Hearing "Time-Savers"

In most *ad hoc* situations, the impartial third man arrives at the scene of the hearing armed with only two salient facts—the names of the parties and perhaps the knowledge that the issue concerns discipline, seniority, overtime distribution or what have you. In short, the *ad hoc* arbitrator starts completely cold at 10 A.M. on the day in question. Most practitioners and arbitrators are so accustomed to this condition of ignorance that there have been few systematic efforts to improve the prospects for making an economical and orderly record. In my own *ad hoc* experience, prehearing briefs are a rarity whereas posthearing briefs are becoming increasingly standard practice. This situation should be completely reversed to improve the efficiency of arbitration and make more effective use of the present limited supply of competent, experienced and acceptable arbitrators.

Usually the union is the party objecting to the necessity for filing prehearing statements. Again the villains cited would be understaffing and consequent insufficient time to devote to such "formalism." The argument against prehearing statements would thus be similar to that against dry-run or trial arbitration. The rebuttal to such reasoning is also the same. Prehearing statements can serve, among others, the following functions: (1) a basis for reaching stipulations on undisputed pertinent facts that will eliminate the necessity for considerable testimony, thus saving time and preventing confusion; (2) a basis for defining the arbitrable issue in more precise fashion and (3) an economical way to fill in the "cold" arbitrator.

If Company X and Union Y were already utilizing the dry-run or trial arbitration device, the task of preparing written submissions on the arbitrable issue and prehearing statements of what each intends to show at the hearing would not be burdensome, since much of the essential work would already have been done. The prehearing statement is of particular value to the novice arbitrator who may be less adept than the veteran in securing agreement on the arbitrable issue and in deducing from verbal opening statements what the shooting is all about.

Finally, and most importantly, effective utilization of prehearing statements can greatly facilitate factual stipulations at the hearing and can make it possible in most cases to eliminate the necessity for posthearing briefs. The prehearing statement, properly prepared, will summarize the pertinent facts and indicate the line of contractual argument that each party intends to pursue. These statements can thus be used to narrow, if not eliminate, the range of disagreement on pertinent factual matters. This can often save much time (and possible confusion) by shortening or eliminating the usual parade of lay witnesses. Greater clarity and economy in presentation are the invariable result of the advance preparation that the prehearing statement requires.

Ad hoc arbitrators should perhaps become more "aggressive" than most of them are in requesting *ahead of the hearing* that they be furnished with the contract, a submission agreement, the grievance and employer answers and written statements of what each party intends to show. There is no reason other than past practice that compels arbitrators to begin hearings with zero information. If the arbitrator takes some initiative in the manner suggested, a more economical hearing can result.

Arbitrators can also help matters at the hearing by being less permissive than some are inclined to be. The parties should not be choked off prematurely in their presentations. However, many hearings run far longer than they should because the arbitrator does not meet his obligation to conduct the hearing in an efficient and orderly fashion.

The Expendability of Transcripts and Court Reporters

An arbitrator is generally pleased when he walks into a hearing room and sees a court reporter present. He knows at once that his note-taking burden will be reduced. Yet the arbitrator worthy of his hire should be willing to take his own notes on the average arbitration case. Experienced arbitrators develop their own informal shorthand for noting relevant testimony and keeping accurate track of exhibits introduced. If the management or union representative is going too fast, the arbitrator should remember that it is he who is in charge of the hearing. He can always slow down a practitioner or a witness or ask for repetition on anything he may have missed or failed to record in sufficient detail.

I have been disturbed to find that some arbitrators request the parties to provide court reporters. This is regrettable for many reasons. In the first place, court reporters and transcripts are expensive. Second, use of a transcript entails a certain amount of delay, often several weeks. Perhaps most important, however, is the fact that the arbitrator is not the one who should be dictating the use of a reporter. This decision is for the parties to make.

There are *some* cases where the best interests of both parties suggest the desirability of providing for a verbatim record of the hearing. I refer to technical job evaluation or incentive-pay issues and also to future terms cases concerning wages, pension plan modifications or other technical matters. Wherever technical terminology is crucial to the case, a transcript is certainly a justifiable expense. Transcripts may also be justified in discipline or discharge cases that may hinge on credibility of testimony. In any such case it may be desirable to examine and, more pertinently, to cross-examine witnesses in rapid-fire fashion, too fast for most arbitrators to take competent notes. When credibility is involved, the arbitrator should be free to concentrate on the witnesses under examination.

In the great majority of cases, however, transcripts can be regarded as an expensive luxury. This is particularly true where the employer and union representatives have done a thorough job of grievance investigation and case preparation.

Posthearing briefs seem to be more common in grievance arbitration than in former years. Once again, the busy arbitrator is not likely to protest too vigorously that he does not need briefs when he knows that their filing will put off for two weeks or longer the time when he must study the record and write his decision. The fact remains that posthearing briefs are a time-consuming, expensive luxury and not a necessity in most cases. If the parties are genuinely concerned about improving the grievance arbitration process, they should devote proportionately more effort to investigation and preparation of cases. From the standpoint of reducing delays and improving performance, this is where the payoff should come.

Employers today are increasingly making use of attorneys in labor arbitration. This fact alone may account for the apparent increased incidence of posthearing briefs because attorneys have a natural affinity for this procedure. To them a brief is a familiar and comfortable device. On the other hand, most union practitioners of arbitration are likely to be more articulate

and convincing verbally than they are in writing. They thus have a preference for arguing their contractual position at the end of the hearing, entirely
apart from the desire to avoid delay and added expense.

Arbitrators with experience cannot candidly say that briefs are a
necessity in most situations. In my six years as permanent arbitrator for
John Deere and the UAW (1952–1958), posthearing briefs were received in
only 1 of more than 125 cases. Transcripts were furnished in only about 1
out of 10 cases. Thus, I can state with confidence that arbitration can be
effective without either a transcript or a posthearing brief.

How Can the Arbitrator Improve the Arbitration Process?

As noted earlier, one important contribution the arbitrator can make
is to run "tighter" hearings. He can also be more conscientious in avoiding
the sin of overcommitment. Much of the delay factor is due to the inability
of the busy arbitrator to offer reasonably early hearing dates and the related
factor of long time intervals between the end of the hearing and the appearance of the decision.

The latter difficulty can be overcome to some extent by writing
shorter opinions or by issuing memorandum rulings, followed by full-scale
opinions if requested. Writing short opinions does not necessarily save time
but in most cases it should be effective.

The Potential Uses of "Instant" Arbitration

In some industries the nature of the work requires an approximation
of "instant" arbitration when disputes arise over interpretation or application of the agreement. Two such widely dissimilar fields as the Broadway
theater and West Coast longshoring make use of the instant arbitration
device. The need for a speedy disposition of cases is apparent in each industry
where, for different reasons, the "show must go on" but disputes must also
be resolved.

If an actress suddenly advises that she is leaving the cast of a hit
play and the producer believes her action is in breach of her contract with
him and his contract with Actors Equity, the union in question, he can call
on one of two New York City professional arbitrators named in the Actors
Equity contract to hear the matter and render a decision on virtually an
overnight basis.

In longshoring, disputes may arise on the dock as to the application
of the contract's manning provisions. The tightness of ship turnaround
scheduling makes it mandatory that any such dispute be resolved on the
spot. Such needs are covered in the contract between the Pacific Coast

Shipowners Association and the International Longshoremen and Warehouseworkers' Union (ILWU) by a provision in which an "arbitrator" is designated in each port and employed by the parties on a twenty-four-hour standby basis. The port arbitrators are individuals who are knowledgeable about the contract and the problems of the industry by virtue of extensive prior experience with either the ILWU or the Shipowners Association.

The port arbitrator is to call the dispute as he sees it in a judicial manner. His decision holds and the ruling must be accepted while work continues. However, the contract provides that an appeal may be taken to the permanent arbitrator who is empowered to review the port arbitrator's determination as to its contractual soundness.

What works in the legitimate theater and in longshoring is capable of extension to other types of employer-union relationships if the parties jointly desire to develop a procedure to fit their own circumstances. Building and construction comes to mind as one industry where some form of instant arbitration could prove to be a desirable procedural innovation.

Adaptation of the instant arbitration idea can also be considered for usage in handling the troublesome problem of wildcat stoppages.

Conclusion

Much of this chapter is "bearish" in nature, since there has been a concentration on how to reform procedures. This should not obscure the plus side. There has been general improvement in the conduct of grievance arbitration over the years. The quality of those presenting cases to arbitrators has unquestionably improved.

The strong incentive to restructure procedures is not therefore to be interpreted as evidence that the process itself is working badly. At the same time the supply problem underlines the urgency of doing whatever can be done to make arbitration more efficient, less costly and less time-consuming.

Employers and unions can institute the recommended procedural changes and thereby make grievance arbitration into a more effective instrument of contract administration. The primary responsibility must rest on the users of the process. Yet arbitrators should not be passive. The jurisdiction and authority of the arbitrator are prescribed by contract, but arbitrators should do more than we have done in encouraging needed procedural changes.

Selected Bibliography

Aaron, Benjamin, "Labor Arbitration and Its Critics," *Labor Law Journal*, XX (September, 1959), 605–10, 645.

ABERSOLD, JOHN R., AND WAYNE E. HOWARD, *Cases in Labor Relations: An Arbitration Experience.* Englewood Cliffs, N.J.: Prentice-Hall, Inc., 1967.

BARBASH, JOSEPH, "Due Process and Individual Rights in Arbitration," New York University Seventeenth Annual Conference on Labor *Proceedings*, No. 17, pp. 7–25. Washington, D.C.: The Bureau of National Affairs, Inc., 1964.

BLOCH, R. I., "NLRB and Arbitration: Is the Board's Expanding Jurisdiction Justified?" *Labor Law Journal*, XIX (October, 1968), 640.

CLARK, STEPHEN R., "The Doctrine of Past Practice in Labor Arbitration," *University of Colorado Law Review*, XXXVIII (Winter, 1966), 229–47.

DAVEY, HAROLD W., "The John Deere-UAW Permanent Arbitration System" in *Critical Issues in Labor Arbitration*, ed. Jean T. McKelvey, pp. 161–92. Washington, D.C.: The Bureau of National Affairs, Inc., 1957.

——, "The Supreme Court and Arbitration," *Notre Dame Lawyer*, XXXVI (March, 1961), 138–45.

——, "The Arbitrator Views the Agreement," *Labor Law Journal*, XII (December, 1961), 1161–76.

——, "The Uses and Misuses of Tripartite Boards in Grievance Arbitration," in *Developments in American and Foreign Arbitration*, ed. Charles M. Rehmus, pp. 152–79. Washington, D.C.: The Bureau of National Affairs, Inc., 1968.

——, "Restructuring Grievance Arbitration Procedures: Some Modest Proposals," *Iowa Law Review*, LIV (February, 1969), 560–78.

ELKOURI, FRANK, AND EDNA ELKOURI, *How Arbitration Works* (2nd ed.). Washington, D.C.: The Bureau of National Affairs, Inc., 1960.

FLEMING, R. W., "Reflections on the Nature of Labor Arbitration," *Michigan Law Review*, LXI (May, 1963), 1245–72.

——, *The Labor Arbitration Process.* Urbana, Ill.: University of Illinois Press, 1965.

GETMAN, J. G., "Debate over Caliber of Arbitrators: Judge Hays and His Critics," *Indiana Law Journal*, XLIV (Winter, 1969), 182–90.

GLICK, LESLIE A., "Bias, Fraud, Misconduct and Partiality of the Arbitrator," *Arbitration Journal*, XXII, no. 3 (1967), 161–72.

GROSS, JAMES A., "Value Judgments in the Decisions of Labor Arbitrators," *Industrial and Labor Relations Review*, XXI (October, 1967), 55–72.

HARRIS, PHILIP, "The Arbitration Process and the Disciplining of Supervisors," *Labor Law Journal*, XVI (November, 1965), 679–84.

HAYS, PAUL R., *Labor Arbitration: A Dissenting View.* New Haven, Conn.: Yale University Press, 1966.

LAW NOTE, "Norris-La Guardia Act and Section 301 of the Taft-Hartley Act: Problems of Jurisdiction and Removal in the Enforceability of Collectively Bargained No-Strike Agreements," *Northwestern University Law Review*, LX (September–October, 1965), 489–510.

——, "Section 301(a) and the Federal Common Law of Labor Agreements," *Yale Law Journal*, LXXV (April, 1966), 877–93.

——, "Judicial Enforcement of Labor Arbitrators' Awards," *University of Pennsylvania Law Review*, CXIV (May, 1966), 1050–66.

——, "Section 301(a) and the Employee: An Illusory Remedy," *Fordham Law Review*, XXXV (March, 1967), 517–30.

——, "New Look at Arbitration—Enforcement of a No-Strike Clause by Injunctive Relief," *Syracuse Law Review*, XIX (Summer, 1968), 957–69.

McDERMOTT, THOMAS J., "Enforcing No-Strike Provisions via Arbitration," *Labor Law Journal*, XVIII (October, 1967), 579–87.

——, "Arbitrability: The Courts Versus the Arbitrator," *Arbitration Journal*, XXIII (1968), 18–37.

ROBERTS, BENJAMIN C., AND G. ALLAN DASH, JR., "How to Get Better Results from Labor-Management Arbitration," *Arbitration Journal*, XX, no. 1 (1967), 1–23.

ROSE, GEORGE., "Do the Requirements of Due Process Protect the Rights of Employees Under Arbitration Procedures?" *Labor Law Journal*, XVI (January, 1965), 44–58.

ROSS, ARTHUR M., "Distressed Grievance Procedures and Their Rehabilitation," in *Labor Arbitration and Industrial Change*, ed. Mark L. Kahn, pp. 104–45. Washington, D.C.: The Bureau of National Affairs, Inc., 1963.

SAMOFF, BERNARD, "Arbitration, Not NLRB Intervention," *Labor Law Journal*, XVIII (October, 1967), 602–31.

SCHWARTZ, ALAN, "Procedural Arbitrability under Section 301 of the LMRA," *Yale Law Journal*, LXXIII (July, 1964), 1459–76.

SEITZ, PETER, "Value Judgments in the Decisions of Labor Arbitrators: 'Comment' and 'Reply,' " by James A. Gross, *Industrial and Labor Relations Review*, XXI (April, 1968), 427–32.

SELIGSON, HARRY, "Minority Group Employees, Discipline, and the Arbitrator," *Labor Law Journal*, XIX (September, 1968), 544–54.

SHAPIRO, DAVID L., "Some Thoughts on Intervention before Courts, Agencies, and Arbitrators," *Harvard Law Review*, LXXXI (February, 1968), 721–72.

SHULMAN, HARRY, "Reason, Contract, and Law in Labor Relations," *Harvard Law Review*, LXVII (April, 1955), 999–1024.

SMITH, RUSSELL A., AND DALLAS L. JONES, "Supreme Court and Labor Dispute Arbitration: The Emerging Federal Law," *Michigan Law Review*, LXIII (March, 1965), 751–808.

————, "The Impact of the Emerging Federal Law of Grievance Arbitration on Judges, Arbitrators, and Parties," *Virginia Law Review*, LII (June, 1966), 831–912.

STEIN, BRUNO, "Loyalty and Security Cases in Arbitration," *Industrial and Labor Relations Review*, XVII (October, 1963), 96–113.

TAYLOR, GEORGE W., "Effectuating the Labor Contract Through Arbitration," in *The Profession of Labor Arbitration*, ed. Jean T. McKelvey, pp. 20–41. Washington, D.C.: The Bureau of National Affairs, Inc., 1957.

TRACY, ESTELLE, R., ed. *Arbitration Cases in Public Employment*. New York: American Arbitration Association, 1969.

RESOLUTION
OF FUTURE TERMS DISPUTES
principles and procedures

CHAPTER EIGHT

Use of economic force to resolve disputes over the terms of a future contract continues to be comparatively rare in U.S. labor relations. Nevertheless, whenever there is a general upturn in strike activity in any particular year or a strike occurs in an industry regarded to be of critical importance, the general public's impatience is quick to surface. The contemporary bias against strike activity is especially noticeable in the public sector, where strikes by teachers, firemen and garbage workers have produced severe adverse reactions.

How to eliminate economic force as a means of labor dispute resolution has thus come to achieve an increasingly high priority in the public mind, if not always in the minds of the collective bargaining participants. Strikes, boycotts and lockouts are constantly under attack as anachronistic and inimical to the public interest. The origins of particular labor disputes

191

or their merits are seldom given the attention they deserve. The emphasis is an almost overwhelming one to develop somehow a labor relations condition where production of goods or services is assured indefinitely without interruption.

THE CHALLENGE TO RESOLVE
FUTURE TERMS DISPUTES PEACEFULLY

Such a generalized preference for reason over muscle is both understandable and logical. At the same time it is important to appreciate fully why employers and unions are reluctant to forego their right to resort to economic force, where necessary, as an ultimate means of producing agreement on the terms of a future contract. Their reluctance is based on a joint understanding that the possibility of a strike (or lockout) if agreement is not reached at the expiration of the current contract is in itself the most powerful inducement to reach agreement. This is what keeps the parties at the bargaining table in exhausting marathon sessions. It is rarely the case that any party involved in a labor dispute seeks to resort to economic force in preference to peacefully reaching an agreement. The critical point is that it is the right to use economic force when negotiation fails that gives meaning and substance to the collective bargaining process as we know it in the United States. It is in fact *the* distinguishing hallmark of "free" collective bargaining.

Collective bargaining, as we have seen, is an institutionalized process of joint decision-making. The task of the participants in bargaining is to resolve short-run conflicts in viewpoints and desires on a wide range of economic and noneconomic issues—and to do so peacefully whenever possible. Although employers and unions have done a commendable job of institutionalizing conflict relationships in contract administration (as noted in Chapter 7), the challenge to *improve the level of performance in achieving peaceful resolution of disputes over future contract terms* is a more difficult and compelling one. The stressed language in the preceding sentence was carefully chosen to avoid setting a goal of eliminating economic force entirely. In the first place, it is impossible. Furthermore, such a target would convey the false impression that labor peace is synonymous with health. In *some* circumstances, economic warfare may be a healthier and necessary condition. The absence of conflict may be evidence of either a coercive or a "sweetheart" relationship, neither of which would be regarded as constituting a constructive or mature employer-union relationship.

I do not intend to glorify economic force at the start of a chapter whose purpose is to consider viable alternatives to the use of economic force in labor relations. It is important to appreciate, however, that many employers and unions strongly believe (perhaps correctly so) that there is no *satisfactory* substitute for economic force as an *ultimate* means of producing agreement at the bargaining table. In this same vein, it is argued that there cannot be *meaningful* collective bargaining in the public sector when the right to strike is prohibited.[1] The key word is "meaningful." As we shall see in Chapter 13, collective bargaining is taking hold rapidly in the public sector at all levels of government. I do not believe that the participants in public sector labor relations regard their activities as lacking in meaning or significance. However, many public sector unions seek the same right to strike now enjoyed by their counterparts in the private sector.

As we begin analysis of how to improve performance levels in avoiding use of economic force in future terms cases and to consider alternatives to its use, the first consideration is to acknowledge that if by law we choose to eliminate the right to use economic force there must be at the same time *provision for "suitable" alternative procedures* for producing agreement on future terms. "Suitable" here is defined to mean "acceptable and feasible in the eyes of the parties to the bargaining." Anything short of this involves an end to collective bargaining in the customary sense.

THE STRIKE PERFORMANCE RECORD

Use of economic force is not, in my judgment, a problem of unusually serious magnitude. The overall record on labor peace is a reasonably good one. BLS figures indicate a substantial upturn in strike activity in calendar 1967 and 1968 by comparison with most of the years since 1946, the peak strike year of our history. As noted in Chapter 3, the man-days of idleness in 1946 due to strike activity amounted to 1.43 percent of the total estimated amount of "private nonfarm" working time for the year. In the intervening years prior to 1967 the percentage of lost time due to strike activity seldom exceeded .25 percent of total working time. In 1967, however, the figure was .30 percent and in 1968 it rose to .32 percent.[2]

The increased strike activity is explainable on multiple grounds. One factor was a considerable increase in public sector work stoppages. Another was the customary increase in strike activity during a period of rising prices when union leadership is under severe pressure to obtain substantial wage increases. Still another factor was the upswing in membership rejection of ratified settlements, discussed earlier in Chapter 5.

Aggregative data can be misleading unless carefully used. Although

---

[1] For a forceful, if not completely convincing, statement of this point of view, see Allan Weisenfeld, "Public Employees are still Second Class Citizens," *Labor Law Journal*, XX (March, 1969), 138–50.

[2] See U.S. Department of Labor, Bureau of Labor Statistics, *Work Stoppages in 1968* (Selected Final Tabulations), mimeographed (June, 1969), Table 1.

approximately 2.6 million workers were involved in the slightly more than 5,000 stoppages in calendar 1968, 32 major strikes, each involving 10,000 or more workers, accounted for about two-fifths of all workers idled by strikes during the year and about the same proportion of total strike idleness.[3] The bare figure of 5,045 strikes in one year may sound ominously large. However, we should keep in mind that the "major" stoppages numbered only 32 in the same year.

The significance of the increased strike activity in 1967 and 1968 should not be minimized. It bears witness to the fact that economic force is still very much in vogue among American employers and unions. We have a considerable way to go before becoming satisfied with our record on labor peace. The figures for 1967 and 1968 should give us pause before we speak glibly of the decline and fall of the strike. Furthermore, to me a most disturbing aspect of the 1968 figures is that nearly one-third of the stoppages took place during the term of agreements. This underlines the seriousness of the wildcat strike problem. There are comparatively few contracts providing a basis for "legal" strikes during the life of an existing agreement.

Certain types of strikes and certain types of employer retaliatory conduct during strikes are declining, although not disappearing entirely. Strikes to enforce union recognition as bargaining representatives are comparatively infrequent. Unions customarily utilize the NLRB's representation case election machinery to establish their claim under the law to exclusive bargaining rights. Furthermore, as we noted in Chapter 3, several types of strike are prohibited by federal and/or state legislation. In this category are jurisdictional strikes, secondary or sympathetic strikes, government employee strikes, strikes to achieve unlawful objectives and so on. Their legal prohibition is an important reason for the comparative infrequency of 'strikes in these categories. It is not the only factor. Some credit can properly be given to a maturing labor movement and growth of more constructive relationships between employers and unions.

CHARACTERISTICS OF A CONTEMPORARY STRIKE

The most common strike may be described as a *primary* strike by Union X against Employer Y when negotiations on future terms (the new contract) have failed to produce an agreement. Disputes over proposed general wage adjustments continue as the most important single cause of work stoppages.

As a general rule, when Employer Y is struck by his employees

---

[3] *Ibid.* BLS defines a "major" work stoppage as one involving 10,000 or more employees.

represented by Union X the process of conflict has become institutionalized to the point where Employer Y does not invite violence by initiating a back-to-work movement, by refusing to negotiate further or by seeking to import strikebreakers.

This does not indicate that employers have gone "soft," nor can we say that labor dispute violence is entirely a thing of the past. The general absence of violence and strikebreaking activity can be regarded as evidence that today's employer recognizes the legitimacy of strike activity in such a primary dispute. Furthermore, he views his relationship with the union as a *continuing* one, even though his employees are on strike.

Typically, when a primary strike occurs, the parties lock horns by application of economic pressure, but there is an underlying confidence in the enduring nature of the relationship. Each strike, in other words, does not become a grim battle for survival. On the contrary, most strikes resemble the classic view of a strike as *a continuation of bargaining by other methods.* The union has no intention of breaking the employer. The latter has no intention of using the strike as a method of ridding himself of the union. Both parties assume they will resume relationships with one another after a few days, a few weeks or, in severe cases, a few months.

This is a significant change in basic attitudes. It deserves emphasis. It reflects a maturing conception of a union-management relationship that does not rule out the possibility of industrial conflict. There is an acceptance of the proposition that conflict may at times be necessary as a means of resolving a dispute. Both the employer and the union, however, know that the institutional process of living together will be resumed after the resort to economic pressure has produced a new agreement that in the short run may be "favorable" to the employer or to the union, as the case may be. This attitude may seem hard-headed (or even misguided) to those who equate the absence of conflict with the ideal in union-management relations. To me it is a pragmatic, psychologically sound approach to the realities of labor relations.

A critically important characteristic of today's work stoppage concerns the disappearance of the romantic notion of the union as the underdog. On the contemporary scene whenever employees go on strike, the burden of justifying the use of economic force falls on the union for a number of reasons. In the first place, the wider acceptance of unionism and collective bargaining carries with it a higher premium on avoiding economic force wherever possible. Since 1935 the right to organize and to bargain collectively have been protected by law. This factor alone serves to reduce the acceptability of a strike in the minds of the public at large. The nation has become conditioned to the proposition that labor peace should be the norm. Thus when a strike is called, the "blame" invariably attaches to the union since it has seemingly initiated the conflict. Employer intransigence in a particular situation may have made a strike unavoidable from the union standpoint. Nevertheless, under contemporary conditions the employer rarely takes the step of locking out his employees. The union may be forced into the overt action of calling employees out on strike. The lay observer is therefore prone to consider the union as responsible for the lost production, employment and wages—not the employer. Seldom do the merits of any labor dispute achieve accurate or complete coverage by the media. A related consideration is that few unions have developed skills in communicating the union story on labor disputes to the general public through the media. When a building trades craft union is striking in 1969 for wage increases that will bring the journeyman's rate over the next three years to the neighborhood of $10 per hour, it is somewhat disconcerting and incongruous to see and hear on the evening news a ham-fisted business agent of said craft union seemingly close to tears about how "far behind" his men are in terms of wages. One can easily imagine the impact this particular television vignette had on viewers already predisposed to regard unions as self-seeking and parasitical. The impact on those viewers contemplating the costs of building a home can also be envisaged.

In summary, few strikes under contemporary conditions have been popular in terms of public support. The days of union support from the underdog role are gone forever (except perhaps in agricultural labor). The psychological climate has shifted to the point where labor peace and uninterrupted production are regarded as good *per se*. A work stoppage is considered regrettable *per se*. This strong statement on public attitudes should perhaps be qualified by observing that the right to strike as part of the collective bargaining process is generally much better understood than in former years. At the same time, impatience with use of the strike seems to be on the increase.

In this chapter the focus is mainly procedural. We shall review private and governmental approaches designed to minimize, if not eliminate, the use of economic force as a means of resolving disputes over future contract terms. The concern relates both to the prevention of economic force and the quicker ending of work stoppages already in progress. Some widely discussed "alternatives" to economic force are *not* considered here because their usage, in my judgment, would ultimately put an end to collective bargaining. Chief among these unacceptable alternatives is *compulsory arbitration*, defined here as the requirement that unresolved future terms disputes must be concluded through final and binding arbitration with the right to use economic force at any stage of the dispute being legally prohibited.

Analysis of the viable alternatives will be preceded by a summary of "first principles" that condition my evaluation of both private and public procedures for more effective dispute resolution.

SOME "FIRST PRINCIPLES" RELATING
TO CONFLICT RESOLUTION

A more accurate heading for this section would be "my value judgments on the subject at hand." What follows stems from a basic conviction that private solutions are better than governmental solutions. I therefore consider the optimal role of public policy to be one of encouraging and strengthening the practice and procedure of collective bargaining. This view has been expressed in Chapter 3 and thus requires no further elaboration.

The fundamental test for evaluating the merits of any proposed conflict resolution procedure is whether it contributes to strengthening collective bargaining as an institutional process. This is why a procedural alternative such as compulsory arbitration simply will not pass muster. On the other hand, a procedure such as mediation, when intelligently performed and properly timed, can serve to improve collective bargaining rather than weaken it.

Some "first principles" in line with such thinking are set forth below:

1. In today's complex, interdependent society economic force as a means of resolving labor disputes must be regarded by the parties as a last-resort instrument for producing agreement. However, the right to strike and the right to lock out should be preserved. Usage in the private sector must remain a possibility. The possibility of usage should be available in the public sector as well on a limited basis (to be spelled out subsequently).

2. In any situation where use of economic force is conditioned or prohibited by law effective dispute settlement machinery must be available that will encourage rather than discourage bargaining to finality.

3. Public policy on labor dispute settlement should not be predicated on the proposition that peaceful solutions are always possible, or even always desirable. A primary aim of public policy should be to establish a climate that facilitates informed and rational decision-making by employers and unions in future terms disputes.

4. Part of the democratic credo has always been that truth emerges from the marketplace of free ideas. Public policy can aid the labor relations process to the degree that it can reduce the nonrational tensions and pressures affecting the negotiators at the bargaining table. A principal means of doing so would be to aid the factualization of bargaining and increase the professional capabilities of neutrals assisting the parties in dispute resolution.

If we hold that private dispute resolution is to be preferred over governmental, it is clear that public policy should be designed to strengthen private procedures. Whenever government fails to encourage the parties to achieve their own final solutions to future terms disputes, the likely result is that government will become the agency of first resort rather than last resort in dispute settlement.

PRIVATE MECHANISMS FOR FUTURE TERMS DISPUTE RESOLUTION

Constructive attitudes are more powerful than any procedures. There can be no adequate substitute for the joint will to reach agreement. When such mutual willingness is present, the need for dispute settlement mechanisms, private or governmental, will be minimal. If the will to agree is absent, no procedure yet devised is sure to prevent ultimate use of economic force.

Positive attitudes in management-union relationships will correlate highly with joint efforts to institutionalize the bargaining process in such a way as to minimize the possible need to resort to economic force. For example, employers and unions still on a hostile basis are not likely to create joint study committees for handling continuing problems. Such committees are usually the product of mature bargaining relationships.

Assuming that improved knowledge is an aid to the agreement-making process, we can count as plus factors the increased capabilities and resources of negotiators for both employers and unions. It is logical further to assume that the higher the level of agreed-upon information at the bargaining table the less chance there will be of negotiations breaking down. Here we can note with approval that some employers and unions engage in exploratory sessions as much as one year ahead of formal negotiation time as part of the information-gathering process and also as a way of defusing or reducing the ultimate tensions of the actual bargaining.

Comparatively few "public-be-damned" employers and unions remain on the contemporary bargaining scene. Most parties are alert to the growing public intolerance of work stoppages noted earlier. Thus another positive element can be counted in, that is, widespread and growing joint recognition of the desirability of avoiding the use of economic force wherever and whenever possible. This is not something that can be verified in statistical fashion, but I believe it to be a fact.

Related to this increasing awareness of public impatience is the hard knowledge with which some unions are faced—the technological obsolescence of the strike.[4] In telephonic communications, electric and gas utilities, petroleum refining, chemicals and other highly automated fields the orthodox

---

[4] James L. Stern was one of the first to underline technological and other factors contributing to the reduced effectiveness of the strike weapon. See his "Declining Utility of the Strike," *Industrial and Labor Relations Review*, XVIII (October, 1964), 60–72.

strike has lost most of its punch. Management can use supervisory personnel to continue production for long periods of time even when all bargaining unit personnel support the strike. In such cases, the strike is more of a public information instrument than an exercise in economic strength.

When one surveys the various private procedures for future terms dispute resolution, there seems to be nothing of a genuinely new character in sight. There is nothing new about joint study committees, although they are receiving great attention as a means for avoiding crisis bargaining. Nor is there anything new about the nonstoppage strike, a procedure that is enjoying something of a renaissance in terms of academic interest if not in actual usage.[5]

Perhaps the most significant procedural development of a private nature is the greater disposition to consider voluntary adoption of final and binding arbitration as a way of resolving future terms disputes. In years past nearly all employers and unions systematically shunned this device. However, I have the firm impression (hard to document) that there is something developing here that may soon become prominent enough to be called a trend.

Several factors are at work that may serve to soften traditional employer and union hostility to the idea of giving outside neutrals authority to render final and binding awards on future terms issues. One is the sensitivity to public impatience with use of economic force. Another is recognition of the disutility of strikes in many industries. Both have already been noted. A third factor is a realization that where arbitration has been utilized in future terms cases the results have not been too far from what might have been reasonably expected had the parties bargained to a final solution of their own.[6]

Voluntary acceptance of future terms arbitration may come into vogue in the private sector for these reasons, although I do not predict any substantial increase in usage unless and until employers and unions are

---

[5] A bibliographical footnote could be extensive, but will be limited here to two references. David B. McAlmont sought to meet some of the pragmatic objections in his article, "The Semi-Strike," *Industrial and Labor Relations Review*, XV (January, 1962), 191–208. More recently, Donald E. Cullen has reviewed perceptively the pros and cons of the nonstoppage strike in his monograph, *National Emergency Strikes* (Ithaca, N.Y.: New York State School of Industrial and Labor Relations, 1968).

[6] Such a finding was first made by Irving Bernstein in his *The Arbitration of Wages* (Berkeley and Los Angeles: University of California Press, 1954). Richard U. Miller has analyzed future terms wage awards for the years 1953–1965. Miller's study shows continued rare usage. Miller also found that awards have become "considerably more conservative" since the Bernstein period (1945–1950). See Richard U. Miller, "Arbitration of New Contract Wage Disputes: Some Recent Trends," *Industrial and Labor Relations Review*, XX (January, 1967), 250–64. For the text of selected future terms wage arbitration decisions in recent public sector disputes see Estelle Taylor, *Arbitration in Public Employment* (New York: American Arbitration Association, 1969).

confronted with a serious threat of governmentally imposed compulsory arbitration. Should such a threat materialize, a rush to adopt private procedures can be anticipated as a means of staving off unpalatable legislation.

One other private procedure deserves comment before considering governmental mechanisms for future terms dispute resolution. This is the possibility of greater usage of informed neutrals in a private mediation capacity. In some relationships the contract permanent arbitrator performs in an advisory or mediatory capacity at negotiation time. In other situations a neutral in whom both parties have confidence may be called into a crisis bargaining situation on an *ad hoc* basis in preference to using the FMCS mediator. I have no information as to the prevalence of the practice of using outside neutrals in such capacities. Nor have I had any personal experience that might provide a basis for evaluating the utility of private mediation.

This section can conclude on the assured note that there will be greater experimentation with private measures for avoiding economic force than ever before, stimulated both by the growing maturity of employer-union relationships and the rising threat of more pervasive governmental controls.

GOVERNMENTAL PROCEDURES FOR FUTURE TERMS CONFLICT RESOLUTION

What governmental procedures should be available when negotiations reach an impasse and a strike is imminent or in progress? Keeping in mind our previous reservations and stated principles, we do not consider here procedures that are properly regarded as incompatible with the requirements of a free society.

In reviewing public dispute settlement procedures I am both intrigued and discouraged by the fact that there appears to be nothing of a genuinely novel nature on the horizon. There is, however, a new stress on the potential of such "old" procedures as fact-finding with recommendations and its blood brother, advisory arbitration, related to the needs of those engaged in public sector bargaining.[7] There is also renewed interest in the potential utility of the statutory strike.[8]

---

[7] See Jean T. McKelvey, "Fact Finding in Public Employment Disputes: Promise or Illusion?" *Industrial and Labor Relations Review*, XXII (July, 1969), 528–43.

[8] See footnote 5 above, especially the 1968 monograph by Donald E. Cullen, pp. 102–3, and references cited therein. See also the short paper by Stephen H. Sosnick, "Non-Stoppage Strikes: A New Approach," *Industrial and Labor Relations Review*, XVIII (October, 1964), 73–80.

THE OVERRIDING IMPORTANCE OF EFFECTIVE MEDIATION

Much of what follows is strongly influenced by the running debate as to how best to institutionalize labor relations conflict situations in the public sector. In the main, however, the essential story line of the government's role in labor dispute settlement remains unchanged. Dominating the consideration of every procedural switch or refinement that one can call to mind is the fundamental fact that *the optimal function of government in labor dispute settlement is that of mediation*. When the parties are unable to resolve disputes in bilateral fashion, there is no better instrument, in my mind, than skilled, knowledgeable and well-timed mediation.

The role of government as a conciliator or mediator of labor disputes has been historically accepted in principle, although perhaps resented in particular situations. The role of the neutral peacemaker has undeniable plus values in labor relations as in other types of conflict situations. The mediation function rests on two important basic considerations: (1) the public interest as well as the interest of the parties immediately concerned will normally be better served by achieving a solution to the dispute that does not require (or which minimizes) the use of economic force; (2) in a conflict situation, third party intervention of a voluntary kind frequently can produce a psychological climate that will lead to settlement of differences impossible to achieve when the parties are left indefinitely to confront one another. There is, however, no intrinsic magic in the conciliation or mediation function. Its effectiveness depends almost entirely on two things: (1) acceptability of the function to the parties; and (2) the knowledgeability and skill of the mediators.

The mediation function had gained increasing acceptance at both the federal and state level. Most of the key industrial states have regularly established mediation agencies whose services are utilized by employers and unions as the need arises.

The Federal Mediation and Conciliation Service, an independent agency since the 1947 amendments to the National Labor Relations Act, has become a truly professional agency. Its staff mediators are more highly respected and utilized with a much greater level of confidence than in years past. FMCS insists on previous labor relations experience as a prerequisite for becoming a staff mediator. It then puts all recruits through a rigorous academic and field regimen. The results are visibly more satisfactory. Both the mediation function and those performing it are more highly regarded by employers and unions utilizing the service, an indispensable factor in successful dispute resolution.

Professional mediation is the most desirable (least undesirable) form of third-party intervention in future terms disputes. In most cases there should be no need for other forms of procedural intervention for final resolution of the conflict. My preference for mediation as the most salutary form of neutral assistance to employers and unions does not connote ignorance of the fact that in some *critical* situations mediation alone will not be adequate to the challenge. The word "critical" is stressed in the previous sentence to avoid the more familiar terminology of "emergency dispute" and "impasse" for reasons presently to be outlined.

A Note on Preventive Mediation

Before considering other procedural forms of trilateralism in dispute resolution, brief comment may be in order on one of FMCS's favorite techniques, preventive mediation. Virtually all FMCS staff mediators are engaged in preventive mediation as well as in the more customary activity of attempting to prevent an imminent strike or end one in progress. The operational aim of preventive mediation is to work informally with employers and unions between contracts, when tempers are cool and negotiation deadlines are not pressing, in an effort to head off future crisis situations.

In the eyes of FMCS, an ounce of preventive intervention is worth a pound of subsequent poststrike cure. It is difficult to quarrel in the abstract with such a praiseworthy concept. I am currently more sanguine about the value of preventive mediation than in former years, when I shared the views of Allan Weisenfeld and other critics who condemned the process as a contradiction in terms and an unjustifiable interference with the right of the parties to run their own affairs.[9] The true function of mediation is to assist the parties in reaching a solution of their dispute that they were unable to achieve bilaterally. One of the dangers in preventive mediation is that it *could* develop into continuous monitoring in the area of contract administration—a consequence that would be harmful. It would inhibit the parties from strengthening their joint abilities to solve their problems unaided.

FMCS is so pleased with its experience record, however, that it is increasingly difficult to be critical. While retaining a strong preference for private mediation during the life of agreements, assuming the aid of neutrals is essential, I would nevertheless agree that many employers and unions can benefit greatly from professional guiding hands. Nor can I quarrel with the idea of defusing potentially explosive issues before they become a focal point in future terms negotiations.

We consider next the role of government in any "critical" dispute

---

[9] See Allan Weisenfeld, "Some Thoughts on Labor Mediation," *Proceedings of Sixth Annual Meeting, Industrial Relations Research Association* (Madison, Wis.: IRRA, 1954), pp. 276–83.

where negotiations are deadlocked, a strike is imminent or in progress and conventional mediation has proved unsuccessful.

PROCEDURES FOR RESOLUTION OF "CRITICAL" DISPUTES OTHER THAN CONVENTIONAL MEDIATION

My approved arsenal of procedures includes:

1. Fact-finding panels, boards or single neutrals, with power to recommend substantive solutions.
2. Voluntary submission by the parties to final and binding arbitration by a single neutral or tripartite board or an all-public board.
3. High-level "executive" mediation.
4. Use of injunctions to prevent or end use of economic force, with provisos that require continuing negotiation during the effective period of the injunction.
5. Seizure of the enterprise, with operation by government personnel rather than the regular managerial personnel, coupled with an all-public neutral panel with power to recommend a solution.
6. Advisory arbitration, including the proviso that failure to accept recommendations would make the rejecting party subject to a show-cause proceeding.
7. The statutory strike.
8. Special legislation for the particular dispute.

A review of my earlier thinking shows that in 1954 I was much less interventionist-minded. My inventory of *blacklisted* procedures in 1954 included:

1. Compulsory arbitration.
2. National emergency dispute procedures of Taft-Hartley.
3. Fact-finding boards or boards of inquiry lacking the power to recommend substantive solutions.
4. Seizure of the facility.
5. Injunctions.
6. A "permanent" agency for dispute settlement.
7. Strike votes.[10]

In the years since 1954 I have become less adamant in my opposition to Title II procedures for settlement of disputes that in the president's judgment constitute a danger to the national health and safety. In some circumstances I now concede that seizure and injunctions may be both necessary and appropriate. Still inadmissible are compulsory arbitration

---

[10] See Harold W. Davey, "Government Intervention in Labor Disputes," *Labor Law Journal*, V (November, 1954), 739–42, 800.

and/or a "permanent" peacetime board or agency for dispute settlement. Finally, required strike votes, particularly those on employer last offers, appear to be an exercise in futility.

My increased receptivity to additional interventionist procedures is based on the following factors:

1. Consideration of the declining utility and palatability of strikes as the economy becomes increasingly interdependent and complex in structure.
2. Awareness of the difficulties in changing the Title II approach.
3. Recognition that Title II procedures have not worked as badly as the volume of criticism might suggest.

The Durability of Title II Procedures

Title II has been invoked only twenty-nine times over the period from 1947 through 1968.[11] With the possible exception of Section 14(b), no other provision of Taft-Hartley has come under such critical fire. Most of the negative comments end by concluding that Title II procedures are too rigid and too predictable. Once the president determines to utilize Title II, the sequence of steps is pretty much cut and dried. This has doubtless been an important reason for the comparatively few instances where the president has determined that a threatened or actual labor dispute "will, if permitted to occur or continue, imperil the national health or safety. . . ."

Having made such a determination, the president is required to appoint a "board of inquiry" to investigate and report back to him on the issues. The board is *not* permitted to make recommendations. The president may then direct the attorney general to seek an injunction in federal district court to prevent or terminate the strike (or lockout). While the injunction is in effect, the status quo on wages and working conditions is preserved. If a strike continues or begins, the strikers would, of course, be subject to jail for contempt of the district court order. Employer and union are obligated to make efforts to resolve the dispute with FMCS aid. If after sixty days the dispute is not resolved, the board of inquiry is reconvened to make an updated status report, again with no recommendations. The second report must indicate the employer's last offer for settlement on which the NLRB must poll the employees within fifteen days and certify the result to the attorney general within five days. After this step the injunction must be dissolved. The employees are then free to resume (or begin) the strike.

This brief recital of the steps in the Title II minuet reveals the rigidity and predictability we have noted. Yet no alternative procedures

---

[11] See U.S. Department of Labor, Bureau of Labor Statistics, *National Emergency Disputes*, Bulletin No. 1633 (Washington, D.C.: Government Printing Office, 1969).

have been successfully urged since 1947. What factors then account for the durability of the procedure?

For one thing, the critics are of one mind only in attacking Title II. There is no consensus as to a preferred alternative. The favorite substitute would give the president a greater range of discretion and choice of procedures in handling emergency disputes. The model for most of these proposals is the law drafted for Massachusetts by the late Sumner H. Slichter.[12] Although the choice-of-procedures concept has wide support, the critics do not agree on which procedures to include in the president's arsenal of weapons. For example, my list of acceptable procedures would be regarded as too interventionist by some and as not tough enough by others.

Another reason why Title II has remained intact is that it has not been as ineffective as the volume of criticism might suggest. Studying the chronology of the disputes in which Title II has been invoked over the years shows that injunctions were issued in twenty-five of the twenty-nine cases and were effective in all but the 1949–1950 bituminous coal dispute. In only seven cases were strikes resumed after the eighty-day cooling-off period of the injunction. Five of these were in the stevedoring industry in Atlantic and Gulf Coast ports. However, in no case has a dispute been ended by employees voting to accept the employer's last offer.[13]

A third factor in Title II survival has been its sparing use. All White House occupants since 1947 have frequently avoided use of Title II in favor of a variety of informal procedures for inducing settlement. Finally, the restrictive semantics of Title II are such that it cannot be wheeled into action unless the dispute can fairly be characterized as one which constitutes a genuine threat to the national health and safety. The severity of the statutory language comes close to defining away the problem. It is even possible to make a learned demonstration that we have never experienced a true national emergency work stoppage in the Title II sense.[14]

SUGGESTED APPROACHES FOR RESOLUTION OF "CRITICAL" LABOR DISPUTES

The preceding discussion suggests the wisdom of changing our terminology along the lines advocated by Donald E. Cullen in his thorough critique of various alternative procedures.[15] Cullen wisely prefers the word

---

[12] For an early appraisal of the so-called Slichter law, see George P. Shultz, "The Massachusetts Choice-of-Procedures Approach to Emergency Disputes," *Industrial and Labor Relations Review*, X (April, 1957), 359–74.

[13] BLS Bulletin No. 1633, cited in footnote 11 above.

[14] For one such effort, see Edgar L. Warren, "Thirty-Six Years of National Emergency Strikes," *Industrial and Labor Relations Review*, V (October, 1951) 3–19. I submit that there have been no strikes since the period covered by Warren's analysis that would measure up to the kind of economic paralysis Title II language brings to mind.

[15] Donald E. Cullen, *National Emergency Strikes*, cited above in footnote 5.

"critical" to the highly restrictive definitional language of Title II. If the president or appropriate executive agency heads were authorized by Congress to deal with "critical" labor disputes in flexible, imaginative fashion, we would be taking a giant step toward effective realism. Cullen tends to favor the statutory strike approach, although he admits that it may not be politically acceptable.

As Cullen observes, the statutory strike addresses itself squarely to the three goals of an "ideal" strike control, although not meeting any one completely. These goals are "continued operation for the protection of third-party interests; an even-handed impact of government on the power relationship of labor and management; and a strong inducement for the private parties to settle their dispute by themselves."[16]

If Cullen's statements of the "ideal" are accepted, we then must consider *feasible* procedures calculated to achieve such goals. Hopefully, no extreme interventionist measures such as compulsory arbitration will gain favor. By the same token, it is unlikely that the statutory strike (or, if one prefers, the nonstoppage strike) will achieve congressional acceptance. Nor is Congress likely to enact a federal version of the Massachusetts Slichter law.

If the foregoing analysis is accurate, how can the effectiveness of the federal government's performance be improved in aiding the parties to resolve "critical" disputes over future contract terms? Here, I wish to stress once more that the most effective and feasible method of intervention continues to be skilled professional mediation. There is no magic procedural panacea for dispute resolution.

A choice-of-procedures law might be preferable to the present Title II, but such legislation does not appear to be in the cards. If we must "make do" with what we have, the emphasis should be on further professionalizing the FMCS and on training chief executives in the delicate art of timing, personal suasion and avoidance of premature White House intervention.

Simply coming out in favor of more effective mediation will be deemed inadequate because there will be disputes requiring governmental efforts *beyond* mediation. It is therefore appropriate to conclude this chapter with a brief examination of pertinent considerations in such "critical" disputes.

---

[16] *Ibid.*, p. 129. The essential attribute of a statutory or nonstoppage strike is continued operation of the enterprise, with the parties putting settlement pressures on themselves through heavy deductions from the workers' pay and the employer's income.

How to Achieve More Effective Results in "Critical" Disputes Requiring More than Straight Mediation

Whatever form governmental intervention takes beyond straight mediation should be aimed at keeping the negotiating parties on the hook. Once the intervention permits the disputants to evade their continued obligation to bargain, the proper focus has been lost, even if the particular use of economic force is ended or prevented. Employer X and Union Y must somehow be kept in stage center.

The public sector comes to mind readily because relative inexperience on both sides of the bargaining table frequently requires more than straight mediation. In many jurisdictions the law requires utilizing of fact-finding procedures when negotiation and mediation have failed to resolve the dispute. In these circumstances, should the single fact-finder or board be content to hold formal hearings in the judicial manner and then to issue substantive recommendations, staying aloof from the parties throughout the proceedings?

The burden on the fact-finder is a severe one when the dispute has already assumed critical proportions. However, the most effective approach for both the short run and the long run is to maintain regular contacts with the disputing parties and to keep them actively involved in trying to find their own solution. To put it bluntly, fact-finders should attempt to mediate solutions. The prestige and personal skills of the neutrals involved should be directed toward cutting through to the heart of the matter and keeping the parties engaged.

Some disputes lend themselves to "rational" solutions once the true factual circumstances have been highlighted and generally understood. In other cases the actual or threatened strike has nonrational or personal grounds as a root cause. In such a case, the task of the neutral in paving the way to a peaceful settlement is difficult in the extreme. Logic and total candor won't work. What may be required is skilled window-dressing and unobtrusive face-saving prior to announcing the "solution" to the dispute.

In conventional or straight mediation it is often possible to work with the disputing parties outside the glare of publicity. When the dispute has gone beyond straight mediation, however, there may be no way to avoid considerable publicity and open speculation. This complicates the neutral's task. It also creates the temptation to make fact-finding or advisory arbitration a formal hearing procedure akin to that with which we are familiar in grievance arbitration.

In my view, this temptation should be resisted. In a formal hearing pattern the disputing parties will no longer be actively responsible in the search for an acceptable, workable solution. In some cases the best strategy may be for the neutral agent or board to put public heat on the party whose intransigence is blocking a satisfactory settlement. Generally speaking, however, it is preferable to keep the "pressures" of logic and the facts on both parties.

In grievance arbitration under an existing contract the neutral is empowered to issue a final and binding award based on his best judgment as to what the contract means rather than on the "acceptability" of the award. In a future terms dispute, however, acceptability and workability are the heart of the matter. The "solution" has to be lived with for the next two to three years. Thus the best offices of neutrals should be *involving the disputing parties in the development of viable solutions.* Continuous involvement is the best insurance of ultimate acceptability and responsibility.

The burden on the neutral is greater if an injunction is in effect or a facility has been seized in order to keep production going. The level of tension and hostility will be higher in such circumstances. Whatever the difficulties may be, in some fashion the pressure must be kept on the parties themselves. They must be given constant encouragement to end the crisis through their own initiative and effort.

When talented neutrals concentrate on continued involvement of the disputants, the "critical" conflicts are likely to become less difficult. Cases of "impasse" and "deadlock" lose some of their paralyzing significance. The parties will develop confidence in their own abilities to find solutions instead of abdicating their responsibilities to the "third man." In such a fashion the use of neutrals can serve to strengthen rather than weaken collective bargaining institutions.[17]

Robert G. Howlett, chairman of the Michigan Employment Relations Commission, might take exception to some of these remarks. In Michigan, writes Howlett, representatives of public employers and unions "resent too much flexibility in the fact-finding procedure. By the time they have requested fact-finding, they expect someone who will listen to evidence, find facts, and make a recommendation."[18] He adds that Michigan staff fact-finders are instructed to play a quasi-judicial role and to mediate "only if an opportunity develops." This last phrase perhaps offers the bridge between my views and those of Howlett. In the hierarchy of dispute-resolving steps in most public sector statutes, fact-finding invariably follows mediation. It is undertaken when mediation presumably has been tried and failed. In many cases, however, the parties may be "looking ahead" (of mediation)

---

[17] See Harold W. Davey, "The Use of Neutrals in the Public Sector," *Labor Law Journal*, XX (August, 1969), 529–38.

[18] Personal correspondence from Robert G. Howlett to Harold W. Davey, November 12, 1969, commenting on the Davey article cited in note 17 above.

to the fact-finding step and thus have made no genuine effort to negotiate on their own or with the aid of the mediator. If this *is* the situation and the fact-finder then plays a quasi-judicial role, collective bargaining never takes place. The parties have been "off the hook" from the beginning as far as contributing to the solution of their own future terms crisis.

A Note on Binding Arbitration of Future Terms Disputes

Binding arbitration for resolving future terms disputes is rarely used in U.S. labor relations, even in the public sector. It is doubtful whether this type of arbitration will increase appreciably in the years ahead. However, there is a logical basis for expecting some further utilization on a voluntary basis. The available evidence suggests that the parties have no real basis for fearing the outcome.[19] If and when binding arbitration is employed, there are some prudent considerations to be noted.

Of first importance is a careful defining of the nature and scope of the issue(s) to be arbitrated. Future terms arbitration need not be open-ended in character, nor should it be. Second, the essentially political nature of the function calls for use of a tripartite board rather than a single neutral or an all-neutral board. The flanking of neutrals with "partisan" arbitrators can help to keep the parties involved, thus enhancing the possibility of achieving a mediated solution (consent award). Future terms arbitration will necessarily be more formal than most other types of neutral intervention. Even when arm's-length formality may prove to be a necessity, the partisan members of the arbitration board can be of value in "selling" the award.

Public Sector Strikes: A Special Case?

Much of the literature on public sector bargaining appears morbidly preoccupied with how to resolve impasses and prevent strikes.[20] The prevailing sentiment remains negative on granting government employees at any level the right to use economic force as an ultimate means of resolving future terms disputes. Federal employees have been denied this right since 1947 (Taft-Hartley Act). The bumper crop of state laws in recent years on

---

[19] Richard Miller's findings support this conclusion. See his article cited above in footnote 6.

[20] One noteworthy exception is Kurt L. Hanslowe. He has done an excellent job of summarizing the basic issues. See *The Emerging Law of Labor Relations in Public Employment*, ILR Paperback No. 4. (Ithaca, N.Y.: New York State School of Industrial and Labor Relations, 1967).

public employee bargaining exhibits an astonishing variety of policies and procedures in most respects. However, only two of some twenty-five state public sector laws, those of Hawaii and Pennsylvania, provide for the strike option after exhaustion of dispute settlement procedures. About half the states still have no special legislation on public sector labor relations. In such jurisdictions the courts follow common law concepts of sovereignty and grant injunctive relief to any government employer, state or local, faced with an employee work stoppage.

Among government employees and the unions or associations who represent them there is a division of opinion as to the propriety of using the strike as a bargaining instrument. Some oppose use of the strike whereas others insist that government employees will continue to be second-class citizens until they achieve the same rights as their counterparts in the private sector, including the right to use the strike if and when necessary.

Government unionists who oppose use of the strike do not believe they are thereby giving up the possibility of meaningful collective bargaining. They point to the rapid growth of unionization and bargaining in the public sector since January, 1962, when President John F. Kennedy issue Executive Order 10988. The impact of E.O. 10988 was substantial on state and local government workers as well as on federal employees. Government employee unionization in recent years has been advancing at the rate of about 1,000 new members per day.[21] The unavailability of the strike has not been a significant source of discouragement to workers who have made up their minds to be represented by a union or association for collective bargaining purposes. How the strike ban may have affected negotiated terms is an impossible question to answer.

The strong general sentiment against use of the strike by government employees has stimulated considerable creativity in developing alternative procedures for resolution of future terms disputes, especially at the state and local level. There is widespread recognition and acceptance of the viewpoint that "bargaining to finality" in the private sector sense of the strike as a "continuation of bargaining by other methods" is simply not feasible in most public sector labor disputes.

Yet all but the most naive realize that strikes cannot be eliminated simply by making them illegal. Nor can we be confident that even the most carefully structured set of alternative mechanisms for dispute resolution will succeed in all cases in avoiding strikes by government employees. The most that we can hope for is that government agencies and the unions or associations representing their employees will learn quickly the superior wisdom of joint problem-solving, a theme to be developed presently.

---

[21] This estimate is that of Howard Anderson, senior editor of The Bureau of National Affairs, whose *Public Employee Organization and Bargaining* (Washington, D.C.: Bureau of National Affairs, Inc., 1968) is an excellent study.

No one is neutral on the issue of whether government employees should have the right to strike and the companion question of whether it is possible to distinguish between critical and noncritical occupations in this connection. For many the compelling folklore of sovereignty maintains a powerful bias against legitimizing the strike weapon for public employees. This bias admittedly affects my thinking to a considerable extent. Yet I am convinced that the incidence of strikes among government employees is *not* essentially determined by whether the law in question prohibits or permits strikes. The amount of strike activity is going to be determined mainly by *how professional a job the bargainers do*, assisted where necessary by competent neutrals.

Sweeping legal prohibition of the strike with harsh penalties for violation is not a salutary approach. Such legislation tends to concentrate attention on the negative instead of the positive side of labor relations. Although it is too early to make judgments with confidence, my view currently favors the Hawaii-Pennsylvania approach.

Although I hold to the conventional view that policemen and firemen should never strike, it is impossible for me as a professional student of labor relations to draw an equitable dividing line between critical or essential occupations and those which are not. Most discussions on this issue seem to me to arrive at a dead end. The realistic outcome of attempting a division is that those employees who could benefit from strike activity would not be allowed to do so, whereas those with little or no bargaining power could strike as they please. Such a result is neither fair nor equitable and would satisfy no one. Such dividing lines are at best hard to draw and probably should not be drawn. Even so there are a few of such an obviously critical nature that the sentiments against striking are overwhelming. This factor should give pause to responsible employee groups in these categories. To illustrate, my list includes policemen, firemen, garbage collectors (in the summertime), rapid transit workers in large urban centers, light and gas workers, hospital nurses and perhaps a few other categories. I would *not* include teachers on my "critical" list.

Conclusion: Accentuating the Positive

We have already noted the excessive preoccupation with the strike issue in both the private and the public sector. Although such a preoccupation may be understandable in terms of the assumed political realities, I should like to conclude this chapter on a positive note. I believe we should be emphasizing *how to make collective bargaining work better* in both private and public sectors. In the public sector in particular we must observe the following imperatives: (1) need for trained negotiators on both sides; (2) need for an effective state mediation service; (3) need to avoid use of neutrals whenever possible and (4) development of an attitude that equates effective bargaining with reaching joint solutions to future terms disputes instead of building up to impasse situations.

Eva Robins, one of the best of the professional mediators, has been perceptively critical of the ways in which government agencies and unions have misused the procedures established for neutral assistance in dispute settlement.[22] Miss Robins notes that in some cases the parties have viewed both negotiations and mediation "merely as necessary steps to fact-finding," thus arriving at the fact-finding step without prior agreement on any of the union's or the agency's proposals. She properly warns that such tactics, if continued, will destroy the collective bargaining concept.

There is no need for public sector labor relations to experience the turbulent and hostile record of private sector bargaining in the 1930s. It should be possible to counter and to avoid the stereotyped attitudes that led to many private sector conflict situations. It also should not be too hard to appreciate that *one learns to bargain by bargaining* rather than by constant reliance on neutral assistance.

The welfare of public sector labor relations demands that the emphasis be a positive one. The sought objective should be to become as professional as possible as quickly as possible in the demanding tasks of both contract negotiation and contract administration. Success will not come overnight, but the alternatives to learning how to bargain constructively are not attractive. As government agencies and unions develop the habit of bargaining to finality on future terms and of professionalizing their contract administration, the current overriding concern with strikes and strike penalties should fall into proper perspective. It should not be a serious problem. The answer to strikes does not lie in harsh and punitive legislation. Enduring solutions can only be found through mature joint involvement of the parties.

SELECTED BIBLIOGRAPHY

AARON, BENJAMIN, "Observations on the United States Experience with Public Interest Disputes," *Labor Law Journal*, XIV (August, 1963), 746–52.

BERNSTEIN, IRVING, HAROLD L. ENARSON AND R. W. FLEMING, eds., *Emergency Disputes and National Policy*. New York: Harper & Row, Publishers, 1955.

BLACKMAN, JOHN L., JR., *Presidential Seizure in Labor Disputes*. Cambridge, Mass.: Harvard University Press, 1967.

---

[22] Eva Robins, "Penalties in Strikes Against a Public Employer," mimeographed (A paper delivered on June 11, 1969, at the New York University 22nd Annual Conference on Labor), p. 25. Miss Robins' analysis is broader than the paper's title suggests. It should be required reading for all students and practitioners of public sector labor relations.

BOULDING, KENNETH E., "Is There a General Theory of Conflict?" *Industrial Relations Research Association Proceedings* (Spring, 1967). Madison, Wis.: Industrial Relations Research Association, 1967, 4–11.

CHAMBERLAIN, NEIL W., "Strikes in Contemporary Context," *Industrial and Labor Relations Review*, XX (July, 1967), 602–16.

COLE, DAVID, *The Quest for Industrial Peace*. New York: McGraw-Hill Book Company, Inc., 1963.

CULLEN, DONALD E., *National Emergency Strikes*. Ithaca, N.Y.: New York State School of Industrial and Labor Relations, 1968.

CUSHMAN, BERNARD, "Voluntary Arbitration of New Contract Terms: A Forum in Search of a Dispute," *Labor Law Journal*, XVI (December, 1965), 765–77.

EPSTEIN, DAVID G., "Impasse in Collective Bargaining," *Texas Law Review*, XLIV (March, 1966), 769–84.

FELDESMAN, WILLIAM, "Another Approach to Strikes: Inducements to Voluntary Arbitration," *George Washington Law Review*, XXXIII (December, 1965), 457–66.

FOEGEN, J. H., "A Qualified Right to Strike in the Public Interest," *Labor Law Journal*, XVIII (February, 1967), 90–102.

GOODWIN, BERNARD, AND PAUL P. HARBRECHT, "Strikes: Trial by Battle or Due Process," *Journal of Urban Law*, XLIV (Fall, 1966), 25–38.

HANSLOWE, KURT L., *The Emerging Law of Labor Relations in Public Employment*. Ithaca, N.Y.: New York State School of Industrial and Labor Relations, 1967.

HUTCHINSON, JOHN G., *Management under Strike Conditions*. New York: Holt, Rinehart and Winston, Inc., 1966.

KAUFMAN, JACOB J., "The Railroad Labor Dispute: A Marathon of Maneuver and Improvisation," *Industrial and Labor Relations Review*, XVIII (January, 1965), 196–212.

KELTNER, JOHN W., "The United States Federal Mediation and Conciliation Service: Catalyst to Collective Bargaining," *International Labor Review*, LXXXVIII (November, 1963), 476–89.

LAW NOTE, "Interest-Balancing and the Use of Economic Weapons in Labor Disputes: A New Look at Management's Arsenal," *Rutgers Law Review*, XX (Fall, 1965), 102–22.

LAW NOTE, "Labor Lockouts: New Weapon in Management's Bargaining Arsenal," *Northwestern University Law Review*, LX (November–December, 1965), 689–714.

MARSHALL, ANTHONY P., "New Perspectives on National Emergency Disputes," *Labor Law Journal*, XVIII (August, 1967), 451–59.

MARSHALL, HOWARD D., AND NATALIE J. MARSHALL, "Nonstoppage Strike Proposals —A Critique," *Labor Law Journal*, VII (May, 1956), 299–304.

MCKELVEY, JEAN T., "Fact-Finding in Public Employment Disputes: Promise or Illusion?" *Industrial and Labor Relations Review*, XXII (July, 1969), 528–43.

MCLAUGHLIN, RICHARD P., "Collective Bargaining Suggestions for the Public Sector," *Labor Law Journal*, XX (March, 1969), 131–37.

MCLENNAN, KENNETH, "The New York Transit Strike: Misconceptions about Bargaining Power," *Management of Personnel Quarterly*, V (Summer, 1966), 25–33.

MILLER, RICHARD U., "The Arbitration of Disputes over Reopened Wages," *Arbitration Journal*, XXII, No. 1 (1967), 24–30.

MORAN, R. D., "State Subsidized Arbitration—The Massachusetts Experience," *Labor Law Journal*, XIX (October, 1968), 628–39.

NORTHRUP, HERBERT R., *Compulsory Arbitration and Government Intervention in Labor*

Disputes. An Analysis of Experience. Washington, D.C.: Labor Policy Association, 1966.

NORTHRUP, HERBERT R., "Fact-Finding in Labor Disputes: The States' Experience," *Industrial and Labor Relations Review*, XVII (October, 1963), 114–34.

NORTHRUP, HERBERT R., AND HARVEY A. YOUNG, "The Causes of Industrial Peace Revisited," *Industrial and Labor Relations Review*, XXII (October, 1968), 31–47.

PHELPS, ORME W., "Compulsory Arbitration: Some Perspectives," *Industrial and Labor Relations Review*, XVIII (October, 1964), 81–91.

ROBERTS, HAROLD S., *Compulsory Arbitration: Panacea or Millstone?* Honolulu, Hawaii: Industrial Relations Center, 1965.

ROSS, ARTHUR, *Changing Patterns of Industrial Conflict.* New York: John Wiley & Sons, Inc., 1960.

SHULTZ, GEORGE P., "Massachusetts Choice of Procedures Approach to Emergency Disputes," *Industrial and Labor Relations Review*, X (April, 1957), 359–74.

SHUTKIN, J. J., "Preventative Arbitration—A Path to Perpetual Labor Peace and Prosperity," *Labor Law Journal*, XIX (September, 1968), 539–43.

SLOANE, ARTHUR A., "National Emergency Labor Disputes: The Need for a Presidential Buffer Zone," *Personnel Journal*, XLVI (December, 1967), 703–9.

SLOANE, ARTHUR A., "Presidential Boards of Inquiry in National Emergency Disputes: An Assessment after 20 Years of Performance," *Labor Law Journal*, XVIII (November, 1967), 665–75.

SOSNICK, STEPHEN H., "Non-Stoppage Strikes: A New Approach," *Industrial and Labor Relations Review*, XVIII (October, 1964), 73–80.

STEVENS, CARL M., "The Analytics of Voluntary Arbitration: Contract Disputes," *Industrial Relations*, VII (October, 1967), 68–79.

STEVENS, CARL M., "Is Compulsory Arbitration Compatible with Bargaining?" *Industrial Relations*, V (February, 1966), 38–52.

WILSON, BERNARD, "Critical Disputes: Compulsory Arbitration vs. Bargaining," *Canadian Personnel and Industrial Relations Journal*, XIV (November, 1967), 38–43.

JOB SECURITY
industrial jurisprudence revisited

CHAPTER NINE

Job security has many faces. We shall examine such familiar aspects as seniority and protection against arbitrary discipline. We shall also consider both old and relatively new approaches to the perennial problem of adjusting to technological change.

The challenge to the bargainers is often a complex one. Employee job security requirements need to be related to a constantly changing work environment. Job content changes. Work locations and job assignments may need to be shifted frequently in response to management needs. The structure and location of the employer's operations can change in dramatic fashion. All these developments have a direct impact on the job security objectives of unions in collective bargaining. So do such federal laws as the Civil Rights Act of 1964 and the Manpower Development and Training Act of 1962, as amended in subsequent years. In short, job security as a policy objective is never a simple or a one-time thing. The problem concerns a complex, ever-changing set of multipurpose targets. Achieving mutually satisfactory, workable contract provisions is thus a demanding task for both management and union representatives.

CONTROL OF JOB OPPORTUNITIES THROUGH COLLECTIVE BARGAINING

In his pioneering theory of the labor movement, Selig Perlman stressed the job-consciousness of American unions.[1] Union policy was guided by an underlying assumption of job scarcity. The goal was to conserve such limited job opportunities for the membership. Perlman wrote at a time when craft unionism was the dominant structural form. However, his thesis as to the primacy of job control in union thinking can be transferred legitimately to industrial unionism, which has long since proved its durability. It is abundantly clear that industrial unions in their fashion are just as job-conscious as craft unions. Union efforts to conserve job opportunities are concentrated on controlling one end of the employment process or the other. Craft unions generally seek to control the supply of labor and thus limit employer discretion in hiring. The industrial union seeks to negotiate a variety of on-the-job conditions that promote employee security and protect against arbitrary discipline or layoff. It is neither necessary nor feasible for a union to condition or limit the employer's discretion at both ends.

Both craft and industrial union approaches to the job security problem are considered in this chapter. The basic objective must be to reach an accommodation between the employer's interest in maintaining an efficient operation and the worker's interest in job security. Such an accommodation is often hard to achieve, especially when fairly rapid changes in the structure and composition of available jobs are required.

The analysis is conditioned by two basic propositions, stated in Chapter 1.[2] Honoring the two together can provide a basis for short-run conflict. These propositions are repeated for ready reference as follows:

1. Management must retain freedom to innovate in terms of technology, structure of industrial operations and location of plants, involving the shutting down of obsolete installations and the construction of optimal size units.
2. Employees are entitled to contractual protection of bargaining unit work opportunities to the maximum extent consistent with point 1 above and to negotiated provisions for cushioning the impact of either technological

---

[1] Selig Perlman, *A Theory of the Labor Movement*, (New York: The Macmillan Company, 1928).

[2] See Chapter 1, p. 10.

displacement or loss of employment due to plant closures and/or removal to a different location.

Job Security and Industrial Jurisprudence

A useful way to position the job security problem in its proper context is to do so in terms of "industrial jurisprudence," a term introduced in 1941 by the late Sumner H. Slichter.[3] In Slichter's usage, "industrial jurisprudence" embraced many nonwage aspects of collective bargaining, including (1) control of entrance to the trade, (2) seniority as a vehicle for regulating layoffs, promotions and transfers, (3) negotiated controls on worker output and job assignments and (4) negotiated provisions concerning methods of wage payment. Also embraced by Slichter's conception was the basic problem of utilizing collective bargaining as a vehicle for adjusting to the impact of technological change.

Finally, and perhaps of greatest importance, Slichter contemplated "industrial jurisprudence" as using collective bargaining to protect employees against arbitrary discipline or treatment on the job.

In company with most if not all students of labor relations, I consider the function of collective bargaining in establishing a system of industrial jurisprudence as of greater meaning and value to the individual employee than the more familiar function of negotiating the price of labor and various economic fringe benefits.

The individual worker is always concerned about the size of his pay envelope. However, he has a keen interest in being protected against arbitrary discipline or treatment. He wants his union to protect his job security to the fullest possible extent. Many workers may not recognize the term "industrial jurisprudence," but they are nevertheless insistent that their union succeed in achieving the twin objectives of such a system: job security and protection against arbitrary treatment.

Essential Elements of Effective Industrial Jurisprudence

The key concepts in an effective system of industrial jurisprudence are: (1) uniformity, (2) consistency, (3) fairness and (4) predictability. The basic aim of the negotiators is to fashion policies and procedures governing

---

[3] Sumner H. Slichter, *Union Policies and Industrial Management* (Washington, D.C.: The Brookings Institution, 1941). Slichter's analysis retains an essential modernity that makes it of continuing value. An expanded treatment, based on extensive field research, was undertaken (with the help of Harvard associates) as Professor Slichter's last major project before his death in 1959. See Sumner H. Slichter, James J. Healy and E. Robert Livernash, *The Impact of Collective Bargaining on Management* (Washington, D.C.: The Brookings Institution, 1960).

on-the-job relationships so that each employee covered by the contract will know exactly where he stands in relation to his fellow employees. He will also have assurance in the knowledge that he will be treated in the same manner as all other employees in like circumstances. In short, the essence of industrial jurisprudence lies in uniform written policies and procedures, applied in a consistent, nondiscriminatory fashion.

To put it another way, under an effective system of industrial jurisprudence the contract provides intelligible, consistent rules of the game on such matters as employee discipline, layoffs, recalls, promotions, transfers, distribution of overtime opportunities, methods of wage payment and so on. For each subject covered there is one policy only. The antithesis of industrial jurisprudence would be two (or more) standards on the same subject. Contract ambiguity and uncertainty are foreign to the spirit of industrial jurisprudence.

THE DISCIPLINE FUNCTION AND INDUSTRIAL JURISPRUDENCE

The classic illustration of industrial jurisprudence in action concerns the exercise of the managerial right to discipline employees in accordance with principles and procedures spelled out in the contract. Guarantees of fair treatment by supervision and protection against arbitrary managerial action are basic to the concept of democratized industrial relations.

The right to fire (or to administer lesser penalties in the form of a disciplinary layoff or written warning) is traditionally a management prerogative. It should remain so. Most collective agreements recognize this, although a few require union consent to disciplinary action. However, exercise of the disciplinary prerogative is manifestly one that must be subject to check and challenge if employee rights and personal dignity are to have meaning. Prior to unionization, discharged workers had no effective recourse from arbitrary action by line foremen or top supervision. The need to insure against such wrongful exercise of the discipline function has been in many instances more compelling as a motive for unionization than purely economic factors.

Most collective agreements limit management's right to discipline. A common requirement is that the discipline must be only for "cause" or for "good and just cause." In some contracts an effort is made to spell out the various offenses calling for discipline and to distinguish between the more serious ones calling for immediate discharge and lesser violations calling for disciplinary layoff or warning. Most contracts, however, state the general principle governing all discipline matters, leaving application on a case-by-case basis. This approach is preferable because it recognizes the fact that no two disciplinary cases are alike. No two sets of facts are identical any more than any two individuals are the same or likely to behave in the same fashion.

Another variable is that the severity of a particular offense often depends on the circumstances. For example, smoking on the job calls for immediate discharge in a chemical plant or an oil refinery. It may be only a minor offense in a plant where there is no appreciable danger from fire or explosion. Certain types of employee conduct are regarded as proper grounds for discharge in almost all situations the first time they occur. These include such breaches of conduct as fighting on the job, reporting drunk on the job, stealing company property, malicious destruction of company property, direct insubordination to supervision, instigating a wildcat strike and so on. On the other hand, discharge for such offenses as chronic absenteeism, unsatisfactory work performance or persistent inability to meet accepted production norms should be preceded by cumulative corrective discipline with clear notice that discharge will be the ultimate consequence of failure to improve performance.

Fair treatment by supervision is one factor that shows up high on any worker's listing of the requisites of a "good job." Since it seems to be human nature to blame others for one's own shortcomings, many management disciplinary actions are protested by workers who assert that they are "not guilty" of the offense with which they are charged or who consider the penalty to be excessively harsh. No worker likes to have a disciplinary penalty on his personnel record. It may jeopardize his chances for advancement. Also, if he is discharged, it is hard to find other employment even in a fairly tight labor market. For these reasons, discipline grievances will make up a substantial part of the case load. Typically, about one out of four arbitration cases involves a discipline issue.[4]

Discipline grievances are troublesome and often explosive. However, any employer and union should be able to develop policies and procedures that will safeguard management's interest in maintaining an efficient and orderly establishment and the union's interest in insuring that no worker is disciplined arbitrarily or without cause.

From time to time complaints are heard that under union contracts employers have been deprived of their power to discipline workers. Some employers are allegedly afraid to discharge employees because they fear they might incur reprisals, such as a wildcat protest stoppage. If such an unfortunate condition exists in any enterprise, the blame can fairly be placed on management's doorstep for not exercising its contractual right to discipline,

---

[4] This estimate is that of Joseph S. Murphy, vice-president of the American Arbitration Association. Reliable figures are hard to come by and estimates will vary somewhat. However, it is beyond any question that discipline and discharge issues rank at the top of the list as the most common type of issue submitted to arbitration.

including discharge, for "good and just cause." There is no valid reason why a good faith employer should abstain from disciplining employees in a fair and nondiscriminatory manner.

Of course, the employer must be prepared to prove that he had good cause to discipline. Some local union leaders will not press a grievance over discipline to arbitration if the employer's evidence and/or their investigation of the case satisfies them that the employee merited the discipline imposed. Others, however, will carry most, if not all, discharge cases to arbitration, even where they may think the employer has a good case. Their reasoning presumably is that a discharged employee is always entitled to full contractual due process. I can understand this viewpoint, but I do not agree with it. I believe the union has a responsibility to screen out grievances that lack contractual merit. Discipline and discharge cases should not be an exception to this responsibility.

In any event, any employer who for any reason "gives up" on disciplining employees has only himself to blame for results which are bound to be unfortunate.

DIFFICULT TYPES OF DISCHARGE CASES

Possibly the most troublesome type of discharge case is one where management concludes that the employee's performance has been so unsatisfactory as to require firing. Discharge for this reason is often resisted strenuously, especially when alternative employment opportunities are scarce. The union contends typically that management had ample opportunity to gauge the employee during his probation period. Once past this period, with seniority acquired, in the union view the worker has developed an equity in his job akin to a property right. Discharge should never be warranted except in the most extreme circumstances after failure to heed repeated warnings.

One can agree in principle that discharge, as the ultimate disciplinary sanction, should be resorted to only when all efforts to rehabilitate the deficient employee have proved unsuccessful. At the same time the employer must retain freedom to insure and maintain an efficient operation. In matters of discipline and discharge the employer's prerogative to take action for "just cause" must be preserved.

Subject to reasonable standards sufficient to protect workers who are doing a conscientious but uninspired job, management should always be able to discharge chronically inefficient, lazy or indifferent employees. When the reason for unsatisfactory performance is that the task is beyond the employee's abilities, he should be transferred to a less taxing assignment. This alternative is certainly preferable to discharge since discharge must be considered an admission of failure from a personnel standpoint.

The optimal approach requires searching out the root causes for poor performance and then removing these causes. When the unsatisfactory performance of the employee is shown to be a product of poor mental attitude, personal troubles outside the shop or physical or mental deficiencies, responsible employers will make an effort through counseling to correct the condition. Discharging for poor performance has the effect of passing on the problem to another employer or to the community.

In arbitration of discipline cases two basic issues usually arise. First, did the company prove cause for the discipline? Second, did the punishment imposed fit the crime? A union will invariably challenge management discipline if it feels that the answer to either of these questions is negative.

IMPORTANCE OF SOUND PROCEDURES IN DISCIPLINE CASES

An effective system of discipline requires the development of a uniform procedure for handling any and all cases where the employer believes that discipline or discharge is required. If the same procedure is used in each case, all employees know that they will be treated similarly both as to due process and as to penalties. Such knowledge is important in preventing misunderstanding and reducing hostilities.

It is essential in any disciplinary investigation to discover the facts in the case at the earliest possible time before memories can fade. One effective technique is to provide for a disciplinary action hearing within twenty-four hours after the incident that led to discipline. At such a hearing the charged employee can state his case and call witnesses on his behalf. The supervisor calling for the discipline presents his evidence. Such an internal hearing is usually conducted by the head of the employer's labor relations department. The employee is represented by his union steward or the chairman of the local union's grievance committee. Written minutes are usually kept.

Under such a procedure, the *formal* decision on disciplinary action is made after this hearing. Up to this point, the employee is under suspension. He can be regarded in a sense as being under indictment by his supervisor. In some cases, the disciplinary action hearing record reveals that the employee was not at fault and no action against him is taken. Where management believes the evidence warrants discipline, the employee and his union representative are notified as to the reason for and content of the discipline. The employee and his union are then free to grieve the company's action as having been taken without just cause.

A procedure similar to the one described above has been in use for many years at John Deere plants where production and maintenance employees are represented by the UAW.[5] In the Deere-UAW relationship discipline and discharge cases typically constitute only 10 to 15 percent of the grievances appealed to the arbitration step. This percentage is significantly lower than the estimated national average of one out of every four cases. It is my view that the prompt internal hearing in such cases before imposition of formal discipline is an important factor in explaining the comparatively low incidence of discipline issues reaching arbitration.

DISADVANTAGED WORKERS: SPECIAL DISCIPLINE PROBLEMS

In recent years many employers, with union knowledge and approval, have undertaken to hire and train varying numbers of disadvantaged workers or so-called hard-core unemployed. Such efforts have produced some difficult problems in contract administration. One of the more troublesome arises in the discipline area. How can an employer and a union satisfy the requirements of industrial jurisprudence, outlined above, while still making realistic allowance for the special characteristics of the new recruits that may necessitate differential treatment (double standard?) for some period of time? This critical question will be treated briefly.

The term "hard-core unemployed" is an unfortunate one and will be dropped henceforth in favor of the term "disadvantaged worker." We are referring in some cases to individuals who have been unemployed for long periods of time and in other cases to those who seek to enter the labor force for the first time. In many cases these individuals have no marketable skills. Some have never been employed. Many are black or, more accurately, nonwhite, since Mexican-Americans, American Indians and Puerto Ricans are frequently affected. Our summary profile of the disadvantaged shows many to be males and females aged sixteen to twenty who have dropped out of the educational system.

The most difficult dimension of the disadvantaged employee is a psychological one related to the characteristics just noted. If a prospective employee is black, young and unskilled, he frequently will have "hang-ups" or behavior patterns that make the adjustment to work difficult. Learning how to fit into the work environment is hard for the new worker, for his supervisors and for his fellow employees. Incumbent employees may hold antagonisms toward the new recruit. The latter in turn may regard the "regular" employees as "square" or as racist.

---

[5] I served as permanent arbitrator for John Deere and UAW for approximately six years, 1952–1958. This experience caused me to develop a high regard for the disciplinary action hearing as an administrative procedure. My understanding is that such hearings continue to play an important role in Deere-UAW contract administration.

A NOTE ON TEMPORARY NEGOTIATED DOUBLE STANDARDS

Employers and unions continue to cope in various ways with the difficulties inherent in the employment of the disadvantaged. One contractual approach utilized in agreements between the Communication Workers of America and employers participating in the National Alliance of Businessmen Jobs Program (NAB) provides in effect for a year's grace for the disadvantaged or underqualified employees. In a written memorandum of understanding, the employer and union recognize that the NAB hiring program will include persons who may not meet the employer's normal hiring standards. The memorandum contemplates that such employees "will be given special and exceptional consideration during the early period of their employment."

Extensive quoting from one such memorandum is desirable as a means of illustrating the joint effort of employer and union to cope with the special characteristics of the new hires while also recognizing the wisdom of avoiding a dual standard of treatment for a long period of time. The agreement used for illustration is a 1969 memorandum of understanding between The Chesapeake and Potomac Telephone Company of Virginia and the Communications Workers of America (CWA).[6] The employer is participating in two types of programs initiated by NAB, one for full-time hiring into a Basic Jobs Program and the other for summertime employment of young people. The policy and procedure sections of this memorandum read as follows:

> The program is intended to include persons who may be unable to meet the Company's normal hiring standards, and contemplates that such employees will be given special and exceptional consideration during the early period of their employment.
>
> The Company and the Union have mutually recognized that participation in such a program will require that exceptions to normal, established, and still existent practices, methods, standards, and agreements, such as those referred to herein, be made in the employment and working conditions for a limited period of time and for a limited number of special trainee employees who may be hired on a probationary basis in connection with the program.
>
> In order to do their fair share, the Company and the Union have

---

[6] Agreements of this type were first called to my attention by a management representative at an American Arbitration Association seminar. Further information about the nature and prevalence of such agreements can be obtained from either the National Alliance of Businessmen or from the AFL-CIO's Human Resources Development Institute, the Federation's "manpower arm." George E. Gill, executive vice president of CWA, advised the writer by letter on April 16, 1970, that the CWA had nine such special agreements currently in effect.

agreed to participate in this program and to look upon such exceptions as may be made for the special trainees from normal and established practices, methods, standards, and agreements, including contract provisions, as "social contributions" which are being made by them in order to help solve a social problem considered by both the Company and the Union to be of paramount importance to the welfare of the urban communities in which the NAB program has been or may be established.

The Company and the Union agree to work closely together to assure the success of the program and to keep each other currently advised of developments in the program.

It has been mutually agreed by the Company and the Union that persons hired under the program and who are assigned to job classifications within the scope of the bargaining unit will be eligible for Union membership. In connection with this program and within the limitations later outlined, it also is agreed that the Company may make exceptions from normal, established and still existent practices, methods, standards, and agreements in such employment and working conditions as those that relate to the training, tutoring, coaching, guiding, assigning, transferring, retaining, disciplining, and dismissing of such special trainee employees. The Company is supported and joined by the Union in this "social contribution," and the Union agrees that it will use no exception applied to any special trainee employee hired in connection with this program as a claim of contract violation or as establishing or tending to establish a precedent which should be applied to any other employee not hired under this program on any such exception that may be made for a special trainee.

This agreement is subject to the following limitations:

1. The agreement may be cancelled by either party at any time upon thirty (30) days' written notice to the other party, but such cancellation will not apply to employees already hired under the program.

2. The Company will not establish any additional exceptions, as referred to above, for any special trainee hired under this program beyond a probationary period not to exceed one year of service. In other words, not later than one year after employment, such special trainee employee from that date will be treated in all respects as other employees not in the special trainee program.

3. The Company will maintain records that will clearly identify the special trainee employees and will indicate the probationary period and other significant information for each such employee.

4. The Company will notify the Union when each such special trainee employee is hired and also when each such employee is removed from the special trainee status.

5. It is contemplated by both parties that participation in this program will be limited to the hiring of a number of employees from the program somewhat corresponding to the fair-share responsibility of the Company as based on the approximate quantitative relationship of all its employees to the total number of all persons employed in a given locality or area, subject to further discussion and agreement between the parties.

The Company and the Union understand that this program, including the requirement for making the type of exceptions to usual employment, training and work performance standards, as set forth above, is being carried on under the cognizance of the United States Department of

Labor. Because both the Company and the Union are making this "social contribution" in good faith and in a sincere effort to help solve a pressing social problem, and because they believe that responsibility for helping to solve this problem is inherently shared by all employers and all unions in the area and that a few should not be expected to carry out the responsibility of all, they agree that they will endeavor to urge other employers and other unions in the area to cooperate similarly in fulfilling their fair-share responsibility in this program.

CONTRACT ADMINISTRATION OF CASES INVOLVING DISADVANTAGED EMPLOYEES

Hopefully, the experience under such specially negotiated temporary double standards will be worthwhile and comparatively trouble free. Also, one hopes that research of a participant-observer type is being carried on in connection with such programs. Such experiments in assimilation can work well when the difficulties are faced candidly by both the employer and the union as they are in the quoted memorandum. Difficult and troublesome cases will arise, however, even under the best of conditions. Some will find their way to the arbitration hearing room. It is logical to expect a high incidence of grievances from disadvantaged new employees who may be disciplined by the employer *after* the probationary year has ended and the employees have been removed from their special trainee status.

One type of case might arise from a claim by a former special trainee that he was discriminatorily disciplined by the employer after the expiration of his special trainee status. Cases could also arise from "regular" employees contending that they were disciplined more harshly than former special trainees for the same offenses and were therefore subjected to unequal treatment.

The first type of case will probably raise an issue as to whether the discipline was racially motivated. The second type of case illustrates the difficulties in making the transition from a special circumstance double standard to the long-run single standard required by the concepts of industrial jurisprudence.

Some cases will arrive in arbitration no matter how intense a joint effort may have been made to avoid and prevent discrimination against the former special trainees either by supervision or by "regular" employees. When there has been in fact no discrimination, the case may still be pushed by the grievant, who is likely to be oversensitive on such matters. The union may appeal to arbitration because it wishes to avoid a charge that it is not performing its statutory duty of fair representation. Arbitrators will be ruling on some touchy, difficult factual situations, where serious conflicts of testimony and issues as to credibility are likely to arise.

The Stance of Arbitrators:
Single or Double Standard?

Arbitrators should not be making their decisions on such cases in terms of a double standard unless they are sitting on a case arising under a special-treatment proviso of the type quoted earlier. The contract is still the arbitrator's only proper guide. When the grievant is a *former* special trainee he comes under the system of industrial jurisprudence applying to "regular" bargaining unit employees. The arbitrator's decision-making criteria must remain those he would use in any "normal" case.

The problems under discussion will plague employers and unions alike for some time to come. Much can be learned from early experience with the negotiated temporary double standards of treatment. The intensity and the dimensions of the problem will vary greatly from one employment relationship to another. Although it is dangerous to be dogmatic on policy at this stage, two general points can be made in conclusion:

1. When special employment and training programs are undertaken for disadvantaged employees, a negotiated agreement is essential covering the policies, procedures and time horizon of these programs.

2. The negotiated agreement should make clear that the special trainee ceases to be special in any way once he or she is retained beyond the terminal date of special status. The new employee then becomes subject to the contract in the same way and to the same degree as any other employee. Adjustment of grievances filed by former special trainees must follow whatever may be the single standard of consistent and equitable treatment prescribed by the "regular contract."

If assimilation has been successful, there *should be* no higher incidence of problems arising among the former special trainees than among the so-called regular employees. Realistically, however, a considerable number of cases involving charges of discriminatory treatment can be anticipated.

Discharge Cases Raising the Racial
Discrimination Issue

The discussion of contractual problems posed by employment of the disadvantaged requires noting a related problem of comparatively recent vintage and broader scope. I refer to cases of discipline or discharge involving a black or a nonwhite where the grievant sincerely believes that his discipline was motivated by racist considerations and was thus a violation of the contract's no-discrimination clause.[7]

Cases of this type often go to arbitration because the union seeks to avoid the charge that it is failing in its duty of fair representation. If the evidence fails to substantiate the discrimination charge and establishes that the grievant was disciplined for "just cause," the grievance will properly be denied by the arbitrator. When this happens, however, the employer may feel vindicated but the grievant and his fellow blacks may view the award as an example of "white justice." The union will get small credit for having carried the matter to arbitration and may be criticized for not having done a proper job of case preparation and presentation.

Turning the tables around, if the arbitrator finds discriminatory intent to have been the actuating factor and rule for the grievant, the employer who denied racist motivations will doubtless be outraged by the award and may charge the arbitrator with using a double standard to reach his decision.

The above possibilities are realistic rather than hypothetical, although they are not based on actual cases. In work environments characterized by racial tension and suspicion such cases will continue to arise. There is no easy or painless end to such problems. Real or fancied racial discrimination is not new in labor relations, but the current level of intensity is greater in some bargaining relationships. In some quarters black arbitrators are being asked for on all cases involving black grievants. Fortunately or unfortunately, the supply cannot match the demand. Most black grievants must take their chances with white justice.

Urgency of Maintaining Industrial Jurisprudence

There is no need to begin a search for new principles or procedures in discrimination cases. The principles and procedures of industrial jurisprudence outlined in preceding pages remain completely valid. The worst

---

[7] The treatment of the problem here is necessarily brief. For a thorough review and analysis, including the advocacy of alternative forums for handling racial discrimination cases, see William B. Gould, "Labor Arbitration of Grievances Involving Racial Discrimination," *The Arbitration Journal*, XXIV (Fall, 1969), 197–227. Professor Gould doubts that black workers can obtain justice where employers and unions select the arbitrator. In his view we must devise "special procedures for racial problems—particularly in the case of black workers," (p. 227). At this point I find myself in disagreement with Professor Gould, but I believe the reader will find his persuasively reasoned and documented analysis to be of great interest and value.

The literature on the multiple problems of black workers in reference to unionism and collective bargaining has become extensive in recent years. It is recommended that the reader consult the references cited in *Black Workers and the Unions*, Selected References No. 152, (Princeton, N.J.: Princeton University Industrial Relations Section, May, 1970).

thing that could happen would be to depart from industrial jurisprudence norms in favor of some naively contrived double standard. There is no room for a double standard in contract administration of discipline cases, including the appellate stage of grievance arbitration. The sole legitimate exception would be a negotiated special standard with carefully articulated goals and time limits.

In the sections to follow we shall consider industrial jurisprudence as reflected in two other major components of employee job security, that is, seniority as a contractual control mechanism and the role of collective bargaining in adjusting to the impact of technological change.

Seniority as a Mechanism
for Control over Job Opportunities

In many collective labor agreements the seniority article is the longest and most detailed, running as many as ten to twenty printed pages. In other contracts seniority may occupy only a paragraph or so. Variety and diversity characterize seniority contract provisions. This is one subject in collective bargaining that requires custom tailoring to specific local conditions.[8] Seniority is a controlling or significant factor in determining the order of layoff and recall from layoff in many contracts. In every case the governing principles and procedures must be articulated with care. Seniority also plays an important and sometimes decisive role in determining the filling of vacancies, in access to overtime work opportunities, in ordering of interplant transfers and other facets concerning the control, assignment and direction of the work force.

The multiple ramifications of the seniority issue will not be treated here. Our concern will be mainly with seniority as a job opportunity control mechanism and as another important illustration of industrial jurisprudence in action. The focus will thus be on provisions negotiated by industrial unions. Craft unions who control entrance to their trade use seniority as an internalized control within the union. Seniority is thus not an important bargaining matter for these unions. Most industrial unions, however, continue to place strong reliance on seniority provisions as a job control mechanism. They do so because the bargaining units represented by industrial unions typically contain a high proportion of semi-skilled workers and a relatively

---

[8] One of the best and most interesting ways for the reader to develop an understanding of the variety, complexity and difficulty of seniority issues in contemporary bargaining is to read a number of recent arbitration decisions involving different industries and unions. Many seniority disputes going to arbitration have long histories as issues in labor relations, but new applications arise constantly with different factual situations. Also, new contract language on an old topic may prove to be a source of controversy.

small number of craft employees and unskilled. The great majority of the union's "constituents" thus lack the economic power as individuals that attaches to possession of special skills. Most industrial workers are easily trained and easily replaced in a loose labor market. They frequently work at jobs whose content is defined in ways that minimize potential for differential performances based on human effort. The organization of many production operations is such that the output from the worker is machine-paced or group-paced. Job design affords little opportunity for recognition of individual differences in ability, attitude or effort. In these circumstances seniority (length of service) has a strong appeal to the individual worker as a mechanism for retaining employment during cutbacks or for securing advancement in the occupational hierarchy.

As a clear-cut, impersonal, objective yardstick, straight seniority also has considerable appeal for many employers as the basis for determining the order of layoff and recall from layoff. Within large bargaining units in particular seniority satisfies one of the essential requirements of an effective system of industrial jurisprudence—substitution of a uniform policy for managerial discretion, which can at times be arbitrary.

Employer Opposition to Straight Seniority in Layoff, Recall, and Promotion

Many employers continue to question the merit of length of service as the primary, if not sole, criterion governing layoffs and recalls. Employer opposition is stronger when unions seek to make seniority the governing factor in promotions. The employer thesis is that seniority places a premium on mediocrity, that it discourages initiative by making it impossible to recognize individual differences in ability and zeal and, finally, that it hampers seriously management's need for flexibility in work assignments as dictated by the requirements of a changing job mix and a dynamic technology. In the eyes of such critics seniority becomes a barrier to efficient operation of the enterprise.

How seniority affects employee efficiency continues to be a matter of serious debate in some bargaining relationships. Many employers consider seniority to be a prime factor in contributing to lower employee productivity and increased labor costs. On the other hand, defenders of seniority claim that it can contribute to increasing managerial efficiency by forcing employers to be more selective in their hiring and more thorough in their training programs. It is urged that seniority helps to lower costs by reducing labor turnover. Some contend that improved employee morale flowing from enhanced job security has a positive effect on worker productivity. Finally, the proponents of seniority urge that any alleged losses that might flow from inability to recognize properly differences in individual abilities are more than offset by the elimination of grievances and resentment that invariably result from unfettered managerial discretion on layoffs, promotions, recalls and transfers.

The argument over the vices and virtues of seniority varies in scope and intensity from one relationship to another, but the union pressure for retention of seniority restrictions continues. Many employers have reconciled themselves to utilizing seniority as the main governing criterion in connection with layoffs and recalls, particularly if they have been successful in negotiating some flexibility and discretion for themselves to retain some key employees without regard to seniority and to avoid the phenomenon of multiple or chain bumping.

SENIORITY AND THE MANAGERIAL DRIVE FOR EFFICIENT PRODUCTION

Employers find they can live with seniority if they can negotiate certain essential qualifications on the undiluted or straight seniority application. One employer-oriented proviso, for example, aims at avoiding the need to do training in connection with a layoff. An employee who wishes to exercise his seniority to bump another must always be able to do the latter's job without any training.

When a layoff is necessary, any employer has an understandable desire to minimize the number of job switches and assignment changes. How successful he is in attaining such an objective depends in great measure on how the contract's seniority article reads. Does it provide for straight seniority with no deviations on a plant-wide basis? If so, the employer's objective cannot be achieved. The employer therefore usually tries to define seniority units in fairly narrow terms based on occupational categories or clusters of related jobs. If the working force is clearly and neatly departmentalized, it may suit the employer's objective to define seniority along departmental lines. Whatever the situation, most employers seek to assure minimal movement whenever the impact of a layoff removes X as the most junior man in his seniority unit. If X then wishes to "go plant-wide" he is often restricted by the contract to bumping the most junior (least senior) employee whose work he is qualified to perform, if he wishes to remain at work rather than taking the layoff. The sequence of chain or multiple bumping is thus successfully avoided.

The foregoing pattern of limited bumping is clearly illustrated in Paragraph H, Section 5, Article XIV of the 1967–1970 John Deere-UAW contract, which reads as follows (p. 86):

> An employee with one (1) or more years of seniority being laid off from his seniority unit may elect to exercise his seniority to displace the employee,

if any, junior to him with the least seniority in the bargaining unit whose work assignment he is qualified to perform.

How the parties handle the many difficult pragmatic questions posed by seniority is a most crucial factor in determining the overall character of the employer-union relationship. The potential is great for constructive cooperation on the one hand or for destructive friction and antagonism on the other. Over the years many employers and unions have been able to work out contract provisions that reflect a workable compromise between the union's interest in protecting the job security of long-service employees and the employer's interest in maintaining an efficient work force under all conditions. Doing so necessarily involves negotiating *some* departures from the straight seniority application, as indicated above.

Maintaining the viability of a negotiated compromise between efficiency considerations and protected seniority is a constantly evolving responsibility whenever the technology is a dynamic one and the work force mix thus changes over fairly short spans of time. Many employers could use to advantage more flexibility than their contracts currently permit on such matters as intrafirm transfers and shifts in job assignments. How to negotiate the desired flexibility into the contract is one of the more important challenges currently facing many bargainers.

The task should be eased somewhat if employee job and income security fears have been reduced via the medium of an advanced "income security benefit plan" such as those in the automobile and farm implement industries. Such plans are the final product deriving from the original 1955 SUB plans (supplemental unemployment benefits). Under the 1967-1970 version the worker with more than one year seniority receives about 95 percent of his customary wage when he is on layoff up to as long as 104 weeks.

The future impact of technology is never easy to anticipate. It is evident, however, that the employer requires some degree of freedom in manipulting his work force, retraining incumbents as necessary and transferring those whose jobs have been drastically changed or eliminated. Seniority provisions negotiated for a former job mix frequently need to be revised if the transition is to be reasonably smooth and efficient. Further reference will be made to seniority as related to technological change in the concluding section of this chapter.

SENIORITY AND PROMOTIONAL POLICY

Most employers appear to have adjusted to seniority as *the* criterion governing the ordering of layoffs and recalls, particularly if they have secured contract language giving assurance that they will have qualified personnel manning the available jobs at all times.[9] Few employers, however, are sympathetic to union contentions that length of service should be the determining factor in promotions. This is a policy area where employers generally prefer full discretion to choose among applicants for vacancies on the basis of ability. In management eyes, ability is more relevant than comparative length of service.

Management and union thinking on promotional policy remains in conflict in a considerable number of bargaining relationships. I can recall some situations where a policy evolution has taken place from contractual silence (full employer discretion) to conclusive preference for the senior applicant when qualified. This latter provision has been extended to provide a trial on the job for the senior applicant held not qualified by management in the initial review of applications. Management still retains authority to determine what qualifications are needed to fill any vacancy. It also exercises administrative initiative in determining which applicants are qualified and which are not qualified. However, the senior applicant who has been held not qualified can still get a crack at the position under the following language from the 1967–1970 John Deere-UAW contract if there are no qualified workers seeking employment with the company at the time:

> When the vacancy has been posted for two (2) working days (48 hours), the Company shall remove the posting from the bulletin boards and accept no more applications for the vacancy. From the applications filed, the Company shall determine those who are qualified, and from this group, if there be more than one (1), shall fill the vacancy under the following procedure:
> a. The senior qualified applicant.
> b. If it is determined by the Company that there are no qualified applicants and there are no qualified workers seeking employment with the Company, then the Company shall give consideration to those applicants whose records would seem to indicate they could learn satisfactorily to perform the required work before a new inexperienced employee shall be hired and trained for the work assignment.
> c. Assuming there are no experienced qualified applicants and there are no applicants whose record would seem to indicate that they could learn satisfactorily to perform the required work, then the Company may fill the vacancy by the transfer or hire of any employee or applicant.

To my knowledge John Deere does not feel unduly restricted under the above language. In many bargaining relationships, however, the parties still operate with provisions stating in substance that the promotion will go to the senior applicant *if* relative ability and fitness are equal or relatively equal. Such a policy appears to give management considerable discretion in

---

[9] For a representative sampling of contract provisions dealing with seniority as a factor in promotion and transfer situations, see Winston L. Tillery and William V. Deutermann, Jr., *Seniority in Promotion and Transfer Provisions*, Bureau of Labor Statistics Bulletin No. 1425–11 (Washington, D.C.: Government Printing Office, March, 1970).

selection, but real difficulties and conflicts can arise in particular cases over whether employees X and Y are in fact equal or relatively equal in ability and fitness.[10]

The importance of length of service as a promotional criterion is not a matter on which a scientific judgment can be made. It is an area of continuing disagreement between employer and union over what an optimal policy should be. The weight accorded to length of service in particular contracts appears to depend principally on how strongly the parties hold their contrasting viewpoints. If the contract remains silent on promotional policy, this usually indicates that the union has not seen fit to make seniority a prime negotiation demand, although such a demand is clearly within the scope of mandatory bargaining. Frequently the contract reflects a negotiated compromise of two polarized views similar to the Deere-UAW provision quoted above. In many cases employer and union are continuing to operate with the familiar provision that calls for seniority to govern where abilities of applicants are deemed to be equal or relatively equal.

Putting to one side for the moment the issue of the contractual restriction of management discretion and speaking solely in terms of sound principles of personnel administration, one can find a broad consensus on the values of promotion from within as a general rule. Furthermore, when it is recalled that only slightly more skill and responsibility is required to move up successfully in most lines of job progression, the traditional objections to seniority as a promotional yardstick lose much of their force. This is especially the case where management has assured itself the right to determine which applicants are qualified. Under those circumstances where management has ruled the senior applicant to be not qualified either before or subsequent to a trial on the job, such a discretionary determination by management should not be open to successful challenge unless it can be shown that the decision was arbitrary, capricious or discriminatory—a difficult burden to maintain.

SENIORITY AND INTERPLANT TRANSFERS

Seniority is properly cited as a good example of a bargaining issue that should be a "local item" in negotiation of a master contract between

---

[10] The reader can appreciate how troublesome disputes can arise on issues of relative or equal ability and fitness for performing higher-rated jobs. When such cases go to arbitration, the union is often undertaking a difficult and thankless task. It must show that the employer's judgment was faulty, arbitrary or discriminatory—a difficult burden to maintain. The task is thankless because if the union "wins" the case it make the grievant happy, but only at the cost of making unhappy the employee who received the promotion originally.

For a recent perceptive analysis of criteria used for measuring ability, written by an experienced and highly respected arbitrator, see Thomas J. McDermott, "Types of Seniority Provisions and the Measurement of Ability," *The Arbitration Journal*, XXV (Summer, 1970), 101–24.

Union X and Employer Y with several plants in different locations. Differing job mixes from one plant to another frequently require that seniority arrangements be tailor-made for particular locations. It is difficult in a master agreement to provide a set of principles and procedures that would fit the variety of local circumstances.

One of the more thorny seniority problems facing multiplant firms is how to provide for interplant transfers of employees displaced at their original location by a shutdown of the facility or by technological change. The job security objectives of most unions require that some consideration be given to providing transfer rights under such circumstances. Many difficult questions arise. How shall such employees be treated in seniority terms in their new locations? Must they be regarded as new employees when transferring in or shall they carry with them some, or even all, of their seniority at their former location? An optimal solution is not possible because gains to one group of employees are regarded as losses or infringements by another. Merging of seniority lists in any situation is invariably a headache for all concerned.

The transfer rights problem underlines an important attribute of seniority not mentioned up to this point. *Seniority is acquired only by contract.* It can be retained only by contractual agreement and not by inherent right. Thus the very possibility of a transfer of an employee displaced at one plant to a job at another facility of the employer is contingent entirely upon what the master contract (multiplant agreement) provides. If we are talking about two different contracts, there is no way in which seniority rights acquired under one contract can be "imported" into the second and separate contract. Only when the same contract governs both plants does the possibility arise of an employee taking himself, together with some of his former seniority, to the new location.

Interplant Transfers
in the Meat Packing Industry

Job security is a worrisome problem for employees working for a multiplant employer in a technologically dynamic industry. In the meat packing industry, for example, a complete metamorphosis has taken place. Technological advance and changed marketing practices have made the large-scale, multiproduct packing plant virtually a thing of the past. Today's plant is one of much smaller dimensions, highly automated and devoted to a single type of meat product. Furthermore, the newer plants are more often than not located in small midwestern towns rather than in large urban centers.[11]

---

[11] For a general discussion of labor relations problems in meatpacking with considerable attention to the job security problem, see Harold W. Davey, "Present and Future

Union leadership recognized that these locational changes as well as the new job skills demanded in a modern packing plant would compound the problems of the old-style packinghouse worker. The policy of providing for interplant transfer rights was negotiated initially in the 1961 contracts and has been a feature of all subsequent contracts. Thus the transfer option has been one approach for the displaced packinghouse worker whose seniority antedates 1961. He can exercise such seniority in his new location over any workers hired since 1961 if this proves necessary. In actual practice only a small percentage (somewhere between 3 to 5 percent) of those eligible to transfer actually do so, according to Jesse Prosten, a principal union negotiator in the packing industry for many years.[12] It seems clear that interplant transfer rights solve the adjustment problem for only a small number of packinghouse workers displaced for either locational or technological reasons.

SENIORITY AS A RESTRICTIVE INFLUENCE ON INTERNAL FLEXIBILITY IN JOB ASSIGNMENTS

Many employers claim to be hampered by the restrictive impact of contractual seniority provisions on internal transfer and reassignment of employees to meet changing production needs and job requirements. They urge their inability to stay effectively competitive under modern conditions when faced by a restrictive web of seniority entanglements that solidify employee positions within the plant and inhibit free transfers from one job to another. Such employers seek a condition characteristic of many small firms or job shops where the work at hand gets priority without regard to particular job classifications. In this view the new technology has served to outmode established job classification lines and has underlined the need for greater freedom of worker movement from one category to another or one type of assignment to another.

We shall not treat the merits of this particular complaint. The nature and dimensions of the problem vary markedly from one industry to another. In my view, greater progress could be made in labor relations and contract administration if we shifted our emphasis from concentrating on the seniority of the worker to focusing on his trainability or retrainability. Some years ago Neil W. Chamberlain put the emphasis where it belongs, in my judgment, by emphasizing that the worker's only true security in a dynamic economy lies in the provision of continuing vocational education on a scale much more ambitious than we have yet attained. Chamberlain noted the essentially short-run and static quality of seniority in underlining

---

. Labor Relations Problems in the Meat Packing Industry," *Labor Law Journal*, XVIII (December, 1967), 739-51.

[12] Interview at National Academy of Arbitrators annual meeting, Montreal, Canada, April 7, 1970.

its shortcomings as an instrument for achieving genuine security in an age of rapidly evolving technology and changing product lines.[13] The ultimate goal must be that of provision for the continual upgrading of a worker's skills over his productive lifetime. This will require a combination effort by the private sector and governmental agencies. It is unlikely that industry will go beyond the training associated with the immediate vocational welfare of its employees. Government will thus have to pick up the tab for much of the proposed lifetime upgrading assignment.

COLLECTIVE BARGAINING AND TECHNOLOGICAL CHANGE

At least a volume would be needed for proper analysis of how collective bargaining has been and can be used to respond to the impact of technological change on bargaining unit personnel. In this section we shall hit only a few high spots, recognizing that we are giving short shrift to some truly difficult policy issues in this aspect of the job security problem.[14]

In his pioneering study, cited earlier in this chapter, Sumner H. Slichter classified union policies toward technological change as being of three kinds; (1) obstruction, (2) competition and (3) control. Slichter's empirical research dealt with bargaining practices of the 1920s and 1930s. Slichter identified comparatively few unions with policies of outright obstruction of technological change or of competition with such change. Most unions have recognized the legitimacy of the employer's felt need to improve work methods and to develop more efficient operations even when the net effect has been to change his factor mix in such a way as to reduce permanently his requirements for bargaining unit personnel. Nevertheless, nearly all unions, with varying degrees of tenacity, have sought and will continue to seek to control the manner and rate of introduction of technological change whenever such change contributes to reduced manpower. In surveying the collective bargaining scene as a whole, it is hard to generalize without oversimplification of the picture, but generalize we must. It is well to outline some familiar but diverse examples of union policy.

In some cases, such as coal mining, the union has chosen the route of aggressive economic bargaining while ignoring adverse effects on employ-

---

[13] These thoughts by Professor Chamberlain were expressed at a Cornell University conference dealing with seniority issues in grievance arbitration held in New York City on April 15, 1965.

[14] The literature on collective bargaining and technological change is so extensive and varied that citation of only one or two sources must be an arbitrary act. For perspective and a balanced consideration of the problem as a whole, the reader should consult Gerald G. Somers, Edward L. Cushman and Nat Weinberg, eds., *Adjusting to Technological Change* (New York: Harper & Row, Publishers, 1963). See also John T. Dunlop, ed., *Automation and Technological Change* (Englewood Cliffs, N.J.: Prentice-Hall, Inc., 1962).

ment. The extensive mechanization of the mines is a familiar story. Over the years the demand for coal has remained relatively constant while the productivity of the individual miner has been drastically increased by mechanization. The result of this combination of circumstances has been a sharp decline in employment and in the membership of the United Mine Workers. The bargaining objective of the late John L. Lewis was to make the employed coal miner the highest-paid semi-skilled worker in the world. Lewis viewed the resultant unemployment as a macro-economic problem with which the union was not particularly concerned.

A different union stance toward the impact of technological change is well illustrated in the building and construction field. Many craft unions associated with this industry have long pursued restrictionist policies in bargaining that blocked or retarded the introduction of new technological developments. These unions did not hesitate to use their strong market power to do so. Only fairly recently have the major unions in construction moved to "modernize" their bargaining policies to accommodate important technological developments. Many contractors would still urge that the unions have an excessive amount of restrictionism built into their contracts.

Another category would be that of a fundamental shift from union restrictionism to receptivity toward technological innovation. Longshoring on the Pacific Coast provides a graphic example. The full story of the longshoring mechanization agreement of 1961 and subsequent developments is told in a carefully researched study by Paul T. Hartman.[15] The shipping industry continues to move steadily toward "containerization."[16] This trend means that still further "adjustments" will be required of the bargainers. Although longshoring is just one industry with some individual special twists, the Hartman study contains some valuable insights for nearly any employer and union endeavoring to cope effectively and equitably with the continuing problem of accommodating the employer's need to innovate with the incumbent employees' drive for job security.

In no case is such an accommodation an easy task. However, a giant step toward adjustment has been taken with general management recognition that meeting job security needs must be held to be a proper cost of introducing technological change.

Negotiated approaches take many and diverse forms. However, those that appear to be working the best have the common characteristic

---

[15] Paul T. Hartman, *Collective Bargaining and Productivity: The Longshore Mechanization Agreement* (Berkeley, Cal.: The University of California Press, 1969).

[16] The containers in question are large, rigid boxes filled by the shipper or terminal operator, ranging at present from five to twenty tons when loaded. They are handled throughout the journey from origin to point of destination with special equipment such as large gantry cranes or specially designed trucks or jitneys. Ships also have to be modified to the new requirements of container loading. The productivity gains are enormous in going from the old break-bulk approach to containerization. See Hartman, *ibid.*, 160–161.

of joint acknowledgement that incumbent employees (with varying levels of minimum seniority) should not be adversely affected by technological change, either as to employment or income, whenever it lies within the private capabilities of the parties to prevent such impact. There is, for example, general recognition that a regular cost of introducing technological change will be carrying through the retraining or relocating of workers affected by the change or, in the alternative, providing "just" compensation to those workers who cannot be absorbed and must therefore be defined as "permanently displaced."

Practically speaking, there is a good deal of variation in the degree to which this principle can be honored operationally in particular situations. On the current scene, however, most employers concede their obligation to cope with the problem as effectively as possible. Success is easier for employers whose market demand is such that they can expand rather than contract bargaining unit personnel, even while extensive technological change is being instituted. Substantial gains in labor productivity due to mechanization can be achieved under these happy circumstances with no serious employee job security or income security problems.

In many cases the manpower adjustment problem will not be painless and friction-free. If manpower adjustments are likely to be severe, as in meatpacking, to name one example, employer and union bargainers face a continuing challenge. In meatpacking the parties have apparently done their best as private negotiators in several successive agreements to cope effectively with the following fundamental question: How can we introduce X amount of Y type of technological change over the next contract period without affecting adversely job and income security of incumbent employees?[17]

NEGOTIATED POLICIES FOR COPING WITH TECHNOLOGICAL UNEMPLOYMENT

Where actual unemployment is contemplated as a consequence of technological change, there are a variety of ways in which collective bargaining can be utilized to deal directly with such unpleasant prospects. These include the following:

---

[17] The contracts in meat packing contain numerous provisions designed to cushion or ease the burden of adjustment, such as interplant transfers, six months advance notice of plant closings, training and retraining opportunities and technological adjustment pay. All in combination, however, have not been sufficient to prevent *some* unemployment of structurally (relocated plants) or technologically displaced employees. Collective bargaining cannot be expected to do it all, in other words.

1. *Adjusting by attrition* to reduced manpower needs by phasing in the new or changed technology gradually to conform to the normal employee turnover rate from quits, death, retirement and so forth, with little or no new hiring.
2. *Planned retraining of incumbent employees* to fit into other jobs as their old positions are eliminated or phased out.
3. *Permanent transfer* of employees to other plants where their abilities can be fitted to job needs elsewhere in the employer's domain.
4. *Early retirement plans* to encourage voluntary reduction of the work force to accommodate reduced manpower requirements caused by technological change.[18]
5. *Severance pay plans* with amounts related to employee's overall length of service or to his average income in years immediately preceding separation.

Which one or which combination of the foregoing will be used must depend on the conditions in the particular employer-union relationship. In a surprisingly large number of situations planned adjustment in terms of normal employee turnover (attrition) may prove to be sufficient alone to prevent any actual employee displacement. In other cases, however, there will be a need for a combination approach.

Direct joint efforts of this type are becoming a familiar component of bargaining in a wide range of relationships. Such straightforward approaches do not require extensive treatment because the goals and the rationale are clear, even though operational success may not be complete.

We must take notice, however, of a considerable number of normal or conventional union bargaining demands not visibly related to technological change but which are often intimately although indirectly related. I refer to such matters as subcontracting, premium pay clauses, working rules and the like.

Subcontracting and Job Opportunities

Nothing is more certain to arouse employee fear and suspicion than the news of an employer intention to subcontract work. If over a long period of years an employer has customarily subcontracted certain types of work not directly related to that performed by bargaining unit employees, no serious problem will arise. This is especially true when the subcontracted work is of such a nature that current bargaining unit employees do not have the know-how to handle the work in any event.

---

[18] Many "early retirement" plans currently in effect utilize the age 62 for optional retirement instead of the conventional 65 for mandatory retirement. The UAW in the 1970 negotiations had a priority demand for retirement *at any age* after thirty years of service at a minimum monthly figure of $500.

Opposition will be generated, however, when the employer seeks to subcontract work currently performed by bargaining unit personnel or which *could* be performed by incumbent employees. Any actual or prospective diminution of bargaining unit work activity due to subcontracting is almost certain to be challenged by the union in question. The employer will argue typically that subcontracting is a managerial prerogative. He will urge further that the business of staying competitive requires him to get the work done in the most economical and efficient manner possible. When doing so requires him to farm out (that is, to subcontract) certain duties, he will maintain that his right to do so should not be restricted by union contract. The union response will typically be that the employer has no right to subcontract bargaining unit work for any reason, particularly when a reduction in work opportunities within the bargaining unit is the likely result.

The range and limits of employer discretion to subcontract have been extensively explored in many industries via the medium of grievance arbitration. The subcontracting issue has exposed significant differences among arbitrators, particularly on the matter of how to interpret contractual silence in such cases. The more "conservative" school of arbitrator thinking supports the conventional managerial view expressed as follows: "If we have not limited ourselves by contract, we still have discretion to subcontract as necessary according to our best judgment." The more "liberal" school of arbitrator thinking often applies "implied limitations" reasoning to restrict employer discretion to subcontract when the effect of such subcontracting is to diminish bargaining unit work opportunities.[19]

A 1969 BLS study of contractual provisions relating to subcontracting reveals a wide variety of ways of handling this potentially explosive issue.[20] As already noted, there are still many contracts that maintain silence on the subject. One can presume that in some cases of this type the contractual silence reflects the fact that subcontracting is not a problem. In others it might reflect a situation where management does not in fact do any subcontracting. In still others the silence would underscore the fact that management is subcontracting certain types of work, with the union having won or lost on its challenges depending on the arbitrator's philosophy as to how the silence should be construed.

---

[19] According to Paul Prasow and Edward Peters, when the contract is silent on subcontracting, a "large majority" of arbitrators will not sustain management if the subcontracting results in layoffs or impairment of established employee benefits. Prasow and Peters immediately qualify this generalization, however, by noting exceptions where the subcontracting has been customary in the past or where there has been "a drastic change in underlying conditions of the jobs in question." See Paul Prasow and Edward Peters, *Arbitration and Collective Bargaining: Conflict Resolution in Labor Relations* (New York: McGraw-Hill Book Company, 1970), p. 47.

[20] U.S. Bureau of Labor Statistics, *Subcontracting*, Bulletin No. 1425–28 (Washington, D.C.: Government Printing Office, 1969).

The BLS study contains examples of contract provisions wherein the employer agrees to do no subcontracting other than what he has customarily done in the past. Many employers would be wary about limiting themselves in this fashion. However, it should not be surprising to find unions seeking to enforce through collective bargaining a policy statement on subcontracting that would either prevent altogether or limit as much as possible the contracting out of work normally done by bargaining unit personnel. Perhaps the most consistent pressure exerted by employees on any union leaders is to maintain job opportunities to the maximum degree possible.

Many contracts contain provisions containing a joint recognition of the desirability of maintaining a stable work force while also recognizing the employer need for some flexibility in making arrangements to have work done. In such cases the contract language clearly reflects intent but is not unduly restrictive of the employer need for some flexibility. The John Deere-UAW 1967–1970 agreement (Article II, Section 9, pp. 11–12) is a good example of such an approach. It reads as follows:

> It is not the Company's intent to have subcontractors working in the plant on work normally performed by bargaining unit people unless the affected bargaining unit people are working a maximum number of hours (i.e., at least 48). In such cases the Union will be notified prior to the work being performed.
>
> In other situations the Company shall make decisions as to whether work shall be performed by the Company forces in any Company plant, or by others consistent with an intention to maintain as far as practicable, a stable workforce. The Company shall make decisions of such nature with such intention taking into consideration such factors as the scope of the project or production requirements, relative cost, possession and availability of Company equipment and of employees qualified to accomplish the production without undue overtime or delay either of the specific production or of any other scheduled activity, desirability of continuity of relations with historic sources of supply and believed best utilization of all of the Company's plants with a view to a long-term stability and health of the enterprise as a whole."

Either contractual silence or contractual ambiguity can lead to serious disputes whenever an employer elects to subcontract in a manner that takes work opportunities away from bargaining unit personnel. The problem is one that calls for clarity and mutual understanding if the parties are going to avoid recurring instances of friction and resentment.

PREMIUM PAY PROVISIONS AND JOB SECURITY

Conventional union pressure to increase premium pay rates for daily or weekly overtime is another instance of a continuing type of issue that does not at first seem related to job security. Looked at more closely, however, these demands can be viewed as a strong inducement to the employer to carry more employees in his regular or normal work force than he might need to fill "normal" needs in order to avoid the financial penalties of recurringly expensive overtime.

The matter of how much to pay for overtime or for holidays when worked is frequently an issue in current bargaining. Some contracts now carry what employers must regard as truly exorbitant rates for holidays when worked (triple time is no longer unusual) or for the sixth and seventh consecutive days in a work week. The contractual cost of using regular employees under these conditions is so high that it provides a most powerful incentive to the employer not to schedule work under such circumstances if he can possibly avoid doing so. Thus the temptation might be present to carry a "regular" force of more employees than he might "normally" need in order to be sure the requisite amount of production can be obtained in straight-time scheduled hours.

CONTRACTUALLY PRESCRIBED WORKING RULES AND TECHNOLOGICAL CHANGE

Any technologically dynamic situation provides the opportunity for a confrontation between the new and the old ways of getting work done. One of the stickiest areas in bargaining concerns such matters as work pace, work load and proper crew size for a given operation. The union thrust in such cases will be to pursue a course which will preserve a fixed quantum of bargaining unit job opportunities. The typical employer will be extremely reluctant to go along with any contractual specifications that will bind him to using x number of employees on given work operations or that require him to continue doing work in a certain way. The employer desires to maintain complete freedom over "control and direction of the working force." He thus comes into conflict with the union's objective of using the contract to assure maximum employment opportunities for bargaining unit employees.

The semantics are important if we are to obtain a true picture of this potential conflict area. If its demand is one that involves outright featherbedding or make-work under current conditions, union leadership will be hard pressed to develop a plausible rationale. There are comparatively few union practitioners that will unabashedly seek to enforce such policies as a way of life. But when the manpower issue is put in less obvious and extreme terms, legitimate differences in viewpoint can and do develop between management and union. To take a familiar example, problems frequently arise when a change in method or a change in machinery leads the employer to conclude that a given operation can henceforth be performed by one man instead of two. Another familiar situation arises when a sweeping technological change makes it possible for the employer to contend plausibly that producing a given amount henceforth requires a production worker component of only 100 men instead of the former 150 or 200 men.

The difficulty and seriousness of such manning controversies can be easily appreciated when one recalls such lengthy and bitter struggles of recent vintage as those concerning the diesel fireman in the railroad industry, the flight engineer position in jet aircraft and the conversion in the municipal bus field from two men (motorman and conductor) to one man. Whenever a technological development calls for reduced manpower, there may be a serious dispute as to whether the reduction can be instituted under the current collective bargaining agreement. Whenever revision of contractual provisions on work rules or manpower components is under consideration, the union position is often that management wants to move too fast or that it is trying to cut corners by using technological change improperly to conceal an alleged increase in work load for remaining employees.

To write in meaningful fashion about such disputes would require going into the details of specific situations. Each such case has its individual variations. Sticking here to general terms, my view is that the employer must retain sufficient contractual freedom to take advantage of opportunities to utilize technological development to aid him in achieving his objectives of staying competitive by increasing productivity and by cost reduction. At the same time there must be contractual recognition of worker equity in jobs. Where net displacement is known to be a consequence of an anticipated technological change, collective bargaining should be directed to minimizing or cushioning the adverse impact on incumbent employees.

There is no optimal answer to the work rules and manpower component problem. Furthermore, it is often hard to predict with accuracy how a given technological innovation will affect manpower requirements in a specific case. Resolution of such disputes will be a thorny problem for most bargainers, even in a full employment economy. I regard it as unfortunate, however, whenever any union chooses to use bargaining power "muscle" to force employers to maintain outmoded working rules or methods.

Achieving satisfactory accommodations between conflicting but legitimate differences in viewpoint as to proper manning on particular jobs will always be a part of the negotiators' task at the bargaining table. In most cases, detached assessment of the circumstances will reveal whether the union stance is in reality an obstructionist one designed to make the cost of instituting technological change prohibitively high. In any such case there should no longer be any question as to proper policy direction. Union leadership and union membership must reconcile themselves to the need for accepting the change. They must be realistic on the matter of removal of outmoded working rules from the collective agreement. Stubborn adherence to old patterns can be sustained by "muscle" in the short run, but the consequent damage to the relationship between the parties will be irreparable. The damage goes far beyond the particular relationship. Society's interests are injured by the perpetuation of enforced restrictions on production that have been made obsolete by technological improvements.

A COMMENT ON "AUTOMATION" AS A SPECIAL FORM OF TECHNOLOGICAL CHANGE

Reference to "automation" has been avoided intentionally in this discussion of technological change as a way of avoiding the confusion from the loose usage of the word "automation" in many discussions. In 1959 I concluded that the term "automation" should be limited to technological developments which made possible the *use of machines to control other machines*. I continue to hold this view. Such restricted usage reserves the term to cover the development of electronic control devices (servomechanisms) applying the basic principles of automatic self-regulation. It is the development of self-regulative control machinery that has provided the key to what I consider to be true automation. The ramifications of this technological revolution in such fields as computerization of office processes, automatic foundries, automatic engine block plants and the like are today a familiar story. Controversy still endures as to the impact of this type of technological change on employment opportunities and the job mix. In particular cases the net result has been drastic reduction in the level of bargaining unit employment. In others, however, the technological changes have been instituted in firms with expanding market and employment horizons so that the net displacement effect has been slight. Many of the fears expressed in the late 1950s as to the negative employment consequences of automation have proved to be exaggerated. The fact remains, however, that decisions to automate any work operations, either fully or in part, necessarily pose a most difficult challenge to bargaining practitioners. The challenge covers many other aspects of industrial relations as well as job security.

For example, the new automatic technology generally requires a scrapping of conventional wage incentive systems based on individual effort. Either day work or some type of group incentive payment must be substituted. The new technology also involves wholesale revision of other conventional policies because of its effect on job mix, on raising the level of supervisory skills required and on greatly increasing the ratio and value of equipment to men. Formidable difficulties are posed by the required training, retraining and transfers to new or changed tasks accompanying such fundamental change. Conventional seniority arrangements are no longer suitable for the new technology that puts a premium on a mobile, versatile and highly interchangeable work force.

CONCLUSION: THE LOGIC
OF INDUSTRIAL JURISPRUDENCE RESTATED

We have examined several critical components of the job security problem. The discussion has been structured in such a way as to illustrate the important role of collective bargaining in instituting and implementing a system of industrial jurisprudence. Whether talking about individual discipline, seniority provisions or adaptation to technological change, the recurring theme has been the use of collective bargaining to develop jointly policies and procedures spelling out clearly the rules of the game on dealing with the problem at hand.

In each case, the acid operational test must be whether the policies and methods jointly decided upon measure up to the basic demands of industrial jurisprudence—clarity, consistency, predictability and equality of treatment in like circumstances. The long-run health of collective bargaining as a process will be determined by how conscientiously the parties stick to the imperative of a single standard of fair and equitable treatment in their specific efforts to insure a maximum of job security to incumbent employees in a technologically dynamic and volatile labor relations scene. In the long run there is no satisfactory alternative to the single standard for achieving and maintaining stability and equity in contract administration.

SELECTED BIBLIOGRAPHY

Note: Most of the references in this chapter bibliography are germane to the discussion of collective bargaining and job security problems posed by technological change, shifting manpower requirements, industrial relocation and the like. There are few references from the vast literature on employee discipline and seniority issues. The slighting is intentional because I am convinced that a reading of recent arbitration decisions on discipline and seniority issues is the most productive way to achieve better understanding of their significance in the general scheme of contract administration.

ARMOUR AUTOMATION COMMITTEE, "Adjustment to Plant Closure; Cooperation in Planning for the Transfer of Negro Workers into a White Community," *Monthly Labor Review*, XC (January, 1967), 42–46.

BAITSELL, JOHN M., *Airline Industrial Relations, Pilots and Flight Engineers.* Boston, Mass.: Division of Research, Graduate School of Business Administration, Harvard University, 1966.

BARKIN, SOLOMON, "A Systems Approach to Adjustments of Technical Change," *Labor Law Journal*, XVIII (January, 1967), 29–38.

————, *Technical Change and Manpower Planning: Coordination at Enterprise Level; a Series of National Case Studies.* Industrial Relations Aspects of Manpower Policy No. 4. Paris: Organization for Economic Cooperation and Development, Social Affairs Division, 1967.

BARRES, STEPHEN J., "Subcontracting: A Persistent Labor Problem," *Labor Law Journal*, XVIII (October, 1967), 588–96.

BEAUMONT, RICHARD A., *Management, Automation, and People*. Industrial Relations Monograph No. 24. New York: Industrial Relations Counselors, 1964.

BECKER, JOSEPH M., *Guaranteed Income for the Unemployed; the Story of SUB*. Baltimore, Md.: Johns Hopkins Press, 1968.

BLUM, ALBERT A., "Job Skills for Automated Industry," *Management of Personnel Quarterly*, IV (Winter, 1966), 24–31.

BRANDT, FLOYD S., "Unions, Management and Maintenance Subcontracting— An Industry Experience," *Labor Law Journal*, XIV (July, 1963), 601–13.

BRANDWEIN, SEYMOUR, "Manpower Implications of Technological Change: Research Findings of the United States Dept. of Labor," *Labor Law Journal*, XIV (August, 1963), 655–69.

CAMPBELL, RALPH, "Employing the Disadvantaged: Inland Steel's Experience," *Issues in Industrial Society*, I, No. 1 (1969), 30–41.

CHAMPAGNE, JOSEPH E., "Job Recruitment of the Unskilled," *Personnel Journal*, XLVIII (April, 1969), 259–68.

COHEN, WILBUR J., *Womanpower Policies for the 1970s*, 40 pages. Washington, D.C.: Dept. of Labor, Manpower Administration. Office of Manpower Policy, Evaluation and Research, 1967.

COLEMAN, JOHN R., "Public Policy, Collective Bargaining, and Technological Change in the United States & Canada," *Labor Law Journal*, XV (December, 1964), 802–14.

DAYKIN, WALTER L., "Arbitration of Work Rules Disputes," *Arbitration Journal*, XVIII (1963), 36–45.

DUNLOP, JOHN T., ed., *Automation and Technological Change*. Englewood Cliffs, N.J.: Prentice-Hall, Inc., 1962.

FABRICANT, SOLOMON, *Measurement of Technological Change*. Washington, D.C.: Dept. of Labor, Manpower Administration, Office of Manpower, Automation and Training, 1965.

FISHER, ROBERT W., "Arbitration of Discharges for Marginal Reasons," *Monthly Labor Review*, XC (October, 1968), 1–5.

FREEDMAN, AUDREY, "Office Automation in the Insurance Industry," *Monthly Labor Review*, LXXXVIII (November, 1965), 1313–19.

FRYE, JACK, "Attrition in Job Elimination," *Labor Law Journal*, XIV (September, 1963), 809–17.

GINZBERG, ELI, ed., *Technology and Social Change*. New York: Columbia University Press, 1964.

GITELMAN, H. M., "Occupational Mobility Within the Firm," *Industrial and Labor Relations Review*, XX (October, 1966), 50–65.

GORDON, ROBERT A., ed., *Toward a Manpower Policy*. New York: John Wiley & Sons, Inc., 1967.

———, "Unemployment Patterns with Full Employment," *Industrial Relations*, VIII (October, 1968), 46–72.

HABER, WILLIAM G., AND HAROLD M. LEVISNON, *Labor Relations and Productivity in the Building Trades*. Ann Arbor, Mich.: University of Michigan Press, 1956.

HARBISON, FREDERICK AND CHARLES A. MYERS, *Education, Manpower and Economic Growth*. New York: McGraw-Hill Book Company, Inc., 1964.

HARTMAN, PAUL T., "Union Work Rules: A Brief Theoretical Analysis and Some Empirical Results," *Proceedings, 1966*, pp. 332–42, Industrial Relations Research Association. Madison, Wis.: Industrial Relations Research Association, 1967.

————, *Collective Bargaining and Productivity: The Longshore Mechanization Agreement.* Berkeley and Los Angeles: University of California Press, 1969.

JACOBSON, JULIUS, ed., *The Negro and the American Labor Movement.* Garden City, N.Y.: Doubleday and Company, Inc., 1968.

JAFFE, ABRAM J., AND JOSEPH FROOMKIN, *Technology and Jobs; Automation in Perspective.* New York: Frederick A. Praeger, 1968.

KILLINGSWORTH, CHARLES C., *Jobs and Income for Negroes.* Policy Papers in Human Resources and Industrial Relations No. 6. Ann Arbor, Mich.: Institute of Labor and Industrial Relations, University of Michigan–Wayne State University, 1968.

LEVINE, MARVIN J., "State and Local Retraining Programs and Legislation: A Case for Federal Action," *Labor Law Journal,* XVI (January, 1965), 27–43.

————, "Training and Retraining in American Industry: An Appraisal of the Evidence as an Ameliorative for Unemployment," *Labor Law Journal,* XV (October, 1964), 634–48.

LEVITAN, SAR A., AND GARTH L. MANGUM, *Federal Training and Work Programs in the Sixties.* Ann Arbor, Mich.: Institute of Labor and Industrial Relations, University of Michigan–Wayne State University, 1969.

LUCE, CHARLES F., "Consolidated Edison and the 'Hard Core,'" *Training in Business and Industry,* VI (March, 1969), 46–53.

MANGUM, GARTH L., *MDTA: Foundation of Federal Manpower Policy.* Baltimore, Md.: Johns Hopkins Press, 1968.

————, *The Emergence of Manpower Policy.* New York: Holt, Rinehart and Winston, Inc., 1969.

MANN, FLOYD C., AND L. RICHARD HOFFMAN, *Automation and the Worker.* New York: Holt-Dryden, 1960.

MANSFIELD, EDWIN, *The Economics of Technological Change.* New York: W. W. Norton & Company, Inc., 1968.

MARSHALL, F. RAY, *The Negro and Organized Labor.* New York: John Wiley & Sons, Inc., 1965.

————, AND VERNON M. BRIGGS, JR., *The Negro and Apprenticeship.* Baltimore, Md.: Johns Hopkins Press, 1967.

MORGAN, C. BAIRD, JR., "The Adequacy of Collective Bargaining in Resolving the Problem of Job Security and Technological Change," *Labor Law Journal,* XVI (February, 1965), 87–99.

NORTHRUP, HERBERT R., *The Negro in the Aerospace Industry.* Philadelphia, Pa.: University of Pennsylvania Press, 1968.

PALEN, J. JOHN, AND FRANK J. FAHEY, "Unemployment and Reemployment Success: An Analysis of the Studebaker Shutdown," *Industrial and Labor Relations Review,* XXI (January, 1968), 234–50.

PERLINE, MARTIN M., AND KURTIS L. TULL, "The Impact of Automation on Collective Bargaining Agreements," *Labor Law Journal,* XIX (February, 1968), 112–16.

PHELPS, ORME W., *Discipline and Discharge in Unionized Firms.* Berkeley, Cal.: University of California Press, 1959.

PIORE, MICHAEL J., "On-the-Job Training and Adjustment to Technological Change," *Journal of Human Resources,* III (Fall, 1968), 435–49.

PORTER, ARTHUR R., *Job Property Rights.* New York: King's Crown Press, 1954.

ROSS, ARTHUR M., AND HERBERT HILL, eds., *Employment, Race and Poverty.* New York: Harcourt, Brace and World, Inc., 1967.

ROWAN, RICHARD L., *The Negro in the Steel Industry.* Philadelphia, Pa.: University of Pennsylvania Press, 1968.

Rubinstein, Kenneth, "Plant Relocation and Its Effects on Labor-Management Relations," *Labor Law Journal*, XVIII (September, 1967), 544–55.

Samoff, Bernard, "Individual Job Rights and Union Functions: Compatible or Conflicting Forces," *Proceedings, 1965*, pp. 88–98. Industrial Relations Research Association. Madison, Wis.: Industrial Relations Research Association, 1966.

Scoville, James G., *The Job Content of the U.S. Economy, 1940–1970*. New York: McGraw-Hill Book Company, Inc. 1969.

Shils, Edward B., *Automation and Industrial Relations*, New York. Holt, Rinehart and Winston, Inc., 1963.

Simler, Norman J., "The Economics of Featherbedding," *Industrial and Labor Relations Review*, XVI (October, 1962), 111–21.

Simon, Herbert A., *The Shape of Automation for Men and Management*. New York: Harper & Row, Publishers, 1965.

Slichter, Sumner H., *Union Policies and Industrial Management*. Washington, D.C.: The Brookings Institution, 1941.

———, James J. Healy and E. Robert Livernash, *The Impact of Collective Bargaining on Management*. Washington, D.C.: The Brookings Institution, 1960.

Somers, Gerald G., Edward L. Cushman and Nat Weinberg, eds., *Adjusting to Technological Change*. New York: Harper & Row, Publishers, 1963.

Stern, James L., and David B. Johnson, *Blue- to White-Collar Job Mobility*. Madison, Wis.: Industrial Relations Research Institute, University of Wisconsin, 1968.

Stieber, Jack, ed., *Employment Problems of Automation and Advanced Technology: An International Perspective*. New York: St. Martin's Press, 1966.

Stoikov, Vladimir, "Increasing Structural Unemployment Reexamined," *Industrial and Labor Relations Review*, XIX (April, 1966), 368–76.

U.S. Bureau of Labor Statistics, *Impact of Office Automation in the Internal Revenue Service: A Study of the Manpower Implications During the First Stages of the Changeover*. Bulletin No. 1364. Washington, D.C.: Government Printing Office, 1963.

———, *Implications of Automation and Other Technological Developments: A Selected Annotated Bibliography*. Bulletin No. 1319–1. Washington, D.C.: Government Printing Office, 1964.

———, *Technology and Manpower in the Textile Industry of the 1970s*. Bulletin No. 1578. Washington, D.C.: Government Printing Office, 1968.

U.S. Office of Manpower, Automation and Training, *Manpower and Automation Research Sponsored by the Office of Manpower, Automation and Training, 1963–64*. Washington, D.C.: Department of Labor, Manpower Administration, 1964.

Weber, Arnold R., and David P. Taylor, "Procedures of Employee Displacement: Advance Notice of Plant Shutdown," *Journal of Business*, XXXVI (July, 1963), 302–15.

———, "The Role and Limits of National Manpower Policies," *Proceedings, 1965*, pp. 32–50. Madison, Wis.: Industrial Relations Research Association, 1966.

Weinberg, Edgar, "Reducing Skill Shortages in Construction," *Monthly Labor Review*, XCII (February, 1969), 3–9.

Weinstein, Paul A., ed., *Featherbedding and Technological Change*. Boston: D.C. Heath and Company, 1965.

WILCOCK, RICHARD C., AND WALTER H. FRANKE, *Unwanted Workers: Permanent Layoffs and Long-term Unemployment*. New York: Free Press of Glencoe, 1963.

ZELLER, FREDERICK A., AND ROBERT W. MILLER, eds., *Manpower Development in Appalachia; An Approach to Unemployment*. New York: Frederick E. Praeger, 1968.

ZUCKERMAN, GEORGE D., "The Sheet Metal Workers' Case; a Case History of Discrimination in the Building Trades," *Labor Law Journal*, XX (July, 1969), 416–27.

COLLECTIVE WAGE DETERMINATION

micro-economic aspects

CHAPTER TEN

The union's demand for upward wage or salary adjustments continues to be the paramount issue at the bargaining table. Other issues may take the spotlight on occasion in particular negotiations, but the principal business of the American union remains that of improving the economic position of the employees it represents.

Satisfying such an obligation to the membership in an affluent, inflation-prone society means that the employer is confronted at each negotiation with a serious union demand for a substantial general increase in wages or salaries, plus a miscellany of satellite cost demands. The latter may include extra wage increments for skilled craftsmen, additional paid holidays, a "sweetened" pension plan and perhaps proposals for guaranteed annual and monthly "income security benefits."

Employees and the union representing them are *income-conscious*.

Employers are necessarily *cost-conscious*. The stage is thus set for short-run conflict that sometimes assumes serious proportions.

Wage or salary negotiation is no longer a simple task, if indeed it ever was. The union's ultimate economic proposal is a blend of several ingredients that make up the "price of labor," broadly defined. The day of the straightforward wage adjustment has about vanished. Contemporary bargaining is generally concerned with economic "packages" of various shapes and sizes. The employer must translate the union's combination proposal into accurate labor cost estimates. He must know what agreeing to the whole and to each of the various elements of the union-proposed package will mean in terms of unit labor costs.

In most of the analytical discussion we shall oversimplify matters for purposes of convenience by discussing wage or salary adjustments as if they were the *only economic issue* at the bargaining table. In reality, nonwage benefits in most negotiations account for twenty to thirty percent of the labor cost dollar.

Three Principal Types of Decision-Making on Wage and Salary Issues

Collective wage determination is a micro-economic process. This holds true whether we are considering a truly small employer negotiating with a local union or analyzing the triennial negotiations between such giants as General Motors and the UAW. In times of concern about inflation there is often strong sentiment for instituting direct governmental control of wages and prices combined with compulsory arbitration. However, analysis of the relationship between macro-economic goals and micro-economic decision-making is deferred until the next chapter.

The central focus in this chapter is on wage determination by Company X and Union Y. In each contract negotiation the parties must confront jointly on three basic categories of wage problems. First (and usually foremost), an agreement must be reached as to whether a general (that is, across-the-board) wage increase (decrease) should be effected and, if so, how much it should be. Second, a number of "structural" wage problems cry for solution. The key structural question often relates to the differential appropriate between the rates of top skilled craftsmen and those of semi-skilled production workers.

Structural headaches can also arise over alleged intrafirm inequities in occupational rates among existing job classifications and over where to slot new job classifications within the labor grade hierarchy.

The third category of decision-making concerns methods of wage administration. Disputes over administration of incentive systems are hardy perennials in this category. Union pressure for converting production workers from an hourly to a salaried method of wage payment is another issue that can be troublesome.

The complexity of the task for management and union representatives in current wage bargaining should be evident. When other economic issues are injected into the calculations (as is usually the case), the need for considerable expertise is apparent.

Policy decisions in all the foregoing categories must be made also in some fashion by nonunion employers. The latter must consider periodically the amount and type of wage increase (decrease) he will institute. He must also review his intrafirm structure of occupational rates to insure that it remains balanced and equitable. Finally, the nonunion employer's methods of wage and salary administration may need revision or change from time to time. The prudent nonunion employer thus strives to achieve a sound policy in all aspects of wage determination. He enjoys greater flexibility and discretion than if he were negotiating with a union. However, he has the same need for developing operationally feasible wage policies.

Many nonunion employers take a leaf from the union book in the industry or area in which they operate for two important reasons: (1) they recognize the intrinsic merit of some wage policies in the unionized sector; (2) following the economic pattern of unionized firms is a sound way of "keeping up with the Joneses." Such an approach will often facilitate recruitment and retention of employees. It can also prove to be a good way to remain nonunion in some cases, especially when the employer decides to top the union pattern.

Scope and Limits of the Wage Treatment in This Analysis

Certain distinguishing characteristics of collective wage determination as an institutionalized process should be identified as an aid in understanding the differences between most textbook explanations of labor factor pricing and what actually happens at bargaining tables. We shall also consider in realistic terms what factors determine the wage objectives of unions and the main considerations affecting employer decisions on meeting union economic demands.

We shall also review briefly some of the challenges posed in Chapter 1 pertinent to the micro-economic sphere, such as the following:

1. Converting from hourly or incentive payment plans to weekly, monthly or yearly salaried bases.
2. Achieving an "appropriate" wage differential for craftsmen without alienating production workers.
3. Negotiating an effective relationship between wages as such and such economic fringe benefits as paid vacations and retirement plans.

We shall consider also whether we can develop objective criteria for determining the soundness of wage decision-making under collective bargaining. To what extent can we objectify the familiar phrase "equal pay for equal work"? Is there an objective way of deciding the appropriate spread or differential between the rate paid to a toolmaker (top skilled job) and a janitor or sweeper (common labor job)? Can we say, objectively, that all like jobs should pay the same, regardless of geographic location and local labor market demand-supply relationships? Should employers gear their wage policies to those of their competitors or to the policies of other firms in their labor market area? Should unions gear their wage demands to those of other unions, regardless of the localized conditions they may face? What *are* the relevant criteria or variables that *should* condition the thinking of management and union leadership in facing various wage issues at the bargaining table?

The analysis will be concluded with a summary review of recent evidence on the economic impact of the union at the level of the individual firm and industry. We shall end with a modest effort at bridge-building between micro and macro through noting one way in which Company X and Union Y can make their wage bargaining compatible with national economic policy goals while also meeting their own economic requirements.

The first order of business is to outline the distinguishing characteristics of wage determination under collective bargaining.

Negotiated Wages in an Institutionalized Market

When employer and union meet at the negotiating table they are generally engaging in a serious economic confrontation. The ultimate joint product will usually cost the employer more money. Negotiating a general wage increase or incorporating a special increase in the rates for skilled workers or agreeing on substantial additions to the present complex of money fringe benefits—any and all of these will boost the price of labor as a factor of production. When this is determined at the bargaining table, the process is a different breed of cat from the marketplace interaction of labor demand and supply forces.

Clark Kerr pointed out many years ago that in wage bargaining between employer and union traditional market forces are replaced by institutionalized controls on both sides of the bargaining table.[1] In the

---

[1] Clark Kerr, "Labor Markets: Their Character and Consequences," *Proceedings, Second Annual Meeting*, Industrial Relations Research Association (Champaign, Ill.: Industrial Relations Research Association, 1950), pp. 69–84; and "Wage Relationships—The Comparative Impact of Market and Power Forces," in *The Theory of Wage Determination*, ed. John T. Dunlop (New York: St. Martin's Press, 1957), pp. 173–93.

short run at least, one important consequence has been drastically different behavior in the *wage* market than one might expect from looking at the condition of the *job* market.

Economists are accustomed to reasoning that an abundant supply of labor in a particular labor market will cause the price of such labor to fall. Conversely, when labor is "tight" (that is, in short supply) and demand for such labor is intense, the price of such labor can be expected to rise to reflect this market condition. Under collective bargaining, however, these "logical" developments may not take place. The price of labor may actually increase rather than decline, even though supply is plentiful. In fact, as Kerr suggested in his 1950 and 1957 papers, in some highly organized employer-union relationships labor supply and demand may well adjust to the wage rate rather than the other way around.

Certain structural developments noted in Chapter 2 need to be reviewed that reflect the manner in which the institutional market has become *the* dominant force in negotiated wage behavior.

These include:

1. Extensive coverage and importance of centralized structures for bargaining, on both management and union sides.
2. The customary control of policy formation (especially on wages and other key bargaining issues) in the hands of international union officers.
3. The growth and vitality of formal multi-employer bargaining arrangements.
4. Recent emphasis on coalition or coordinated bargaining on the union side to cope with giant management concerns (chiefly the conglomerates, operating over a wide range of industries under one central management).
5. Closer integration of union policies through mergers of formerly competing unions and through more direct, continuing research and organizational assistance from the AFL-CIO itself.

The foregoing structural developments, reinforced by the follow-the-leader aspect of pattern bargaining, can be seen as nudging the economy toward an approximation of national collective bargaining—in the sense of a tacitly accepted (if not agreed upon) overall wage policy for a particular contract year.

We have not yet developed formal machinery such as a council of top union and industry representatives meeting with the Council of Economic Advisers for hammering out a tripartite consensus on a "responsible" wage policy applicable to all employers and unions whose contracts are up for negotiation in a particular year. A consensus mechanism would be preferred over direct government wage and price fixing. The prospects for voluntarism in developing an entente of this nature are reserved for Chapter 11.

Pattern-Following on Wage Policy

Pattern-following remains of vital significance in many sectors. Wage increases won by the UAW in the automobile industry for 1967–1970 were followed closely in subsequent negotiations in the farm equipment industry and in other UAW contracts open in 1967. The rubber workers had served as a pilot for the UAW earlier in 1967 by gaining substantial economic improvements after a rather lengthy strike against several of the major rubber companies. The same chronology of developments occurred in 1970. Negotiations in the rubber tire industry served in a sense as a pilot for the automobile negotiations, with the latter in turn setting the pattern for subsequent demands in farm equipment.

In the 1967 meat packing industry negotiations, Armour and Company and the two unions involved at the time led the way by concluding negotiations peacefully for the 1967–1970 contract several months in advance of the contract's expiration date. The Armour package was subsequently adopted by most major and independent packers later in 1967. The 1970 pioneer settlements were reached with Armour and Swift. These were subsequently followed closely throughout the industry. Once again the key contract negotiations were successfully consummated without a strike about five months ahead of the expiration date of the 1967–1970 agreement. The 1970 negotiations were more centralized in the sense that the two unions involved, the United Packinghouse Workers of America and the Amalgamated Meat Cutters and Butcher Workmen, had merged organically in the summer of 1968, adopting the name of the Amalgamated.

Perhaps the most significant model in the 1968 negotiations was the substantial package gained by the United Steelworkers of America without a strike in its negotiations with the major steel companies. The Steelworkers were under pressure to do as well or better than the UAW had done in 1967. The same will be true when steel contracts open in 1971. The Steelworkers will be looking back on what the UAW achieved in its 1970 bargaining.

The point is clear that no part of the collective bargaining scene escapes the eyes of other employers and unions. Any change of fashion on wage policy (or on anything else, for that matter) inaugurated in a key employer-union relationship is likely to be reflected in other negotiations if the parties wish, for their own purposes, to follow suit. On wage policy there is generally pressure to match (although not necessarily to exceed) the average increase being negotiated elsewhere. When it became known that the 1968 steel compact called for about a $6\frac{1}{2}$ percent across-the-board wage boost, this percentage became almost a guiding light affecting negotiations in other fields. The comparison compulsion is invariably stronger than

purely economic factors might suggest. Collective bargaining is not necessarily a rational process at all times.

THE PATTERN-FOLLOWING SYNDROME
AND ITS RELATIONSHIP TO LONG-TERM CONTRACTS

Employers do not like to be too far apart from their fellow employers on wage policy, no matter how competitive they consider themselves to
be. Unions are also motivated to "keep up with the Joneses." The union
leader's constituents keep careful tabs on whether he is doing as well for them
on wages and other key economic issues as other unions appear to be doing
for their membership.

Pattern-following is also highly visible on such matters as the length
of contracts. We note here one famous illustration linking the duration of
contract with the shape of negotiated wage provisions nationally ever since
1950. We refer to the unique experiment of General Motors and the UAW
with a five-year contract for the period 1950–1955. Prior to this imaginative
experiment most contracts in this country were negotiated and renegotiated
on an annual basis or, at most, for two years at a time.

The *quid pro quo* for an agreement lasting as long as five years in a
dynamic field such as labor relations had to be a mutually satisfactory formula on the wage issue, one which would accommodate the employees'
economic aspirations and also be one that the employer could live
with under potentially shifting economic conditions for such a lengthy
period.

GM and UAW first tried a "dry run" with their two-pronged wage
formula between 1948 and 1950. They then decided to plunge for five years
with their controversial combination of an Annual Improvement Factor
increase (related to the annual trend rate increase in physical productivity
per man-hour for the economy as a whole) and a quarterly review, with
wage rate adjustment upward or downward, related to changes in the BLS
Consumers' Price Index (the so-called escalator clause).

The five-year span was a shocker to many employers and unions.
Many continued with more conventional bargaining arrangements. Five
years in actuality proved too long for GM and UAW themselves, but they
established conclusively the wisdom of breaking away from the traditional
annual wage bargaining. The GM-UAW formula for determining wage
increases over a long-term contract has met the hard test of experience
since 1955, although all subsequent contracts have been for three years
each.

The Dynamics and Determinants
of Union Wage Policy

Arthur M. Ross' classic study, *Trade Union Wage Policy*,[2] appeared first in book form in 1948, but most of the analysis remains fresh and pertinent for current understanding. Operating from the central proposition that the trade union is a political agency operating in an economic environment, Ross employs this deceptively simple generalization as the key to understanding unionism as an institutional phenomenon. Another eminent labor economist, Harold M. Levinson, has made a significant improvement in our understanding of the economic side of unionism with his 1966 study of the *determining forces* in collective wage bargaining. Through meticulous empirical analysis of bargaining on wages *and* major fringe benefits in four sharply different industries, Levinson moves beyond the Ross dichotemization of "political" and "economic" variables by introducing an important analytical component, the "pure power" variable.[3]

Of crucial importance to understanding *why unions behave like unions* rather than as cost-conscious employers might wish them to behave is an appreciation of the fact that union leaders are not sellers of a commodity (labor) in the usual sense. Union leaders *represent* groups of employees who have selected or designated them to perform the representation function. Union leaders are *agents* of the employees they represent. More importantly, both the local union leadership and the national union leaders are *elected agents*. As agents who must satisfy their clients, union leaders cannot act always as economic men. Over any period of time the union leader must satisfy the needs and aspirations of his constituency—the membership—or face the prospect of losing power. Union leadership behavior and demands in negotiations, therefore, are frequently not as businesslike or as responsible as employers and economists might like.

Employees in the United States are the most economically affluent

---

[2] Arthur M. Ross, *Trade Union Wage Policy* (Berkeley and Los Angeles: University of California Press, 1948). The final draft of this chapter was completed before word was received of the sudden death of Arthur M. Ross in June, 1970. I regard the Ross contribution to our understanding of the dynamics of union wage behavior as essentially timeless in nature. He continues to live in his contributions to analysis of union wage policy and in his many fair-minded and perceptive decisions as an arbitrator of labor disputes. My analysis reflects at many points a major obligation to Dr. Ross.

[3] Harold M. Levinson, *Determining Forces in Collective Wage Bargaining* (New York: John Wiley & Sons, Inc., 1966). The Levinson work is one of the most illuminating studies of recent vintage for understanding union behavior. Another excellent treatment is that of Frank C. Pierson, *Unions in Postwar America: An Economic Assessment* (New York: Random House, Inc., 1967).

workers in the history of the world. They are also the most economically secure in most unionized situations, even with as little as one year's seniority. Such favorable considerations have not diminished by one iota the individual worker's desire for "more" of everything. It was once considered smart by some critics to talk in disparaging terms of Sam Gompers' dedication to bread-and-butter unionism. His concentration on economic goals was condemned as too parochial or self-centered, with insufficient emphasis on what is often called social unionism. Although *some* union leaders do have *some* crusading spirit left,[4] union leaders appear to be more bourgeois and middle class than ever before. Employees who are more affluent and secure than any of their predecessors appear determined to achieve still greater affluence. They have little sympathy for union leaders who fail to satisfy their escalated expectations. Few employees have any memory of "how tough it used to be," nor are they interested in hearing about the old days.

The typical worker is in his late twenties or early thirties. He has probably never been unemployed. He lives up to or beyond his assured income of $120 to $150 (or more) per week. He is so accustomed to an annual wage increase of a substantial nature that he equates it in his mind with his constitutional rights. His conception of a "fair" wage or salary is likely to be "at least 10 percent more than whatever I'm making today." This psychological law of wage determination bedevils any union leader who must deal with employers who simply may not be economically capable of satisfying such soaring expectations.

The wage objectives of the rank-and-file may not be reconcilable with the cold economics of a particular situation. The workers' goal may involve maximizing the total wage bill for the membership in some cases. In other situations, reaching the desired end may involve appreciable unemployment in the bargaining unit. Ordinarily, rank-and-file workers do not associate a given set of wage demands with the volume of employment opportunities, nor are they likely to be concerned about the nexus between wage rates and productivity. On the other hand, in almost all cases they have unbounded faith in employer ability to absorb successive wage increments. Worker perception of the *external impact* of a particular wage bargain is likely to be lacking.

The prime determinant of rank-and-file wage demands continues to be the Ross "standard of equitable comparison." Its importance helps to explain why union leaders are so intensely concerned about matching the

---

[4] The tragic and untimely death of Walter P. Reuther in an airplane accident in May, 1970, mutes considerably the force of this generalization. The longtime president of UAW was by all odds the outstanding leader among those socially concerned unionists who sought to involve themselves with such basic community problems as poverty, racial discrimination, urban housing and the like. No figure of stature comparable to Reuther is likely to emerge for some time to come.

gains made by rival unions and why the percentage amount of the adjustment is frequently of greater importance than the absolute amount.

Informed trade union leaders are concerned about the economic
consequences of wage demands. Nevertheless, they are operating from a
political basis of authority. They must deliver to the satisfaction of the membership (or at least to the satisfaction of the employed portion of the membership) if they expect to remain in office. Careful regard must also be given
to the *survival and growth requirements of the union as an institution,* aside from
the demands of the membership.

Such union institutional needs help to explain why strikes occur
when the employer and the union are only a few cents apart in the amount
of wage increase demanded and the amount offered. When a strike is thought
to be necessary to maintain the integrity and standing of the union as an
institution, the figures as to how many years it will take the workers to make
up the paychecks lost while they were striking over what appears to be a
negligible wage gap are almost irrelevant to the union leader and to the
membership. If the alternative to striking is thought to be the destruction
or emasculation of the union, the strike is worth it in their eyes.

How and by Whom are Union Wage Policies Formulated?

In stressing the desires of employees for higher and higher wages
and bigger and better fringes, it should be noted at the same time that the
functions of formulating economic policy and also negotiating on wages
and other key issues are generally performed by top union leadership. Collective bargaining has become much too technical, complex and specialized to
be planned and conducted on a town meeting basis.

The preliminary reciprocal communication between union membership and leadership goes on months ahead of negotiation time. Firm decisions on what to press for at the bargaining table are then made by the
national union leadership. There are notable exceptions, such as the building
trades unions, who still leave bargaining pretty much in the hands of the
locals in particular labor markets. Generally speaking, however, national
union leaders call the shots for their affiliated locals. Such centralized control
over wage policy formation will continue to be the way of life for most major
industrial unions and many craft unions as well. In fact, as we noted in
Chapter 2, structural trends do not show any likely diminution of national
authority on major policy matters. Coalition or coordinated bargaining
arrangements among unions with related interests are likely to continue.
The AFL-CIO is developing ways of computerizing relevant bargaining
data to be made available for the use of all affiliates in bargaining. I under-

stand the Steelworkers' union is prepared to furnish computerized data to its representatives.

The dynamics of union wage policy are substantially different from those of management in bargaining. As political institutions, there is generally a degree of responsiveness and interaction between union leadership and the rank and file that one does not find in most management organizations. Such communication can be noted even in the most autocratically administered unions.

Unions cannot operate on a chain-of-command basis as do many business firms. There is more two-way communication in the union hierarchy, notwithstanding the usual high degree of centralization. The final formation of union wage policy, however, is the function of top leadership in most instances.

The main factors responsible for this centralization in policy formation should be briefly restated. First, wage bargaining is a technical, complicated process. It demands a degree of expertise and a fund of information not ordinarily found among most local union leaders, let alone the rank and file. This factor alone is a powerful argument for increased centralization.

Second, union policy goals such as the standard rate and industry-wide stability in wage relationships cannot be reached through uncoordinated local union bargaining. Centralized control is essential. The consequences for big unionism in this respect are similar to those for big business. Large-scale organization precludes the luxury of pure democracy in the sense of complete rank-and-file participation.

Most union members nevertheless have a more effective voice on wage policy than the foregoing remarks suggest. Union constitutions, for example, generally require that agreements with employers be negotiated subject to approval by the membership. In the large, highly centralized unions, ratification was often a rubber stamp or *pro forma* kind of thing. More recently, there has been a significant increase in membership rejections of contract settlements negotiated in good faith by the union leadership. The rejection phenomenon is a matter of serious concern to employers, union leaders and federal and state mediators. A former director of the Federal Mediation and Conciliation Service, William E. Simkin, notes that some aspect of the wage problem ranked foremost among causes of rejection. Simkin's study shows only 16 percent of the rejections not involving wages as a factor.[5] Our Chapter 5 observations on contract rejections need not be repeated. If the high rejection rate should continue, we can expect some fundamental changes in employer approaches to bargaining and also some drastic revision of many union constitutional policies.

---

[5] William E. Simkin, "Refusals to Ratify Contracts," *Industrial and Labor Relations Review*, XXI (July, 1968), 518–40.

Better communication is needed between union membership and union leadership if we are to achieve improved stability in labor relations. Procedures must be developed to assure that *the negotiators on both sides of the bargaining table are known to have the authority to bind their constituents to an agreement.* The technical character of contemporary bargaining requires that negotiation be conducted by top union leadership as well as by top management in most cases. Internal conflicting pressures within a union must be reconciled effectively before going to the bargaining table. Union leadership needs a free hand when actually facing management across the table. The needs of a national union negotiator are similar to those of a labor relations employer association representing large numbers of diverse small employers in a multi-employer bargaining arrangement. In each case the internal pressures must be accommodated ahead of negotiation through development of an integrated bargaining posture.

Factors Unions Consider in Shaping Wage Demands

What factors determine what the union leadership will press for at the bargaining table in any particular negotiation? In the listing to follow, some factors are primarily economic; others are more political than economic. Still others fit the Harold Levinson category of "pure power" considerations.

Our prototype of a prudent, well-informed union, Union X, will need to know and consider the following:

1. Wage increases (and economic fringes) recently negotiated by other unions with which Union X is accustomed to comparing itself, either in the particular labor market area, in the industry in question or nationally.
2. The comparative strength within Union X of the employed and unemployed segments of its membership.
3. The nature and extent of differences or conflicts among various interest groups within Union X (for example, the familiar problem of the skilled-unskilled differential).
4. A pragmatic, down-to-earth estimate by Union X's research department of what is feasibly obtainable from Company Y or Industry Z with which Union X is about to bargain for a new contract.
5. An estimate of current bargaining power on economic demands, related to past union economic gains and to the anticipated future bargaining strength of both parties at the negotiations three years in the future. (This is assuming that the current economic package, whatever its ultimate content, will be for a three-year period.)

Union X will also need to make a careful evaluation of the extent to which bargaining demands can (or should) be affected by *external* variables, such as the need (or absence of the need) to rationalize the union's proposals in terms of federal government pressures, direct or indirect.

When operating in a partially unionized industry such as textiles, Union X must consider the probable impact of its demands on the economic health of the particular firm as it relates to labor cost competition from the nonunion sector.

When labor cost is a substantial element in the total cost of the employer's product or service, a careful appraisal must be made of the employer's ability either to absorb or to pass on the increased money costs of what Union X hopes to obtain at the bargaining table. It must also make an objective estimate of its power to enforce its economic demands through strike action if necessary and, correspondingly, the employer's or the industry's *disposition* and *capacity* to "take" such possible application of economic force. This involves, among other things, making a realistic assessment of the membership's enthusiasm (or lack of enthusiasm) for strike action as a guide to how hard and how long to press at the negotiating table before either striking or retreating from original demands.

These are among the many elements that should be considered by union leadership in preparation for and conduct of negotiations on economic issues. The listing is representative but not exhaustive. For example, the question as to whether union leaders can or should consider the employment effect of their wage and other economic demands has not been included. This question interests professional economists far more than it does union leaders. Academic protocol, if nothing else, suggests that the employment effect issue be reviewed before going on to consider the dynamics and determinants of employer wage policy.

Do Union Leaders Consider the Wage Rate-Employment Ratio?

Some economists contend that union leaders (and employers, for that matter) should demonstrate their "responsibility" by exhibiting concern over the relationship between wage rates and volume of employment opportunities. Arthur Ross's 1948 statement remains pertinent today as the most forceful expression of the view that it is difficult, if not impossible, to estimate accurately the wage rate–employment ratio. His blunt conclusion is as follows:[6]

> The volume of employment associated with a given wage rate is unpredictable before the fact, and the effect of a given rate upon employment is

---

[6] Arthur M. Ross, *op. cit.*, p. 80.

undecipherable after the fact. The employment effect cannot normally be the subject of rational calculations and prediction at the time the bargain is made, and union officials are normally in no position to assume responsibility for it. It is the exceptional case which is so widely celebrated in the literature of labor economics as a model of responsible behavior which all unions could do well to emulate.

To support such reasoning Ross first sets forth four links by which the wage rate may be connected to the demand for labor: (1) wage rate to labor costs; (2) labor cost to total cost; (3) total cost to price and (4) price to volume of sales and production. He then stresses that there is such a great deal of free play at each one of these four links in the chain of the wage-employment bargain that "as a result, the initial and final links are so loosely connected that for practical purposes they must be regarded as largely independent."[7]

Ross was promptly charged with underestimating the extent to which unions take into consideration the employment effect of wage decisions. In 1950, George P. Shultz and Charles A. Myers took issue with Ross's conclusion that instances in which wage-cost-price-employment relationships are clear and predictable (and therefore taken into account) are the exceptional cases. Shultz and Myers contended that employment opportunities vitally affect wage decisions in many areas, particularly in job shops as distinguished from continuous production plants, in industries where there is strong competition in the product market and in industries that are only partially organized.[8]

Instead of emphasizing general wage settlements, Shultz and Myers stressed the many other wage decisions that union leaders must make, contending that employment effects are an important influence on such decisions. In his study of the shoe industry in Brockton, Massachusetts, Shultz emphasizes the preoccupation of union leaders in that industry with the employment effect of changing piece prices, changing product lines and the impact of technological change.[9]

The informed reader will recognize that both Ross and his critics are right in terms of the industries they have selected for analysis. Their divergent conclusions reflect differences in the industries and product markets involved. Ross concentrated on oligopolistic industries with administered prices, such as automobile and steel. Shultz and Myers, on the other hand, considered such competitive industries as shoes, clothing and textiles, where labor cost is a substantial element in total cost and where consequently the

---

[7] *Ibid.*, p. 90.

[8] George P. Shultz and Charles A. Myers, "Union Wage Decisions and Employment," *American Economic Review*, XL (June, 1950), 362–80.

[9] George P. Shultz, *Pressures on Wage Decisions* (New York: John Wiley & Sons, Inc., 1951).

wage change-price change-product demand relationships are more readily visible.

The perennial interest of labor economists in the relationship of wages and employment was given fresh stimulus some years ago by the British economist, A.W. Phillips.[10] The famous Phillips curve approach has been applied to U.S. data by several American economists. The *ex post* results of such efforts appear to suggest an almost mystical property in a 5 percent unemployment rate for maintaining price stability in the United States—a result similar to the Phillips data for the United Kingdom covering the period from 1861 to 1927.

We can hope the day is not too far distant when we can reduce our normal or frictional unemployment rate to as little as 2 or 3 percent without sacrificing our price stability objective. There is nothing inexorable or pre-destined about the 5 percent figure.

We are departing from the main thrust of this micro-oriented chapter. Devotees of Phillips curve analysis are mainly concerned with macro-economic policy. We shall conclude the discussion by noting that *some* unions *do* take into account the impact of a given wage rate on employ-ment *when they are in a position to do so*. Even in such cases, however, the employment effect is not likely to be a matter of prime concern. Union leaders are concerned mainly with satisfying their employed rather than their unemployed members.

ADDITIONAL FACTORS AFFECTING UNION WAGE POLICY DETERMINATION

In addition to factors already noted, the following are often influ-ential in determining union wage demands:

1. The expressed desire of the membership on economic demands, bearing in mind the need to temper the "blue-sky" tendencies of rank-and-file proposals.
2. The minimum economic necessities of the employees, a factor of parti-cular relevance in chronically low-paying industries such as laundries and dry cleaning, which remain at or near the legal minimum wage level.
3. Maintenance of weekly take-home pay at previous levels whenever a bargaining demand is in the mill for a permanent reduction in the length of the work week from, for example, forty to thirty-five hours.
4. Increases in the productivity of labor (not stressed by unions, of course, when such productivity is static).

---

[10] A. W. Phillips, "The Relation Between Unemployment and the Rate of Change of Money Wage Rates in the United Kingdom, 1861–1927," *Economica*, XXV (November, 1958), 283–300.

5. Increases in the cost of living (a potent factor to justify union demands when the CPI is rising, but played down when it is stable or declining).
6. The employer's ability to pay (stressed by unions when the employer's profit picture and outlook are rosy, but disparaged as a factor in the opposite case).
7. Wages and economic fringes paid by the employer's competitors in the same industry or labor market area (stressed as relevant whenever the employer in question is below par, but minimized if he is an economic leader except to the extent of appealing to his pride in remaining a leader).

SUMMARY ON UNION WAGE POLICY CONSIDERATIONS

When such a complex of considerations is viewed as an entity, what can we conclude? First, it is clear that to be prepared for all contingencies in bargaining on economic issues, union leaders must do a great deal of homework ahead of negotiations. Second, in particular circumstances certain factors will be of overriding importance that at other times will be of minimal concern.

For example, in the years 1966–1970 the United States experienced sharp increases in consumer goods prices, interest rates and wholesale prices following several years of relative price stability (1962–1966). The CEA's wage guidepost thus crumbled under the united union onslaught. The chief rationale for wage demands since 1966 has been the catch-up argument, triggered by rising living costs and soaring corporate profits.

In wage bargaining, as in most phases of their activity, union leaders are pragmatists. As political animals they do not operate (in fact, cannot operate) on economic and cost considerations alone. They consider the essentially political variable of comparison. Furthermore, they are seldom reluctant to take advantage where feasible of Levinson's "pure power" variable.

When dealing with marginal firms or sick industries, however, the wage policies of particular unions (both craft and industrial) will usually be geared to the operating necessities of particular industries or plants. The influence of local labor demand and supply factors is then of considerable (though not necessarily determinative) importance.

Ross shows the comparison factor as one of the two most significant equalizing tendencies in collective wage determination. The second is the tendency toward consolidated bargaining structures. Among the more compelling factors tending to produce what Ross terms "orbits of coercive comparison" are centralized bargaining within the union, common ownership of establishments, governmental participation in wage determination and rival union leadership. Each of these exerts a pressure for uniformity. Similarly, a pressure toward uniformity in occupational rates and uniformity in wage adjustment patterns develops from consolidated bargaining structures, either of the multi-employer or multi-union type (an employer dealing with several unions jointly).

The need for institutional security is a powerful influence toward union acceptance of multi-union or multi-employer bargaining. Through multi-union bargaining, as Ross points out, unions "protect themselves against participating in the establishment of inequities. They eliminate the possibility of making what appears to be a satisfactory settlement, and then witnessing another union making a better settlement which renders their own embarrassing or untenable." Similarly, the chief advantage of multi-employer bargaining to the union lies in the institutional security it provides against "the apathy of workers, the hostility of employers, and the inroads of rival organizations."[11]

Unions usually outdo employers in their interest in comparisons. It is difficult to see a union's rank and file passing up a wage increase or settling for, say, a 5 percent increase when it is known that other unions are securing higher general increases. *The union leader is under pressure to deliver at least the average increase being obtained elsewhere.*

This compulsion to match the gains of other unions is one that cannot be ignored. The rank and file is neither informed about, nor interested in, distinguishing features that make a 10 percent increase logical in one industry and no increase logical in another. Since employees are interested in wages as income, their concern about an employer's competitive position is not as great as perhaps it should be. Furthermore, as noted earlier, unbounded faith seems to exist in the employer's capacity to absorb a succession of wage increases.

The test of trade union leadership emerges in severe fashion in such cases. We should not assume that a sheeplike rank and file is being led down a suicidal path of high wage policy by an overmilitant trade union leadership. The opposite is more likely to be the case. Trade union leaders often face the uncomfortable task of explaining to a militant rank and file why their desired wage adjustment cannot be achieved.

Many union leaders are becoming more aware of the *external* significance of their wage bargains. They are in a better position than the membership to appreciate the cumulative impact of a series of separate wage bargains. In an inflationary period such as 1966–1970, union members are concerned usually with one factor—the rising cost of living. They are not impressed with arguments for a "responsible" wage policy when they can see their purchasing power whittled away by the mounting prices of consumer goods.

Union leaders therefore cannot be too statesmanlike. Pressures upon

---

[11] Arthur M. Ross, *op. cit.*, p. 71.

them can develop quickly. The Korean war impact is one example. Another is the continued pressure that has been exerted on union leaders to deliver substantial wage increases since prices began to rise rapidly from 1966 forward. In the Korean emergency a prior recession-oriented stress on pensions was quickly forgotten in the face of demands to match rapid increases in the cost of living and to beat the gun on anticipated wage and price controls. Employer resistance to such wage pressures was weak in most cases. In the latter half of 1950 many substantial wage increases were negotiated. Concern over the rising CPI and the force of the comparison factor overpowered any considerations that might have been present concerning the need for restraint to prevent inflation.

Similarly, in every negotiation since 1966 union leaders have felt a mandate to press for as much as the employers were willing and able to concede. Such aggressive wage bargaining was conducted in complete disregard of the CEA's pleas for restraint in terms of productivity trend rate guideposts. In 1967 and 1968 most employers found themselves in a fairly good position to institute substantial wage increases and did so. The 1968 income tax surcharge did not visibly dampen inflationary pressures. Catching up with cost of living increases was still the name of the game in 1969 and 1970 wage negotiations.

Union leaders negotiate with employers in a frame of reference that is basically micro-economic. They are not moved to fight the battle of inflation single-handed. In a time of rising prices such as the economy has experienced since 1966 the role of escalator clauses tied to the CPI brings out clearly the conflict of interest between national economic policy and a micro-economic bargaining orientation. Economists tend to oppose such clauses as constituting engines of inflation. The union leader, however, gets heavy pressure to protect his constituents by insisting on escalator clauses. In the late 1960s some union leaders were audibly regretting their commitments to contract "ceilings" on escalator clauses. Prices had increased in each of the years 1967–1969 considerably beyond the annual percentage limitations of contract cost-of-living adjustments. In 1970 negotiations the union watchword once again was catch-up for past losses in real wage position and removal of ceilings on any future escalator arrangements.

In final summary on union wage policy we conclude as follows:

1. Formation of union wage policy (and other economic demands) is necessarily a function of top leadership.
2. Economic demands of the union are shaped mainly by the comparison factor—the gains made by other unions—and by membership needs and aspirations. The requirement of accommodating and reconciling conflicting internalized interests among the membership is a "must" before going to the bargaining table.
3. Union wage and other economic demands are thus shaped by political as well as by economic calculations. The vigor with which these demands

may be prosecuted is often influenced greatly by Levinson's "pure power" variable.

4. The impact of external variables such as the CEA's wage guideposts had *some* degree of influence with *some* unions and employers from 1962 to 1966. However, since 1966 even the major unions that must operate in a goldfish bowl of national publicity have negotiated economic bargains considerably in excess of CEA criteria.

5. Local labor market factors are less persuasive with union leaders than they are with employers. In some cases, notably building and construction, the time-honored practice of localized negotiation aimed at achieving whatever the traffic will bear is still in vogue. On the whole, however, the increasing centralization and institutionalization of the wage determination process has contributed to reducing the significance of local labor supply and demand factors.

THE DYNAMICS AND DETERMINANTS OF EMPLOYER WAGE POLICY

When analyzing the decisive factors in the employer's approach to economic issues in bargaining, it is hard to generalize. As with unions, the questions must always be asked, "Which company?" and "Under what type of conditions?" Employers are themselves pragmatic. There is thus no one standardized approach to wage determination.

The employer's task is less complex than the union leader's. The employer can concentrate on *cost* as the dominant consideration. A prudent employer needs the same type of data and know-how for economic decision-making, whether he is dealing with a union or operating unilaterally. In a negotiating situation the employer's approach may appear to differ from that of a nonunion firm. This appearance is more illusory than real because it is the negotiated economic settlements that call the tune for many nonunion employers.

Most of what the employer needs to know is of an economic nature, although some factors are political for the employer as well as for the union. An employer, for example, wishes to remain in good standing with his business peers. He thus desires to stay in line with what other firms are doing, even when he is in a position to do far better (or far worse) in terms of economic demands. This consideration is the employer's version of the union comparison factor.

The wise employer at the bargaining table should consider the following:

1. His firm's current competitive position in the industry and in relation to possible substitute products.

2. His cost picture related to his current and anticipated factor mix, that is, percentage of labor cost to total cost for whatever product(s) or service(s) may be involved.

3. Accurate comparison of his wage rates and fringe costs with those of his chief competitors in the industry and those of comparable firms in his labor market area.

4. An informed estimate of his absorption potential for increased labor costs in the coming contract period at different assumed levels relating to union economic proposals.

5. An estimate of his own economic bargaining power, involving his ability to take a strike of varying levels of duration and intensity, including an accurate estimating of his own and his customers' inventories and the goodwill of the principal customers and suppliers upon whom he relies.

6. An informed appraisal of the probable cost impact of the union's economic demands, if granted, and the necessary revisions, if any, in price policy. Future price revisions in turn entail knowledge of current and prospective market conditions and the nature of demand for the firm's product(s), for example, how might consumers be expected to react to a price increase of x percent.

7. Analysis of the macro-economic outlook as related to the probable outcome of his negotiations.

8. Estimate of the tightness or looseness of the local labor supply, relating this to recruitment and retention of labor under his probable new labor costs after negotiations.

Life for the employer on economic issues is never simple any more than it is for his union leader counterpart. His decision on a general increase is only part of the battle. The employer will need to review his internal occupational rate structure. His idea of an appropriate skill differential may be at variance with what the union is pressing for in negotiations. Most employers are partial to intraplant rate adjustments suggested by their industrial engineers. These often differ sharply from union demands for correction of alleged intraplant inequities. Also, in negotiation of such structural wage problems, the employer will usually pay more attention to local labor supply and demand factors than the union.

CONVERSION FROM HOURLY TO SALARIED METHODS OF WAGE PAYMENT

Many employers face intensified union pressure to pay their blue-collar production and maintenance employees on a salaried basis. Honoring such demands will require careful calculations on the employer's part. More is involved than agreement on the conversion formula.

"Going on salary" can have either favorable or unfavorable practical results from a labor productivity standpoint. When paying by the hour, the employer had the satisfaction of knowing that he was never—in theory at least—paying for work not performed. An employee who clocked in late or clocked out early was usually not paid for such time lost. When absent from work, *even for legitimate reasons*, the employee was usually not paid (unless under a negotiated sick-leave plan or on a contract-specified paid holiday). In other words, the general rule under the old system was no work–no pay.

In going on a salaried method of payment, production workers expect more than just psychological satisfaction from their presumed status increase. They anticipate receiving also what *they believe to be* the greater freedoms of the white-collar salaried employee, such as taking occasional days off or reporting late or leaving early without incurring any income loss thereby. Many blue-collar workers have an exaggerated idea of the amount of freedom enjoyed by salaried employees. The employer negotiating a conversion plan must therefore make clear what the new ground rules are going to be on absenteeism, tardiness and the like. His doing so may complicate the conversion process and furnish a source of conflict and misunderstanding early in administration of the new plan.

Anticipated difficulties in the conversion process will not diminish pressure on the part of many blue-collar unions for switching to salaried methods of payment. In one form or another, many blue-collar workers already have reached an approximation of salaried status through guarantees of so many hours of work or pay each week (as in the meatpacking industry) or through the medium of monthly and annual income security provisions for those with one or more years of seniority (as in the automobile and farm equipment industries).

Summary on Employer Wage Policy Determinants

All employers are necessarily concerned with the cost implications of union wage demands, but employer wage policies are not cast from one mold. Some firms with plants in different geographic locations prefer to follow a policy of wage uniformity throughout the chain. Others adapt their wage or salary structures to prevailing rates in the local labor markets. Some prefer to be leaders or pacesetters in wage policy whereas others prefer to follow a pattern. Some employers act on the view that high wages will bring lower unit labor costs because of increased productivity and better employee morale. Others lack faith in wage increases as a stimulus to worker productivity. The latter may try to get by with the lowest possible money wage scale.

Most employers are better prepared for wage negotiations than in former years. They are generally well informed on labor costs internally. They also know the relevant *external* wage data. As indicated in Chapter 5, both employer and union currently begin negotiations with better data. A measure of agreement can often be reached on what data are relevant to their respective wage proposals.

This improving quality of employer and union preparation for wage bargaining should not be overstressed. The cold logic of data does not always prevail at the negotiation table. An experienced management negotiator told me in confidence that he sees little to be gained by extensive economic research prior to negotiations because (in his view) union demands are based invariably on purely political factors. The resigned pessimism of this comment is not very encouraging, but it underscores the fact that the political rationale behind union wage demands must always be a part of the employer's advance calculations and preparations.

Few employers will delegate responsibility for formulating policy on economic issues. This must remain a function of top management in any situation because of its clear importance to all aspects of the enterprise. Authoritative perspective cannot be achieved through hunch or intuition. No employer should approach the bargaining table *prepared only to react* to whatever the union proposes. He must be fully prepared to support his policy, especially when he anticipates that the union's demands will be geared to political factors rather than economic. Whatever the union's imperative, the employer must stay with labor cost as his principal yardstick when negotiating wages and other economic union demands.

Standards for Evaluating Joint Decision-Making on General Wage or Salary Increases (Decreases)

Let us assume that Company X is hit with a demand by Union Y for a straight across-the-board wage increase amounting to 10 percent and the company's top counterproposal reaches 5 percent. A two-month strike ensues ending with a wage agreement for a $6\frac{1}{2}$ percent general increase for each of the next three years. On what basis can the rightness or wrongness of such a settlement be evaluated? Are there objective criteria by which the economic soundness of such a settlement can be judged?

I suggest that there are none. There is no *scientific* basis for concluding that particular wage settlements are right, wrong, too high, too low or about right. Collective wage determination thus remains the despair of those who yearn for scientific validity and predictability. Some economists maintain that a wage bargain not consistent with local labor demand-supply relationships is in some fashion wrong. Those who favor the bargaining power theory rather than the market theory of wage determination (see Chapter 4) are more tolerant of indeterminacy. They nevertheless continue to advocate "responsible," "rational" or "restrained" wage adjustments. These are all plus-type adjectives, awarded whenever it can be shown that the wage increases under the new contract are unlikely to increase unit labor costs.

The fact of the matter is that *all* evaluations of wage settlements are *necessarily subjective.* They are conditioned by the views and positions of those who make them. What is held to be a "responsible" bargain by a labor economist may be characterized as a "sell-out" by the union membership because it does not match the increases won elsewhere in the industry (or area) or because it lacks an escalator clause in a period of rising prices for consumer goods.

Management and union practitioners must work out in the final analysis an agreement on economic issues that permits the parties to live together for the period of the contract (usually three years) in a comparatively harmonious pattern of accommodation. They are not interested in breaking lances for the pleasure of professional economists or the White House. Their bargains on wages and other cost items may thus be disturbing to economists on both micro and macro grounds. There were very few contracts negotiated in 1968, 1969 or 1970 that received good marks from economists on responsibility. Yet they satisfied the operational necessities. These agreements met the crucial pragmatic test of mutual acceptability to the parties.

In summary, many of the criteria for evaluating general wage adjustments cited in the economic journals as being relevant determinants of wage policy are not objective in nature. Nor are they generally used in an objective fashion by the negotiators. Such criteria as cost-of-living changes, productivity changes, industry rates and area rates are in fact always coins with two sides. Their pertinence is stressed or minimized by the participants to rationalize their respective bargaining postures before, during and after negotiations. The level of objectivity in economic negotiation has risen somewhat as more reliable data became available. It seems unlikely, however, that academic standards of rational economic behavior will ever be achieved in collective wage determination.

Scientific precision and pure objectivity are thus not realistically attainable. Can a labor economist say in a particular bargaining situation that industry rates should be used as *scientific* guidelines for wage adjustments rather than area rates (or vice versa)? Similarly, can we claim *scientific* support for determining what share of the fruits of increasing productivity per man-hour should go to employees in the form of wage increases, what share to the employer in the form of profits and what share to the consumer in the form of lower prices? I suggest that we cannot do so.

We can affirm only that employees should benefit *in some degree* from productivity gains. To go beyond this would reveal quickly the lack of a consensus on a formula for allocation of productivity gains. Wage negotiations are "easier" when employer and union can agree on what *are* the relevant economic facts and criteria. Such an understanding often will point directly to what the wages should be.

Once we put aside the notion that we can achieve *total* objectivity or rationality in performing what must remain in part a political function, we have made considerable progress. We can then proceed toward *greater* objectivity and regard for rational (economic) considerations. We can do so by achieving agreement on the relevant data and criteria. A joint employer-union wage policy framework for decision-making can then become a reality.

One durable illustration is the understanding between General Motors and the UAW that *to produce more with the same amount of human effort is a sound economic and social objective.* This has served as the joint rationale for annual improvement factor increases negotiated by GM and the UAW since they first agreed on the proposition in their 1948–1950 and 1950–1955 agreements.

SELECTED STRUCTURAL WAGE PROBLEMS

Many difficult issues can arise over structural or "relative" wage problems, the second basic category of wage decision-making. Perhaps the most troublesome structural question relates to the proper differential between the rate for the top-skilled job in the bargaining unit and that for common labor.

How do Employer X and Union Y decide what the differential shall be? On what basis can they conclude at any given time that the differential is too narrow (too broad)? Should the problem be resolved by scientific methods or by orthodox bargaining? Can the differential be negotiated in objective fashion or must it inevitably be affected by shifting internal pressures within the union and other political variables?

Industrial engineers as a professional group prefer that occupational wage structures be derived from complete job analysis and job evaluation. In their view such a procedure can lead to a correct differential between the highest-skilled and lowest-skilled jobs in the bargaining unit hierarchy. It can also be used to develop a logical ordering of occupational rates for all other jobs at intermediate levels, in the industrial engineer's view.

The economists, if they remain true to their code, would contend that the skill differential should be determined by market forces of demand and supply. In such a view, the market over time will reflect suitable differences among jobs as to skill, effort, previous training and experience and other components.

Management and union negotiators are not as confident of their proper stance. Union negotiators, for example, are seldom impressed by the objectivity claims of the industrial engineer. Employer and union alike may consider the market to be an unsatisfactory guide to what is operationally necessary in *their* particular situation. The practitioners favor the pragmatic approach in resolving structural wage issues. They both seek a wage structure that they can live with for the duration of the agreement.

An accommodation of views among the industrial engineers, economists and labor relations negotiators is always possible if we make our proposed generalization sufficiently broad. It would be difficult, for example, for anyone to quarrel with the basic goal of equal pay for equal work. In labor relations this target is the moral equivalent of home, mother, flag, country and Yale. Consensus is thus available until we become more specific. In negotiation of job rate hierarchies significant conflicts of interest develop that must somehow be accommodated. The net result may square with one party's view of equal pay for equal work while doing violence to the other party's conception of how the goal should be achieved. How does one develop wage standards for machine-paced jobs and worker-paced jobs? Should a toolmaker (highest skill) receive twice as much or three times as much as a yard laborer (lowest skill level)? Clearly, the principle of equal pay for equal work requires paying the toolmaker more than the janitor. The question is how much more?

In the 1967–1970 Deere-UAW contract each of the many job classifications paid on an hourly basis has been allocated to one of eleven labor grades indicated below:

Labor Grade	Rate Range	
*	$4.595	$5.060
1	4.110	4.720
2	3.870	4.485
3	3.655	4.245
4	3.410	4.010
5	3.210	3.775
6	3.075	3.605
7	2.975	3.440
8	2.920	3.285
9	2.870	3.120
10	2.825	3.010

The above schedule shows a differential ratio of about five to three (that is, less than two to one) between the highest-paid and lowest-paid hourly jobs. This reflects substantial narrowing of the gap compared to the days of World War II when highly-skilled jobs were paid about three times as much as common labor. Is it "wrong" to pay a toolmaker three times as much as a janitor? Is it "wrong" that a janitor should be paid more than half as much as a toolmaker? These questions cannot be answered scientifically.

Within any particular occupational rate hierarchy serious disputes between employer and union arise as to where certain jobs should be slotted on the labor grade ladder. The adjustment of alleged occupational rate inequities is an endless task in any relationship. Especially when the employer's technology is a dynamic one, there is a continuing need to revise the content of existing jobs, to create new job classifications and, in some cases, to abolish certain classifications.

Any such changes in job patterns and job mix will produce grievances by employees who believe their work has been improperly classified. Two of the more common structural wage issues heard by arbitrators are the following:

1. Did the company violate the contract by reclassifying the work of John Doe into Labor Grade 6?
2. Was there a substantial change in the content of Job X within the meaning of the contract?

Some Thoughts on Job Evaluation

Most employers and all industrial engineers have a preference for job analysis and job evaluation as a method of resolving structural wage problems. The following thumbnail summary represents my conception of what is needed for effective job evaluation.

A job evaluation plan requires the following:

1. Accurate and complete descriptions for all distinct jobs in the appropriate bargaining unit.
2. Identification of factors common to all jobs to be evaluated, such as (a) degree and type of skill required; (b) previous training or experience needed; (c) responsibility for materials and equipment and for safety of other employees; (d) physical working conditions; (e) employee effort required; (f) education required, such as high school diploma, shop math and so forth.
3. Assignment of weights to these basic factors, followed by the evaluation and rating of each described job in terms thereof.
4. Classification of all jobs into labor grades in terms of the evaluation findings.

Assuming that the practice faithfully follows the theory, the results from such an undertaking will be a rational, logical and equitable hierarchy of all jobs in the unit.

A job evaluation expert is not properly concerned with monetary values. His primary function is to develop accurate, complete descriptions for all distinct jobs and then to evaluate each one in objective fashion by rating the described duties in terms of the factor elements common to all jobs. His focus must always be on the job itself rather than on the man performing the job. The job evaluator should not be concerned with or affected by wage rates currently being paid or sought.[12] His task is one of comparative analysis of jobs in terms of degree of difficulty, skill, educational requirements and the like. Determination of actual wage rates is the joint responsibility of the employer and union negotiators. Their ultimate structural solution may not always correspond to the job evaluator's findings.

Experience indicates that the success or failure of job evaluation depends not so much on the type of plan used as upon the manner of its introduction and administration. Many plans that seemed excellent from a technical standpoint have failed in execution because of improper or insufficient attention to the human aspects of the program. The latter must include union and employee understanding and, hopefully, acceptance.

Whatever the plan, it should be introduced with great care and with top management's full approval. A clear understanding is needed with the union involved on the relationship between the job evaluation plan and wage setting. Of particular importance are the procedures for implementing a job evaluation plan in daily administration. There must be a clear understanding of the procedure for evaluating and rating new and changed jobs under the plan.

Certain intraplant rate differentials may not agree with the logic of the job evaluation plan's occupational hierarchy. If such differentials have been in existence for many years, it may not be wise to attempt to force them to conform to the plan's logic overnight.

For example, a difficult situation can arise whenever a technological improvement makes it possible for an employer to assign a machine-paced, automatic duty to a semi-skilled job classification, thus achieving a product result formerly done by employees in a highly skilled classification. When this occurs, the employees in the semi-skilled classification are likely to confuse the product result with the skill required to produce it. They will therefore contend that *their work* should promptly be reclassified upwards, even though the new duties are no more demanding (or even less so) than their former assignment. Such cases can be "sticky" and they are not uncommon.

Union Attitudes toward Job Evaluation

Unionism's historical opposition to job evaluation has been vigorous and, in some cases, justified. Job evaluation plans were sometimes used in

---

[12] This statement is a bit sweeping. I do not mean to suggest that industrial engineers should live in a world divorced from reality. My intention is to stress that the evaluator's judgment when ranking jobs should not be affected by what those jobs are paid.

the past as a sophisticated cover-up for rate-cutting. On the other hand, during World War II job evaluation plans were used by some employers to rationalize rate increases and upgrading of jobs to get around the National War Labor Board's wage stabilization restrictions. These tactics produced considerable union mistrust and cynicism concerning the objectivity of industrial engineers.

Under current conditions, many unions accept job evaluation as a process, in some cases wholeheartedly and in others grudgingly. Some union leaders recognize the values of a fairly administered job evaluation plan in wage administration. However, nearly all union leaders face difficult problems at times in reconciling and accommodating the conflicting internal pressures of a heterogeneous union membership.

For example, an industrial union certified as exclusive bargaining representative for an appropriate unit consisting of all production and maintenance employees, excluding clerical and supervisory, periodically encounters difficulties in balancing the divergent interests and claims of highly skilled craftsmen (for example, toolmakers) with those of semi-skilled production workers (for example, assemblers or machine operators). Friction, even hostility, between such groups within the same bargaining unit is often severe.

Craftsmen are generally paid on a straight hourly basis whereas the semi-skilled production workers may be taking home handsome weekly earnings from an incentive system based on output. In some instances, the latter's take-home pay may actually exceed the craftsman's. The resultant internal political problem makes it difficult for the union to live with the logic of a formal job evaluation plan. It is not surprising, therefore, that union leaders generally prefer to handle occupational rate disputes by negotiation rather than be restricted by the impersonal mechanism of job evaluation.

During the life of agreements, particularly those that run three years or longer, the technological imperative will produce substantial changes in the content of many existing jobs, requiring that such jobs be reclassified upward or downward. Also, new jobs will make their appearance during a contract's lifetime. Disputes are bound to arise as to whether changed or new jobs are properly placed within the hierarchy of occupational rates.

Grievance arbitration is frequently of value to employers and unions under these circumstances. As noted in Chapter 7, a frequent issue before arbitrators relates to whether under the contract particular work duties are properly classified. Issues can also arise as to whether particular employees are slotted into the proper classification in terms of the work they do. Thus arbitration can be an aid to the parties in their never-ending task of seeking to maintain a rational, equitable hierarchy of occupational rates in a dynamic job design milieu.

In summary, the major structural problems continue to be two-fold in character: (1) the avoidance of excessive compression or stretching of occupational differentials, and (2) effectuating rate changes as they may be needed to reflect changes in job content, job method and so forth.

WAGE AND SALARY ADMINISTRATION PROBLEMS

Our third category of wage decision-making relates to a number of troublesome issues in wage or salary administration. These include such basic decisions as whether to pay employees on an hourly, weekly or monthly basis or whether to gear payments to output through some form of incentive system. Grievance machinery for resolving alleged occupational rate inequities during a contract's lifetime has already been touched upon in the preceding discussion of structural wage problems. It can also properly be viewed as a key problem area of wage administration.

Among the questions requiring an answer in an effective plan of wage and salary administration we can list the following:

1. If the employee is to be paid by the hour, day, week or month, should his compensation be in terms of a single occupational rate (that is, job rate) or a rate range? If rate ranges are used, how should an employee be advanced from the minimum (entrance rate) to the maximum?
2. On what basis shall the rate on an existing job be changed when job content changes?
3. Are incentive methods of compensation worth the time and trouble required to install and administer them?
4. Assuming that rates of pay for blue-collar and nonsupervisory white-collar employees are administrable through conventional techniques, should professional employees be handled under the same administrative rubric or should they be accorded separate attention?
5. How can the complications from extensive monetary fringe payments be administered most effectively?

These are but a few of the questions that make life difficult for the wage and salary administrator and for the union involved. Each deserves a chapter in itself, but can be given only brief attention here.[13]

SINGLE RATES OR RATE RANGES?

The single rate concept has the appeal of simplicity in administration. It also ties in with worker and union notions of egalitarianism. On balance, however, a system of rate ranges answers more problems more

---

[13] For a perceptive analysis of many of these problems, related to both the firm and the economy as a whole, see Leonard R. Burgess, *Wage and Salary Administration in a Dynamic Economy* (New York: Harcourt, Brace & World, Inc., 1968).

satisfactorily. Management generally seeks sufficient flexibility in wage administration to permit recognition of individual differences in merit, effort and experience. It cannot do this under a single or standard rate approach. When the rate range between minimum and maximum is a suitable one (that is, neither too narrow or too wide) the possibility exists of starting new employees at the minimum, then advancing them to the midpoint by specified increments after specified intervals of service. Midpoint to maximum of the range can then be reserved for recognition of superior merit and effort. In some cases, however, unions have been successful in negotiating automatic progression to the maximum of the range by regular step-ups every three or six months. From a management standpoint automatic progression to the top of the range doesn't make sense. An optimal blend of management and union thinking would call for progression to the midpoint at regular time intervals and advancement from midpoint to maximum on the basis of merit. This approach is based on viewing the midpoint of the range as the monetary equivalent of what the job would pay if it were on a single rate basis.

ADMINISTRATION OF MERIT INCREASES

Granting or withholding of merit increases can prove to be an administrative headache. This need not be the case if management knows what it is doing and the union leadership understands the policy and the procedure. The NLRB has held consistently that the employer's obligation to bargain extends to negotiating with the union on merit increases upon request. The employer is also required to furnish information to the union as to merit increases granted or withheld. Many unions prefer to leave the matter entirely in management's hands, subject to challenge through the grievance procedure in any case of alleged favoritism or discrimination. Merit increase disputes are a thankless hot potato from the union leadership standpoint in much the same fashion as are many seniority issues and disputes over denied promotions.

In my arbitration experience the challenged denial of a merit increase has been rare. The denial of a merit increase is a discretionary managerial act. It is difficult to challenge successfully unless it can be shown that the action was arbitrary, capricious or discriminatory. Such a burden of proof is a difficult one to maintain. Furthermore, many unions seek to avoid becoming embroiled in too many individual disputes. They will not challenge to the point of arbitration unless they think the company in question is deliberately discriminating in its administration of the merit increase program, or unless they fear a charge of neglecting their duty of fair representation.

Incentive Systems: Are They Worth the Trouble?

Many employers are less sanguine than in years past about the virtues of incentive methods of wage payment. For what this prediction may be worth, it is my impression that the days of the incentive system are numbered in many work relationships. I suspect that in many cases a candid cost-benefit study of an incentive plan's installation and operation would reveal that this time-honored method of rewarding employee effort is not accomplishing what the employer had anticipated.

This conclusion is based on such considerations as the following:

1. An incentive system is expensive to install and costly to maintain in proper fashion.
2. If incentive dispute arbitration costs are figured into the reckoning, it is questionable in many cases whether the game is worth the candle.
3. Apart from economic considerations, it is probable that employee morale and rapport with management will be easier to achieve and maintain under a sound system of occupational rate ranges than under an incentive payment plan.

Incentive plans may be on the wane. However, there are still many lines of work that lend themselves to a system of payments related to worker output. Also, many instances could be cited where the employees are pleased with operating on an incentive basis. They remain deaf to the pleadings of their national union leadership, which officially opposes piece-rate systems.

In recent years there has been considerable experimentation with joint administration of wage-incentive systems. Some plants have joint time study operations; others have a joint committee to review production standards and piece rates set in terms of those standards. In most cases, however, the methods analysis and time study operations remain management functions. The establishment of production standards and the setting of piece rates are also usually management functions, with the union reserving the right to challenge the fairness of the standard or the rate through the contract's grievance machinery.

Union opposition to incentive methods of payment is often deep-rooted. The direct relating of earnings to effort works against the union principle of wage uniformity. However, when the union's institutional status is secure and job operations lend themselves to an incentive method of payment, there is less union opposition.

Most unions are not equipped for joint participation with management in administration of a wage-incentive plan. Nor do most unions wish to share responsibility for the effective operation of such plans. They prefer to insist upon the right to challenge managerial exercise of administrative initiative. If the right to challenge is secure, most unions are not interested in going further.

ELEMENTS OF A SOUND INCENTIVE SYSTEM

Variety is still the hallmark when one reviews the field of incentive systems. Some generalizations can still safely be made concerning principles to be observed for successful operation in a unionized context. These include the following:

1. In union-management relations a constant piece-rate plan is the most feasible and acceptable. The principle of one for one will produce the least opposition and the best results.
2. The average normal operator should be able to earn approximately 20 to 30 percent above his guaranteed base rate.
3. The guaranteed base rate should not be set at an unrealistically low figure to create the illusion that piece-work earnings are exceptionally high. It should correspond to what the job would pay on an hourly rate basis.
4. Piece rates should not be reduced unless there has been a *substantial* change in methods, materials, design or equipment.
5. The contract's grievance and arbitration machinery should be available both for challenging rates alleged to be too tight and for reviewing those alleged to be too loose (that is, runaway standards).

SALARY ADMINISTRATION FOR PROFESSIONAL EMPLOYEES

Should the employer's wage and salary administration program treat unionized professional employees as a breed apart? How to answer this question becomes increasingly important in terms of intensified collective bargaining activity by teachers, nurses and some categories of engineers.

Professional employees are nearly always paid on a salaried basis. There is no evidence that they prefer another method. The prestige status of being on salary remains such that it would not make sense to remove professional employees from this category at a time when pressure is strong from blue-collar and nonsupervisory clerical employees to go on a salaried basis. In fact, the conversion of the latter to salaried status may provide the logical basis for greater homogeneity in the employer's administrative system.

Most unionized professional employees appreciate the need for a salary system that recognizes individual differences in value to the firm. There is not likely to be any objection to differential performance recognition as long as the salary classification plan clearly provides for established minima and subsequent advancement. A familiar illustration of this can be taken from union policies in the performing arts. The stress in negotiations is on improving "scale" for the various categories such as pit musician, supporting actor, extra work and the like.

We shall return to the special nature of collective bargaining for professional employees in Chapter 13. This brief discussion of individual recognition in the case of professional employees should serve as a reminder that the future will witness in all probability a similar stress on individualism on the part of all unionized workers once the latter's drive for basic security has succeeded to the point where their economic aims can become more varied and complex. Bok and Dunlop have pointed out that the trend toward individualized choice is visible in the form of such varied negotiated accomplishments as expanded employee choice in selection of vacation periods, employer-financed training and education programs, choice of shifts, bidding opportunities and grouping of certain fringe benefits into individualized lump-sum accounts. The last-named arrangement would permit employees and their families to adjust their contributions to their age and style of life.[14]

Administration of Equal Pay for Equal Work Principles

Administering contracts to preclude discrimination against employees on the basis of sex or color is a great deal easier than in the recent past. Most employers and unions are playing it straight. They have abandoned such discriminatory devices as labeling work as "female jobs" and "male jobs." This kind of terminology often covered a tacit understanding that the former paid less although the duties were essentially the same. There has also been an encouraging decline in the use of "black only" or "white only" work categories where the basis for the distinction was both racial and economic. Federal and state legislation has helped to improve a formerly shabby picture. However, joint moves toward nondiscriminatory application of equal pay for equal work policies have occurred without the external push being necessary.

This is not to say that the problem of discrimination in wages based on sex or race no longer exists. Deeply ingrained patterns of discrimination do not vanish overnight in response either to the law or to the letter of labor relations agreements. Grievance arbitrators can testify that women still face barriers in successfully bidding on job vacancies traditionally regarded as beyond their capacities. Black workers face similar difficulties in certain cases even though the law and the union contract are unambiguously in

---

[14] Derek C. Bok and John T. Dunlop, *Labor and the American Community* (New York: Simon and Schuster, Inc., 1970), Chapter 12, "Frontiers of Substantive Bargaining," pp. 342–60.

their favor. The encouraging fact remains, however, that wage discrimination based on sex or race is on its way to being a matter of historical interest only.

SETTING WAGE RATES ON NEW OR CHANGED JOBS DURING THE LIFE OF A CONTRACT

No discussion of administrative decision-making on wage and salary matters can end without some consideration of the perennially difficult task of setting wage rates on new or changed jobs during the life of a contract. The pace of technology and changing job design in recent years has been such as to make this phase of union-management relations more rather than less demanding. The future shape of work patterns is certain to differ drastically from what we take for granted today. Assuming the continued prevalence of three-year agreements, we have reason to anticipate that employers and unions will need to devote considerable amounts of time and energy to this phase of contract administration.

In any one plant the content of most jobs will not change during the life of a contract. In a dynamic industrial system, however, there always will arise a number of new jobs that cannot be fitted into existing classifications, or situations in which the duties on existing jobs may have to be changed. What procedure should be followed in setting rates on new or changed jobs?

Practice varies considerably on this question. In some cases the parties will sit down and negotiate the rate every time a new job appears or an existing job has its duties changed appreciably. In others it is customary for management to set the rate on the new or changed job, subject to challenge by the union through the grievance procedure. Many contracts in effect prohibit management from changing the duties or rate on a job existing at the time of the contract's signing for the life of the contract.

As a general rule, the most practical and efficient approach would appear to be one which permits management to set the rate on a new job, reserving to the union the right to challenge this rate within a specified time period, such as thirty, sixty or ninety days. This is a frequent practice on incentive jobs and has validity for new hourly jobs as well. In plants with well-established job evaluation systems the problem of setting rates on new or changed jobs is not likely to be as troublesome as in plants with no definite system of wage administration.

Even under a job evaluation program, however, disputes may frequently arise, particularly in connection with changes in the content of an existing job. The normal direction of technological change is toward work simplification with the breaking down of complex tasks into simpler, more specialized assignments. Hence, the resultant wage change is likely to be downward and therefore productive of considerable employee and union resistance.

An even more difficult issue relates to whether disputes over rates on new or changed jobs should be arbitrable or subject to strike action under the contract. An arbitrator under contracts that exclude such disputes from the arbitration step well might be grateful for the exclusion, since such disputes do not lend themselves to the "judicial" type of arbitration. The proper rate for a new job is essentially a "political" question that should be worked out by the parties. At the same time, there are real advantages in using arbitration as an alternative to economic force for any contract dispute during the life of an agreement. Majority practice seems to favor making such disputes arbitrable.

ECONOMIC EFFECTS OF UNIONISM AND COLLECTIVE BARGAINING

This brief consideration of the economic impact of unionism will be framed in terms of our discussion of three types of decision-making on wages: (1) general wage or salary adjustments; (2) the structure of occupational rates and (3) methods of wage or salary administration.

In reviewing wage increases of an across-the-board type, the question of greatest interest is whether unionism as such has proved to be a source of differential economic advantage to employees. The answer in simple terms appears to be yes in the short run and no in the long run. One must stick to the hard facts and ignore the partisan claims and counterclaims on this explosive question.

The evidence marshaled by H. Gregg Lewis offers sufficient documentation for the basic conclusion that unionism over time has not been a significant source of wage advantage. Harry M. Douty's study covering the years 1946–1966 shows that the nonunion sectors in our economy display somewhat greater sensitivity to changing market conditions and greater flexibility in both the form and timing of wage adjustments.[15]

Price behavior in recent years, combined with a relatively low unemployment level (until 1970), served to place union leaders under severe pressure to negotiate agreements to prevent erosion of their real wage positions. Somewhat ironically, the data show that wages increased more in such largely nonunion segments of the economy as agriculture, services

---

[15] See H. Gregg Lewis, *Unionism and Relative Wages in the United States: An Empirical Inquiry* (Chicago: University of Chicago Press, 1963), and Harry M. Douty, *Trends in Labor Compensation in the United States, 1946–1966* (Washington, D.C.: Government Printing Office, 1967), p. 9.

and retail trade than they did in the more highly organized manufacturing field.[16] It could fairly be said that unionists were hard-pressed to keep up with their nonunion "brothers."

The constraints of the typical three-year contract in unionized segments of the economy are of obvious importance in reducing the ability to respond quickly to sharp changes in the economic picture. In an inflationary period only those long-term contracts with escalator clauses (without a ceiling) can keep pace. The nonunion employer is free to up the ante for his employees at any time and for any amount he elects. Evidence is available to indicate that nonunion employers have in fact used their discretion as a means of retaining personnel and also, in some cases, of forestalling unionization. The prudent nonunion employer senses intuitively the correctness of Milton Friedman's dictum that inflation makes strong unions rather than strong unions causing inflation. He is therefore not loathe to utilize the wage increase as a tactical weapon in his arsenal of policies aimed at maintaining his nonunion condition.

In summary we can say that the union's ability to deliver wage increases significantly greater than those obtainable in (otherwise) comparable nonunion situations has been exaggerated by both opponents and supporters of unionism and collective bargaining. There is little doubt that in particular circumstances unions have been able to exert their market power to extract wage increases higher than might have been forthcoming in a nonunion setting. Such has been the case in many urban areas in the building and construction field. In such cases the true monopoly position of the involved craft unions has enabled them to impose and maintain an artificially high differential over a period of years. In the main, however, unionism over time has not proved to be a source of independent wage advantage. For evidence of significant union impact we must turn to our second and third categories of decision-making, structural and administrative.

IMPACT OF UNIONISM ON RELATIVE WAGE RATES

Unionism's greatest economic impact has been on wage rate structures and on managerial approaches to wage or salary administration. Most unions strive to achieve a politically acceptable ordering of occupational rates within a particular bargaining unit. Elimination of alleged inequities within a firm's rate structure is a continuing union objective in contract administration. Union concern in this area has been a potent factor in

---

[16] Bok and Dunlop observe that increases in the largely nonunion agricultural and retail trade sectors were 37 and 32 percent respectively over the years 1960–1967. This compares with 25 percent for the same period in manufacturing, which is fairly well organized. Bok and Dunlop, *op. cit.*, p. 285.

causing employers to do a thorough, consistent job of policing their rate structures.

An employer will generally claim that his rate structure is determined solely by objective criteria whereas the union's wishes are based on internal pressures that, if honored, would in some fashion distort the picture. The goal of equal pay for equal work is subscribed to by both management and union with equal vigor in the abstract. Implementation, however, can yield sharply divergent views. The typical union will dispute the accuracy of any employer charge that internal politics is the guide to union claims as to appropriate job slotting. The union rejoinder usually is that the employer's allegedly scientific ranking is a cover for maintaining or creating unduly low rates for the work involved.

When one cuts through the rhetoric relating to inequities, it is relatively clear that union policy in negotiating changes in occupational rates has had an important impact on employer policy. Many employers today have well-developed programs of occupational rate adjustment that can only be regarded as an improvement over the pre-union condition. The impact of the union has been such as to compel the employer to think through the logic of his rate program. Whether the managerial approach has been an optimal one in all cases is certainly open to question. In general, however, the conclusion must be that internal wage rate rationalization has reached a more sophisticated and equitable level in many relationships.

One who doubts the impact of unionism on internal rate structures should consult any experienced grievance arbitrator. Abundant evidence of unending contract administration concern for intrafirm occupational rate adjustment can be found in the files of most arbitrators. Next to discipline and discharge cases the most prolific source of grievance arbitration disputes comes from alleged improper slotting of employees into the job classification hierarchy or other types of internal rate adjustment issues.

Disputes over proper slotting or over the proper occupational rate for new or changed jobs constantly occur. Not a few of these end in arbitration. In many cases the employer is operating under a unilaterally developed job evaluation plan, with the union choosing to remain aloof and process its rate grievances under its own standards of internal equity. In many situations, however, as noted earlier, both the employer and union use the job evaluation plan as their point of departure for arguing the merits of particular cases of alleged inequitable rate determination.

Most economists acknowledge the force of union impact on internal wage rate structures within particular firms and industries. Union policies have also served in many instances to reinforce and ratify general economic tendencies toward a narrowing of occupational and geographical differentials. Union influence on interindustry differentials, however, has been slight, if not nonexistent. Over the years, traditionally high-paying industries remain high-paying and those with low wage standards tend to remain low. This generalization holds true without reference to the presence or absence of unionism. Clearly, collective bargaining has not proved to be a deterrent to high profits or to substantial productivity gains. Correspondingly, where unionism exists in low-paying fields the economic factors that explain the relatively low pay cannot be overcome by the presence of the union. All the union can do in such cases is to make every effort to inhibit any employer moves to gain an edge by paying an exploitative wage.

Bridge-Building Between Micro-Economic Needs and National Policy Goals

Earlier in this book reference was made to the need to make a switch from bilateral to trilateral thinking in collective bargaining. The emphasis on trilateralism is most directly pertinent to the peaceful resolution of management-union disputes over future contract terms discussed in Chapter 8. The strictly economic hue of trilateralism becomes more prominent when a three-year bargain appears likely (or certain) to call for increased labor costs that cannot be compensated for by increased productivity. The results of such economic bargains are certain to be criticized as incompatible with national anti-inflation objectives. The semantic shorthand word for such a bargain is "irresponsible." An economic package consistent with productivity gains is a "responsible" bargain.

Such terminology is used appropriately at the conclusion of a micro-oriented chapter because we have arrived at the point in our thinking where we expect from employers and unions *some* tangible concern beyond lip service for the macro-economic impact of their bargains. At the same time there is no disputing the fact that the bargainers must be expected to pursue their own calculated economic self-interest as they see it. The result of this pursuit may often be inimical to national policy objectives of price stability.

More intensive analysis is reserved for the next chapter. It is logical, however, to end a micro-oriented chapter with a brief description of one neglected way to bridge the alleged chasm between national goals and practitioner needs. The writer's favorite illustration remains the union-management cooperation plan. This deceptively general term has a restricted meaning. It is reserved for describing *joint efforts by employers and unions to increase productivity and reduce costs.* If the efficacy of such plans had to be judged on the basis of their proved general acceptance over the years, there would be little point in continuing the discussion. Such plans have never enjoyed any vogue among employers and unions, principally because employers were worried about their managerial prerogatives and employees were fearful about working themselves out of jobs. The only time when union-management cooperation plans were plentiful was during World War II under the special stimulus of a national emergency psychology. We can also note some scattered examples of such joint efforts born in desperation to save particular firms from going to the wall.[17]

The union-management cooperation plan nevertheless remains a logical vehicle for facilitating negotiation at the individual firm level that can satisfy simultaneously the employer desire to keep labor costs stable, the employee desire for increased income and the community interest in promoting noninflationary bargains. These plans have high potential, in my view, for those employers and unions who *on their own initiative* would like to adopt policies that are clearly compatible with national economic goals. Requirements for successful operation of such plans are dealt with in the next chapter.[18] Here we conclude by noting that effective joint efforts to increase productivity and reduce costs of production (with built-in safeguards for incumbent employees) must *by hypothesis* be regarded as in aid of national policy objectives of price stability at high employment levels.

The bridge is thus available for those employers and unions who wish to use it.

SELECTED BIBLIOGRAPHY

ADAMS, J. STACY, "Wage Inequities, Productivity and Work Quality," *Industrial Relations*, III (October, 1963), 9–16.

ALLEN, BRUCE T., "Market Concentration and Wage Increases: U.S. Manufacturing, 1947–1964," *Industrial and Labor Relations Review*, XXI (April, 1968), 353–65.

ANDREWS, I. R., AND MILDRED M. HENRY, "Management Attitudes Toward Pay," *Industrial Relations*, III (October, 1963), 29–39.

BEHMAN, SARA, "Wage-Determination Process in U.S. Manufacturing," *Quarterly Journal of Economics*, LXXXII (February, 1968), 117–42.

BOK, DEREK C., AND JOHN T. DUNLOP, *Labor and the American Community*. New York: Simon and Schuster, Inc., 1970, especially Chapters 9 and 10.

BURGESS, LEONARD RANDOLPH, *Wage and Salary Administration in a Dynamic Economy*. New York: Harcourt, Brace & World, Inc., 1968.

CARTER, ALLAN M., *Theory of Wages and Employment*. Homewood, Ill.: Richard D. Irwin, Inc., 1959.

CLOVER, VERNON T., "Compensation in Union and Nonunion Plants, 1960–1965," *Industrial and Labor Relations Review*, XXI (January, 1968), 226–33.

---

[17] The classic treatment of joint efforts to save individual firms remains that of Sumner H. Slichter, *Union Policies and Industrial Management* (Washington, D.C.: The Brookings Institution, 1941). The best account of World War II plans is that of Dorothea de Schweinitz, *Labor and Management in a Common Enterprise* (Cambridge, Mass.: Harvard University Press, 1949).

[18] The detailed discussion in Chapter 11 borrows extensively from Harold W. Davey, "Union-Management Cooperation Revisited," *Business Perspectives*, IV (Winter, 1968), 4–10.

DOUTY, HARRY M., *Trends in Labor Compensation in the United States, 1946–1966*. Washington, D.C.: Government Printing Office, 1967.

DUNLOP, JOHN T., ed., *The Theory of Wage Determination*. London: Macmillan & Co., Ltd., 1957.

GARBARINO, JOSEPH W., *Wage Policy and Long-Term Contracts*. Washington, D.C.: The Brookings Institution, 1962.

HICKS, JOHN R., *The Theory of Wages* (2nd American Ed.). New York: St. Martin's Press, 1964.

KAUN, DAVID E., "Union–Non-Union Wage Differentials Revisited," *Journal of Political Economy*, LXXII (August, 1964), 403–13.

LESTER, RICHARD A., "Negotiated Wage Increases, 1951–1967," *Review of Economics and Statistics*, L (May, 1968), 173–81.

LEVINSON, HAROLD M., *Determining Forces in Collective Wage Bargaining*. New York: John Wiley & Sons, Inc., 1966.

———, "Unionism, Concentration, and Wage Changes: Toward a Unified Theory," *Industrial and Labor Relations Review*, XX (January, 1967), 198–205.

LEWIS, H. GREGG, *Unionism and Relative Wages in the United States: An Empirical Inquiry*. Chicago: University of Chicago Press, 1963.

PEN, J., *The Wage Rate Under Collective Bargaining*. Cambridge, Mass.: Harvard University Press, 1959.

PIERSON, FRANK C., *Unions in Postwar America: An Economic Assessment*. New York: Random House, Inc., 1967.

REDER, M. W., "Unions and Wages: The Problems of Measurement," *Journal of Political Economy*, LXXIII (April, 1965), 188–96.

ROSS, ARTHUR M., *Trade Union Wage Policy*. Berkeley, Cal.: University of California Press, 1948.

SEGAL, MARTIN, "The Relation Between Union Wage Impact and Market Structure," *Quarterly Journal of Economics*, LXXVIII (February, 1964), 96–114.

———, *Wages in the Metropolis*. Cambridge, Mass.: Harvard University Press, 1960.

SHULTZ, G. P., AND MYERS, C. A., "Union Wage Decisions and Employment," *American Economic Review*, XL (June, 1950), 362–81.

COLLECTIVE BARGAINING
and national economic policy

CHAPTER ELEVEN

Wage bargaining between employers and unions is no longer a strictly private matter. Nor is it likely to become so again as our national economy becomes more complex and interdependent. The third man theme will be played in some fashion in future negotiations, even those involving such staunch devotees of bilateralism as bargainers in construction and trucking.[1] How dominant the third man music may be depends, of course, on how

---

[1] In 1970 the Chicago Teamsters achieved the height of something or other by striking long and hard to secure a higher wage settlement than had been obtained earlier in negotiations at the national level. The Midwest truckers ultimately capitulated and signed for a 13 percent wage increase. An unusual clause in the national agreement permitted its reopening if a higher adjustment was secured in local negotiations. The Chicago breakthrough spread nationally in the trucking industry, thus putting a considerable strain on any anti-inflationary impulses the UAW might have entertained as it struck GM in September, 1970.

seriously we wish to work toward a national incomes policy to prevent price inflation, excessive unemployment and income maldistribution.

The main challenge concerns whether we can achieve a judicious blend of private decision-making with national economic policy that will retain a maximum of private discretion in bargaining while at the same time insuring relative price stability and an improved performance in reducing unemployment to a frictional minimum of perhaps as low as 2 to 3 percent.[2] The magnitude of the challenge is made clear simply by listing the major national economic policy goals which command general support. In doing so we are obligated to note that simultaneous achievement of all these goals is extraordinarily difficult because of varying degrees of noncomplementarity.[3]

Price stability and low unemployment lead the list of national policy targets. In addition, we seek to achieve the following macro-economic goals:

1. A "sound" annual economic growth rate.[4]
2. Achieving and maintaining an equilibrium condition in our international balance of payments.
3. Elimination of poverty income levels.
4. Improved performance in labor mobility.
5. Removing structural imperfections in the labor market.[5]

These ambitious policy goals are not beyond our grasp. We have the economic sophistication to do a pretty fair job of hitting these targets, even when proper allowance is made for foiling the noncomplementarity dragon. Whether we succeed depends partly on desire and partly on recognizing the indispensability of a coordinated approach at the public policy level. Of critical importance also is the performance level of employers and unions in both the private and public sectors on economic bargaining. How

---

[2] I have selected a price stability goal of about 2 percent per annum to accompany a target level of unemployment at the 2 to 3 per cent level. See the discussion on pp. 295–96.

[3] The most serious of the built-in goal conflicts concerns the trade-off effect between price stability and unemployment. Most economists hold that when unemployment is reduced to less than 5 percent, price stability is endangered. We should be able to do better at having our cake and eating it.

[4] The term "sound" is value-loaded. I have in mind a growth rate of about 3 percent per annum. However, "sound" from now on will include necessarily something more than purely physical gains in output. We shall be considering seriously the ecological implications of everything we produce, including a reorienting of production goals toward the retrieval and reutilization of many products currently handled as waste.

[5] We shall not attempt to cover the many and varied efforts of federal agencies in recent years to remove structural imperfections in the workings of the labor market. Some attention was given to these problems in Chapter 9. In a era of still considerable unemployment existing side by side with critical shortages in many skilled occupations we have much farther to go in both governmental and private efforts to make the labor market a more efficient allocative mechanism.

completely can a macro-economic consciousness be infused into the negotiators short of direct governmental controls?

Focus on Private Decision-Making

Considering various *feasible* policies and procedures will be the
main business of this chapter. We shall resist the temptation to beat to death
once more the issue of the degree of responsibility unionism and collective
bargaining should bear for inflation. The academic output on this subject
appears to be endless.[6] When it is all added up, I believe Bok and Dunlop
are close to the mark in concluding that "most economists would express the
judgment that collective bargaining has added only modestly to inflation in
America since the end of World War II; a much larger role would be ascribed
to monetary and fiscal policy and to the war-related expenditures of government."[7]

I propose to hew to the pragmatic line by concentrating on various
ways to make collective bargaining more effective as an anti-inflationary
instrument. Doing so involves recognizing the obvious fact that private
economic decision-making can be shaped either to aid or to detract from
national price stability and employment objectives.

The Inflationary Bias of Collective Bargaining

Union pressure for steadily increasing wages and economic fringe
benefits clearly introduces an inflationary bias. This bias is less conspicuous
in periods such as 1967–1970 when factor prices and product prices in some
nonunion industries actually have risen faster and by greater amounts than

---

[6] For the reader who wishes to explore the overall problem of reaching macro-
economic objectives, recent knowledgeable analyses include: Walter Heller, *New Dimensions
of Political Economy* (New York: W. W. Norton & Company, Inc., 1967); Arthur M. Okun,
The Political Economy of Prosperity (New York: W. W. Norton & Company, Inc., 1970);
Martin Bronfenbrenner and Franklyn D. Holzman, "Survey of Inflation Theory," *American
Economic Review*, LIII (September, 1963), 593–661; Melvin W. Reder, "The Public Interest
in Wage Settlements," in *Frontiers of Collective Bargaining*, ed. John T. Dunlop and Neil W.
Chamberlain (New York: Harper & Row, Publishers, 1967), pp. 155–77; Kenneth O.
Alexander, "Unionism, Wages, and Cost-Push: A Summary Statement," *American Journal
of Economics and Sociology*, XXIV (October, 1965), 383–95; George L. Perry, *Unemployment,
Money Wage Rates, and Inflation* (Cambridge, Mass.: Massachusetts Institute of Technology
Press, 1966); Adrian W. Throop, "The Union-Nonunion Wage Differential and Cost-Push
Inflation," *American Economic Review*, LVIII (March, 1968), 79–99; Edmund S. Phelps,
"Phillips Curves, Expectations of Inflation and Optimal Unemployment Over Time,"
Economica, XXXIV (August, 1967), 254–81.

[7] Derek C. Bok and John T. Dunlop, *Labor and the American Community* (New York:
Simon and Schuster, Inc., 1970), p. 292.

in many unionized fields, as noted in Chapter 10. In recession periods, however, the force of collective bargaining in enforcing wage rigidities becomes clear. A decline in demand is invariably met by a decrease in output and employment rather than by lower prices and wages. Such wage rigidity in unionized sectors during an economic downturn means that wages and prices invariably start from a higher plateau during the next upswing.

Seeking to generalize further as to the contributory impact of unionism on inflation is likely to be misleading. Of course, if we wish to pick our spots we can prove anything. Numerous illustrations can be found where collective bargaining has raised unit labor costs (with little or no productivity gains) compensated for by increased prices with the result being reduced output and increased unemployment because the firm in question had not built into the demand curve for its product sufficient inelasticity to accommodate the increased prices.[8] Illustrations can also be found where prices and profit margins were increased involving a considerable amount of "float," using the wage increases as an excuse.[9] In still other situations the seemingly substantial negotiated wage increases with the familiar "front-end loading" (that is, a bigger amount in the first year of a three-year agreement) were of a make-up or catch-up nature rather than of a triggering type. In such instances, the price increases had clearly preceded the wage increases both in timing and in amount.[10]

The specific impact of a given wage increase on labor cost and employer price policy varies considerably from one situation to another. The cause of understanding has been poorly served by anti-union polemicists assessing total blame or by unionists and their supporters claiming total innocence. It would be misleading, for example, to label the inflation of 1966–1970 as having been sired solely, or even primarily, by union economic demands on the one hand or by corporate price-profit policies on the other. Both realism and candor compel the conclusion that *some* causative significance can be attributed to an impressive variety of factors including, among others, the Vietnam war's stimulus of demand for capital goods and armaments, widened corporate profit margins, union wage increases, wage increases in nonunion sectors, excessive internal financing, low or even negative productivity gains in some sectors and, last but not least, inadequate or ineffective monetary policy controls.

The analytical Pandora's box in the preceding paragraph will not

---

[8] The reader will recognize this readily as the now familiar villain of cost-(wage-) push inflation.

[9] Perhaps the most scorching of the many union indictments of corporate profits as *the* cause of inflation is the open letter from the late Walter P. Reuther to all members of the American Economic Association in December, 1969.

[10] Many of the key wage settlements negotiated since 1968 have been of the catch-up variety.

be opened. I shall also resist the temptation to adopt the alluringly over-simplified Friedmanian view that inflation is made solely in Washington by the Federal Reserve System's Board of Governors. Unfortunately, perhaps, inflation is not a simple phenomenon. Furthermore, we do not yet possess the certainty of understanding that would permit differential apportioning of degrees of blame among the various causes of inflation.

The assumption is made, therefore, that collective bargaining, as conducted in most cases, introduces an inflationary bias. The better part of wisdom, valor and comparative advantage influences the decision to dwell principally on how collective bargaining can be geared toward producing results that will aid or complement rather than conflict with national economic objectives. The first essential in this regard is facilitating the vital switch from bilateral to trilateral thinking on the part of the negotiators themselves. In my view, the optimal way for employers and unions to avoid direct government intervention is for them to face up to the desirability of introducing *on their own* policies and procedures to complement rather than conflict with national goals. Thinking in trilateral instead of bilateral terms will involve some hard adjustments for many employers and unions, but the incentive is there. It is the real threat of sweeping government intervention.

THE ROLE OF PUBLIC POLICY

The emphasis on private decision-making via collective bargaining should not be interpreted as minimizing the crucial importance of sound governmental fiscal, monetary and manpower policies. The United States can succeed in maintaining price stability with minimum levels of unemployment only through greater virtuosity in public policy than has been displayed so far. Fortunately, our defined emphasis permits us to avoid the turbulent waters of monetary and fiscal policy.

Public policy analysis is confined to certain governmental efforts bearing directly on the practitioners of collective bargaining. We shall review the rise, fall and possible resurrection of the CEA's wage-price guideposts. Also of direct concern to practitioners of bargaining are federal efforts to remove structural imperfections in the labor market in the variety of programs stemming from the Manpower Development and Training Act of 1962 as amended.[11] Also relevant are governmental efforts to avoid strikes.

---

[11] The relevant manpower literature is far too extensive to capture in a footnote. Among the many recent analyses I would mention the following: Garth L. Mangum, *MDTA: Foundations of Federal Manpower Policy* (Baltimore, Md.: Johns Hopkins Press, 1968); Arthur M. Ross, ed., *Employment Policy and the Labor Market* (Berkeley and Los Angeles: University of California Press, 1965); Arnold R. Weber, Frank H. Cassell and Woodrow L. Ginsburg, eds., *Public-Private Manpower Policies* (Madison, Wis.: Industrial Relations Research Associa-

These can be viewed as a plus factor in achieving productivity, cost reduction and price stability objectives. We can thus logically incorporate by reference the Chapter 8 discussion of feasible procedures for peaceful resolution of future terms disputes.

COLLECTIVE BARGAINING APPROACHES CONSISTENT WITH NATIONAL ECONOMIC POLICY

Sufficient attention has been paid elsewhere to the pressures on both Employer X and Union Y to pursue their own calculated economic self-interest in collective bargaining. That discussion is incorporated by reference as we analyze a climate in which Employer X and Union Y are assumed to understand and appreciate the macro-economic impact of their own and thousands of other privately negotiated agreements. The level of economic sophistication among practitioners of bargaining can be assumed to be such that they will be willing to consider the "public interest" as a relevant variable in negotiating economic issues. How much consideration they may be expected (or required) to give depends greatly on how we define the "public interest" in this context.

For discussion purposes, we shall equate "public interest," generally speaking, with seeking the national economic policy goals as outlined earlier. We shall concentrate particular attention on how private decision-making can produce results that are compatible with our national price stability and low level unemployment objectives.

How the exercise of private discretion is viewed will depend on the price stability and unemployment concepts we have in mind. It makes a big difference whether we are willing to accept an unemployment level around 5 percent and consumer price increases in the neighborhood of 3 percent per annum or whether we set our sights in more exacting fashion at holding consumer price increases to around 1 percent per annum and keeping unemployment in the range of 2 to 3 percent.[12] Value judgments differ on both the optimality and achievability of such varying alternative national economic policy goals.

Keeping firmly in mind both feasibility and a strong value prefer-

---

tion, 1969); also Garth L. Mangum, *The Emergence of Manpower Policy* (New York: Holt, Rinehart & Winston, Inc., 1969). The reader will also find valuable a series of "Policy Papers in Human Resources and Industrial Relations" on specific labor market problems, published by the University of Michigan–Wayne State University Institute of Labor and Industrial Relations. Twelve papers in this series were released between January, 1967, and January, 1969.

[12] The implications of goal choices are perceptively discussed by Frank C. Pierson, *Unions in America: An Economic Assessment* (New York: Random House, Inc., 1967), pp. 123–24.

ence for retaining a maximum of private discretion in bargaining, my targets are 2 to 3 percent per annum on the price increase goal and between 2 and 3 percent on the unemployment level.[13]

The price stability target contemplating increases of 2 to 3 percent per annum in my view approximates the proper rate for encouraging the requisite economic growth and new investment while at the same time incurring minimal risk of inducing either recession or hyperinflation. The 2 to 3 percent unemployment level goal is based on a firm conviction that we can reduce normal or frictional unemployment considerably below the 4 to 5 percent levels which economists have too long been accustomed to regarding as the watershed level in relation to price stability.

Dating from the initial impulse of the Manpower Development and Training Act of 1962 there has been an encouraging and continuing experimentation with a variety of manpower programs aimed at reducing structural unemployment. We have learned from some of the early failures in MDTA operations. The new breed of manpower economists appear to have increased confidence in their ability to determine which programs are suited to the task of upgrading skills, productive unemployment of the disadvantaged, relocating of structurally or technologically unemployed and so on.[14]

With reference to the price stability target, I recall that the late Sumner H. Slichter was criticized severely when he suggested in the late 1950s that a little inflation was a modest price to pay for insuring a sound economic growth rate. Slichter's critics doubted the ability of fiscal and monetary authorities to prevent relatively small annual increments in the price level from escalating into an inflationary binge. They subscribed to the conventional wisdom that where inflation was concerned there was no possibility of remaining a little bit pregnant.

Fortunately, we have made progress in dispelling the fear that inflation cannot be prevented from becoming a runaway affair. Even the severe inflation of 1966 to 1970 did not get seriously out of hand before yielding to disinflationary pressures.

Nevertheless, the policy goals just outlined are demanding in nature. Achieving them would exceed any performance level to date. We shall need more than greater sophistication and virtuosity in the public policy complex of programs and controls. We shall also need a concerted effort from private decision-makers in collective bargaining in achieving the trilateral orientation already referred to. It is to the private potential for aiding national economic objectives that we turn first.

---

[13] These targets do not reflect any specially researched macro-economic know-how. Rather they are a personal judgment as to optimality, fortified by a strong dose of faith that in the years ahead both federal expertise and private determination will increase sufficiently to bring these goals within the realm of the possible.

[14] See references cited in footnote 11 above.

COLLECTIVE BARGAINING POLICIES
AND PROCEDURES COMPLEMENTARY TO PRICE STABILITY
AND LOW LEVEL UNEMPLOYMENT OBJECTIVES

Taking inventory of feasible policies and procedures for practitioners in adapting their mutual goals to national economic objectives is in itself an important step on the plus side. None of the various approaches noted below is to my knowledge a new or impractical idea. These policies and procedures are workable rather than visionary. Their effective use can be reassuring to those who fear to venture into the unknown. No policy or procedure is designed to detract from private self-interest in favor of the public interest. The sole objective is to spotlight what will work both for the benefit of the practitioners and the community at large.

The inventory of complementary policies and procedures includes the following (not listed in any particular order of preference):

1. The productivity-gains-sharing approach, as illustrated by the Kaiser Steel-Steelworkers plan at Fontana, California.[15]
2. The "productivity unchained" approach (my description for the West Cost Longshoring agreement wherein the union removed its contractual blocks to introduction of mechanized loading and unloading equipment in exchange for substantial job security safeguards).[16]
3. Prenegotiation conferences aimed at greater factualization of the bargaining process, as discussed in Chapter 5.
4. Institutional reforms in bargaining structures in industries currently plagued by costly inefficiencies in bargaining and excessive economic packages traceable to multicraft friction and competition, as in such industries as building and construction, shipbuilding, newspaper, maritime and railroads.
5. Union-management cooperation plans of the classical Slichter type, involving the use of joint committees to increase productivity and reduce costs.
6. Three-year contracts instead of annual or biennial negotiations, featuring a wage and economic fringe formula consistent with price stability goals.
7. Discontinuance of escalator clauses, but with provision for a wage reopener should public policy controls fail to satisfy assumed price stability limits.
8. Intensified efforts to avoid strikes over future contract terms, including acceptance of carefully defined binding arbitration.

---

[15] For a readable discussion of the origins and early experience under the plan see James J. Healy, ed., *Creative Collective Bargaining* (Englewood Cliffs, N.J.: Prentice-Hall, Inc., 1965), pp. 244–81.

[16] See Paul T. Hartman, *Collective Bargaining and Productivity: The Longshore Mechanization Agreement* (Berkeley and Los Angeles: University of California Press, 1969).

The above listing should be sufficient to point up the private potential for economic bargaining in ways that can satisfy the needs of the parties while remaining consistent with macro-economic objectives. Employers and unions *can* develop the habit of thinking in trilateral rather than bilateral terms. As they do so, the potential of the suggested policies will be better appreciated.

The prudent, intelligent approach to preserving private discretion in bargaining involves voluntarily infusing macro-economic criteria into the bilateral picture. The simplistic approach to negotiating economic packages epitomized in the famed "I look first to cigars" slogan must be viewed as outmoded and, in fact, square. Our state of sensitive interdependence is such that considering the requirements of the "public interest," as defined earlier,[17] is essential to effective pursuit of private interest.

Many of the various approaches listed speak for themselves or have been discussed elsewhere in this volume. Here we shall give expanded consideration only to two: structural bargaining reforms and union-management cooperation plans.

STRUCTURAL BARGAINING REFORMS AS AN AID TO "PUBLIC INTEREST" BARGAINING

Basic structural reforms are needed in the special circumstance of multicraft institutional rivalry existing among enterprises that have considerable product-market power but are not well organized to resist union demands. Bok and Dunlop note the inflationary pressures generated in such an environment when an increase negotiated by one union becomes a target to be exceeded by a second or third union which in turn produces pressure for readjustment of the first settlement, and so on. When this occurs under tight labor market conditions, with ample profits, and in a climate where workers feel they have a past score to settle, Bok and Dunlop find that ". . . very large settlements may emerge, often after a long strike which, in itself, may raise the settlement price. *These pathological bargaining structures are themselves a major independent factor contributing to wage inflation.* Large wage increases gained in such circumstances are also contagious affecting other negotiations in the same localities or in contiguous industries (emphasis added)."[18]

Bok and Dunlop have singled out the newspaper, construction and maritime fields, where employers bargain with several craft unions. The railroad industry should be added, in my view. Bok and Dunlop do not go beyond pointing out the need for structural reform. The needed structural

---

[17] See above, p. 295.
[18] Derek C. Bok and John T. Dunlop, *op. cit.*, pp. 290–91.

changes will not be self-generating. How to achieve coordinated bargaining among powerful, autonomous craft unions who are suspicious and envious of one another is no light challenge. Employers in the affected industries have much to gain by seeking to persuade the many unions with which they deal to adopt a cooperative bargaining stance. It is perhaps naive to suggest the long-run wisdom of organic merger in many multiple craft situations. We should urge upon the various craft organizations in the industries under discussion that they abandon internecine warfare in favor of coordinated bargaining with common contract expiration dates. It is appropriate also to ask the parties to consider the need for abandoning obsolete working rules and outmoded apprenticeship regulations that have contributed to serious productive inefficiencies and labor supply shortages.[19]

I stop just short of advocating abandonment of craft unionism in favor of industrial unionism for two reasons: (1) my lack of substantial experience in the industries named[20] and (2) awareness of the odds against achieving such a sweeping structural reform. It would be instructive, however, to have the results of an empirical survey testing the hypothesis that structural bargaining reforms are indispensable to a successful effort in achieving compatibility with public interest objectives of price stability and low level unemployment.

UNION-MANAGEMENT COOPERATION PLANS

Joint management-union efforts to increase productivity and reduce costs have been few and far between, as already noted in Chapters 9 and 10.[21] The logic of such joint efforts is clear and should be appealing. Nevertheless, these plans are not likely to be embraced eagerly by employers and union leaders under prevailing conditions. The employer will continue to maintain that productivity is management's business. The union leader will continue to shy away from a joint venture that seemingly might result in reduced employment opportunities.

If this is true, no union-management cooperation plan has a chance unless it contains built-in safeguards relating both to management rights and job security.

---

[19] There are still, regrettably, many employers and unions in a variety of industries for whom the shoe would be a perfect fit if they would but try it on. The Hartman study, cited in footnote 16 above, offers convincing proof that leopards can change their spots when they jointly desire to do so. For a comprehensive review of the problem, see Paul A. Weinstein, ed., *Featherbedding and Technological Change* (Boston: D. C. Heath and Company, 1965).

[20] As an arbitrator I have had only two or three cases involving newspapers, none in the maritime field, very few in construction and one docket of thirty plus cases as a referee for the National Railroad Adjustment Board.

[21] This section is freely adapted and updated from my article, "Union-Management Cooperation Revisited," *Business Perspectives* (Winter, 1968), pp. 4–10.

Several factors make it logical to conclude that the potential for success is greater than ever before. In the first place, there is the strong emphasis that collective bargaining has given in recent years to strengthening employee job and income security. We have reviewed the job security scene in Chapter 9. In the next chapter we shall consider recent developments in negotiated economic security. It all adds up to giving the individual employee more of a visible stake in his particular firm. It follows that the employee is or should be more concerned than he has usually been with the economic health of his employer.

Second, the era of the wage-price guideposts had the plus value of making the nexus between productivity and real wages clear to millions of Americans who perhaps never thought about it before. Employees in many industries grasped the fundamental point that they can continue to improve their economic position only when new ways are found to increase productivity and reduce costs. In many lines of endeavor the economic saturation point has perhaps been reached where some kind of special effort is required if the pie is to be enlarged.

Third, it is currently fashionable to think in terms of modernizing collective bargaining procedures to make them more responsible and responsive to current requirements. We have discussed such techniques as pre-negotiation conferences, joint study committees, use of neutrals for dispute settlement in future terms cases and so forth in earlier chapters. Much of this intensified interest in better bargaining performance derives from legitimate concern about the real prospect of sweeping government intervention.

Collective bargaining is considered to be on trial by many friends as well as critics. In the welter of criticism it is easy to overlook the evidence that generally collective bargaining has proved to be flexible and adaptable to meet the requirements of the changing scene.[22] How the practitioners are performing, however, is almost beside the point. The image is more relevant than the reality at this stage. The picture of bargaining has been sufficiently tarnished that it behooves employers and unions to be receptive to a way of working together for their own mutual advantage that will also serve as an aid rather than a threat to national economic goals.

The union-management cooperation plan offers employers and unions an opportunity to do so.

---

[22] For a strong defense of the continuing utility of collective bargaining, see Vernon H. Jensen, "The Process of Collective Bargaining and the Question of its Obsolescence," *Industrial and Labor Relations Review*, XVI (July 1963), 546–56. In a similar vein see Harold W. Davey, "The Continuing Viability of Collective Bargaining," *Labor Law Journal*, XVI (February, 1965), 111–22.

Conditions for Effective Operation of a Union-Management Cooperation Plan

We need to be realistic about the fears of employers and unions that have obviously discouraged support for the union-management cooperation idea in the past. We must think in terms of a plan specifically tailored to lay these fears at rest. This means that the prospects for success are brightest in technologically dynamic growth fields where labor-saving and cost-saving proposals would accompany employment increases rather than reduced job opportunities. In fields where for market or technological reasons the employment prospect is static or declining, the odds would appear heavy against introducing a plan successfully. Even in such cases, however, the idea need not be written off completely. Ways could be worked out to coordinate joint private efforts with ongoing public programs for alleviating structural unemployment and continuous training for upgrading work-force skills.

For the moment we will summarize essentials of a viable plan assumed to be operating in a growth environment that minimizes employee insecurity. The first requirement is purely educational. That is, top management, union leadership and the affected employees must all have a clear understanding and acceptance of the nature and objectives of the plan. This will require some fundamental rethinking and changing of entrenched attitudes in many cases.

Assuming the necessary re-education and initial enthusiasm for the venture, what are the essential features of a "model" plan? In my view, the heart of the matter lies in appointing a joint committee whose membership is related to experience and interest in productivity gains and cost reduction rather than to the individual's position in the management or union hierarchy. It is also critically important that the joint committee's jurisdiction be carefully defined. It should be made clear that the committee is advisory in nature. Its findings and recommendations should not be binding on the employer and union in their collective bargaining operations, although much of the committee's work will have great importance for the negotiators.

The range of the committee's jurisdiction will vary from one relationship to another. My view is that the committee's charge should be a broad one, encompassing consideration of any proposal from any source that gives promise of gains in productivity or cost reduction. In addition to the customary attention to improving methods and technology, the committee might well consider also the merits of ideas for new products or style changes in current products. Improved marketing and distribution methods might also be made a part of the committee's responsibility. This latter function can become one of major significance in an era of growing concern for the negative ecological implications of many of industry's conventional operations. For example, a great deal of imaginative know-how is called for in tackling the problem of recapturing and re-utilizing product waste.

Greater worker acceptance of the committee's role will be forthcoming if intentional stress is placed on development of ideas for simultaneously increasing productivity *and* job opportunities.

The joint committee's proposals will have, at times, a direct impact on critical issues in negotiations. Whenever a committee recommendation is one that will affect bargaining unit employees (for example, proposals on such matters as job mix, manning requirements, hiring qualifications, temporary or permanent layoffs and so forth) it must be reported to and discussed with the appropriate management and union labor relations representatives.

In this respect, the proposed joint committee would be performing a function similar to joint study committees in such industries as meatpacking. Here again the necessity is apparent for stressing the advisory, extracontractual character of the proposed joint committee. Finally, the parties may wish to consider providing for the *ad hoc* assistance of "informed neutrals" to the joint committee. In my view, use of outside expertise should be provided for but not required.

UNION-MANAGEMENT COOPERATION PLANS AND "PRODUCTIVITY BARGAINING"

The Kaiser Steel-Steelworkers productivity-gains sharing plan initiated in 1962 aroused considerable academic interest as an example of "creative" collective bargaining.[23] More recently the British have placed a great deal of stress on cost savings through productivity bargaining as a condition for wage increases.[24] The British appear finally to be facing up to a serious problem posed by inefficient work practices and numerous wildcat strikes. They are stressing productivity bargaining as a means of coping simultaneously with these problems and with the spectre of resultant inflation.

The Kaiser Steel experiment and the British stance are mentioned in this context to underline the relative modesty of the union-management cooperation joint committee concept and also to reaffirm its clear complementarity with both price stability and low level unemployment objectives of national policy.

---

[23] See discussion in James J. Healy, ed., *op. cit.*, cited in footnote 15 above.

[24] Several illuminating articles will be found in "Symposium on Productivity Bargaining," *British Journal of Industrial Relations*, V (March, 1967), 1–62.

Bok and Dunlop note that "unlike the situation in England, there is no general need in America for productivity bargaining or plant-level reorientation of collective bargaining, although there are instances, of course, where such changes would contribute to efficiency and stability."[25] This may well be true. At the same time there is no valid reason why we should not be encouraging any plan or procedure that can benefit the bargainers themselves while at the same time aiding in achieving national economic goals. Employers and unions owe it to themselves as well as to the community at large to consider seriously the positive values in a union-management cooperation plan of the type described.

Most problems have been analyzed in this book in unvarnished fashion as they exist. This has led to prescriptive analysis where the situation seemed to call for it. Practitioners may have found that words like "should" and "ought" appear with irritating frequency. Perhaps the value judgments have been overdone. However, a conscious effort has been made to avoid too much of this.

The stress on union-management cooperation plans is deliberate on my part. It is clear that employers and unions need to take a hard look at their bargaining policies and procedures with a view to making them compatible with price stability and low level unemployment goals. Among the various approaches for achieving greater complementarity the union-management cooperation plan has great appeal to me, perhaps because its potential has been virtually ignored for so long.

The Role of Public Policy in Promoting Responsible Collective Bargaining

Public policy must carry the main burden of preventing inflation, achieving a low level of unemployment and the other national economic objectives noted at the start of this chapter. Because such problems are macro-economic in nature, they demand the best efforts of those administering a complex of federal measures in the areas of monetary policy, fiscal policy, manpower policy and so on. They cannot be solved by the practitioners of collective bargaining, but it has been important to review various ways in which the microbargainers can aid in the achievement of these national economic goals.

The following review of public policy instruments will be limited to those which apply *directly* to management and union at the bargaining table. I recognize the crucial importance of the indirect controls of monetary

---

[25] Derek C. Bok and John T. Dunlop, *op. cit.*, p. 306.

and fiscal policy. I shall nevertheless forego analysis of indirect controls. These areas I consider to be beyond my specialized competence.

The consideration of *direct* federal policy instruments will be confined to those that appear to be workable and feasible. This restriction will drastically shorten the chapter. Excluded therefore are such pervasive governmental control mechanisms as wage and price controls, *cum* rationing, and compulsory arbitration of future terms disputes tied to a general legislative prohibition of strikes and lockouts. These instruments are neither feasible nor workable except under conditions of total emergency such as World War II. Furthermore, compulsory arbitration and wage-price controls remain anathema to the great majority of American employers and union leaders.

Opinions differ as to the effectiveness of World War II regulation of prices and wages and the handling of labor disputes by the National War Labor Board. In company with most other "alumni" of the National War Labor Board, I believe that this agency did an excellent job of handling labor disputes between January, 1942, and the Board's termination in December, 1945. One reason for the NWLB's commendable record has sometimes been forgotten. The NWLB was operating in a very real sense with the consent of the governed. The Board was established by President Roosevelt's Executive Order in January, 1942, pursuant to a voluntary consensus reached by top management and union representatives convening shortly after Pearl Harbor. The conferees pledged no strikes and no lockouts for the duration of the national emergency with the understanding that disputes affecting the war effort would go to the new agency.

The consent of the governed remains, in my judgment, a critically important consideration in evaluating the potential effectiveness of any federal policy or program that impinges directly on the practitioners of bargaining.

Is "Jawboning" Enough?

If extreme controls are to be excluded from our policy frame of reference, what instruments qualify for consideration as being necessary, feasible and desirable? Do we need something more than periodic presidential pleas for restraint? Is what has at various times been called the "economics of admonition," "exhortation" or, more recently, "jawboning" enough to induce the desired degree of restraint in wage bargaining and price setting?

The performance record suggests that we have not yet succeeded in persuading any considerable number of employers and union leaders that they have a clear obligation to accommodate their bargaining and corporate decision-making to whatever specifics the presidential speech-making may suggest as essential in any particular year. In other words, it seems that "jawboning" is not enough.

If this conclusion is valid, what more can or should be done in the way of direct federal action relating to the wage bargainers and the price setters while still avoiding the excluded extremes of sweeping wage-price controls and compulsory arbitration? The question suggests the answer, I believe. I am convinced that it is possible to make a fresh start on developing what could ultimately approximate a national incomes policy, utilizing the Council of Economic Advisers and the Executive Office of the President as the two agencies to assume the necessary initiatives.

THE CEA AND A PROPOSED ANNUAL NATIONAL MANAGEMENT-UNION CONFERENCE

Since the Employment Act of 1946 we have been committed as a nation to maintaining a "maximum" of employment opportunities, production and purchasing power. This responsibility is to be achieved in a manner calculated to foster and promote free competitive enterprise and the general welfare. All is to be done in a manner consistent with other needs and obligations of the federal government and with the assistance and cooperation of "industry, agriculture, labor and state and local governments."

President Truman described the 1946 Act (Public Law 79–304) as constituting "a commitment to take any and all of the measures necessary for a healthy economy." This admittedly could be an awesome undertaking. No one would contend that we as a nation have achieved as yet the full measure of what is clearly contemplated by the sweeping prose of the 1946 law.[26] Nevertheless we have an encouraging base from which to move toward a more complete honoring of the original congressional intent.

The Congress has become accustomed each January to receiving from the White House three important documents: (1) the president's state of the union message; (2) the proposed budget for the fiscal year beginning the following July 1 and (3) the annual *Economic Report* of the president.

The *Economic Report* is prepared by the professional staff of the Council of Economic Advisers, itself a creation of the Employment Act of 1946. The Report is received and studied by the Joint Committee on the Economic Report. The Joint Committee is charged with submitting whatever legislation it may believe is called for by the findings of the *Economic Report*.

---

[26] We have perhaps gone further than the Congrees in 1946 could have envisaged. Nevertheless, there is still more that can be done under the elastic language of the original 1946 "enabling" law.

The value and impact of the *Economic Report* could be enhanced considerably if the president by Executive order would set up an annual conference of top management and union representatives whose specific charge would be to study the forthcoming *Economic Report's* findings on the current and prospective state of the national economy. The conference would strive for a voluntary consensus on a wage-price-profit "line" for the coming calendar year. What I am referring to as a "line" would be suggested norms or models for wage-price-profit decisions. These could be widely publicized for the information and guidance of those employers and unions who are agreeable to dovetailing their micro-economic concerns with macro-economic objectives.

The success of such a proposed annual conference depends on both the composition and caliber of the delegates. It is critically important that all segments of the economy be represented—not just the industrial and union giants with visible market power. Included in the must category for representation would be construction, trucking, service trades, railroads, textiles, needle trades and many other lines whose negotiations with unions in recent years have taken place in comparative obscurity with little regard, in many cases, for public interest considerations.[27]

The suggested conference should also include representatives from management and labor in the public sector as well as the private. Government is our largest "industry." At the state and local level it is also our key growth industry.[28] Unionization of public employees continues to proceed at a rapid pace. As we shall see in Chapter 13, the bargaining on economic issues between government agencies and employee organizations can have serious unstabilizing effects.

Some skeptics may think that the proposed charge to the conference to achieve consensus each year on a "line" or parameters for guiding negotiated economic packages, corporate price policies and profit levels is so ambitious that the undertaking is doomed at the start. However, if the conference can be broadly representative and staffed with appropriate professional expertise and if the whole operation is run in close cooperation with the Council of Economic Advisers, I believe there is a genuine possibility for achieving a consensus in most years. In a particular year when a consensus is not forthcoming there would at least be the educational impact of an informed division of opinion that would in itself be illuminating.

---

[27] The 1970 Teamsters contract again comes to mind as a classic example of total commitment to extracting whatever the traffic will bear. See footnote 1 above.

[28] The number of government employees at all levels rose from 6 million to 10 million between 1950 and 1965, according to George Hildebrand. The growth is occurring mainly at the state and local government level. The public sector is continuing to expand. Unionization is also proceeding briskly. See George H. Hildebrand, "The Public Sector," in *Frontiers of Collective Bargaining*, ed. John T. Dunlop and Neil W. Chamberlain (New York: Harper and Row, Publishers, 1967), pp. 125–26.

The conference idea stems from a deep sense of lost opportunity in the original development and use of the CEA's wage-price guideposts in the period 1962–1966. Much can be learned from the tactical and substantive errors of the CEA's initial approach. The guideposts may well be dead at this writing, unmourned by most in their original form. The experience with them can nevertheless be most instructive in furthering the search for effective and feasible policy instruments beyond the level of exhortation.

In the summer of 1970 a National Committee on Productivity was convened to recommend, in President Nixon's words, how to "achieve a balance between costs and productivity that will lead to more stable prices."[29] This presidential conference must be regarded as a step in the right direction, but it falls short of what I have in mind in *my* proposed annual conference. So also does President Nixon's instruction to the CEA to prepare what he calls a "periodic Inflation Alert."

The Origins and Rationale of the CEA's Wage-Price Guideposts

Presidents Truman and Eisenhower periodically urged upon management and union representatives the need to be restrained and responsible in their negotiations on wages and economic fringes. These presidential statements were aptly characterized as "the economics of admonition."[30] President John F. Kennedy, however, advanced from admonitory rhetoric to something much more specific in his wage-price guidepost approach, one which had a controversial, well-publicized and comparatively short life.

The CEA's wage-price guideposts had an impeccable rationale when looked at by the professional economist from a macro-economic standpoint. They underscored the proposition that gains in real income derive only from economic growth, that is, increases in physical output per manhour. The CEA made clear that wage increases or price increases unaccompanied by increasing output per man-hour produced inflationary consequences, that is, reduced real national income.

Instead of paraphrasing, I shall set forth the CEA's rationale as stated in the 1962 *Economic Report*. In analyzing these paragraphs the reader may wish to think back to the famed General Motors-UAW annual improvement factor increase rationale, discussed in Chapter 10. There is a haunting similarity between the GM-UAW joint statement as to the mutual benefit deriving from productivity gains and the following language from the 1962 *Economic Report*:

---

[29] Address by President Richard M. Nixon on the state of the economy, June 17, 1970 (mimeographed).

[30] This phrase is credited to Professor Ben Lewis.

The general guide for noninflationary wage behavior is that the rate of increase in wage rates (including fringe benefits) in each industry be equal to the trend rate of over-all productivity increase. General acceptance of this guide would maintain stability of labor cost per unit of output for the economy as a whole—though not of course for individual industries.

The general guide for noninflationary price behavior calls for price reduction if the industry's rate of productivity increase exceeds the over-all rate—for this would mean declining unit labor costs; it calls for an appropriate increase in price if the opposite relationship prevails; and it calls for stable prices if the two rates of productivity increase are equal.[31]

INITIAL MISTAKES IN THE WAGE-PRICE GUIDEPOST POLICY

Blessed with the customary advantages of hindsight, it is not hard to see why the wage-price guideposts had a rocky road from the start and why the house came tumbling down when the CEA unblushingly refused to follow its own formula in connection with the 1966 guideposts. Several of the more serious errors or flaws should be noted.

In the first place, the consent of the governed apparently was not solicited in advance. There was a failure on the part of both the CEA and President Kennedy to take top management and AFL-CIO leaders into their confidence to secure understanding and support of the new policy. This communication gap came back to haunt the CEA and the White House in short order. Although contacts were frequent and intense in connection with efforts to secure adherence to the guideposts as specific negotiations took place, the requisite sympathetic rapport was not often there.

The story of the 1962 steel negotiations is a case in point. The Steelworkers went along with the new restrained approach. The union and the president understood that Big Steel would do likewise when it came to price increases. When steel management broke the faith, as President Kennedy saw it, they ran into a buzz saw. The awesome power of the presidency manifested itself through a dismayingly quick, varied series of thrusts designed to effectuate the rescinding of the announced steel price increases. In a matter of days Big Steel capitulated.[32]

Even if one grants that President Kennedy's anger was justified as to what he regarded as a stab in the back, it cannot be denied that mobilizing such diverse federal "weapons" as the Department of Justice's antitrust division, the Defense Department's purchasing arm and the Federal Trade

---

[31] *Economic Report* (January, 1962), p. 189.

[32] For an absorbing account of the confrontation between President Kennedy and Big Steel see Grant McConnell, *Steel and the Presidency, 1962* (New York: W. W. Norton & Company, Inc., 1963).

Commission in a sudden hard-line concentration on steel price policies was hard to reconcile with the propaganda sell that adherence to the wage-price guideposts was voluntary.

A second major flaw in the wage-price guidepost approach, as conceived by Walter Heller, chairman of the CEA under President Kennedy, was the single-minded concentration on the trend rate in physical productivity per man-hour as *the* criterion for evaluating negotiated economic packages and corporate price changes. The CEA's textbook logic may have been sound, but from a practical standpoint it left much to be desired.

In the real world of micro-economic decision-making many factors must be considered by management and union at the bargaining table. Corporation X and Union Y could not blithely agree on a 3.2 percent increase (covering wages and economic fringes) simply because 3.2 was the magic number in the CEA's calculations. In Chapter 10 we described at some length the various factors that the employer and union must consider and weigh in making their wage and fringe policy decisions. To refresh understanding of the importance of this consideration, the following statement of John Dunlop is directly in point:

> The wage and price guideposts are not expressed in criteria that are meaningful to private decision makers. The "trend rate of overall productivity increase" and the relative rate of an industry's increase in productivity compared to the average are scarcely standards which are meaningful to decision-makers on wages and prices. These concepts are not congenial or directly applicable in their operating experience. Wage decisions are typically argued in terms of comparative wages, living costs, competitive conditions, labor shortages, ability to pay, specific productivity, job content, and bargaining power. Negotiators and their constituents understand these concepts. Pricing decisions are considered in terms of specific competitive prices, quality, advertising, market prospects, responses to changes in other prices, costs, and the like. The diffuse structure of collective bargaining and pricing makes the standards of the guideposts appear remote and unrealistic. The guideposts simply "do not come through." The macro-standards not only have no simple application to specific wage or price decisions, they do not appear relevant, controlling or decisive to micro-decision-makers. You cannot effectively prescribe micro-decisions with macro-precepts. I suggest that unless guidepost standards are formulated in terms much more directly applicable and specific for decision-makers, in terms they ordinarily utilize, the guideposts will command neither respect nor application."[33]

If a decision is ever made to resurrect the wage-price guideposts, there should be realistic concern and empathy for the multiple headaches faced by the bargainers.

---

[33] John T. Dunlop, "Guideposts, Wages and Collective Bargaining," in *Guidelines, Informal Controls and the Market Place*, ed. George P. Shultz and Robert Z. Aliber (Chicago: University of Chicago Press, 1966), p. 86.

A third defect in the implementation of the wage-price guideposts was the discriminatorily uneven burden of their impact, even though it could not be said that this was intentional on the CEA's part. Perhaps unavoidably the bright light of guidepost policy was focused on our major oligopolistic industries and the giant unions with which they bargain, notably steel and automobiles. It was an easy matter to wheel the guideposts into position for close monitoring of negotiations involving "big business" and "big labor" where the market power of the participants was clearly visible. It was not long, however, before it became evident to both professionals and laymen alike that some of the most severe inflationary pressures of a cost-(wage-) push nature were emanating from construction, trucking and a variety of service trades and professions (college and university teaching, for example) rather than from the market giants. At the same time that appropriate restraint was initially displayed in steel and automobile agreements, wage and salary increases far in excess of the 3.2 yardstick, most of them totally unjustified by the CEA's cherished productivity consideration, were being instituted in these areas seemingly beyond the reach of the CEA's educational efforts. In these situations wages and salaries were being blithely escalated at a 5 to 10 percent annual clip in tight labor markets. No effective way was found to carry the guidepost message to negotiators in these fields. Steel and automobile negotiators were understandably irked about being singled out for federal attention while the decentralized bargainers were able to do their bit to feed inflationary fires in enviable obscurity.

These are some of the chief errors and flaws in the original use of the guideposts. They must be avoided in any future effort to develop private support for macro-economic targets.

THE REVOLT OF THE AFL-CIO IN 1966

Looking backward we see clearly that management had less to complain about than did organized labor. The CEA contends that it gave as much attention to implementing the price guidepost as it did to the wage guideline of the year. This contention is not supported by the evidence. The spotlight was mainly on collective bargaining rather than on corporate price policy (with the conspicuous exception of the 1962 steel "high noon" showdown). Be that as it may, it is essential to probe more deeply into the reasons for the AFL-CIO's profound resentment which surfaced in 1966.

The Federation was probably never happy with the guidepost policy, mainly for the reasons already noted. An additional sore point with union leaders was that no federal effort was made to curb soaring corporate profits and executive salaries. It is gospel with most union leaders that the inflation which began in the mid-1960s after several years of relative price and wage stability was basically attributable to unrestrained increases in corporate profits.[34] Although the late Walter Reuther and Federation President George Meany were at sword's point on many labor issues they agreed completely in naming corporate profits as the villain of the piece in the late 1960s.[35]

Most union leaders thought that they and their constituents were singled out to bear the brunt of the federal drive to prevent or curb inflation. Open revolt, however, did not occur until the CEA in the 1966 *Economic Report* announced that it was sticking with the familiar 3.2 percent wage guidepost even though it conceded that its own productivity trend rate rationale suggested a figure in the neighborhood of 3.6 percent. The CEA's reasons for sticking to 3.2 may have made sense to other professional economists because of the swelling inflationary tide that had become clearly visible. To the unions, however, it amounted to sophistry.

Another contributing factor in triggering the AFL-CIO's blast against the 1966 guideposts was the bitter disappointment over losing once more in the fight to persuade Congress to repeal Section 14(b) of the Taft-Hartley Act. In early 1966 the AFL-CIO leadership became convinced that President Johnson was dragging his feet on applying White House pressure in relation to 14(b). At the same time the CEA, a staff agency in the Executive Office of the President, was urging unions to display restraint on wage demands, with no visible effort to reduce profit margins or prices as unit costs declined.

The CEA's 1967 report contained a strong retrospective justification of its wage-price guidepost policies. In 1967, however, it made no effort to spell out a percentage guideline for negotiations. The Council discussed with pride its procedures for preventing price increases already put into effect. These remarks were obviously intended to rebut the AFL-CIO charge of overemphasis on the wage guidepost.[36]

The 1967 report acknowledged that there might be merit in the AFL-CIO's position that trend rates in physical productivity per man-hour should not be the sole criterion in evaluating whether a given wage increase is consistent with macro-economic price stability objectives.

The AFL-CIO Executive Council's denunciation of the guideposts represents one instance where it can be said with assurance that the Federation spoke truly as the voice of all its affiliated unions. The building trades never had paid any particular attention to the CEA's admonitions. The unions that felt compelled to do so were the industrial union giants that

---

[34] Every statement of the AFL-CIO Executive Council from 1966 onward hammered away at this thesis.

[35] Reference has already been made to Reuther's open letter to members of the American Economic Association in December, 1969.

[36] The AFL-CIO remained unimpressed.

always bargain in the national spotlight, such as the Steelworkers and the UAW. By the CEA's own admission in its 1966 report, wage behavior in the unionized manufacturing sector for several years past had been generally consonant with guidepost requirements.

The Federation reiterated throughout 1966 and ever since that organized labor was prepared to sacrifice as much as anyone else for as long as anyone else provided that there was equality of sacrifice. If extraordinary stabilization measures are held to be necessary, says the Federation's Executive Council, they should be designed to bring all costs, prices and profits, as well as wages and salaries, under even-handed restraint.

Briefly summarized, the Federation's case against the guideposts stresses the following points:

1. The CEA considered only the trended rate in productivity as a criterion for judging whether wage increases were consonant with the public interest. Many other factors, which neither management nor unions can afford to ignore, must affect wage negotiations.
2. The CEA and other concerned federal agencies have always concentrated on labor's adherence to the wage guidepost. Similar zeal was not shown with reference to the price guidepost. Nothing was said by the CEA, the White House or anyone else about soaring profits.
3. The wage guidepost impact was unfair because it spotlighted some negotiations and overlooked others.
4. The CEA's exceptions were not sufficient to allow for appropriate wage adjustments in industries with much higher than average productivity gains.
5. The CEA guidepost made no allowances for increased consumer prices.[37]

THE IMPACT OF THE GUIDEPOSTS

Did the CEA's wage-price guideposts really guide? The answer must be a qualified "yes." The CEA did a good "p.r." job that made it difficult for either management or organized labor in major negotiations from 1926 to 1966 to avoid consideration of the percentage guidepost in reaching agreement on wages plus fringes. They may often have exceeded the guidepost in fact. However, they usually found it desirable to develop some kind of rationalization for doing so. Correspondingly, whenever the negotiated wage increase plus fringe increments was within the guidepost, the parties seldom failed to call public attention to their "restrained" and "responsible" action.

Quantifying the impact of the guideposts is hard to do. We have no certain way of knowing what the pattern of wage increases plus fringe

---

[37] Since January, 1967, however, the CEA has conceded that unions must consider increases in consumer prices in evaluating what to shoot for in wage negotiations.

improvements might have been between 1962 and 1966 had there been no guideposts. The CEA's evidence of general wage and price stability between 1961 and 1966 does not "prove" guidepost impact. During this period the unemployment level was considerably above the frictional norm. Also, there was substantial unutilized plant capacity. These factors may have been more important than any subtle restraining pressure from the much-publicized guideposts.

Robert Solow of MIT offered some interesting, though not necessarily persuasive evidence that the wage guidepost did make a difference.[38] Whether Solow is correct or not, there can be no doubt that the publicizing of the guideposts had considerable educative impact on the parties at interest and, to a degree, on the lay public. The media did their bit by making adherence or nonadherence to the guidepost standard the lead in any story on a major wage negotiation. When the wage guidepost was cracked in a particular case, this seemed to be regarded as more newsworthy than a case of adherence.

The guidepost saga has intrinsic appeal for the economist who is concerned about the problem of economic literacy. Our brief, unhappy experience can also be illuminating on the still unresolved problem of how to infuse the "public interest" concept into private decision-making on wage policy or price policy without imposing direct controls. Ironically, the CEA standard in actuality weakened the strong and strengthened the weak. Employers and unions negotiating in the Levinson framework (high economic concentration ratio, high degree of unionization and high profits) were always on the spot.[39] They were urged not to take advantage of their market economic strength to raise wages and administer prices to compensate for labor cost increments. Employers and "weak" unions in highly competitive industries, where wages are characteristically "low" and where the union's bargaining power could not produce any appreciable wage increase, were encouraged implicitly by the CEA standard to negotiate for a higher figure. Finally, the negotiators in industries where bargaining is customarily geared to local labor market conditions (for example, building and construction) were able to ignore the collective macro-economic impact of their cozy micro bargains.

Nearly all Western countries have tried some type of national incomes policy in recent years. These vary widely as to the degree to which they control and limit private decision-making on wages and prices. The evidence suggests that direct controls have not been particularly effective in curbing inflationary wage and price increases. Edelman and Fleming

---

[38] Robert M. Solow, "The Case Against the Case Against the Guideposts," in George P. Shultz and Robert Z. Aliber, eds., *op. cit.*, pp. 41–54.

[39] Harold M. Levinson, *Determining Forces in Collective Wage Bargaining* (New York: John Wiley & Sons, Inc., 1966).

emerged with a marked pragmatic preference for indirect controls (that is, monetary controls).[40]

Except for the comparatively mild wage and price controls of the Korean War period, the United States has depended since the end of World War II on a combination of indirect controls and various degrees of exhortation. The wage-price guideposts are a good example of what can be termed *explicit admonition*. In 1970 there was considerable discussion over whether to return to something like the guideposts. Those who retained their faith in the guidepost approach, however, were generally aware of the importance of avoiding the mistakes of the 1962–1966 period.

Of first importance to my mind is candid advance consultation with representatives of all segments of our economy. For this purpose the annual conference of management and union representatives would be appropriate. This could be an excellent way of inducing micro-economic decision-makers to use their discretion on wages, prices and profits in responsible fashion.

Perhaps the conference idea is too ambitious or utopian. The temptation is strong to take the easy road by concluding: "We'll do the best we can with a combination of indirect monetary and fiscal controls and let the market mechanism operate as it pleases." I suggest that this would be a cop-out on everybody's part. The severe inflation of 1966 to 1970 should have demonstrated convincingly the insufficiency of this approach.

One thing is certain. The basic problem to which the guideposts were addressed will not go away of its own accord. We must therefore press for the following: (1) improved virtuosity in the use of indirect monetary and fiscal controls, (2) improved performance by micro-economic decision-makers in voluntary dovetailing of their own interests with the public interest and (3) use of an annual conference to work in conjunction with the CEA to develop a "line" for the coming calendar year on wage, price and profit policy that will be compatible with the needs of the economy as shown by the CEA's findings as disclosed in the January *Economic Report*.

I am convinced that such a three-pronged offensive, if pressed in vigorous and determined fashion, could enable us as a nation to have our cake and eat it. We could accomplish the seeming miracle of simultaneously achieving relative price stability, low level unemployment and sound economic growth while at the same time leaving the bargainers *comparatively free*. We can thus avoid the extremes of compulsory arbitration and sweeping wage-price controls that hardly anybody really wants.

SELECTED BIBLIOGRAPHY

AKERLOF, GEORGE A., "Relative Wages and the Rate of Inflation," *Quarterly Journal of Economics*, LXXXIII (August, 1969), 353–74.

---

[40] Murray Edelman and Robben W. Fleming, *The Politics of Wage-Price Decisions: A Four Country Analysis* (Urbana, Ill.: University of Illinois Press, 1965).

ALEXANDER, KENNETH O., "Unionism, Wages, and Cost-Push: A Summary Statement," *American Journal of Economics and Sociology*, XXIV (October, 1965), 383–95.

BOK, DEREK C., AND JOHN T. DUNLOP. *Labor and the American Community*. New York: Simon and Schuster, Inc., 1970, Chapters 9 and 10.

BOWEN, WILLIAM G., *The Wage-Price Issue*. Princeton, N.J.: Princeton University Press, 1960.

BRONFENBRENNER, MARTIN, AND FRANKLYN D. HOLZMAN, "Survey of Inflation Theory," *American Economic Review*, LIII (September, 1963), 593–661.

CHRISTIAN, JAMES W., "Bargaining Function and the Effectiveness of the Wage-Price Guideposts," *Southern Economic Journal*, XXXVII (July, 1970), 51–65.

EDELMAN, MURRAY, AND R. W. FLEMING, *The Politics of Wage-Price Decisions: A Four Country Analysis*. Urbana, Ill.: University of Illinois Press, 1965.

HELLER, WALTER, *New Dimensions of Political Economy*. New York: W. W. Norton & Company, Inc., 1967.

JOSEPH, MYRON L., "Wage-Price Guideposts in the U.S.A.", *British Journal of Industrial Relations*, V (November, 1967), 311–21.

KASSALOW, E. M., "National Wage Policies: Lessons to Date, Europe and the U.S.A.," *Proceedings, 1966*, Industrial Relations Research Association. Madison, Wis.: Industrial Relations Research Association, 1967, pp. 125–38.

LAW NOTE, "Wage-Price Guidelines: Informal Government Regulation of Labor and Industry," *Harvard Law Review*, LXXX (January, 1967), 623–47.

LUCAS, ROBERT E., Jr., AND LEONARD A. RAPPING, "Real Wages, Employment and Inflation," *Journal of Political Economy*, LXXVII (September–October, 1969), 721–54.

McCONNELL, GRANT, *Steel and the Presidency—1962*. New York: W. W. Norton & Company, Inc., 1963.

MORTON, WALTER A., "Trade Unionism, Full Employment, and Inflation," *American Economic Review*, XL (March, 1950), 13–39.

OKUN, ARTHUR M., *The Political Economy of Prosperity*. New York: W. W. Norton & Company, Inc., 1970.

PERRY, GEORGE L., *Unemployment, Money Wage Rates, and Inflation*. Cambridge, Mass.: Massachusetts Institute of Technology Press, 1966.

————, "Wages and the Guideposts," *American Economic Review*, LVII (September, 1967), 897–904.

PHELPS, EDMUND S., "Phillips Curves, Expectations of Inflation and Optimal Unemployment Over Time," *Economica*, XXXIV (August, 1967), 254–81.

RYDER, MEYER S., "Collective Bargaining for Greater Productivity: Some Factors in the American Labour Relations System Possibly Generating Greater Productivity," *British Journal of Industrial Relations*, V (July, 1967), 190–97.

SHEAHAN, JOHN, *The Wage-Price Guideposts*. Washington, D.C.: The Brookings Institution, 1967.

SHULTZ, GEORGE P., AND ROBERT Z. ALIBER, eds., *Guidelines, Informal Controls, and the Market Place: Policy Choices in a Full Employment Economy*. Chicago: University of Chicago Press, 1966.

THROOP, ADRIAN W., "The Union-Nonunion Wage Differential and Cost-Push Inflation," *American Economic Review*, LVIII (March, 1968), 79–99.

NEGOTIATED ECONOMIC SECURITY

PACKAGES

and other "fringes"

CHAPTER TWELVE

For more than two decades employee economic security has been a major focus of union and employer negotiators. There is no reason to suppose that economic security issues will not continue to be of prime concern in the years ahead. Progress in the field of retirement programs and health and welfare plans has been dramatic. It must be regarded as one of the most significant developments in the recent evolution of collective bargaining as a process.

As Robert Tilove has observed, there would not have been the conversion from "progressive practices" to "standard practices" had it not been for the pressure of unions at the bargaining tables.[1] A few figures serve to highlight the change that has occurred. Tilove notes that in 1965 at least

---

[1] Robert Tilove, "Pensions, Health, and Welfare Plans," in *Challenges to Collective Bargaining*, ed. Lloyd Ulman (Englewood Cliffs, N.J.: Prentice-Hall, Inc., 1967), p. 37.

three out of four American workers were covered by a health and welfare plan of some sort and two out of four by a pension plan. This stands in sharp contrast with 1940, when employee benefit plans covered no more than one out of every ten workers.[2]

The term "package bargaining" is in itself testimony to the importance of the nonwage economic provisions of contemporary agreements. No story on a negotiated settlement is complete without a journalistic calculation of the percentage or cents per hour increase in so-called "fringes" as well as the wage increase as such. How inappropriate the term "fringes" has become can be appreciated by talking with nearly any employer engaged in collective bargaining.

An estimated 20 to 30 percent of the employer's labor cost dollar customarily goes to nonwage economic benefits. One usually associates the word fringe with a blanket or curtains or draperies, but if any of these had a fringe approximating 30 percent, it would look bizarre to say the least. The inventive minds of practitioners and students of collective bargaining have failed to coin a suitable substitute term, so we must perforce continue to talk of fringes.

The varied range of negotiated employee economic security programs cannot be dealt with in complete fashion in one chapter. We shall be concerned primarily with tracing the evolution, current status and future prospects of negotiated pension plans, health and welfare programs and, more briefly, income security and supplemental unemployment benefit (SUB) plans. In the concluding section of the chapter we shall present a summary overview of recent developments on other standard fringes such as paid vacations, paid holidays and the like.

Many issues that used to be troublesome for negotiators in all these categories have been resolved by a variety of means, including sad experience, grievance arbitration, legislation and so on. To cite one example, one no longer hears debate over the once burning issue of whether a negotiated pension plan should be on a contributory or noncontributory basis. The pension plans of many nonunion firms continue to be of a contributory type. However, the answer at the bargaining table has been overwhelmingly conclusive. Nearly all negotiated plans are noncontributory. We shall therefore forego analyzing the pros and cons on this issue.

There is no shortage of troublesome matters to test the mettle of the negotiators. In one fashion or another most of the difficulties relate to the increasing cost problem. At each negotiation a decision must be made as to how much of the economic package is to be allocated to wage adjustments as such and how much to improvements and innovations in the various employee benefit programs. Notwithstanding the problem of increasing cost,

---

[2] *Ibid.*

the "mix" of benefit programs in most cases tends to become richer and more varied at each contract renegotiation.

An Outline of a Typical Nonwage Economic Package

The two staple items in most negotiated packages are a retirement plan and some type of health and welfare program. The contents of the health and welfare part of the package will vary markedly from one relationship to another as to both the range and level of benefits.

A fairly typical H-and-W plan will embrace the following:

1. A hospitalization care program.
2. A surgical and medical care program.
3. A group life insurance or death benefit plan.

Important features of contemporary H-and-W bargaining, not yet in the typical or customary category, are prepaid medical and dental care. Many unions are also seeking coverage of a number of items, not yet covered by most contracts, that are adding seriously to members' out-of-pocket costs. I refer to outpatient diagnostic services, X-ray and other types of laboratory services, prescription drugs and the like.

In health and welfare bargaining, the trend is to increase the range and coverage of benefits wherever possible. This is not an easy task in the face of constantly mounting costs. Another costly development concerns extending the coverage to dependents of employees. In the pension plan phase of package bargaining, the principal current targets relate to obtaining full or partial vesting and sounder funding. These problems will be treated in greater detail shortly.

The Frustrations of Package Bargaining

Package bargaining typically requires some agonizing choices on the part of the negotiators—more often than not the union representatives, who must face up to a forced choice in many cases between a substantial wage boost and improvements in the complex of employee security benefit plans. The employer's financial position is frequently such that he is unable to grant simultaneously a demand for a hefty wage increase and a considerable "sweetening" of the pension and health and welfare provisions. It is therefore a fairly common practice for the employer to advise the union representatives informally as to approximately how much of an increase in overall labor cost he is capable of absorbing over the next contract period (usually three years), leaving it up to the union as to how this lump sum shall be apportioned between wages and nonwage economic benefits.

This is a tough decision to make in inflationary periods like 1966–1970. Union representatives are getting strong pressure from their constituents to obtain catch-up wage increases *and* to liberalize the benefits program at the same time. If the employer's cost picture is such as to require an either-or choice, it is likely that the wage increase will get priority attention during inflationary periods. In most of the key bargaining relationships, however, it has been possible to obtain some improvements in the important fringe areas in addition to substantial wage increases.

Bargaining on economic security programs is a technical and complex business. It demands a kind of expertise that many management and union negotiators lack. Both parties have thus had to train themselves or hire specialists. The analysis here will not be technical in nature. I claim no specialized knowledge of the subjects at hand.

No area of current bargaining is more dynamic and volatile. Costs are constantly rising. At the same time, pressures for new and varied services are growing more insistent. Policies properly regarded as pioneering and imaginative in the previous two decades are relegated unceremoniously to the realm of the taken-for-granted. The union negotiators are plagued with the familiar refrain, "What have you done for us *lately*?"

The Prospect of Federalizing Health Care

The limits of private ability to handle economic security issues will be reached soon in many relationships. In some cases, the saturation point has been reached. In the light of these considerations, it is pertinent to note that a major effort is under way in the U.S. Congress to federalize some major aspects of employee security, principally in the areas of comprehensive prepaid medical care and health insurance. Bills to commit the federal government to picking up the tab in these areas were introduced in the summer of 1970. One can predict safely that the debate over proposed federalization of the cost of health care will be lengthy and heated before final action is taken either way. Ultimately, the Congress will probably enact legislation authorizing federal payment for doctors' and hospital care, with varying restrictions thereon. How any such action by the federal government will affect negotiated H-and-W plans is obviously a matter of critical importance.

Here we make no assumptions on federal action. However, the probability is that organized labor (and many employers as well) will give strong support to the new proposed federal effort. There is a growing recognition on the part of both employers and unions that even the most broadly based of the negotiated plans are proving to be extremely costly. Furthermore, the private plans pose a continuing psychological problem for the bargainers. Attainment of a certain level and range of benefits invariably produces employee expectations of "more" at the next contract negotiation. Sooner or later this expectation may not be realizable.

PENSION PLANS: PAST, PRESENT AND FUTURE

Prior to World War II there were a few private retirement plans operated by nonunion firms, but there were virtually no negotiated plans. The initial impetus for negotiated pension schemes came during and immediately following World War II. The United Mine Workers in 1946 and the Steelworkers and UAW in 1949 and 1950 formed the vanguard of the drive to make some kind of negotiated retirement plan a "must" item thereafter on collective bargaining agenda.[3]

The proliferation of negotiated plans in the 1950s and 1960s was nothing short of phenomenal. Furthermore, significant improvements have been made steadily in many contracts on the level of benefits, eligibility requirements, vesting rights and the like. Most contemporary negotiated pension plans bear scant resemblance to their forebears. Throughout this twenty-year period of dynamic change, however, both employers and unions of necessity have had to negotiate their revisions in pragmatic fashion in order to achieve adequate benefit levels while at the same time keeping premium costs at a tolerable level. This has not been an easy task, particularly when both parties were serious about the necessity to develop a fully funded, actuarially sound plan.[4]

Robert C. Miljus and Alton C. Johnson, writing on multi-employer pension plans in 1963, estimated that in 1940 there were only 4 million workers covered by private pension plans, whereas by 1961 the number covered had increased to around 22 million, over one-fourth of the work force at that time.[5] These figures include, of course, some employer-initiated plans in nonunion firms, but in recent years nearly all the growth has come in negotiated plans, mostly of the multi-employer type.

Continued growth of negotiated pension plans is logical to anticipate, reflecting the worker's strong interest in security not only on the job (as noted in Chapter 9) but also in his post-working years.[6]

---

[3] The United Mine Workers pension plan was a pioneer negotiated plan in 1946, but it has not been a good model to emulate. Increasing costs have led to uncertainty of benefits and low actual payments in terms of worker expectations.

[4] Many plans do not meet rigid standards of being fully funded and actuarial soundness. Ultimately, much tighter federal control may be needed for adequate protection of worker pension rights.

[5] Robert C. Miljus and Alton C. Johnson, "Multi-Employer Pensions and Labor Mobility," *Harvard Business Review*, XLVI (September–October, 1963), 147–61.

[6] The stress placed on a liberalized pension plan in the UAW's 1970 negotiations in the automobile industry is but one illustration of strong and continuing employee interest.

The other side of the growth coin is the depressing fact that a considerable number of pension plans are terminated each year. A BLS study by Emerson H. Beier shows that approximately 4,300 pension plans were terminated in the period 1955–1965. A high proportion of these involved small firms. The median life span of the plans terminated was six years.[7] In many cases, financial difficulties were the principal factor leading to termination. I do not propose to elaborate on the termination problem. However, it must be a sobering factor for employers and unions to keep in mind as they deal with the pressures to "sweeten" their plans at each renegotiation period.

ANALYSIS OF CONTEMPORARY NEGOTIATED PENSION PLANS: THE VESTING PROBLEM

Reviewing some features of current negotiated retirement plans will show the progress that has been made in disposing of former sources of conflict and uncertainty. As already noted, nearly all negotiated plans are noncontributory. The employee makes no contribution toward the retirement fund. This makes possible a higher benefit level than would be the case in a contributory plan. The case for noncontributory pension plans in a union setting has clearly prevailed.

One of the most critical problems in negotiated plans concerns whether and how to provide for vesting. Vesting is a term that applies to an employee's right to all or some fraction of his pension equities for which the employer has paid when an employee goes to another firm. In the absence of any provision for vesting, the horizontal mobility of workers may be seriously restricted. On the other hand, in many single firm pension plans the cost of providing for complete or even partial vesting of the employer's contribution may prove to be considerable, if not in fact prohibitive.

In spite of such difficulties, however, great progress has been made both in providing for vesting where none had existed previously and also in liberalizing existing vesting arrangements.

A BLS study covering the five-year period between 1962–1963 and 1967 by Donald M. Landay and Harry E. Davis indicates not only substantial growth in negotiated pension plans (principally in the multi-employer category), but also marked increase in and liberalization of vesting provisions (also largely in the multi-employer category).[8] Landay and Davis studied the contents of 1,698 plans for 1967 compared with 1,060 studied for 1962–

---

[7] Emerson H. Beier, "Terminations of Pension Plans: Eleven Years' Experience," *Monthly Labor Review*, XC (June, 1967), 26–30.

[8] Donald M. Landay and Harry E. Davis, "Growth and Vesting Changes in Private Pension Plans," *Monthly Labor Review*, XCI (May, 1968), 29–35.

1963. About seven out of ten workers in this survey were covered by collective bargaining agreements.

The Landay-Davis study shows that four-fifths of the workers covered by contributory plans in 1967 had vesting protection compared with three-fifths of those covered by noncontributory plans. Landay and Davis note that this discrepancy is accounted for mainly because of a heavy concentration in the noncontributory group of multi-employer plans without vesting.

The absence of vesting in many multi-employer plans is perhaps not as bad as it sounds. Under a multi-employer contract the worker enjoys protection of his pension rights as long as he remains within the employment circle of the member firms who are parties to the agreement. In other words, he enjoys what I shall term "internal vesting." However, whenever a worker takes a job outside the bounds of the multi-employer contract, he forfeits his pension rights in most cases. Landay and Davis found an exceedingly low incidence of vesting in negotiated multi-employer pension plans, only about one out of four workers.[9]

Improvement in vesting provisions has taken place in many cases, particularly under plans covering large numbers of workers. According to Landay and Davis, in 1967 nearly one out of five plan members could qualify for full vesting after ten years of service, regardless of age. This figure compares favorably with one out of seventeen only a few years earlier.

Deletion of age requirements is likely to be one of the more important of the "liberalizing" targets in current and prospective negotiations. The aim of many unions is to achieve full pension rights after twenty-five to thirty years of service, regardless of age, or with ten or more years of credited service after reaching age sixty.

The inflation since 1966 has also caused union pressure for escalator clauses on pension benefits and for raising benefits for those who have already retired under a less satisfactory program.

The desired benefit levels in negotiated plans have been figured usually in terms of $5 per month or more for each of the employee's years of credited service. For example, the 1970–1973 meatpacking contracts with Armour and Swift provide for a benefit of $6 per month for each of the employee's credited years of service for those retiring after January 1, 1971. Under this arrangement an employee retiring after thirty years of service would be entitled to a pension of $180 per month. The benefit figure is upped to $6.50 effective January 1, 1972, applying to those who retire in 1972 or thereafter.[10]

---

[9] *Ibid.*, p. 31.

[10] I acknowledge here my appreciation to Frederick R. Livingston for access to multilithed copies of the new Armour and Swift agreements (1970–1973) with the Amalgamated Meat Cutters.

A Note on Portability of Pensions

Portability is a term used to describe an employee's right to transfer earned pension credits from one pension plan to another. The federal Social Security retirement system is the obvious illustration of complete portability. An employee's credits under Social Security continue to accumulate whenever and wherever he works under covered employment, no matter how many individual firms may be involved.

Portability is very difficult to work out under private negotiated plans because of the range and diversity of plans now in existence as to level of benefits, age qualifications and the like. Portability is, of course, possible under multi-employer or multi-plant agreements (same employer), but the benefit is limited, of course, to the confines of the bargaining unit.

Portability and vesting are concepts that are frequently confused in discussing pension plans. As we have seen, vesting refers to a terminating "qualified" employee's right to a pension based on his credits in a particular plan. Many negotiated plans do not yet provide for vesting. Those which do frequently impose qualifications of ten to fifteen years' service and an age requirement of, say, forty years. In contracts that provide for vesting the worker who leaves employment to take a job with another firm must recognize that his vested pension credits go into cold storage until he reaches the retirement age under the plan he left (generally age sixty or age sixty-five). Vesting does not involve a transfer of credits on a taking-it-with-you basis to the new employer. Portability is the proper term applying to the right to transfer pension credits from one pension plan to another.

Future Prospects for Negotiated Pension Plans

Continued liberalization of negotiated pension plans can be anticipated. The union incentive to play catch-up appears to be just as strong in the pension field as it always has been in the drive for continuous upward adjustment of wages or salaries. The improvement drive nevertheless will be affected by pragmatic considerations. Single employers with a small employment base can only be moved so far. Even giant multi-employer plans have finite limitations on the extent to which they can finance fully funded, actuarially sound plans. The pension target of the UAW in the 1970 negotiations probably represents the ultimate in the achievable for most unions.

In 1970 the UAW was seeking to improve upon an already advanced pension plan by removing the $400 ceiling on its early retirement pension formula negotiated in 1964 so that the formula would be fully related to the rate of pay. UAW also is seeking a service-related benefit of at least $500 a month with thirty years' service and with protection of the individual's Social Security benefits.

Other UAW pension goals in the 1970 negotiations include the following:

1. Increase the basic pension benefit for both present and future retirees.
2. Establish cost-of-living protection for all retired workers' pensions.
3. Increase the survivor benefit so that the survivor of the retiree does not suffer a reduction in living standards.

A NOTE ON ADMINISTRATION OF NEGOTIATED PENSION PLANS

The nature and control of administration of negotiated pension plans proves to be a recurring headache for many employers. Most negotiated plans are largely administered and controlled by employers, pursuant to whatever policy guidelines have been developed through negotiation. Most unions are content to leave management in charge of pension administration. Most employers prefer it that way because of their strong views on prerogatives. Furthermore, few unions have full-time specialists in pension plan management. The UAW is the only union reported on in the recent BLS study of large plans that has equal representation on joint union-employer boards handling the day-to-day aspects of single-employer plan management.[11] Of course, attention is paid to the protection of employee rights through contract provisions relating to grievance procedure and arbitration. However, in handling pension grievances there is a major difference between insured and self-insured pension plans. The distinction is best explained by quoting here from the 1970 BLS study by Dorothy R. Kittner and Harry E. Davis, as follows:

> Plans with insured benefits may permit workers to challenge factual data (for example, data on credited service or earnings) submitted to the insurance carrier by the employer in connection with a specific claim, but the insurer's decision is otherwise final and binding. The insurer's decisions are not subject to the grievance machinery in the collective bargaining agreement; to do otherwise would subject to collective bargaining the expert judgment of a neutral party, for which part of the premium is paid. If the plan is self-insured, provisions for handling grievances are explicit in all jointly administered plans and in some administered by the employer.

---

[11] Dorothy E. Kittner and Harry E. Davis, *Major Collective Bargaining Agreements: Administration of Negotiated Pension, Health, and Insurance Plans*, U. S. Bureau of Labor Statistics (Washington, D.C., Government Printing Office), Bul. 1425–12, May, 1970.

However, where the plan doesn't have grievance provisions, one may properly infer that the regular grievance procedure in the collective bargaining agreement is applicable.[12]

Management is in the administrative driver's seat in the overwhelming majority of negotiated plans. It is management therefore that should be in the vanguard of those who are concerned about such serious problems as improper investment of pension funds, termination of plans due to financial deficiencies and, in a few cases, corruption in pension fund administration. Each year Congress receives proposals for tighter control over private pension plans with various suggested policies for better funding, greater portability and improved vesting rights.

There can be little doubt that more needs to be done in assuring the preservation of private pension plans, including the negotiated ones. This goal can best be achieved by carefully drawn federal legislation requiring all private plans to meet if not exceed defined minimum performance standards on each one of the key elements of a viable retirement plan, that is, sound funding, earlier vesting and portability.

The negotiated pension plan arena is one more illustration of the proposition that optimal results can be achieved only through *careful dovetailing of private discretion with public policy.* The goals or targets are reasonably clear, but a consensus has not developed fully as to the nature and shape of the final solution. It seems certain, however, that we require tougher federal legislation assuring adherence to sound minimum performance standards.

The Current Scene in "Health and Welfare" Bargaining

The term "health and welfare" has become a standard shorthand label for an impressive range of negotiated benefits other than pension or retirement plans. The H-and-W umbrella generally covers some if not all of the following: (1) sickness and accident insurance; (2) hospitalization benefits for employees and their dependents; (3) surgical benefits; (4) payments for doctors' charges in hospital; (5) nursing and medical care in the home; (6) various outpatient services such as diagnostic X-rays, laboratory tests for allergies and so forth; (7) prescription drugs and medicines; (8) dental care and (9) eye care.

Some items are doubtless missing in the above enumeration, but generally it covers the principal benefits that unions currently seek to include as integral parts of the total economic security package in contemporary

---

[12] *Ibid.*, p. 3.

bargaining. The union emphasis generally has a dual focus: (1) to extend the range of health benefits and (2) to improve the level of benefits for each of the categories covered. The protean, diverse nature of negotiated health benefit plans is such as to defy thoroughgoing consideration. The modest aim here will be to note trends and problems in health benefit bargaining.

The Spur of Rising Medical and Hospital Costs

It is no secret that the costs of medical and hospital care have been rising at a rapid rate for some years with no ceilings in sight. Hospital care in 1970 was approaching in some quarters the astronomical figure of $100 per day. The spectre of insecurity raised by these rising costs has added to the pressure on unions to negotiate adequate coverage while trying to remain abreast of the cost picture. This is no simple task. Another troublesome concern is the search for increasing efficiency in medical plan expenditures. Some of the larger and more affluent unions and employers, profoundly disturbed at the costs of doctors, hospitals and commercial insurance firms, have gone into the health care business on their own.

The most dramatic of health care developments lies in the field of private prepaid group health plans such as that launched in California some years ago by the Kaiser corporate empire. Both the Kaiser Foundation plan and the Health Insurance Plan of Greater New York lay stress on preventive care through periodic (that is, routine) physical examinations. The Kaiser Foundation plan provides comprehensive health care through its own clinics operated by salaried professionals.

More prepaid group plans can be anticipated. In 1968 the U.S. Public Health Service made a five-year grant of $165,000 a year to the Group Health Association of America for the express purpose of assisting new groups to get started.[13]

The future for union-only plans does not appear to be promising, in the opinion of BLS expert Donald M. Landay.[14] Part of the problem is the tremendous expense and effort required to organize such plans. Another factor is that the official AFL-CIO policy is to lend support to community plans rather than to plans limited to union families. Considerable improvement is needed in those union plans already in operation, chiefly in the matter of extending benefits to dependents. Among the union plans surveyed by Landay about half (with about half the enrollment) cover union members only and do not embrace dependents.

---

[13] Donald M. Landay, "Trends in Negotiated Health Plans: Broader Coverage, Higher Quality Care," *Monthly Labor Review*, XCII (May, 1969), p. 7.
[14] *Ibid.*, p. 8.

PROBABLE TRENDS IN HEALTH PLAN BARGAINING

Union pressure for additional types of health care will doubtless continue in the years ahead. Cost-consciousness will be a factor in seeking to obtain more efficient expenditures of health plan dollars. Union-negotiated plans have clearly been in the vanguard of all private group health insurance programs for the past two decades. By 1969 they accounted for almost half of all employees covered by health benefit plans in private industry.[15]

Most negotiated plans provide reasonably well for the basics of hospital-medical-surgical coverage. However, there is a growing realization on the part of unions and their members that the so-called basics are not enough. A principal goal is to provide for major medical expenses arising from serious accidents or illnesses. Another is the matter of covering expenses currently coming from the union member's own pockets on such items as diagnostic services, X-rays, laboratory work and various kinds of prescribed therapy. These are not yet covered in most plans. Other types of benefits currently sought by unions include the costs of out-of-hospital drugs and mental health care (the UAW has been a leader on this latter item). Last but not least, there may well be a rapid expansion of negotiated dental plans, a late-comer in the benefit field.

In concluding this brief treatment of negotiated health benefits, it is appropriate to mention again the real possibility of federal legislation occupying all or part of the field in the 1970s. Our system of federal Social Security retirement benefits has made private negotiated pension plans a feasible undertaking in many relationships. So also has the federally induced system of state unemployment compensation made viable a negotiated program of SUB (supplemental unemployment benefits), to be discussed presently. By the same token, the ultimate answer on the costly business of adequate health care for all employees may prove to be federalizing of the costs of the "basics" of medical and hospital treatment, leaving leeway for privately negotiated arrangements for security above and beyond the basics.

A COMMENTARY ON SUB AND OTHER FORMS OF INCOME SECURITY

For many years the goal of a guaranteed annual wage (GAW) was in the minds of union negotiators at many bargaining tables. In most cases the goal retained the status of an unrealizable dream. A scattering of success-

---

[15] *Ibid.*, p. 3.

ful early plans, such as that of the George A. Hormel Company, received envious attention periodically by trade unionists. These early plans were also studied carefully by academicians. As far back as 1945, for example, Jack Chernick and George C. Hellickson developed a plausible demonstration that a GAW plan could work in the most unlikely of all fields—building and construction.[16] Yet the GAW did not become a key demand at the bargaining table until the UAW's famed push in 1955.

The ultimate result of the UAW effort in 1955 was the conversion of its demand for a full-dress GAW into the first of the SUB (supplemental unemployment benefit) plans. The initial SUB plans in automobiles and farm equipment (both in 1955) and in steel (1956) could be described as constituting what amounted to two-thirds of a semi-annual guaranteed wage. This is to say that the eligible worker upon being laid off was entitled to an amount from the SUB fund which, when combined with his payments from UC (unemployment compensation) approximated two-thirds of his normal weekly take-home pay. He could receive such payments for up to twenty-six weeks. In subsequent years SUB plans have been liberalized in most cases to the point where the eligible laid-off employee receives from a combination of SUB and UC payments 95 percent of his customary take-home pay when working, less $7.50 for "work-related expenses." Furthermore, the time span for receiving such payments has been extended from an original maximum of twenty-six weeks to as long as two years in many situations.[17]

Although employers and unions found it necessary to argue before state unemployment insurance agencies that the payments from SUB funds were *not* technically "wages" but rather a "social benefit,"[18] in reality it could be said that the current liberalized form of SUB does amount to a nearly complete realization of the original GAW dream in substance.

INCOME SECURITY BENEFITS

The liberalization of SUB plans is far from being the whole story, however, on negotiated income security programs. The main thrust of SUB, in the minds of union negotiators, was a protection for laid-off employees in technologically dynamic industries with considerable job attrition or where production levels (and thus employment) experienced sharp downswings periodically. In these circumstances SUB was not envisaged as an answer, let alone *the* answer, to the goal of continuing and predictable income security

---

[16] Jack Chernick and George C. Hellickson, *Guaranteed Annual Wages* (Minneapolis, Minn.: University of Minnesota Press, 1945).

[17] The example cited here is from the John Deere-UAW 1967–1970 Agreement.

[18] Donna Allen, *Fringe Benefits: Wages or Social Obligations?* (Ithaca, N.Y.: New York State School of Industrial and Labor Relations, 1964), pp. 241 ff.

on a weekly, monthly and/or annual basis for the employee who might continue to work but who might be subjected to downgrading during a general reduction in force or to recall after layoff to a lower-rated assignment.

Income security benefits in such circumstances are considered as wages. They are in essence income maintenance provisions. Although these provisions are designed to meet a different type of problem than SUB, there is a contractual relationship to SUB to prevent an employee with one or more years' seniority but less than ten or more from having the best of both worlds, so to speak. This is best illustrated by quoting directly from Article XVIII, Section 1, III, of the John Deere-UAW 1967–1970 master agreement, which reads as follows:

> *Any hourly paid employee* with one (1) or more years' seniority on layoff from one bargaining unit covered by this Agreement (except for employees with ten (10) or more years of seniority) and who is offered a vacant hourly paid work assignment in a bargaining unit covered by this Agreement in the same labor market area will forfeit his SUB benefits, if any, if he refuses the work assignment. However, if he accepts the work assignment and if the work assignment is lower rated than the work assignment from which he was laid off he will be eligible for Income Security Benefits for the remaining portion, if any, of his period of duration of eligibility for Income Security Benefits based on the date of his removal from his original seniority classification in his original bargaining unit.

A similar type of restriction is also provided for incentive paid employees.

Employees with one or more years of seniority qualify for income security benefits under the following three circumstances under the Deere-UAW agreement:

1. When the employee is subject to layoff from his seniority classification but is reassigned by the Company to a vacant lower-rated work assignment in his seniority unit.
2. When the employee is subject to layoff from his seniority unit but is reassigned by the Company to a vacant lower-rated work assignment elsewhere in the bargaining unit.
3. When the employee is first laid off from his seniority classification and is then recalled to a lower-rated work assignment in another seniority classification in his seniority unit or the bargaining unit before the exhaustion of his period of eligibility for income security benefits.

Under the Deere-UAW program income security benefits are designed in essence to make up the difference between what the employee customarily earns on his regular job and what he is paid under any of the three circumstances outlined above. His regular pay is determined in terms of a "computation rate" established in terms of what he earned during the four pay periods preceding his layoff, excluding any premiums or bonus of any kind. The eligibility period for an employee with one or more years of seniority extends to 104 weeks immediately following his layoff.

TRENDS IN SUPPLEMENTAL WAGE PAYMENT PRACTICES

The major nonwage economic benefit areas summarily reviewed in the preceding pages by no means complete the "fringe" story. It remains to note an ever-expanding network of *supplemental wage payment practices*, a phrase to cover such varied matters as paid vacations, paid holidays when not worked, reporting pay, call-in pay, premium pay practices on overtime, special rates for Saturday and Sunday work as such and similar "extras."

In most bargaining relationships the basic pattern of compensation has been clearly established for some time on the practices just listed. It is increasingly difficult to develop any genuinely new additions to the list. In many cases, however, it is still possible to liberalize or expand upon the prior contractual treatment.

Writing in 1956 the late Arthur M. Ross predicted that the so-called fringes would amount to 25 percent of the average employer's payroll by 1960.[19] Although the Ross estimate might then have seemed exaggerated, the actual pace of fringe thickening has been such that in 1970 a full costing of the major and minor fringes reviewed in this chapter would reveal for many employers percentages as high as 30 percent or more. A 25 percent fringe currently is a bit on the conservative side.

In the second edition of this book I noted employer concern over the mounting costs of fringe compensation, the difficulties in accurately estimating such costs and the lack of integration or flexibility in the overall program of employee benefits beyond basic wages.[20] Presumably many of today's employers are even more concerned than in the late 1950s. However, there is no clear indication of a "they shall not pass" stand being taken by management.

Negotiated supplemental wage payments always stay negotiated. A review of representative new contracts in 1969 and 1970 shows no evidence of any retrenchment. On the contrary, the record shows steady inching upward on many of the staple items. Furthermore, there is nothing to suggest that the end is in sight. Unions generally consider that they have an important institutional stake in maintaining and improving an already impressive pattern of supplemental wage payments.

In this area as in most others union bargaining table objectives faithfully mirror the demands of the constituents. In the minds of employees

---

[19] Arthur M. Ross, "Fringe Benefits Today and Tomorrow," *Labor Law Journal*, VII (August, 1956), 476–82.

[20] Harold W. Davey, *Contemporary Collective Bargaining* (2nd ed.), (Englewood Cliffs, N.J.: Prentice-Hall, Inc., 1959), p. 319.

the matter of improving a particular fringe payment can take on an importance far greater than the actual value or cost of the item would appear to warrant. To illustrate this point, we can mention adding the employee's birthday to the conventional list of paid holidays when not worked. Honoring one's natal day has taken on great importance as a demand in many recent contract negotiations.

Not too many years ago I used to tell what was then a true story about an employee at a Des Moines plant grieving each year on his birthday when his foreman refused to give him the day off with pay. I told the story to illustrate a nonarbitrable but psychologically real grievance. In many contracts today the grievance would clearly be arbitrable. The employee's birthday is joining Labor Day, Christmas, New Year's and so on as a conventional holiday with pay in more and more contracts.

In the next few pages we shall note current and prospective patterns on some but by no means all of the multiplicity of fringes in the supplemental wage payment category.

VACATIONS WITH PAY

I know of no contract of recent vintage that does not provide for vacations with pay. Policies have been consistently broadened to the point where what not too many years ago was the maximum length of vacation (two weeks) has become the minimum. The maximum is often four or more weeks for long-service employees.

Many contracts now provide for vacation pay based on a percentage of the employee's earnings during the year rather than merely multiplying his hourly rate or guaranteed occupational rate by forty hours.

Recent contracts also reflect an expanding of employee freedom of choice as to when to take his vacation. This greater freedom is generally subject to managerial discretion to avoid serious labor shortages that would interfere with regular production commitments.

As an arbitrator, my subjective impression is that employers and unions have largely resolved most of their differences over such matters as eligibility requirements, vacation equities of separated employees, computation of vacation pay and so on. Vacations with pay have been part of the compensation pattern for so long that there appear to be few if any remaining areas of ambiguity and uncertainty.

THE STEELWORKERS' "SABBATICAL" PLAN

The most unusual vacation development is the one negotiated by the Steelworkers' union and eleven firms in the basic steel industry. The contractual distinction between "regular" vacations and EV's (extended vacations) is clearly drawn. The "regular" vacation formula in the 1968–1971 agreement is in no way startling. It provides for one week's vacation for those with service of one year but less than three, two weeks for those with three but less than ten, three weeks for those with ten but less than twenty-five and four weeks for employees with twenty-five or more years' service.

The EV plan is truly innovative. For the top half of each plant's seniority list the contract calls for a thirteen-week paid vacation every fifth year. Not surprisingly, the plan was dubbed the "steelworkers' sabbatical." During his EV year the worker, of course, does not have his "regular" vacation. Those in the lower half of the seniority list receive three weeks on top of their regular vacation every fifth year.

The steel vacation sabbatical rationale rested heavily on job creation rather than on concern for the worker's complete "renewal" of spirit and energy. The thirteen-week span every five years was geared to the pragmatic necessities of the industry in terms of advance scheduling of production.

To my knowledge no other bargaining relationship of consequence has followed the steel industry lead on negotiating EV plans. Other employers and unions continue to add incrementally to their established formulae for relating length of vacation to worker seniority.

For example, the 1970–1973 contract between Armour & Company and the Amalgamated Meat Cutters' union upped the ante a bit, effective January 1, 1971, in the following manner:

1. Three weeks' vacation with pay to employees who have completed eight to fourteen years of continuous service (formerly ten years was required to qualify for three weeks).
2. Four weeks' vacation with pay for employees who have completed fifteen to nineteen years of service.
3. Five weeks' vacation with pay for employees who have completed twenty or more years of continuous service.

PAID HOLIDAYS

An employer who schedules work on a holiday recognized in his union contract is either very affluent, very careless or else in dire need of production. The current tab for scheduling holiday work is frequently at triple the employee's normal rate. Furthermore, the number of holidays for the employer to schedule around continues to increase from contract to contract. In the second edition of this book (1959), the most prevalent provision was six paid holidays when not worked, with a growing number calling for eight and some for as many as twelve.[21] This needs amending to

---

[21] *Ibid.*, p. 321.

ten paid holidays as the most common. Twelve appears to be holding firm as the maximum number of feasible holiday observances.

Holiday pay clauses are a part of virtually all contracts. Most of the administrative headaches or disputed points have been satisfactorily resolved through experience and improved contract language.

The chief administrative problem in holiday pay clauses has always been insuring against excessive absenteeism before and after the paid holiday. Most contracts require the employee to work the day before and the day after the holiday in order to qualify for holiday pay. There is no difficulty in principle with such a provision. Problems still arise in attempting to determine in specific cases whether the failure to work the day before or after the holiday was due to legitimate reasons such as *bona fide* illness, death in the immediate family or the like.

For a contract holiday not worked, the employee generally receives eight hours' straight-time pay. For work on a contract holiday, double-time is still common, but many contracts now call for triple-time.

Employees on layoff during a period in which a holiday falls do not ordinarily receive pay for the holiday. This is proper in line with the theory of holiday pay, since an employee already laid off is not "losing" by not working the holiday. An employee on vacation is in a different category, since his vacation pay is an earned equity for prior service. Many contracts provide an extra day's pay for a holiday falling within the vacation period. It is frequently labeled, however, as an extra day of vacation to be taken on the next scheduled work day following the end of the employee's vacation period.

Most contracts will probably not be liberalized beyond twelve paid holidays. This is one fringe benefit that has rather obvious upper limits.

Reporting Pay and Call-In Pay

When employees report for work at their regularly scheduled time without having been notified in advance not to report, it is customary for the contract to guarantee them either four hours' work or four hours' pay without work. The equity of such a provision is clear.

A related provision found in most contracts guarantees at least four hours' pay to employees who are "called in" or "called back" to work after having completed their regular shift and gone home. Such clauses are usually operative if the worker is called in within sixteen hours after he has completed his regular shift. Some contracts provide for double-time in call-back cases.

Reporting pay provisions usually give the employer an "escape clause" for failure to notify an employee not to report, if the reason for no available work at reporting time is due to causes beyond the employer's control such as a power failure, fire, "an act of God" or a strike.

Premium Pay for Overtime

Premium pay for overtime hours perhaps should not be called a fringe benefit. Discussion of practice on overtime pay is warranted, however, since overtime earnings constitute a principal source of additional worker income above basic occupational rates in many busy industries.

Virtually all contracts specify the length of the working day, define the work week and make special provision for payments on hours worked beyond the normal working day or work week.

For many years in most industries, eight hours was the prescribed normal work day and forty hours the normal work week. There has been, however, a marked increase in contracts specifying less than eight hours per day and forty hours per week as normal. Gradual reduction of the work day and work week is a continuing objective of union policy in many cases.

Premium pay for overtime hours is universal in collective bargaining. The premium or penalty rates exhibit a considerable variety. The most common is still one and one-half times the regular hourly rate for hours in excess of the normal work day, or in excess of the norm for the work week. Many contracts call for going to double-time after an employee has worked more than four hours of overtime in any one day. Also, double-time for Saturday and Sunday work as such has become a common contract requirement.

The pattern of overtime compensation is fairly complete in most unionized industries. Those unions with contracts providing for only time-and-one-half can be expected to push for double-time for ordinary overtime and for triple-time on worked holidays.

In overtime compensation the two most vexing problems are how to share in available overtime opportunities and how to treat the question as to whether an employee can be required to work overtime. To avoid conflict and misunderstanding on these troublesome matters, the contract should be as definite as possible. Many contracts call for a sharing of available overtime work on a round-robin basis among employees in a particular classification or department. There is usually a qualifying phrase such as "so far as practicable" or "as equally as possible." Such language can be productive of disagreement. Employees are watchful over the division of overtime and are quick to protest when they feel the division has been inequitable or contrary to contract policy.

Whether employecs can or should be compelled to work overtime is a controversial matter. The practice varies considerably. To minimize disputes and possible disciplinary actions flowing from refusal to work overtime, it is advisable to spell out the contract policy as clearly as possible. In many contracts the employee is obligated to work overtime upon request. He is thus subject to disciplinary action for refusal to do so. Under other contracts accepting overtime assignments is optional with the employee. No stigma attaches to him for refusal to accept overtime but in such cases each refusal is counted as an offered overtime chance under round-robin or equal division policies.

Overtime and the Shorter Work Week

Discussion of premium pay for overtime leads logically into the trend toward shorter work days and work weeks. We are in the midst of a revolution in thinking on what is a normal work day and work week. The trend is inexorably away from the traditional eight-hour day and forty-hour week pattern, although this standard is still the most common.

The probability is that in the 1970s we shall witness a fundamental change toward either an eight-hour, four-day week of thirty-two hours, or a seven-hour, five-day week of thirty-five hours. It is unlikely that a work day of less than six hours or a work week of less than thirty-two hours will be viewed as technically or economically feasible. Also, half days whether four or three hours are hardly desirable from a productivity or scheduling standpoint in most lines of work.

With many employers and unions moving toward the shorter work day and work week it is logical to expect some "bugs" to arise with the new scheduling, producing an unusual and costly amount of overtime. It is doubtful, however, that the employer can expect "mercy" in the form of reduced penalty rates under the redefined normal day and week. Contract rates for hours in excess of the new normal work day or work week will presumably stay at the usual premium pay levels.

Dismissal or Severance Pay Provisions

No employee likes to be laid off, even for short periods of time. However, a layoff with anticipated return to work when production picks up is not particularly traumatic. In many bargaining relationships the worker with some seniority often has the protection of SUB or the option of going to a lower-rated assignment elsewhere in the plant if bumped out of his own department or seniority unit.

Permanent displacement is another matter altogether. Such job loss can result from technological displacement, from financial failure of the firm or from structural or locational changes in the industry. Any of these circumstances can result in the total disappearance of work opportunities. Another common cause in recent years has been the merger of firms with net employment losses in one or both entities. The shock factor and the economic privation for the displaced employee are severe under the best of circumstances. Nearly all unions therefore seek to negotiate the best severance or dismissal pay provisions they can.

The problems necessitating severance pay have been treated elsewhere in this volume, notably in Chapter 9, in recognition of the primary importance of the job security problem. I am hard pressed to rationalize discussing severance pay in a chapter on major and minor fringe payments. Severance or dismissal pay for permanently displaced satisfactory employees should be considered an independent equity in a category all its own. It is not properly classifiable as an economic fringe or as a supplementary wage payment.

In former years some employers sought to argue against severance pay allowances on the basis that the displaced worker had already been justly paid for all his working time and thus he was not entitled to any additional payments. Such thinking is outmoded and is seldom heard in unionized relationships. There is widespread agreement that a permanently displaced satisfactory employee should have a contractual right to a lump-sum payment, with the amount geared to the worker's prior years of service. Long-service employees often are eligible for a year's (or more) pay when permanently displaced.

Most contracts reflect a major effort on the employer's part to avoid permanent displacement of any employee by providing alternative employment at another plant or in another type of work within the same plant.

Severance pay plans are far more prevalent than when BLS first began to study such arrangements in 1944. The Bureau's most recent study, to my knowledge, was published in March, 1965, covering 1,773 major (that is, with 1,000 or more workers) agreements negotiated in 1962 or 1963. About 30 percent of the agreements, covering about 40 percent of the workers involved, contained some sort of severance pay or layoff benefit provision.[22] SUB plans are regarded as being of a different order since they are designed to help employees on layoffs not expected to be permanent.

Five unions are involved in nearly half of the plans covered in the BLS survey—the Steelworkers, the UAW, the CWA (Communication Workers of America), the IBEW (International Brotherhood of Electrical Workers) and the ILGWU (International Ladies Garment Workers Union). The CWA has negotiated a severance pay provision in all its contracts covered in the survey.

---

[22] U.S. Bureau of Labor Statistics, *Severance Pay and Layoff Benefit Plans* (Washington, D.C.: Government Printing Office), Bul. 1425–2, 1965.

It would be surprising if the number of contracts providing for severance pay did not continue to increase. Our economy witnesses each year a considerable number of plant closings, mergers and multiple instances of labor-displacing technological change. Any and all of these, of course, can produce permanent employee displacement.

CONCLUSION: ARRIVING AT AN OPTIMAL MIX OF WAGES AND FRINGES

The current thickness of the fringe (25 to 30 percent) in the labor cost dollar has already been stressed. It would seem logical to conclude that the feasible limit of nonwage economic benefits of one kind or another has been reached, if not exceeded, in many bargaining relationships. A review of successive contract negotiations in a number of different industries shows no well-defined objective or pattern of optimal mix of wages and economic fringes. We must conclude that there is none, save what the employer and union agree upon.

To the employer, labor cost is labor cost. He has a constant incentive to keep his unit labor costs manageable. However, he is frequently indifferent to whether the cost is attributable to wages or to some other economic payment to his employees. An exception to this would be in the case of those fringes that give shelter from taxes.

If the employer's relative indifference as between wages and fringes is assumed and if we further assume that there is a finite limit soon to be reached on many economic fringes, the ultimate decision as to what constitutes an optimal combination must be made by the employee himself. There are few signs today that employees generally have well-defined views on the best possible blend. The bargaining on economic fringes reflects the same blunt "more" strategy that has traditionally characterized wage negotiations in most instances.

Perhaps it is not too much to expect that in the 1970s there will be an increasing disposition to take stock of the complex of wages and fringes with a view to developing a more logical rationalization than simply "more." One promising avenue for such a development is to establish individual employee accounts covering amounts going into the key economic security fringes. The employee himself can then do his own apportioning of the fringe dollar sums available to him in his personalized account.

Implementing this idea of individual employee decision-making on how and when to use funds accumulated in his security benefit account will require a lot of employee education and a great deal of contractual revision. The latter would happily be in the direction of simplification. The economic security portions of the total package currently require as many or more contract pages in most cases as the basic agreement itself. Going to a system of individual employee accounts could reduce drastically the complex, detailed verbiage now essential on most negotiated economic security programs.

Promoting employee responsibility for managing the economic security funds available to him in his own account has the distinct merit of being in line with the theme of restraint and responsibility on wage negotiation that was leaned on so heavily in the preceding chapter. My judgment is that the advantages of going to such a system far outweigh the disadvantages.

SELECTED BIBLIOGRAPHY

ALLEN, DONNA, *Fringe Benefits: Wages or Social Obligation?*. Ithaca, N.Y.: New York State School of Industrial and Labor Relations, 1964.

BARTELL, H. ROBERT, JR., AND ELIZABETH T. SIMPSON, *Pension Funds of Multi-employer Industrial Groups, Unions, and Nonprofit Organizations*. New York: National Bureau of Economic Research, Occasional Paper No. 105, 1968.

BEIER, EMERSON H., "Terminations of Pension Plans: 11 Years' Experience," *Monthly Labor Review*, XC (June, 1967), 26–30.

DAVIS, HARRY E., "Changes in Negotiated Pension Plans, 1961–64," *Monthly Labor Review*, LXXXVIII (October, 1965), 1215–18.

DONAHUE, THOMAS R., *The Pension Promise—Reality or Illusion?*. Honolulu: Industrial Relations Center, University of Hawaii, 1969.

GARBARINO, JOSEPH W., *Health Plans and Collective Bargaining*. Berkeley and Los Angeles: University of California Press, 1960.

GREENBERG, DAVID H., "Deviations from Wage-Fringe Standards," *Industrial and Labor Relations Review*, XXI (January, 1968), 197–209.

GREENFIELD, HARRY I. (with the assistance of Carol A. Brown), *Allied Health Manpower: Trends and Prospects*. Irvington-on-Hudson, N.Y.: Columbia University Press, 1969.

JAMES, RALPH, AND ESTELLE JAMES, "Hoffa's Manipulation of Pension Benefits," *Industrial Relations*, IV (May, 1965), 46–60.

KOLODRUBETZ, WALTER W., "Reciprocity and Pension Portability," *Monthly Labor Review*, XCI (September, 1968), 22–28.

KRISLOV, JOSEPH, "A Study of Pension Funding," *Monthly Labor Review*, LXXXIX (June, 1966), 638–42.

LANDAY, DONALD M., "Trends in Negotiated Health Plans: Broader Coverage, Higher Quality Care," *Monthly Labor Review*, XCII (May, 1969), 3–10.

LANDAY, DONALD M., AND HARRY E. DAVIS, "Growth and Vesting Changes in Private Pension Plans," *Monthly Labor Review*, XCI (May, 1968), 29–35.

LAW NOTE, "Conflict of Interest Problems Arising from Union Pension Loan Funds," *Columbia Law Review*, LXVII (January, 1967), 162–80.

MELONE, JOSEPH J., *Collectively Bargained Multi-Employer Pension Plans*. Homewood, Ill.: Richard D. Irwin, Inc., 1963.

MILJUS, ROBERT C., AND ALTON C. JOHNSON. "Multi-Employer Pensions and Labor Mobility," *Harvard Business Review*, XLVI (September–October, 1963), 147–61.

SOMERS, ANNE R., *Hospital Regulation: The Dilemma of Public Policy*. Princeton, N.J.: Industrial Relations Section, Princeton University, 1969.

SOMERS, HERMAN M., AND ANN R. SOMERS, *Medicare and the Hospitals, Issues and Prospects*. Washington, D.C.: The Brookings Institution, 1967.

SRB, JOZETTA H., *Portable Pensions: A Review of the Issues*. Ithaca, N.Y.: New York State School of Industrial and Labor Relations, 1969.

TILOVE, ROBERT, "Pensions, Health, and Welfare Plans," in *Challenges to Collective Bargaining*, ed. Lloyd Ulman. Englewood Cliffs, N.J.: Prentice-Hall, Inc., 1967, pp. 37–64.

TROWBRIDGE, CHARLES L., "ABC's of Pension Funding," *Harvard Business Review*, XLIV (March–April, 1966), 115–26.

TURNBULL, JOHN G., *The Changing Faces of Economic Insecurity*. Minneapolis, Minn.: University of Minnesota Press, 1966.

U.S. BUREAU OF LABOR STATISTICS, *Labor Mobility and Private Pension Plan; a Study of Vesting, Early Retirement and Portability Provisions* (Bulletin No. 1407). Washington, D.C.: Government Printing Office, 1964.

U.S. BUREAU OF LABOR STATISTICS, *Private Pension Plan Benefits* (Bulletin No. 1485). Washington, D.C.: Government Printing Office, 1966.

U.S. BUREAU OF LABOR STATISTICS, *Supplementary Compensation for Non-Production Workers, 1963: Employer Expenditures, Employer Practices* (Bulletin No. 1470). Washington, D.C.: Government Printing Office, 1966.

U.S. BUREAU OF LABOR STATISTICS, *The Operation of Severance Pay Plans and Their Implications for Labor Mobility* (Bulletin No. 1462). Washington, D.C.: Government Printing Office, 1966.

BARGAINING BY GOVERNMENT EMPLOYEES AND PROFESSIONAL EMPLOYEES

CHAPTER THIRTEEN

In the ultimate history of the American labor movement it is certain that the explosion of unionization by federal, state and local government employees from 1962 into the 1970s will occupy a prominent place. So also will the intensive drives for collective bargaining rights by such professional employee groups as teachers, nurses and football players.[1]

The public sector labor relations scene is so dynamic that it is difficult to draw a balanced picture that will be recognizable a few years into

---

[1] The public sector unionization drive appears sure to sustain its momentum. If it does so, the 1960s and 1970s will be recalled as the third most explosive period in union history, taking a place alongside the 1880s (dubbed by historians as "the decade of social and economic upheaval") and the 1930s (the decade of the blue-collar workers' unionization thrust).

the future. Hopefully, the analytical points to be developed in this chapter will have some enduring validity.

Public sector labor relations presents a number of problem areas with no true counterpart in the private arena. The differences between public and private sector are significant and real. They justify asking how (or whether) the bargaining parties in government at any level can benefit from the substantial body of experience in private sector labor relations. A similar question can be posed for the newly active professional employee groups—can they utilize the same policies and procedures found to be feasible in blue-collar labor relations?

The answers to these questions will be mixed rather than conclusive. In comparative analysis the most intriguing consideration is what is transferable and why and, conversely, what is not transferable and why not? As we survey some of the major substantive, structural and procedural problem areas in public sector and professional employee labor relations, we shall seek reasonably accurate, if not necessarily happy, answers to these questions.

THE MODERN ERA OF PUBLIC EMPLOYEE UNIONISM

The first requisite is that we make a panoramic survey of recent public sector developments. In doing so we shall identify some of the chief distinguishing characteristics of government as an industry. The transferability question becomes more meaningful in such a context. The special problems of professional employees seeking to bargain collectively with their employers will be treated in a concluding section.

There is nothing new about unionism among government employees. Blue-collar craftsmen working for governmental agencies at various levels have been represented by labor organizations for many years—in some cases quite effectively.[2] Also, in particular circumstances, professionals and technicians have enjoyed an approximation of collective bargaining for long periods of time. The case of TVA employees comes readily to mind.[3] Furthermore, labor strife is not new to the field of government employment. David Ziskind's painstaking research serves to remind us of many past occasions when government employees have gone on strike, notwithstanding the acknowledged illegality of such tactics.[4]

---

[2] For the early history see Wilson R. Hart, *Collective Bargaining in the Federal Civil Service* (New York: Harper & Row, Publishers, 1961).

[3] See Arthur A. Thompon, "Collective Bargaining in the Public Service: The TVA Experience and Its Implications for Other Government Agencies," *Labor Law Journal*, XVII (February, 1966), 89–98; Aubrey J. Wagner, "TVA Looks at Three Decades of Collective Bargaining," *Industrial and Labor Relations Review*, XXII (October, 1968), 20–30.

[4] David Ziskind, *One Thousand Strikes of Government Employees* (New York: Columbia University Press, 1940).

What can justly be called the modern era of public sector labor relations dates from January, 1962, when President Kennedy issued Executive Order 10988. This order was flawed in many respects from a purist standpoint. Nevertheless, it would be difficult to exaggerate its importance as a stimulus to union growth not only among federal government employees but at state and local government levels as well.

THE IMPACT OF E.O. 10988 AND E.O. 11491

The Kennedy order was of first importance because it gave *positive encouragement to collective bargaining as a process*. Prior to 1962 there was no focus on bargaining in the proper sense by many unionized federal employees. For example, the postal employees who had been unionized for many years had become adept in the art of lobbying at the congressional level but had never bargained in a proper sense with their direct employer, the Post Office Department, as an agency. It took more than President Kennedy's order to accomplish this. Only the postal strike of 1970 at long last turned postal labor relations in the direction of true collective bargaining.

E.O. 10988 had a catalytic impact far beyond the confines of the federal establishment. It was of great value in stimulating the drive for unionization among employees of state, municipal and county agencies. Union growth in these areas has been nothing short of spectacular in the period since 1962. The ferment of unionism has produced a rash of state legislation, ranging from complete and fairly sophisticated treatment with full-time administrative agencies in charge (as in New York and New Jersey) to simple legislative affirmations of the right to organize and to bargain collectively, but with no implementation provisions.

E.O. 11491 improves upon E.O. 10988 in several respects. It clarifies the rights and responsibilities of the parties to bargaining. Also, it provides for central determination of key disputed points in labor relations, taking autonomy away from the government agency in question. We shall say more on E.O. 11491 in a later section. Here it is sufficient to note that one of its effects should be still further encouragement of union growth and collective bargaining.

THE DIMENSIONS OF GROWTH

Government is by any measure the major industry in the United States. According to George H. Hildebrand, the number of employees in government at all levels rose between 1950 and 1965 from 6 million to 10 million, about a two-thirds increase. Significantly, about 3.6 million of the

4 million new employees were at the state and local level. Hildebrand projects a 1975 total government employment figure of 14.7 million—12.2 million in state and local and 2.5 million in federal service.[5] In 1969, the growth in government employment at all levels was 380,000, well below the gains of recent years. The increase brought total government employment to 12.2 million.[6]

These figures confirm that government is not only our largest industry—it is also our outstanding growth industry. This should be neither surprising nor alarming. As the most "mature" of the Western economies, the United States should logically be devoting an ever increasing proportion of its energies to the tertiary category (services) as distinct from primary (agriculture and mining) and secondary (manufacturing) fields. Within government as a basically service industry, public education accounts for a constantly increasing portion of employment. This too should be neither surprising nor alarming. The multiple domestic crises that we have been experiencing show that, even with the broadest-based educational program in the free world, we are far from being overeducated. The demands of the new technology, linked together with the ecological thrust against pollution, will place new kinds of pressure on our educational system at all levels, many of which are difficult to anticipate at this juncture. The environmental revolution will unquestionably place new kinds of production in the forefront, thus structuring the demand for professional, technical and bluecollar labor new directions. Societal demands on such matters as race relations and urban redevelopment will also have profound impact on what we expect from our education industry and what we expect from various governmental agencies whose operations relate to these continuing problem areas.

THE PUBLIC EMPLOYEE UNIONIZATION PHENOMENON

Unionization among government employees is playing a profoundly significant but as yet imperfectly understood role in accompanying the phenomenal growth of government as an employer. Hildebrand's figures show that in 1956 a total of 915,000 government workers belonged to unions.[7] Most of these, however, were blue-collar craftsmen or postal employees who did not practice collective bargaining in the modern sense used in this chapter's analysis.

---

[5] George H. Hildebrand, "The Public Sector," in *Frontiers of Collective Bargaining*, ed. John T. Dunlop and Neil W. Chamberlain (New York: Harper & Row, Publishers, 1967), p. 125.

[6] *1970 Manpower Report of the President* (Washington, D.C.: Government Printing Office, 1970), p. 31.

[7] George H. Hildebrand, *op. cit.*, p. 125.

The newer thrust of public employee unionism is best illustrated on the one hand by the rapid sustained growth of the American Federation of State, County and Municipal Employees (AFSCME), an AFL-CIO affiliate, and in another aspect by the complete transformation of the National Education Association in the late 1960s into a genuine bargaining force for public school teachers.[8] The AFSCME in September, 1969, reported a membership of 420,000. It is continuing to grow rapidly at the rate of 3,500 new members per month.[9]

Currently well over 2 million government workers belong to unions, more than double the figure cited above for 1956. Sanford Cohen indicates in 1970 that over one-third of the 2.7 million federal employees belong to employee organizations, with the heaviest concentration in the Post Office Department. Excluding postal workers, Cohen estimates that 21 percent of classified federal employees belong to labor organizations that have won exclusive bargaining rights with various government agencies.[10] The Cohen estimate dramatizes the rapid upsurge in union activity among the federal classified workers who make up about half of all federal employment and nearly all the white-collar workers. In 1967, according to Jack Stieber, less than 10 percent of these classified employees were union members.[11] Cohen's 1970 estimate thus shows a doubling of union membership in this important area of federal employment. Much of the recent growth is accounted for by another AFL-CIO affiliate, the American Federation of Government Employees.

We could continue citing other types and varieties of growth figures, but perhaps we have enough illustrations to provide a factual framework for analysis of some of the more serious problems of public sector labor relations. One of the more important difficulties is the assimilation problem posed by the proliferation of union activity at all government levels.

The first order of business will be to outline and then discuss problems posed by the special characteristics of government as they affect collective bargaining. Next in sequence will be a brief survey of labor relations problems and needs, first at the federal level and then at the state and local government levels. Some consideration will be given to illustrations of sound

---

[8] The literature on teacher bargaining has poured forth in such quantity that limited citation is a difficult task. Some valuable references will be found in the chapter bibliography. Here I shall cite arbitrarily one of many references reporting the NEA transformation in economical fashion. See Michael H. Moskow and Robert E. Doherty, "United States," in *Teachers' Unions and Associations: A Comparative Study*, ed. Albert A. Blum (Urbana, Ill.: University of Illinois Press, 1969), pp. 295–332.

[9] *1969 Supplement to the Report of the National Governors' Conference Task Force on State and Local Government Labor Relations* (Chicago: Public Personnel Association, 1970), p. 1.

[10] Sanford Cohen, *Labor in the United States* (3rd ed.), (Columbus, Ohio: Charles E. Merrill Publishing Co., 1970), p. 299.

[11] Jack Stieber, "Collective Bargaining in the Public Sector," in *Challenges to Collective Bargaining*, ed. Lloyd Ulman (Englewood Cliffs, N.J., Prentice-Hall, Inc., 1967), p. 67.

and unsound practice in public employee bargaining. Finally, we shall take a brief look at bargaining developments among two key professional employee groups—public school teachers and nurses. A summary overview of the prospects for public bargaining will be offered in conclusion.

Throughout the analysis we shall be constantly evaluating the prospects for transferability of experience from the "developed areas" (private sector bargaining) to the "underdeveloped" or "newly developing countries" of the public sector.

Special Characteristics of Government as an Industry and as an Employer

Government affects our lives in so many ways that we tend to take it for granted. We do not pause to think of the ways in which government at any level in a free society has certain inherent distinguishing characteristics that complicate life, to put it mildly, for those engaged in public sector labor relations. Employees of government agencies seeking to bargain collectively through AFL-CIO unions or through genuinely independent labor organizations or associations and the "management" of these government agencies with whom bargaining is conducted must cope jointly with a number of serious problems flowing from the special character of government as an industry.

When government is the employer, that is, management, the following special attributes or characteristics affect the nature and substance of the labor relations picture:

1. The collective labor agreement is being negotiated with a nonprofit organization in almost all instances.[12]
2. The government agency or department in question is performing its service as a true monopoly in most cases, that is, the service in question is not performed by any other agency, public or private, in the particular jurisdiction.
3. The government agency's budget goes largely for employee wages and salaries, thus making any negotiated increases in labor costs highly visible to the legislative appropriating body and also to the true owners of the business, that is, the taxpayers.
4. The scope of negotiations in public sector situations is generally more restricted than in the private sector because many matters covered by contract in the latter are treated by statutes or ordinances in the public sector, for example, civil service classification systems at all levels of government.

---

[12] Some government corporations or agencies do sell services or products (for example, TVA, REA and the Superintendent of Documents). However, in no case to my knowledge are their efforts directed toward making profits.

5. The personnel makeup of many government agencies is such that it is not always easy to draw lines between "management" and the "rank and file" to be represented by the union or employee organization.
6. Bargaining on a contract to a final solution is frequently more difficult in the public sector because the test of economic strength and bargaining power (ultimate resort to the strike or the lockout) is not available to pressure the parties into agreement.
7. When negotiating a contract, difficulties frequently arise in determining who is the employer, partially because of the fiscally dependent status of government agencies on the "third force" (legislative branch) for appropriations, and also because many government agencies are funded from multiple sources and levels of government.
8. The boom in unionism and collective bargaining has underlined the severe shortage of experienced and available negotiators and neutrals, a problem of grave concern to government agencies and employee organizations alike.
9. Finally, a statutory framework for public sector labor relations is nonexistent in about half the states and those states with special legislation enacted in the 1960s are discovering that these efforts can stand improvement in many cases.

I do not offer the above listing as an exhaustive cataloging of all the special characteristics of government that affect public sector labor relations. We now have a skeletal base, however, on which to proceed to a more detailed consideration of important legislative, procedural and substantive problem areas. The order of treatment does not signify a determination as to relative importance. We shall consider first the problem of identifying the employer.

WHO IS THE EMPLOYER?

It is often difficult in the public sector for unions to be sure who speaks for "management." Unions encounter many problems in the private sector, but they have no identity problem in figuring out with whom to bargain. They also know that when an agreement has been reached whoever signs for "management" can make it stick. In the private sector, a more troublesome problem for some unions has been getting agreements ratified by their memberships.[13]

In government, those who negotiate on behalf of the government agency in question and the employee organization with which they are bar-

---

[13] This problem has been considered in Chapters 2 and 10. The contract rejection phenomenon may come to haunt union leadership in the public sector as well should the membership sense the possibility of extracting further gains by application of economic or political muscle.

gaining sometimes experience a common difficulty in their relationships with the *third force* on the public scene, that is, *the elected representative body*, whether it be the Congress, the state legislature, the city council, the county board of supervisors or the consolidated school's board of education. The legislative branch at any level of government has ultimate charge of the purse strings. This is frequently a complicating factor when the negotiators agree on a contract that when costed out exceeds what the agency believes to be its ability to pay.

We are not finished with the problem of employer identification. There is a *fourth force* that has an important role to play in public sector labor relations. This fourth force is made up of the true "owners" of the government unit doing the bargaining, that is, the citizen public, the taxpayers of the district involved.

A profound consequence of the insistent drive for collective bargaining by employees at all levels of government will be some important changes in the structural makeup of the government. Furthermore, with labor cost by far the largest item in the budgets of all government agencies, collective bargaining will be exerting a strong fiscal impact. The structural and fiscal repercussions are already clear in many instances.

Personnel services account for 70 percent or more of the operating budgets of state and local governments. To complicate life a bit further, increasing labor costs in most cases will not be compensated for by the traditional productivity gains we rely upon in the private sector institutions to keep the lid on unit labor costs and actually to increase real wages and salaries. In the public sector negotiated salary increases, however well deserved they may be, simply add to the cost of government by the amount of the increases. The consequences of taxpayer (owner) backlash are already visible in many jurisdictions. Voter rejection of bond issues to defray the mounting costs of education is the best-known example.

Impact of Collective Bargaining on the Structure of Government

Structural changes in many governmental units are mandatory in many cases if collective bargaining is to be conducted on a logical, orderly and reasonably predictable basis. *A first requirement is the need to clarify the identity and authority of management at the bargaining table.* To state the need is much easier than to prescribe how it should be satisfied. At the present writing the very fact of the collective bargaining relationship itself has led to the creation of what Arvid Anderson has perceptively observed to be "a quasi-governmental structure . . . which parallels the legislative and executive functions in decision-making as to budgets and other major public policy issues."[14]

Many of the new bargaining relationships, particularly those involving municipal and state agencies, are revealing the structural unsuitability of the managerial units involved for labor relations purposes. For example, the bad fit of conventional government structures often poses problems in terms of the appropriate unit for employee representation. In the initial years of bargaining, the appropriate unit pattern necessarily developed in terms of the structural status quo. The difficulties encountered by the bargainers, however, have brought an increased understanding of the inadequacy and unsuitability of many governmental units long taken for granted, such as the local school district or the single county, just to name two of the more obvious structural anomalies.

Over time, the requirements for constructive labor relations may prove to be a more powerful factor in bringing about state and local governmental reorganization than all the many studies by public administration experts stressing the merits of county consolidation, statewide school organization instead of autonomous local districts and the like.

It is questionable whether all these fundamental changes can be effectuated in time to prevent a high incidence of chaotic and wasteful bargaining experiences in many jurisdictions.

The most compelling requirement is the creation of a sound statutory basis under which orderly and effective bargaining can go forward at all levels of government. Bargaining in the public sector is here to stay—in some cases on a solid *de jure* basis, but in all too many on a *de facto* basis in the absence of any legislative framework.

In all but a few jurisdictions, such as the writer's adopted state and city,[15] the debate is over on the question as to whether government employees should at long last enjoy the right to bargain with their employers that private sector employees have had protected by federal law since 1935. The significant question is not whether collective bargaining will take place, but rather how it shall take place. Structural considerations here become critically important. Public employees know which operating agency, department or commission pays their salaries and directs their work. They consider said operating agency to be their employer for labor relations purposes.

Proper statutory identification of employers for bargaining purposes

---

[14] Arvid Anderson, "The Changing of the Establishment," mimeographed (An address before the United States Conference of Mayors, Denver, Colorado, June 14, 1970), p. 4.

[15] Iowa at this writing (September, 1970) has no public sector law. State and local government employees have been encouraged, however, by a 1970 Iowa Supreme Court decision holding that government agencies *may* bargain collectively with their employees.

is essential to prevent confusion and buck-passing. The appropriate elected bodies (Congress, state legislature, city council and so forth) must establish firmly the identity and the authority of the operating agency as the employer with whom employees and their representatives engage in bargaining. At the same time the legislative body at whatever level must clearly take itself out of the bargaining business for many cogent reasons. One of these is that collective bargaining as a process requires, as we have seen, authoritative spokesmen representing the parties. Furthermore, these representatives must have the professional know-how to do a responsible job for their constituents. In the public sector the negotiator for management should be the designate of the operating agency, *not* a city council or a county board of supervisors— and, most certainly, *not* the U.S. Congress.

Legislation providing the framework for bargaining must, of course, recognize that fiscal control does not reside with the management representative at the bargaining table as it does in the private sector. The enabling legislative enactment can and should establish the parameters of discretionary authority for the government agencies who do the actual bargaining. It can also relate the timing of negotiations to the legislative year in terms of appropriations. Both the government agency and the employee organization must know what can (and cannot) be done on economic (labor cost) issues.

There are still comparatively few governmental jurisdictions that enjoy the defined bargaining framework held here to be essential for stable labor relations. It is thus remarkable that the advent of collective bargaining has been as peaceful as it in fact has been in most instances. However, conditions of uneasy or unstable peace cannot endure indefinitely. This should be a serious concern to the many states that still have no legislation acknowledging the fact or legitimacy of public employee bargaining. It should give pause also to those states whose laws excessively restrict employee rights or which have not clearly defined the bargaining authority of the agencies or departments that must function as "management" on the bargaining front.

THE NONPROFIT ASPECT OF GOVERNMENT AND THE CONTINUING SERVICE OBLIGATION

The nonprofit nature of government as a service institution to the "owners" (taxpayers) is reasonably well understood. Most of government is genuinely nonprofit in character.[16] This is a source of some distinctive

---

[16] It is the nonprofit character of government service that, in my mind, makes economic force singularly inappropriate as a vehicle for government employees. The nonprofit feature is more persuasive against use of the strike than the tired cliches about sovereignty.

difficulties for those engaged in public bargaining that are not always appreciated. Perhaps the greatest of these is the absence of the normal private sector "Robin Hood" impulse to take from the affluent corporation at the bargaining table. In bargaining with a government agency there can be no logical rationale for far-out economic proposals. Both sides are aware that any increase in labor costs resulting from negotiations must be paid for from appropriated funds, which in turn are contingent upon revenue (principally tax revenue).

Intimately related to this nonprofit feature of government is the fact that in nearly all cases the government agency or department operates as a monopolist with no true competition. The U.S. Post Office Department has no competitor. Neither does the U.S. Mint. Municipalities have one fire department and one police department. There are no viable alternatives available in the market for most government services. Furthermore, government agencies at any one level of jurisdiction (federal, state or municipal) do not compete with one another in performing the respective services for which they have been established. Government agencies may "compete" in legislative halls in the annual or biennial scrambling for adequate appropriations, but *in their functional roles they do not face competition.*

This absence of competition in the private sector sense has a number of implications for collective bargaining. For one thing, in government circles a powerful private constraint on costs is not available. Another consideration is that reliable productivity measurement and cost-benefit analysis for measuring the efficiency of employee services are difficult to come by in government employment. Even assuming such calculations to be reasonably accurate, the restraining effect of findings on the bargainers would be hard to demonstrate.

We have indicated in the briefest of fashions some considerations in public bargaining that bear directly on what the union or employee organization may seek in terms of economic improvements. It can be argued that the absence of competition for the employer would bring forth stronger economic demands. Countering any such tendencies, however, is the presence of constraining ceilings in the form of *third*-force (legislative) and *fourth*-force (taxpayers) reaction against exorbitant economic demands.

Of fundamental importance in its impact on the conduct of the parties in public bargaining is the assumption, nearly universally entertained, that *the government service, whatever its nature, must continue to be performed without interruption.* This assumption is perhaps more responsible than the fact that there are no profits to be shared or squeezed for the continuing vitality of the conviction that government employees should not have the legal right to use economic force as a part of their bargaining equipment. It is better appreciated today that strikes are not necessarily prevented by their being legislated out of existence. Nevertheless, the sentiment in this country continues to be negative on the use of strikes by government employees.

Legislative backing for this sentiment remains in force at the federal level and in all but two of some twenty-five states with general public sector labor relations legislation.[17] If economic force is not to be regarded as a suitable instrument for resolving bargaining impasses, the question arises as to whether collective bargaining for government employees can be truly free and meaningful. Allan Weisenfeld, an experienced labor relations professional at the state level, holds that public employees are necessarily second-class citizens under such an inhibition.[18] However, I believe that most students of public sector labor relations are not this pessimistic. The tremendous upsurge of union membership at all government levels, be it remembered, has occurred and is continuing with full knowledge that the arbitrament of economic force is not legally available for resolving future terms disputes. It must also be recognized that there are many examples of effective collective bargaining in a wide variety of public sector situations. The parties to such successful bargaining would not, I am confident, describe their activities as meaningless.

The Need for Adequate Dispute Settlement Procedures

The pressure of opinion is nearly always quickly and completely against government employees who strike to achieve their bargaining aims. Public support is hard to muster unless it can be clearly shown that the government agency has been unyielding in response to reasonable demands. In some cases also the interested public can be moved favorably if it can be shown that the legislative branch has not provided for procedures to resolve impasses over the terms of future agreements in a peaceful and orderly fashion. Here we shall incorporate by reference the analysis of Chapter 8 on the effective use of mediation, fact-finding, voluntary arbitration and so forth for resolving public sector disputes.

Impasses are frequently the product of a public sector difficulty already discussed, that is, establishing the identity and authority of the employer in particular cases. Illustrations can be multiplied of frustration on the part of a union or employee association bargaining with a particular

---

[17] Pennsylvania and Hawaii are the only two states with general public sector laws specifically authorizing strikes after statutory dispute-resolving procedures have been exhausted without success.

[18] Allan Weisenfeld, "Public Employees are Still Second Class Citizens," *Labor Law Journal*, XX (March, 1969), 138–50.

government agency only to discover that said agency is not empowered (or refuses) to enter into a conclusive agreement on terms and conditions of employment. In such an unfortunate situation the temptation to use either economic force or "politics" is frequently irresistible. Mentioning of "politics" makes it logical to consider next this distinctive feature of public sector labor relations.

THE USE AND MISUSE OF "POLITICS" IN PUBLIC SECTOR LABOR RELATIONS

Before the modern era of public employee unionism was ushered in by E.O. 10988 in 1962, the standard method for employees to register economic gains was to bypass their agency and go to the legislative source of funds, that is, to lobby. *Modernity in public sector labor relations requires placing the government agency* ("management") *first wherever the law not only permits but encourages and protects collective bargaining by employees.* A corollary of this proposition is that neither the agency nor the employee organization should rely on the third force to bail either of them out of an untenable position or to sweeten an already negotiated agreement. This is to say that strengthening collective bargaining requires that the negotiators rely on themselves to the greatest extent possible. This entails avoiding the former habit of lobbying as a way of life. *Bargaining to finality* must become the joint goal of government agencies and employee organizations.

This does not mean that "politics" can ever be entirely absent from public sector bargaining. Both government agency X and union Y are well aware that they are not negotiating in a vacuum.

When economic issues are negotiated, it may already be clear that funds are not available to accommodate the contemplated settlement. In many cases, this may require special joint appeals to the legislative branch. One thing is certain. There must be an improved coordination in public employment between contract negotiation deadlines and final legislative action on appropriations bills. If we are to encourage bargaining to finality, as suggested above, there must be a more realistic calendar so that budgetary limits can be realistically known.

When the negotiated contract goes beyond the bounds of legislative authorization or approval, "politics" will necessarily enter the picture. It may be a situation where the appropriations have been so niggardly that the agency and the employee organization jointly decide to plead their case to the legislative branch and perhaps ultimately to the public at large. Another possible "emergency" can arise when the government agency has agreed to the employee organization's demands, confident in so doing that legislative ratification will not be forthcoming. In either of the cited examples, the legislative branch necessarily becomes involved in the action. The important consideration is how and when it can or should be involved.

Hopefully, it is clear that we are not using "politics" in an invidious sense. In representative government, when administrative agencies and employee organizations negotiate contracts, they must respect the limits on their discretion. If public bargaining is to become mature and stable *there can be only one set of negotiations.* There should not be a second round with the legislative branch to achieve a fatter economic settlement. Such a strategy might yield a temporary advantage to a strong union or association in the short run, but the long-run consequences would be the certain breakdown of regularized bargaining procedures. Chaos would soon be the rule if the government agency or the employee organization believed it could run to the legislative branch in any and all circumstances.

There are only two situations that justify traveling the political route. One is when the elected branch itself has been placing economic or other barriers in the way of constructive collective bargaining. The second circumstance would be a clear case of bad faith bargaining or intransigence of one bargaining party. If there is no administrative labor relations agency to handle the problem as an unfair practice case, the injured party should bring the offending party's conduct to the attention of the legislative branch.

THE LEGISLATIVE FRAMEWORK OF PUBLIC SECTOR LABOR RELATIONS

The discussion has already served in several respects to point up another important difference between the private and public sectors. I refer to the nature of the labor relations law (or absence thereof) affecting the discretion of the public negotiators.

Private sector employers and the unions with whom they bargain are not always happy with the nature and quantum of legislative control over their dealings with one another, but at least they know the regulatory story. They are concerned mainly with one federal statute, the National Labor Relations Act of 1935 (Wagner Act), as amended and enlarged by the Labor Management Relations Act of 1947 (Taft-Hartley) and as further amended with new features in the Labor Management Reporting and Disclosure Act of 1959 (Landrum-Griffin). Both private employers and unions look to the NLRB's decisions and orders under this statutory framework for guidance as to what they can and cannot do in collective bargaining.

In sharp contrast, public sector bargaining at the state and local government level goes on under an amazing variety of conditions from a legislative control or authorization standpoint. As we have already seen, there are still many states and municipalities with no law on the subject at all, good, bad or indifferent. In these jurisdictions, the people's elected representatives have not yet seen fit to give legislative support to the rights of government employees to form and join unions and to bargain collectively with government agencies through unions or employee associations of their own choosing. Bargaining takes place on a *de facto* basis. The results are uneven and frequently inequitable, however, because they depend largely on the mood or stance of the government agency concerned. When the agency is adamantly opposed to bargaining (an attitude still easy to find) the only choice of the employees is to strike (an action enjoinable in most jurisdictions in the absence of legislation authorizing bargaining) or to use the unhappy economic force subterfuges of mass resignations, sick-ins, "blue flu" and so on.[19]

Federal employees are much better off than those in state and local governments with no legislation. There is still no congressional word other than the harsh sanctions against any federal employee who strikes.[20] However, there is a solid basis for effective bargaining under President Nixon's order of October 29, 1969 (Executive Order 11491). Some features of E.O. 11491 will be outlined in a later part of the chapter. Here it is enough to note that federal agencies and employees since October, 1969, have enough to go on to permit intelligent, responsible bargaining. The same cannot be said for many state and local jurisdictions. There are a number of instances of overlegislation—a condition perhaps worse in some ways than no legislation.

The pluralistic, protean character of government at the state and local level defies summary description. The temptation is strong to propose a "model" law, but the sober fact is that no one legislative formula can be devised to fit the infinite variety of circumstances. To mention just one important variable, the more heavily populated states with a considerable government apparatus and a great deal of public employee unionism (such as California, New York and New Jersey) need a separate administrative body for handling representation cases and unfair practice cases in the public sector.[21]

Many states, however, do not need a full-time labor relations agency

---

[19] The public sector has developed its own colorful jargon. The term "blue flu" refers to tactics of policemen in a number of municipalities who became coincidentally ill in uncommonly large numbers when negotiations had reached a stalemate.

[20] Taft-Hartley in 1947 provided bluntly for mandatory discharge of any federal government employee who struck, together with forfeiture of civil service status. Furthermore, a striking employee was not eligible for re-employment by any federal agency for three years following his discharge. These harsh strictures were replaced by 1955 legislation that declared a strike against the federal government to be a felony and a disqualification for federal employment.

[21] Although the larger states probably need a special public sector agency, it would have been more economical (and perhaps more effective) to utilize the existing state mediation services for dispute settlement work.

following the pattern of the New York State PERB (Public Employment Relations Board). They *do* need some type of "mini-board" or *ad hoc* regulatory machinery that can be set in motion as the need arises to carry out the statutory mandate. One feasible approach would be to establish regular panels of neutrals available on an *ad hoc* basis for mediation, fact-finding, supervision of representation elections and the like. This could be done through the administering aegis of a nonprofit organization such as the American Arbitration Association. Such panels could also function in impasse situations at both state and municipal levels under a proper authorizing statute by the state legislature.

A realistic idea of what needs to be covered in an effective public labor relations law can be seen from listing the twenty topics that the Advisory Committee to the National Governors' Conference Task Force on State and Local Government Labor Relations believes should be covered.

As reported in the Task Force's 1969 Supplement report, the twenty topics are as follows:

1. Right of employees to organize and bargain collectively or to refrain therefrom
2. Rights of individual employees
3. Duty to bargain
4. Creation of regulatory agency
5. Coverage of employees
6. Determination of the bargaining unit
7. Determination of employee representatives
8. Exclusive representation
9. Certification of bargaining representative
10. Management rights and the scope of bargaining
11. Protection of merit principles
12. Unfair labor practices
13. Budgetary process
14. Written agreements
15. Payroll deduction
16. Resolution of disputes
17. Strike prohibitions
18. The need for an advisory commission
19. Privacy
20. Effective date of legislation[22]

The same prestigious Advisory Committee[23] has also enunciated five principles that it considers must be honored by any public sector labor law. These principles are as follows:

1. Protection of the right to organize and to bargain collectively, and of the right to refrain therefrom.

---

[22] See p. 3 of the *1969 Task Force Report Supplement*, cited above in footnote 9.
[23] The advisory committee includes such knowledgeable professionals in public sector labor relations as Arvid Anderson, Milton Derber and Martin Wagner.

2. Provision of some apparatus for resolving problems which arise in the administration of employee-management relations, such as the definition of bargaining units, scope of bargaining and representation rights.
3. Provision of some apparatus for resolving disputes and impasses, both in the formulation of an agreement and in the interpretation and application of existing agreements.
4. If an administrative board or office is created for the above reasons, provision for substantial latitude for the board to exercise in individual cases.
5. Recognition that there has been insufficient collective bargaining experience in public employment. There is a need for experimentation. The law should give the board or other administrator latitude and encouragement to experiment.[24]

THE PROSPECT OF FEDERALIZATION

The above listing of twenty topics and five guiding principles should serve to clarify the task facing all states—including many of those whose legislation falls short of the mark on some counts. The current legislative norm is confusing variety, but no one can say that experimentation is not going on. The concept of the states as laboratories for social action is getting a full workout on the issues concerning us in this chapter. From all this action and experience we can hope that a stable, workable pattern will emerge in due course, but this is by no means certain.

The union with the biggest job in terms of coping with all the diversity, the AFSCME, is showing impatience and dissatisfaction to the point of advocating federalization of the field.

One can empathize to a degree with the AFSCME's desire for a federal statute pre-empting the field of state and local government labor relations. This union deals with an incredible variety of employer "opponents" under the most diverse circumstances. In some cases, bargaining is doubtless a pleasure for AFSCME. However, one suspects that in most cases its representatives find themselves yearning for the degree of sophistication and consistency that a federal law would bring into play.

Other unions with extensive bargaining relations at the state and local level can be expected to join forces with AFSCME in pushing for federal occupancy of the state and local labor relations field. A concerted effort has not yet been made to persuade the U.S. Congress—perhaps because in this hectic, chameleonlike environment of new employee organization and first efforts at collective bargaining everyone concerned on both sides is just too busy to do anything beyond coping as best they can with immediate problems and exigencies. This leads us logically to the next problem area,—

---

[24] See p. 3 of the *1969 Task Force Report Supplement*, cited above in footnote 9.

the general lack of specialized labor relations know-how in government agencies and the shortage of knowledgeable neutrals for assistance in dispute resolution.

The Short Supply of Experienced Negotiators and Neutrals in the Public Sector

Somehow or other, a great deal of collective bargaining is going on between government agencies and unions or associations representing their employees. Unfortunately, in many instances, the negotiations and the results are not models to emulate. The flawed character of much public bargaining is not due to bad faith so much as it is to the lack of specialized talent on one or both sides of the bargaining table. The absence of expertise is felt more keenly by "management" (Government Agency X or School Board Y) than by the unions or employee associations, although the latter are often handicapped by lack of funds to procure expert aid.

The solution to the expertise gap is neither quick nor easy. Perhaps the most important consideration is the recognition that collective bargaining does call for specialized talent. Once this fundamental point is appreciated the next step may be more difficult because of the shortage of qualified personnel and their comparatively high cost if and when located.

One of the ablest students of public sector labor relations, Milton Derber of the University of Illinois, observes that for small government units it may be appropriate for a line official (a department head, school superintendent, a city manager or even in some cases a mayor) to be the chief spokesman for management. Professor Derber goes on at once to conclude, however, that beyond the level of approximately 100 employees "the benefits of utilizing a staff personnel or employee relations specialist begin to outweigh the costs."[25] This conclusion of Professor Derber closely parallels my private sector findings on the labor relations problems of small firms. My field investigation convinced me that specialized attention to labor relations can profitably be instituted in a private firm at the level of 100 employees, although my original research hypothesis placed the need for specialized treatment at about 200 employees. My final conclusion was as follows:

> One may conclude that the dividing line is somewhere between 100 and 200, being absolutely certain that a firm with bargaining unit employment of 200 or more cannot operate successfully without specialized attention to

---

[25] Milton Derber, "Who Negotiates for the Public Employer?" reprinted by the University of Illinois Bulletin from *Perspective in Public Employee Negotiation* (Chicago: Public Personnel Association, 1969), p. 53.

the labor relations and personnel functions. A firm whose employment is around 100 and expanding must confront the decision to specialize.[26]

Putting Professor Derber's and my estimates together would seem to make the point clear. Whether the management enterprise in question is a private firm or a government agency, bargaining collectively with employees requires specialized know-how unless the enterprise is very small.

THE SHORTCOMINGS OF THE EXPERTS

Finding the talent is going to be difficult for many governmental units for some time to come for a variety of reasons. Most experienced negotiators in the private sector will not be attracted by government salaries. Even if they could be attracted, they might not be worth the cost because a good portion of their know-how is *not* readily transferable. By the same token, the experienced neutrals currently in great demand for handling mediation, fact-finding and future terms arbitration cases in public sector disputes are often poorly suited for the task at hand because their experience has been mainly or entirely in private sector grievance arbitration.

To speak bluntly, it is important to recognize two considerations applying to the current supply of experienced grievance arbitrators in the United States: (1) many are overcommitted in the private sector to the point where the process of grievance arbitration is losing one of its main virtues, that is, having disputes decided with some dispatch, not after several months to as much as a year after hearing,[27] (2) even when not too busy to accept work as neutrals in the public sector, most experienced grievance arbitrators are not trained or skilled as mediators to handle impasse situations nor are they generally familiar with government as an industry.

The National Academy of Arbitrators has become concerned about the short supply of experienced and acceptable neutrals in the face of the intense demand for neutrals coming in particular from the public sector. A special committee chaired by Eli Rock, long-time arbitrator and labor relations adviser to the City of Philadelphia, was appointed by Academy President James C. Hill in March, 1969, to consider "disputes settlement in public employment." The Rock Committee found at the outset that

---

[26] See Harold W. Davey, "Labor Relations Problems of Small Firms and Their Solution," in *Studies in the Factor Markets for Small Business Firms*, ed. Dudley G. Luckett (Ames, Ia.: Iowa State University for Small Business Administration, 1964), pp. 199–223.

[27] I have been seriously concerned for some years about the shortage of competent, experienced and acceptable arbitrators. In discontinous fashion since late 1967 I have been interviewing management and union practitioners (as well as many experienced arbitrators) on shortcomings of the grievance arbitration process. Delay in decision-making is invariably cited as one of the principal frustrations.

there was an "urgent need for *training* in the new and unaccustomed roles required of the neutral in the public sector."[28] It further found that existing public and private labor relations agencies could not cope alone with the problem. It concluded that ". . . the matter represented an urgent problem of national scope calling for a type of activism not typically associated with the Academy."

In 1969 and 1970 a good many locally sponsored training programs of one sort or another were conducted in various cities. The Academy took the unusual step of preceding its twenty-third annual meeting in Montreal with a special two-day intensive training session in mediation and fact-finding techniques in the public sector for Academy members who recognized their need for additional know-how in these procedures. The caliber of instruction and attendance were excellent at this unique "teach-in." As one of the students, I can testify that I confirmed my initial suspicion that the tasks of a neutral in public sector labor relations are much tougher and more demanding than those of a private industry grievance arbitrator.

Contract administration and grievance arbitration have become fairly sophisticated in the private sector. In most cases the arbitrator has the benefit of case presentation by experienced representatives on both sides. Many of the issues he must rule on are difficult. Nevertheless he performs his decision-making function on an adequate record under a contract that is generally clear as to the nature and limits of his function. Last but not least, the arbitrator's decision in each case is final and binding. He can then move on to the next case in his backlog.

Life is not so easy for a public sector mediator or fact-finder. He is frequently confronted with inexperience and emotionalism on one or both sides of the bargaining table. Furthermore, he is dealing with future terms issues which are frequently explosive in character. The talents and expertise demanded of a public sector neutral are of a high order indeed. Most experienced private sector grievance arbitrators are not currently equipped for these demanding public sector roles without considerable additional training. The Montreal teach-in convinced me that my comparative advantage lies in the private sector. I suspect that many of my experienced fellow arbitrators reached a similar conclusion.

What then is the answer to this critical problem posed by a shortage of experienced negotiators and neutrals? I suggest that the most practical approach, even though it may be frustrating at times, is for the government agencies and unions involved to set patiently about the task of developing from within their own corps of specialized labor relations personnel. In the

---

[28] The text of the Rock Committee report appears as an appendix in the *Proceedings* of the 1970 meeting of the National Academy of Arbitrators, edited by Gerald A. Somers and published by the Bureau of National Affairs, Inc., Washington, D.C.

long run this will be more salutary than continuing to improvise by relying on outside labor relations consultants from one contract to another. Government agencies and the unions with whom they deal would do well to join forces in stimulating the intensive training of professionally qualified individuals who wish to serve as neutrals in the labor relations field.

Some substantial financial aid for an intensive training effort may be forthcoming from the U.S. Department of Labor. The problem and the needs are national in scope so this would be both a welcome and logical development. In the meantime what kind of practical action can government agencies and employee organizations take to ease the pains arising from lack of negotiating expertise and the unavailability of qualified neutrals? Two considerations may be of help: (1) the best solution is to try diligently to make collective bargaining work, recognizing that one can learn best about how to bargain by actually bargaining; (2) the better part of wisdom for the public sector practitioners is to recognize that neutrals may be more trouble than they are worth. Bilateralism, no matter how tough it may be on the participants, is generally preferable to trilateralism in any shape or form.[29]

Bargaining at the Federal Level: An Appraisal of E.O. 11491

Since October, 1969, with the issuance of E.O. 11491, the requisite formal framework for effective bargaining has been established. Neither the government agencies nor the unions with whom they deal are entirely satisfied (for different reasons, obviously) with the fleshed-out rules of the game under 11491. Nevertheless, a detached appraisal warrants the conclusion that E.O. 11491 when fully implemented should be generally adequate for the needs of the bargainers.

Under E.O. 10988 uncertainty and inconsistency often prevailed because the decision-maker of last resort was the department head. E.O. 11491 centralizes decision-making authority on several important substantive policy questions in either the newly established Federal Labor Relations Council[30] or in the Assistant Secretary of Labor for Labor-Management

---

[29] I have argued this thesis more fully elsewhere. See Harold W. Davey, "The Use of Neutrals in the Public Sector," *Labor Law Journal* XXI (August, 1969), 529–38.

[30] The Council is to be chaired by the chairman of the Civil Service Commission. It will also include the Secretary of Labor; an official of the Executive Office of the President; and "such other officials of the executive branch as the President may designate from time to time." The Council is mandated to administer and interpret the Order, to "decide major policy issues, prescribe regulations" and so forth.

Relations.[31] Decisions under the new centralization may not always be applauded by all concerned, but they will have the merits of improved consistency and predictability. This should be helpful to both government agencies and employee organizations. Another plus factor will be the greater labor relations expertise and impartiality under the new procedures.

A second area of improvement over E.O. 10988 is the greater stress on exclusive recognition rights as the basis for bargaining. The new order does away with both "informal" and "formal" recognition. These types of recognition under E.O. 10988 had proved generally unsatisfactory, nebulous and frustrating. The current stress on the familiar private sector concept of exclusive recognition is a mature step forward. The employee organization so recognized is entitled to bargain for and must represent all employees within the appropriate unit in question. The use of secret ballot elections as the sole basis for achieving exclusive recognition status is procedurally desirable.

The 1969 order also provides for something called "national consultation rights." This high-sounding but somewhat vague status is accorded to a labor organization that meets criteria established by the Federal Labor Relations Council (FLRC) as the representative of a "substantial" number of employees of the agency is question. The order makes clear, however, that pluralism in representation will be avoided. No "national consultation rights" status can be conferred in any unit where a labor organization already holds exclusive recognition rights at the national level in such unit.

The 1969 order is specific and clear-cut on several important aspects of contract administration and the scope of collective bargaining. For example, it does away with "advisory arbitration" as an instrument for resolving appropriate unit disputes. This responsibility is assigned to the Assistant Secretary of Labor. The latter's expertise and impartiality should at least equal, if not exceed, that of the corps of *ad hoc* advisory arbitrators that made advisory unit recommendations under E.O. 10988. Also, greater consistency in decision-making is assured. Under the former system, department heads could always decline to accept advisory arbitrator unit determinations.

Another administrative plus in the new order is the added scope and status given to grievance arbitration procedures. The new order stops just short, however, of giving arbitrators' decisions final and binding character. Either party may file "exceptions" to an arbitrator's award with the FLRC. One can reasonably anticipate that few awards will be reversed or modified by the FLRC. Criteria for arbitrator reversal are to be similar to

---

[31] The Assistant Secretary has a considerable amount to do. His duties include the deciding of appropriate unit questions submitted for his consideration, the supervision of elections, deciding questions of labor organization eligibility for national consultation rights and the decision of most categories of alleged unfair labor practices and alleged violations of standards of conduct for labor organizations.

the bases on which arbitration awards can now be reversed or modified by federal courts under Section 301 of the Taft-Hartley Act.

Another innovation of the 1969 order is the establishment of a Federal Service Impasses Panel (FSIP) for resolving negotiation (future terms) disputes. The FSIP will function when "voluntary arrangements," including use of FMCS or other mediation assistance, have failed to produce agreement.

THE PROBABLE IMPACT OF E.O. 11491

Executive Order 11491 also spells out and prohibits six agency management unfair practices and six labor organization unfair practices. The prohibited practices correspond generally to those with which we are familiar in labor relations law in the private sector, with some that are especially tailored to public sector characteristics.[32]

Worthy of special mention is Section 19(b)(5), which prohibits labor organizations from discriminating against an employee because of "race, color, creed, sex, age, or national origin." This provision appears to leave open no possible avenue of discrimination.

E.O. 11491 will not be the last word on federal labor relations. However, the order has removed many of the ambiguities and inadequacies of E.O. 10988. Employee enthusiasm for unionism and collective bargaining will continue to be strong in the 1970s. The impact of the new administrative procedures should be a favorable one on both agency and employee sides of the bargaining table. There is not yet sufficient experience at this writing to be sure whether this prediction is overly optimistic.

A POSTSCRIPT ON THE 1970 POSTAL STRIKE

Canada and other countries have weathered postal employee strikes of varying duration and varying degrees of legality. The 1970 letter-carriers' strike was a unique experience for the United States. Its unusual attributes included the following:

1. The sole disputed issue was the amount of a wage increase, but all concerned agreed that the wage rates in effect at the time of the stoppage were inadequate.

---

[32] The wording of most unfair practices is similar to the prohibitions in Taft-Hartley. However, when necessary the language has been carefully tailored to the needs of federal labor relations. For example, federal agency management "shall not refuse to consult, confer or negotiate with a labor organization as required by this Order," [Section 19(a)(6)]. Also of interest is the declaration that a labor organization "shall not call or engage in a strike, work stoppage, or slowdown; picket an agency in a labor-management dispute; or condone any such activity by failing to take affirmative action to prevent or stop it," [Section 19(b)(4)]. There could be some question as to the validity of the complete ban on picketing.

2. The injunction proved singularly ineffective as a means of bringing the letter-carriers back to work, even though all concerned recognized the illegal nature of the strike and the severe penalties that could flow from the walkout.
3. The effectiveness of the strike proved in dramatic fashion to the federal government the short-sightedness of assuming that no stoppage will ever take place merely because it is prohibited, no matter how stiff the sanctions.
4. The dispute dramatized the shortcomings of bargaining by lobbying with congressional committees instead of directly with the agency heads.

Perhaps the strike could have been avoided if the union representatives and postal department heads had utilized the impasse resolution procedures of E.O. 11491. Had this been done there would have been a better opportunity for professional mediation to bring the issues into perspective and perhaps to resolve them. Instead the parties resorted to a policy of lobbying as usual. There was a failure to appreciate the depth of rank-and-file tension and frustration in the face of what must have seemed like intolerable congressional delay.

Hopefully, the new administrative postal reform legislation will have the salutary result of finally blasting loose postal labor relations from the historic lobbying mold into a structural pattern consistent with genuine collective bargaining.

CURRENT AND PROSPECTIVE PROBLEM AREAS FOR STATE AND LOCAL LEVELS

Most of the key problems in labor relations at the state and local government level have already been considered, directly or by clear inference, in earlier sections of this chapter and in Chapter 8. At the risk of some unavoidable repetition it is necessary in the interests of perspective to restate in summary form some of the principal problems as follows:

1. Considerable confusion, friction and uncertainty arising from the immediate need to cope with historic governmental structural forms that are poorly suited to the pragmatic necessities of collective bargaining.
2. Difficulties associated with rapid growth in unionism and collective bargaining at a time when the governmental units directly affected by such growth are experiencing acute fiscal problems—public education being a good illustration of this problem area and also of the structural unsuitability factor described in point 1 above.
3. Difficulties posed by the need to develop labor relations expertise on a crash basis during a period when talented personnel from the private sector is generally not available for a variety of reasons.
4. Difficulties posed by the absence of a legislative framework for conducting labor relations activities or by the inadequacies or inequities of the initial legislative framework.

5. Special difficulties posed by the passage of labor relations legislation for particular employee groupings in some states, such as policemen and firemen, nurses, teachers and so forth.
6. Continuing inability in many jurisdictions to achieve satisfactory procedural alternatives to economic force as a means of resolving future terms impasse cases.

No claim is made that the above list is a complete cataloging of problems. It should be enough to suggest that in most cases we are a long way from the millenium in public sector relations. The writer makes no claim to having *the* answers in fabricated, easy-to-use form. In company with many private sector-oriented individuals I shall continue to watch with keen interest and considerable empathy the seething, confused labor relations revolution in the public sector. Seeking to inform and enlighten myself, I have attended a number of symposia or conferences devoted exclusively to public sector problems.[33] In addition, I have tried to absorb the veritable Niagara of journal articles and books that have poured forth in the past few years. An eclectic selection from the latter makes up the bibliography at the end of this chapter.

A few clear impressions remain from this study and observation. In summary form these are as follows:

1. The public sector is not inexorably fated to repeat the mistakes of the private sector during the latter's growing pains period of the late 1930s and late 1940s, but there is abundant evidence in many local government situations that this will in fact happen, in some cases because of ignorance and in others because of a deliberate effort to thwart employee efforts to organize and to bargain collectively.

2. Many proven legislative and negotiated policies applicable in the private sector can and should be appropriated freely by public sector practitioners; in this realm of the transferable, I would mention the following as illustrative:

a. final and binding arbitration of disputes over interpretation or application of existing agreements;

b. operating with a general, comprehensive labor relations statutory framework rather than trying to develop particularized legislative treatment for different occupational groups;

c. borrowing wholesale the NLRB's salutary respect for employee preferences in defining bargaining units unless the unit sought is manifestly inappropriate or unworkable;

---

[33] A firm impression from conferences attended was that a great deal of taking in each other's washing was going on. The knowledge gap between the experts and the neophytes was not as great as expected. This should be regarded as a basis for optimism rather than discouragement. The "experts" were in the main willing to learn along with those who came to learn. This was refreshing.

      d. avoiding the difficulties of pluralism by clear legislative sanctioning of exclusive recognition as the foundation for effective bargaining;

      e. banning most of those actions currently prohibited to employers and labor organizations as being unfair practices in the private sector.

      3. A studied effort should be made to avoid certain legislative policies and procedures that have proved to be a source of difficulty in regulation of private sector labor relations, for example, an effort should be made to leave the scope of bargaining discretionary with the parties (except as it may already be restricted by existing law such as civil service classification requirements).

      4. The machinery for resolution of impasse situations should be utilized to keep the emphasis on inducing the bargainers to work out their own solutions instead of resignedly following a formal and totally predictable procedural pattern.

      5. A concentrated effort should be made to develop home-grown expertise as needed rather than becoming dependent on expensive outside talent.

Developing a Sense of Shared Responsibility: Foundation for Optimism

      The stress has been on difficulties, problems and unanswered questions. The impression may have been created that the cause of constructive labor relations in government is virtually hopeless. *This is not the case.* There are many excellent examples of effective bargaining and dispute resolution in many jurisdictions worthy of study and emulation. One outstanding example is the way in which the comparatively new Office of Collective Bargaining (OCB) in New York City has coped patiently, quietly and effectively with an enormously varied, complex congeries of labor relations situations.

      New York City departments and agencies have collective bargaining relationships with approximately 130 local unions, affiliated with some fifty-nine parent unions. The bargaining covers something like 347 bargaining units embracing 211,447 employees according to figures furnished the writer by OCB in October, 1970 by Mr. Ernest Doerfler, OCB Trial Examiner.

      One clue to OCB's success is its tripartite composition. Another is the mediatory talent of its director and deputy director, Arvid Anderson and Eva Robins.

      As far as labor relations are concerned, New York City is often portrayed as a jungle where strikes occur with great frequency. The figures do not confirm this picture, although *some* serious stoppages have occurred in recent years.

According to Mr. Doerfler, in 1968 New York City's bargaining arm, the Office of Labor Relations, reached 128 settlements with public employee organizations covering 490 titles and 54,310 positions. In 1969 OLR reached 136 settlements covering 546 titles and 163,339 positions.

One reason for qualified optimism as to the future of public sector labor relations is the nonprofit, service nature of government employment. This factor should contributed to *a sense of shared responsibility* on the part of *all* government employees for *maintaining and improving the quality of services rendered.*

The business of government in a very literal sense is everyone's business. This fact is known and appreciated by government employees. Therefore, *the obligation of bargaining to finality in peaceful fashion* is one that should be strongly felt by both management and employees.

It is also vitally important that no government agency be permitted to maintain an intransigent stance in any situation by wearing the cloak of sovereignty. In an age of constitutionalism there is no room for using an outmoded political theory to justify denial of employee rights.

BARGAINING BY PROFESSIONAL EMPLOYEES: SOME SUMMARY OBSERVATIONS ON TEACHERS AND NURSES

The following section on bargaining by professional employees comes logically at the end of a chapter on public sector labor relations because our largest group of organized professional employees, the public school teachers, work for government. We shall also consider briefly the problems of nurses, with a note or two on professional football and the performing arts.

Imitation is said to be the highest form of flattery. If so, the unions of this country should take pride in the fact that many groups of professional employees openly seek to bargain collectively with their employers over salaries, hours and working conditions. Furthermore, in some cases these professional groups have not been averse to using economic force as an ultimate weapon in future terms controversies. The procedures and the instruments of unionism have been adopted and used by many units of the National Education Association (NEA) and the American Nurses' Association (ANA). In some instances NEA and ANA units have not hesitated to use the vocabulary of collective bargaining, although in others there is a reluctance to being thought of as doing the same thing that the blue-collar or hard-hat employees have been doing with such effectiveness since the 1930s.

The conversion of the NEA in the late 1960s from what the AFT (American Federation of Teachers) sneered at as a "company union" into a strong, vigorous bargaining force in many jurisdictions is perhaps the most dramatic evidence of the profound shift in the thinking of many professionals about the legitimacy and necessity of collective bargaining. In former years the NEA used a specialized vocabulary to avoid the familiar labor relations terms. It opposed the strike as an instrument, but favored "sanctions" instead. It stressed the term "professional negotiation" and eschewed using the term "collective bargaining." This semantic evasion has been largely abandoned.[34] NEA units often compete with AFT for exclusive bargaining rights to represent teachers in many metropolitan education districts. Furthermore, some NEA units have struck as a means of effectuating their economic and noneconomic demands.

A similar conversion in thinking has permeated the American Nurses' Association, beginning with the first stress on an Economic Security Program for RN's in the early 1950s.[35] In the first years of the Economic Security program the ANA avoided the direct action connotations of collective bargaining. However, ANA has gradually moved toward espousing the view that collective bargaining was necessary and desirable. The stand was taken that it was unprofessional for RN's not to work directly to improve their salaries, their hours, their working conditions and their voice in hospital affairs and patient care.

Nurses who seek to bargain collectively with hospitals still have a long way to go because many hospital administrators still hold that it is in some way unprofessional for nurses to engage in collective bargaining. I am peculiarly conscious of this kind of hospital management and municipal government thinking because of a current laboratory example in my own community, Ames, Iowa.

Mary Greeley Hospital in Ames, Iowa, is municipally owned. Its administrator reports to the Ames City Council and to an advisory board appointed by the Council. By June, 1969, approximately 90 percent of the registered nurses at Mary Greeley had joined the Iowa Nurses Association. When the nurses sought to bargain collectively with the hospital, the city fathers declined on the grounds that bargaining was not possible under Iowa law.

---

[34] Habit dies hard, however. I served recently on a panel discussing effective administration of collective agreements at a national conference of NEA staff representatives in Lincoln, Nebraska, August 13–14, 1970. The program title for this presentation was "Seminar on *Professional Negotiation* in Public Education" (emphasis added). Everyone at the seminar, however, spoke of collective bargaining.

[35] For a detached analysis of collective bargaining by registered nurses, see Joel Seidman, "Nurses and Collective Bargaining." *Industrial and Labor Relations Review*, XXIII (April, 1970), 335–51. Other informative and reliable analyses include Karen Hawley, *Economics of Collective Bargaining by Nurses* (Ames, Ia.: Iowa State University Press, 1967); and Archie Kleingartner, "Nurses, Collective Bargaining and Labor Legislation," *Labor Law Journal*, XVIII (April, 1967), 236–45.

The nurses patiently went the court case route to bring the hospital to the bargaining table. They won this judicial test in terms of a February, 1970, Iowa Supreme Court decision in another case holding in substance that state and local government agencies *may* bargain and enter into collective agreements with employee groups. Some two months later (April, 1970) the Ames City Council authorized the hospital to bargain with the nurses. Seven sessions over a two-month period proved fruitless. The principal differences were over noneconomic issues, but the City Council used budget preparation deadlines for the state as a rationale to break off negotiations.

Frustrated and angry after all this time, the nurses were nevertheless determined to go by the book. Instead of striking they employed the mass resignation device with appropriate notice. The City Council could not be moved. More than half of the hospital's some ninety RN's did in fact resign. Citizen efforts to induce the governor of Iowa to intervene by appointing an arbitration board to mediate or decide the dispute came to naught. The nurses were willing to resume negotiations, to submit to mediation or to binding arbitration of the unresolved issues, but the Ames City Council line was "wait until next year."

At this writing (September, 1970) the crisis remains unresolved. Many nurses have accepted positions at other hospitals, in all cases at substantially higher salaries. The hospital remains critically short of nurses but is seeking to recruit enough student wives to approximate former levels of service. Whether this can be done is questionable. Mary Greeley Hospital has been censured by the Iowa Nurses' Association and the American Nurses' Association.

The unfinished story of the Ames nurses contains most of the elements associated with many first efforts to secure bargaining status in the public sector, including the following: (1) refusal to bargain; (2) uncertainty as to who is the employer (the nurses' representatives were shunted back and forth between the hospital administrator and the City Council); (3) scope of the unit (should head nurses be included or excluded?); (4) misunderstanding of the nature of collective bargaining, combined with lack of expertise and (5) absence of an acceptable procedure for dispute resolution.

Professional employees are in many cases demonstrating an increased enthusiasm for organized dealings with management. However, they generally favor working through their professional associations such as NEA and ANA rather than through AFL-CIO affiliated labor organizations. This avoidance of unionism is partially a consequence of superiority feelings, but perhaps more importantly arises from a genuine conviction that there is merit in blending bargaining with professionalism. Economic improvement and simultaneous raising of professional standards can best be done through the professional association, if I read the thinking of NEA and ANA groups correctly.

A NOTE ON PROFESSIONAL FOOTBALL

Similar thinking clearly prevails among the players of the National Football League. Some years ago the Teamsters made a bid to organize pro football players. This effort received a great deal of publicity but little support from the players themselves. Through their own Players Association, however, the players have begun to bargain collectively with owners of the NFL clubs on a multi-employer basis. In 1970 a brief strike followed the owners' lockout of all but rookies from training camps. For a time there was a threat to the leisure-time pursuits of millions of American males (and not a few females), although the dispute could hardly have been characterized as an emergency endangering the national health and safety. The FMCS, however, did its best to mediate the dispute, which was settled finally in a marathon session a few days before the start of the exhibition game season by the efforts of NFL Commissioner Pete Rozelle.[36] The pro football players appeared to be solidly behind their professional players' association, but there was no sentiment for dealing with the club owners through an AFL-CIO union or through the independent but muscular IBT (Teamsters).

The general aversion on the part of professional employees to joining labor organizations raises the question central to this analysis of whether the bargaining needs of professional employees are truly of a special category. Are these employees a breed apart? Can their economic needs be better served through having their professional associations bargain with management? The answer of experience must be generally affirmative, although there are significant exceptions.

For example, there is a considerable amount of effective bargaining for teachers being conducted by the American Federation of Teachers (AFT), an AFL-CIO affiliate. This organization's highly publicized confrontations with the New York City Board of Education have served perhaps to obscure the fact that New York City teacher contracts and the system of contract administration have served as models for many NEA units elsewhere in the country.

THE PERFORMING ARTS AND COLLECTIVE BARGAINING

Professional employees in the performing arts do their bargaining through labor organizations. They do not consider their artistic stature demeaned in any way thereby. I refer to such organizations as the Screen

---

[36] Commissioner Rozelle was apparently successful in convincing the players in the 1970 confrontation that he was not a captive of the club owners.

370 Bargaining by government employees and professional employees

Actors Guild, Actors' Equity, the American Federation of Radio and Television Artists and the American Federation of Musicians. These unions have a lengthy history of effective collective bargaining.[37] A great deal of the bargaining effort of performing professionals is devoted to negotiating satisfactory minimal salaries for such jobs in the various fields as extra work in movies, walk-on stage and opera parts and the like. In the performing arts no effort is made to interfere with the individual bargaining of star actors, actresses and virtuoso musicians for extraordinarily high salaries, percentages of the gross on a film or the like. The egalitarian focus is always present to assure negotiated minimum standards for all jobs covered by the contracts. This is the artistic version of the blue-collar focus on industrial jurisprudence treated in Chapter 9.

COLLECTIVE BARGAINING IN THE PUBLIC SCHOOLS

Several questions have presented themselves in nearly all jurisdictions where teachers have sought to bargain collectively. These include the following:

1. Should teachers and school administrators be separated for labor relations purposes? In other words, should the bargaining unit consist of teachers only or should it also include school principals? The general answer has been to exclude principals from the teacher units.

2. Should the scope of bargaining be confined to conventional areas of bargaining (that is, salaries, hours and basic working conditions) or should negotiation extend to such "professional" issues as determination of curriculum, size of classes, selection of teaching materials and allocation of time between teaching and nonteaching but school-related functions? The answer of experience is a mixed one, but it is clear that teachers in most cases will seek to expand the scope of bargaining.

3. Should state legislation treat teachers as a separate class or should they be covered by one general statute? Again, the answer is mixed but expert opinion appears to favor one inclusive labor relations law.

4. Do teachers as a professional group have *significantly different* bargaining problems and objectives from other professional employees such as nurses, engineers, government attorneys and the like? The short answer must be "yes and no," as the subsequent discussion should make clear.

5. Do teachers perform such a critical function that they should be denied the right to strike under any circumstances? The pragmatic

---

[37] For a wide-ranging account of labor relations problems in radio and television broadcasting, see Allen E. Koenig, ed., *Broadcasting and Bargaining* (Madison, Wis.: The University of Wisconsin Press, 1970).

answer has been to deny the right to strike, although it would be hard to argue that teachers perform "critical" duties in the same sense as policemen and firemen.

6. Should bargaining for teachers be by school districts or should the structure of bargaining be developed on a multi-employer, state-wide basis or on some intermediate structural arrangement such as consolidated school districts of considerable size? The answer favors consolidated districts and, ultimately, state-wide bargaining for optimal results with funds available for education if the state in question wishes to provide approximately equal quality of education for all pupils.

Currently in many places the bargaining by local school districts, although still a legal necessity, is an exercise in futility from a pragmatic standpoint. The bargaining can never achieve any economic gains because there are simply no funds for the purpose in many small districts.[38]

7. Are grievance procedures with arbitration as the terminal step appropriate for resolving disputes between management (superintendents) and teacher representatives on issues of contract interpretation or application? The answer both in theory and practice would seem to be "yes."

The foregoing questions identify some of the main areas of controversy that have characterized teacher bargaining. The answers are necessarily not all in at this stage. The field remains fluid. However, certain definite trends in practice are evident. These developing trends in teacher bargaining can be noted as indicating something about the probable future of collective bargaining in public education.

Developing Trends in Teacher Bargaining

In the years ahead bargaining for teachers will come to resemble more closely patterns and procedures already standard for other organized employee groups. The significant remaining difference will concern the scope of collective bargaining. As professional employees, teachers will press for a joint voice through bargaining on many matters that traditionally have been regarded by school management as subject only to advisory consultation and not to bargaining. I refer to such problems as nature and content of curriculum, selection of textbooks and other teaching materials, size of classes and assignment of teachers to nonteaching functions. Many teachers regard these as vital professional concerns as well as being working conditions.

Of course, not all teacher units have come to the point of insisting

---

[38] I do not refer to cases where school boards out of habit or choice are deliberately crying poor, but rather to situations where the unhappy combination of exhausted millage limits, no borrowing capacity and uneconomically sized districts offers a truly bleak picture.

on a joint voice in these areas of formerly exclusive managerial authority. Bargaining in many districts still covers only conventional issues of an economic nature. However, as teacher organization becomes more complete, the demand for a voice on curriculum, class size and so forth will become more insistent and pervasive.

The conflict over scope of bargaining as just described is a source of great friction in many school districts.

Having spent some twenty-nine years in teaching at the university level, I find it hard to visualize how public school administrators can cling with any logic or grace to a position that denies teachers a joint voice in these professional matters. Although strangers to collective bargaining, most faculty members at institutions of higher learning in this country consider such matters as curriculum, choice of teaching materials and size of classes to be clearly within the realm of *professorial prerogative*. They would be sure to challenge administrators if the latter sought to determine unilaterally what should be taught and how it should be taught. Thus, one of the most explosive issues in public education bargaining is not regarded as even debatable in the field of higher education.

One qualification should be made. College administrators exercise considerable financial control over teaching and research activities. Austerity budgets necessarily have a direct impact not only on what is taught, but also on the size of classes, teaching loads and so forth. These financial constraints are looked upon by faculty members as necessary evils rather than as expressions of legitimate administrative interference with faculty prerogatives.[39]

Public school teacher negotiators should be able to make effective use of these precedents at the higher education level to strengthen their demands for expanding the scope of bargaining to include professional issues. Confrontations over the scope of bargaining will continue for some time in many districts. Yet I can see no sound basis for excluding legitimate professional concerns from consideration at the bargaining table. In the public sector as well as the private, the optimal route for developing stable and mature relationships is adherence to the proposition developed in Chapter 4 that the scope of bargaining should itself be subject to bargaining. It

---

[39] Perhaps the one factor that could trigger direct action to establish collective bargaining on the part of the staidest of faculty would be unilateral administrative efforts to increase teaching loads and/or to dictate what courses shall be taught and how. For a recent analysis of the prospects for collective bargaining in the field of higher education, see Martha A. Brown, "Collective Bargaining on the Campus: Professors, Associations and Unions," *Labor Law Journal*, XXI (March, 1970), 167–81. See also Tracy H. Ferguson, "Collective Bargaining in Universities and Colleges," *Labor Law Journal*, XIX (December, 1968), 778–804.

should not be restrictively delimited by legislation or by perpetuation of unilateral management discretion.

STRUCTURAL TRENDS IN TEACHER BARGAINING

Centralized and consolidated bargaining structures are probably unavoidable in public education if equity is to be achieved for all teachers while achieving and then maintaining comparable educational opportunities for all pupils, wherever situated. The uneconomically "small" district ultimately will give way to the consolidated school district to provide a viable financial base for proper staffing. Related to such consolidation will be the development of state-wide bargaining of minimal economic standards between a "multi-employer" school board association on the one hand and an NEA or AFT bargaining team on the other.

Institutional roadblocks in the way of such a centralized bargaining structure are admittedly formidable. However, there appears to be no effective alternative. To obtain some reliable first-hand information on these matters I consulted a knowledgeable colleague, Richard P. Manatt, professor of education in Iowa State's College of Education. Professor Manatt advised me in July, 1970, that under current conditions a school district with less than 1,500 pupils cannot be supported adequately on either economic or pedagogical grounds. Per pupil costs of administration and teaching in districts that are "too small" are soaring out of sight in Iowa and elsewhere, according to Manatt. Iowa still has 455 school districts, notwithstanding an extensive amount of recent school consolidation. At least 100 of the 455 can no longer be justified on economic and educational grounds. The number of small districts will decline sharply in the 1970s, but the pace will probably not be swift enough. Many districts will struggle along with an insufficient pupil base to permit appropriate instruction and administration.

In Professor Manatt's view, the ultimate solution lies in "massive" state financial support, accompanied by bargaining for minimum salary standards at the state level. The basic picture is a similar one in many other states. Economic logic will inexorably reshape the structure of governmental units as well as the structure of the bargaining relationships. Thus multi-employer bargaining on a state-wide basis appears to be in the cards in the near future. The resultant "master" agreements should cover only issues requiring uniform policy treatment, such as minimum salary levels for various categories. A wide range of discretion should remain for local district supplementary bargaining.

How to achieve these structural bargaining changes will not be treated here. The pain and discomfort associated with the structural transformation is likely to be considerable in some jurisdictions. Hopefully, school administrators and teacher bargaining agencies can make common cause on the need for creating a structural basis that will permit collective bargaining to satisfy simultaneously the educational needs of all pupils and the economic and professional goals of the teachers. *Pupil needs and teacher bargaining aspirations can be complementary.*

Many parallels exist between the collective bargaining drives of public school teachers and registered nurses. Teachers and RN's have many points in common as they seek to establish bargaining relationships with their employers. These include:

1. Both are clearly professional in nature by the strictest of definitions.
2. Both enjoy a generally good public image.
3. Historically pay levels for both have been low when one considers the nature and amount of education and training required for effective job performance.
4. Both face the need to combat the shibboleth that bargaining is somehow unprofessional.
5. Both experience difficulty in handling two key issues, the unit of representation and the scope of bargaining.
6. Both need to consider the sobering fact that their favorable image can vanish overnight if and when they resort to economic force to achieve their bargaining demands.

COLLECTIVE BARGAINING BY REGISTERED NURSES: A BRIEF ENCOUNTER

The American Nurses' Association has been encouraging its affiliates for some years to engage in collective bargaining as an effective process for furthering both economic and professional objectives. Collective bargaining by registered nurses was a logical next step growing out of the ANA's Economic Security Program, which the Association launched in 1946.

As in the case of the NEA, the ANA must reckon with the fact of lack of enthusiasm (or even opposition) on the part of many local units whose members believe that staying purely professional means avoiding collective bargaining. Such attitudes do not change rapidly, particularly in cases where hospitals and other employers of RN's have been sufficiently farsighted on their own to pay attractive salaries and to give nurses an effective voice in improving standards of patient care and working out an equitable allocation of functions between RN's on the one hand and LPN's and nurses' aides on the other. In many hospitals the chief factor pushing nurses toward collective bargaining has been frustration over the absence of any say-so on standards and procedures for patient care and related issues of a strictly professional nature.

A survey of current collective agreements in the nursing field reveals a wide variety in approaches to handling both economic and professional issues. Much depends on the nature and intensity of interest on the part of the nurses involved and also on the degree to which hospital administrators have been persuaded of the legitimacy of the nurses' bargaining objectives. There is no dearth of model contracts to emulate by those engaged in first-time bargaining. I am most familiar with agreements negotiated by the California Nurses' Association, which are perhaps more "advanced" than those in many other jurisdictions.[40] The CNA was the first of the state units to put a high priority on establishing collective bargaining relationships. ANA affiliates have been successful in achieving bargaining rights in many other jurisdictions, notably Illinois, Minnesota and New York. Experience under contracts with ANA units supports the ANA's firm stand on the compatibility of bargaining and professionalism.[41] The contracts I have seen constitute an intriguing mixture of fairly standard economic provisions (resembling union contract provisions in the private sector) and those tailored to the felt needs of nurses on purely professional matters relating to improving standards of patient care.

In hospitals where the nurses work under the terms of a collective agreement, there appears to be an atmosphere of confidence, personal security and self-respect that is often conspicuously absent where nurses have not sought bargaining rights or where their search has been unsuccessful to date. It must be extraordinarily difficult to be a true professional when one is working in an environment conditioned by a management philosophy that denies to nurses a right to a voice on concerns of either an economic or professional nature.

Predictably, the struggle of registered nurses for bargaining rights will continue to be a difficult one in many jurisdictions. Ultimately, the nurses should succeed as hospital administrators come to appreciate both the equities and the economics involved. The short supply of registered nurses in many jurisdictions should tip the scales in favor of bargaining. Yet in many cases there has been a strange unwillingness of the nurses to use the bargaining leverage inherent in the short supply situation. Such naivete will predictably come to an end. Also, the sophistication of hospital administrators should improve over time.

CONCLUSION: THE CLOUDED CRYSTAL BALL

The length of this chapter suggests the wisdom of not attempting to summarize the principal findings and observations. Instead we shall con-

---

[40] One of my former graduate students, Karen Hawley Dunlap, is director of research for the CNA. Mrs. Dunlap has been most gracious in accommodating my requests for current information on bargaining in California.

[41] Nothing in the literature suggests that experience with collective bargaining has caused the nurses involved to become any less professional toward their work.

clude with a brief forecast that may be more discussable than accurate. The dynamic, mixed state of public sector labor relations increases the risks of generalization. At the same time the temptation to do so is irresistible.

The available evidence suggests that unionization of government employees at all levels will continue for some years to come.[42] The initial momentum generated by E.O. 10988 appears to have been revived by E.O. 11491. The postal strike settlement of 1970 also will have spin-off effects in terms of further unionization among federal employees.

At the state and local level, the brisk pace of unionization will continue. The growing pains of initial collective bargaining efforts should diminish as government agency management and union representatives acquire greater sophistication and skill in dealing with one another. The currently discouraging combination of unreasoning fear, ineptitude and ignorance still prevalent in government management circles should yield ultimately to more informed and rational responses to the new bargaining challenges. Improving management attitudes and performance should in turn produce more "responsible" union or association bargaining demands.

The multiplicity of varied legislative approaches to public sector labor relations should begin to shake down into something approaching a consensus pattern as to the most appropriate statutory framework. The Pennsylvania and Hawaii statutes can be viewed as the first evidence of an appreciation of the point that strikes are not prevented merely by declaring them to be unlawful.

Frustration arising from the unsuitability of many governmental structures for collective bargaining will be a powerful factor in inducing long overdue governmental reorganization. The beneficial effects from restructuring will extend far beyond the immediate needs of those at the bargaining table.

To sum up, during the 1970s public sector labor relations will evolve hopefully into a less controversial, confusing and volatile state. However, considerable difficulty will be entailed in achieving stability and maturity in both contract negotiation and administration. Although instant sophistication is unlikely, there is encouraging evidence that both agency management and employee representatives are jointly determined in some cases to move as quickly as possible from the confrontation stage to the level of mutual accommodation. The immediate picture reveals continued hostility, confusion and uncertainty in many cases. Nevertheless, the prospects for achieving comparatively stable relations over the next few years appear reasonably bright.

The accuracy of such an optimistic forecast depends on how effec-

---

[42] See Abraham L. Gitlow, "The Trade Union Prospect in the Coming Decade," *Labor Law Journal*, XXI (March, 1970), 131–58.

tively agency management and employee representatives develop labor relations attitudes, policies and procedures to satisfy their respective aspirations and requirements. Through surveying the history of private sector experience they can, if they choose to do so, avoid many headaches by a judicious process of selection and avoidance. What is good for the UAW may not necessarily be good for the Iowa Nurses' Association. What works well in answering the needs of the rubber workers in Akron, Ohio, is probably not transferable as a means of answering problems faced by a bargaining unit of nonsupervisory employees of the Small Business Administration. Nevertheless, there is much of value that can be utilized. A policy of thoughtful eclecticism in choosing and rejecting from private sector experience offers the quickest, least painful avenue to mature public sector labor relations.

SELECTED BIBLIOGRAPHY

ANDERSON, HOWARD J., ed., *Public Employee Organization and Bargaining*. Washington, D.C.: The Bureau of National Affairs, Inc., 1968.

BILIK, AL, "Toward Public Sector Equality: Extending the Strike Privilege," *Labor Law Journal*, XXI (June, 1970), 338–56.

BLUM, ALBERT A., ed., *Teacher Unions and Associations: A Comparative Study*. Urbana, Ill.: University of Illinois Press, 1969.

BROWN, MARTHA A., "Collective Bargaining on the Campus: Professors, Associations and Unions," *Labor Law Journal*, XXI (March, 1970), 167–81.

BURTON, JOHN F., Jr., and Charles Krider, "The Role and Consequences of Strikes by Public Employees," *Yale Law Journal*, LXXIX (January, 1970), 418–40.

CARSON, JOHN J., AND JON SWANSON, "Collective Bargaining in the Public Service and the Effect on the Private Sector," *Canadian Personnel & Industrial Relations Journal*, XIV (May, 1967), 11–21.

CLARK, R. THEODORE, JR., *Drafting the Public Sector Labor Agreement*. Chicago, Ill.: Public Personnel Association, 1969.

———, "Public Employee Labor Legislation: A Study of the Unsuccessful Attempt to Enact a Public Employee Bargaining Statute in Illinois," *Labor Law Journal*, XX (March, 1969), 164–73.

CLARY, JACK R., "Pitfalls of Collective Bargaining in Public Employment," *Labor Law Journal*, XVIII (July, 1967), 406–11.

COLE, STEPHEN, "Teachers' Strike: A Study of the Conversion of Predisposition into Action," *American Journal of Sociology*, LXXIV (March, 1969), 506–20.

DAVEY, HAROLD W., "The Use of Neutrals in the Public Sector," *Labor Law Journal*, XX (August, 1969), 529–38.

DERBER, MILTON, "Labor-Management Policy for Public Employees in Illinois: The Experience of the Governor's Commission, 1966–1967," *Industrial and Labor Relations Review*, XXI (July, 1968), 541–58.

DOHERTY, ROBERT E., "Determination of Bargaining Units and Election Procedures in Public School Teacher Representation Elections," *Industrial and Labor Relations Review*, XIX (July, 1966), 573–95.

———, and Walter E. Oberer, *Teachers, School Boards, and Collective Bargaining: A*

Changing of the Guard. Ithaca, N.Y.: New York State School of Industrial and Labor Relations, 1967.

DOLE, R. F., JR., "State and Local Public Employee Collective Bargaining in the Absence of Explicit Legislative Authorization," *Iowa Law Review*, LIV (February, 1969), 539–59.

DONOIAN, HARRY A., "Organizational Problems of Government Employee Unions," *Labor Law Journal*, XVIII (March, 1967), 137–44.

ELAM, STANLEY M., MYRON LIEBERMAN AND MICHAEL H. MOSKOW, comps. *Readings on Collective Negotiations in Public Education.* Chicago, Ill.: Rand McNally & Company, 1967.

FERGUSON, TRACY H., "Collective Bargaining in Universities and Colleges," *Labor Law Journal*, XIX (December, 1968), 778–804.

GARBARINO, JOSEPH W., "Professional Negotiations in Education," *Industrial Relations*, VII (February, 1968), 93–106.

GERHART, PAUL F., "The Scope of Bargaining in Local Government Labor Negotiations," *Labor Law Journal*, XX (August, 1969), 545–52.

HAAK, HAROLD H., *Collective Bargaining and Academic Governance: The Case of the California State College.* San Diego, Cal.: Public Affairs Research Institute, San Diego State College, 1968.

HANSLOWE, KURT L., *The Emerging Law of Labor Relations in Public Employment.* Ithaca, N.Y.: New York State School of Industrial and Labor Relations, 1967.

HART, WILSON R., *Collective Bargaining in the Federal Civil Service.* New York: Harper & Row, Publishers, 1961.

———, "The Impasse in Labor Relations in the Federal Civil Service," *Industrial and Labor Relations Review*, XIX (January, 1966), 175–89.

HAWLEY, KAREN SUE, *Economics of Collective Bargaining by Nurses.* Ames, Ia.: Iowa State University Press, 1967.

KIENAST, PHILIP, "Extended Leisure for Blue Collar Workers: A Look at the Steelworker's Extended Vacation Program," *Labor Law Journal*, XX (October, 1969), 641–48.

KLEINGARTNER, ARCHIE, *Professionalism and Salaried Worker Organization.* Madison, Wis.: Industrial Relations Research Institute, University of Wisconsin, 1967.

———, "Nurses, Collective Bargaining and Labor Legislation," *Labor Law Journal*, XVIII (April, 1967), 236–45.

KRINSKY, EDWARD B., "Public Employment Fact-Finding in Fourteen States," *Labor Law Journal*, XVII (September, 1966), 532–40.

———, "Avoiding Public Employee Strikes—Lessons from Recent Strike Activity," *Labor Law Journal*, XXI (August, 1970), 464–72.

KRUGER, DANIEL H., AND CHARLES T. SCHMIDT, *Collective Bargaining in the Public Service.* New York: Random House, Inc., 1969.

LAW NOTE, "Collective Bargaining and the Professional Employee," *Columbia Law Review* LXIX (February, 1969), 277–98.

LEFKOWITZ, JEROME, "The Taylor Law, Discrimination and Nontenured Teachers," *Labor Law Journal*, XX (September, 1969), 575–80.

LIEBERMAN, MYRON, AND MICHAEL H. MOSKOW, *Collective Negotiations for Teachers: An Approach to School Administration.* Chicago, Ill.: Rand McNally & Company, 1966.

LOVE, THOMAS M., "Joint Committees: Their Role in the Development of Teacher Bargaining," *Labor Law Journal*, XX (March, 1969), 174–83.

MAYER, MARTIN, *The Teachers Strike: New York, 1968.* New York: Harper and Row, Publishers, 1968.

McKELVEY, JEAN T., "The Role of State Agencies in Public Employee Labor Relations," *Industrial and Labor Relations Review*, XX (January, 1967), 179–97.

McLAUGHLIN, RICHARD P., "Collective Bargaining Suggestions for the Public Sector," *Labor Law Journal*, XX (March, 1969), 131–37.

MOSKOW, MICHAEL H., "Collective Bargaining for Public School Teachers," *Labor Law Journal*, XV (December, 1964), 787–94.

———, *Teachers and Unions: The Applicability of Collective Bargaining to Public Education*. Philadelphia, Pa.: Wharton School of Finance and Commerce, 1966.

NIGRO, FELIX A., ed., "Symposium on Collective Negotiations in the Public Service," *Public Administration Review*, XXVII (March–April, 1968), 111–47.

RINGER, JAMES M., "Legality and Propriety of Agreements to Arbitrate Major and Minor Disputes in Public Employment," *Cornell Law Review*, LIV (November, 1968), 129–44.

SHILS, EDWARD B., AND C. TAYLOR WHITTIER, *Teachers, Administrators, and Collective Bargaining*. New York: Thomas Y. Crowell, 1968.

STERN, JAMES L., "The Wisconsin Public Employee Fact-Finding Procedure," *Industrial and Labor Relations Review*, XX (October, 1966), 3–29.

STURMTHAL, ADOLF F., ed., *White-Collar Trade Unions: Comtemporary Developments in Industrialized Societies*. Urbana, Ill.: University of Illinois Press, 1966.

TAYLOR, GEORGE W., "Public Employment: Strikes or Procedures?" *Industrial and Labor Relations Review*, XX (July, 1967), 617–36.

THOMPSON, ARTHUR A., "Collective Bargaining in the Public Service: The TVA Experience and Its Implications for Other Government Agencies," *Labor Law Journal*, XVII (February, 1966), 89–98.

U.S. DEPARTMENT OF LABOR, Bureau of Labor Statistics, *Work Stoppages in Government, 1958–68* (Report No. 348). Washington, D.C.: Department of Labor, 1970.

VOSLOO, WILLEM B., *Collective Bargaining in the United States Federal Civil Service*. Chicago, Ill.: Public Personnel Association, 1966.

WAGNER, AUBREY J., "TVA Looks at Three Decades of Collective Bargaining," *Industrial and Labor Relations Review*, XXII (October, 1968), 20–30.

WARNER, KENNETH O., ed., *Collective Bargaining in the Public Service: Theory and Practice*. Chicago, Ill.: Public Personnel Association, 1967.

———, and Mary L. Hennessy, *Public Management at the Bargaining Table*. Chicago, Ill.: Public Personnel Association, 1967.

WEISENFELD, ALLAN, "Public Employees Are Still Second Class Citizens," *Labor Law Journal*, XX (March, 1969), 138–50.

WOLLETT, DONALD H., "The Public Employee at the Bargaining Table: Promise or Illusion?" *Labor Law Journal*, XV (January, 1964), 8–15.

———, and Robert H. Chanin, *The Law and Practice of Teacher Negotiations*. Washington, D.C.: The Bureau of National Affairs, Inc., 1970.

ZACK, ARNOLD M., "Why Public Employees Strike," *Arbitration Journal*, XXIII, no. 2 (1968), 69–84.

COLLECTIVE BARGAINING
IN PERSPECTIVE

CHAPTER FOURTEEN

Many challenges to collective bargaining as a process and the nature of the responses to these challenges have been evaluated in earlier chapters. In these concluding pages we must be mindful once again of the heterogeneous character of collective bargaining relationships. No summary overview can reflect faithfully the entire collective bargaining spectrum.

It is always easy to view with alarm. All this requires is listing some conspicuous collective bargaining failures and then somberly concluding that the process is doomed. It is also easy (and equally misleading) to describe several success stories and then to conclude that all goes well. The whole objective truth about how collective bargaining is working defies summary analysis. However, it is possible to pull some of the major strands together in the interest of an improved perspective.

A logical approach involves taking an inventory of collective bar-

380

gaining accomplishments and shortcomings. This summary is based on both academic study and practical experience as a grievance arbitrator. Arbitration can give one a true reading of the pulse of collective bargaining. It has frequently served to reinforce my faith in the continued viability of collective bargaining.[1] Yet I have witnessed enough labor relations failures to avoid any soaring generalizations as to the perfected permanence of collective bargaining.

COLLECTIVE BARGAINING AS A PRAGMATIC PROCESS

Much criticism of collective bargaining comes from frustrated idealists or crusaders who expect too much from the process. Criticism also comes from those who think collective bargaining has worked too well, that is, that unions are too powerful. Such critics yearn for the days when unions were weak or nonexistent. In this analysis we have not been concerned particularly about criticisms from these two camps. The focus has remained on how collective bargaining is working for those who utilize it conscientiously as a method of determining the price of labor and other conditions of employment.

Collective bargaining is not championed as an ideal system by anyone close to the scene. At best it is an imperfect institutional process that works reasonably well in an imperfect society. It is the best we have. No one up to now has come forth with any alternative procedure that will work any better.

Collective bargaining is necessarily a pragmatic process. The standards for its evaluation should also be pragmatic. We are concerned mainly with two questions: (1) How well has collective bargaining worked? (2) Where it has not worked well, what is needed for its improvement? These questions are central to the analysis and this summary statement.

Although perfection is not a realistic goal, *striving for improvement* is an imperative for a constructive employer-union relationship. Experienced good faith bargainers understand intuitively that *change is a pragmatic necessity* if collective bargaining is to continue to perform effectively. The distinctive characteristic of a progressive and mature collective bargaining relationship is the capacity to adapt and to stay attuned to changing requirements at the micro-economic level. There must also be an awareness of the need to follow policies and procedures that will be complementary with national goals and aspirations.

---

[1] The phrase is borrowed from a 1965 article. See Harold W. Davey, "The Continuing Viability of Collective Bargaining," *Labor Law Journal*, XVIII (February, 1965), 111–22.

Collective bargaining performance regarded as effective for current requirements can become outmoded rather quickly if the parties should fail to adjust to changed conditions and circumstances. Collective bargaining can become a failure if the joint willingness and ability to adapt should somehow be lost along the way. For example, bargaining in the construction field has been justifiably under severe fire on two main counts: (1) blithe disregard for the inflationary impact of outsized wage settlements and (2) slowness in admitting blacks to union membership in metropolitan centers. For these reasons, collective bargaining in this industry has been labeled a failure by some critics.[2]

My inventory of pluses and minuses for collective bargaining will now be set forth in outline fashion.

PLUS FACTORS FOR CONTEMPORARY COLLECTIVE BARGAINING

1. Effective approaches to solution of such continuing problems as adjustment to technological change through joint study committees and other negotiated approaches to job security matters.

2. Improved caliber of both management and union negotiators and contract administrators; acknowledgement of the professional and technical character of the labor relations task; increasing availability and use of reliable data in negotiating economic issues.

3. Joint awareness that collective bargaining can no longer be a matter of solely bilateral concern, but is a process that requires recognition of the public stake in responsible contract negotiation and administration.

Specific developments illustrating the foregoing factors include the following:

---

[2] The available recent evidence shows the major construction unions moving with something less than deliberate speed in admitting blacks to apprenticeship programs and to union membership, although there has been much brave talk (and some action) in the late 1960s. In 1970 the debate centered on the merits of the "Philadelphia Plan," favored by the Nixon Administration, involving commitments by contractors to meet or exceed set quotas of blacks on federal construction projects. The quota concept, related to the percentage of blacks in the population as a whole, has been vigorously opposed by George Meany and other AFL-CIO leaders who favor voluntary black employment agreements between contractors and the affected unions, as exemplified in the "Chicago Plan."

Neither the Philadelphia Plan nor the Chicago Plan appears to be living up to the rhetoric of supporters in terms of visibly satisfying the job placement demands of the blacks. The most telling indictment of the quota approach, to my mind, is that it is likely to enforce discrimination in reverse. The most effective immediate answer to the understandable frustrations of the blacks lies in tough uncompromising application of the fair employment provisions of the Civil Rights Act of 1964; in full use of presidential executive order authority; and last but by no means least, in an aggressive educational campaign among the members of the unions concerned.

a. widespread use of long-term (usually three-year) contracts;

b. nearly universal utilization of binding arbitration for final disposition of grievances raising issues of contract interpretation or application, with no-strike clauses congruent with the arbitrator's authority under the contract; and

c. some evidence of growing inclination to utilize binding arbitration on future terms issues in both the private and public sector.

4. Improved contract administration on such formerly troublesome issues as arbitrability, subcontracting, intrafirm wage structure problems, equitable distribution of overtime and the role of seniority in relation to layoffs, recalls and promotions. (*Note*: Cases still arise on these issues but at a more sophisticated level. Many formerly tough issues have been resolved by better contract language.)

5. Many employers and unions are no longer at odds over union security and scope of bargaining. The union shop prevails. A satisfactory *modus vivendi* has been reached on what is bargainable. The parties have stopped looking over their shoulders to see what is the newest NLRB ruling in the *Borg-Warner* line.

6. The parties are becoming more adept in the demanding task of contract administration. I have been pleased to witness marked improvement in both preparation and presentation of arbitration cases in a wide variety of industries. Few cases in recent years have been easy to decide. This condition I attribute to more effective screening by both management and union.

7. Today's contracts are generally marked by substantial improvement in clarity and force of language. The evidence is convincing that contracts *do change over time* in response to changing conditions.

These favorable developments suggest that the performance record of collective bargaining is better than the torrent of critical comment might indicate. Granted that bargainers have performed poorly in some instances, the process has nevertheless worked rather well on the whole. The quietly successful employer-union relationships do not receive much attention or praise. There is a minus side of collective bargaining, however, that must be reviewed.

MINUS FACTORS IN CONTEMPORARY BARGAINING

1. Neither management nor union is yet prepared in some cases to develop a basis for stable mutual accommodation for the long pull. One party is often labeled as the "villain." Usually, however, neither party is entirely blameless. The NLRB's unfair practice caseload continues to be high. It is obvious that we still have many employers and labor organizations that still are unwilling to observe the law of labor relations.

2. A low level of professionalism exists in some important employer-union relationships. Whenever inept negotiation or irresponsible brinkmanship results in an unnecessary strike, the image of collective bargaining as a whole suffers. This is particularly true when a strike inflicts serious economic losses on noncombatants and causes inconvenience to the public at large.

3. Excessive arbitration continues to be the rule in some relationships. This generally reflects either hostility or poor understanding of how to use arbitration as an instrument of contract administration. Such a condition is doubly unfortunate when there is a serious shortage of competent, experienced and acceptable arbitrators.

4. Employers and unions in some cases have failed to modernize their contracts by eliminating outmoded provisions. To stay competitive most employers need to stay loose in terms of freedom to change methods, introduce new equipment and restructure plant layout. Union concern over the job rights of incumbent employees is one thing, but stubborn refusal to scrap outmoded working rules endangers collective bargaining as a process.

5. Employee rejection of negotiated contract settlements is creating serious difficulties in a number of industries. In some cases such rejection may be a healthy reaction to excessive power centralization and an encouraging example of participatory democracy at work. Too often, however, such rejection of negotiated settlements reflects unrealistic rank-and-file aspirations.[3]

6. Wildcat strikes are presenting a serious problem in some relationships where it was formerly the custom to utilize the grievance and arbitration machinery. Employers are not getting the uninterrupted production span of the contract's lifetime for which many of them have paid a stiff price in economic benefits.

7. In some cases there is evidence of rigid adherence to patterns set in other bargaining relationships instead of attempting to negotiate "custom-made" contracts better suited to the particular needs and requirements of the employer and union in question. Using language or policies from other contracts frequently does not work well when application is attempted in a management-union situation for which they were not originally devised.

8. Bargaining in some cases remains on a strictly short-run horizon. Little attention has been paid to long-range problems that need study on a continuing basis.

9. The potential of joint efforts to increase productivity and lower unit labor costs has been largely ignored. Related to such disinterest is a

---

[3] It would be interesting to ascertain what percentage of the rejections of negotiated settlements can be attributed mainly to anti-establishment sentiments of the membership rather than to disappointment with settlement terms as such.

continuing lack of concern over the macro-economic impact of micro-economic decision-making. The focus of most bargainers remains bilateral. The public interest in responsible and constructive bargaining has not become a significant factor in the parties' assessments of their bargaining posture and demands.

10. An insufficiency of "creative" bargaining can be noted in many cases where innovation is urgently required. In the public sector we can hope that the necessities may prove to be the mothers of invention where private sector experience is not readily or happily transferable.

The Unfinished Business of Collective Bargaining

This inventory of pluses and minuses reveals that there is much unfinished business for many employers and unions. In fact, collective bargaining is never finished. Working out a durably satisfactory pattern of accommodation requires change as our social and economic imperatives continue to evolve and shift.

The term "unfinished business" can be applied to problem areas where collective bargaining can play an effective role but where the performance record in many cases has not been conspicuously successful.

We can do a better job in meeting such challenges as the following:

1. Negotiating special provisions for assimilation into the work force of hard-core unemployed.[4]
2. Opening up construction jobs and union membrship to blacks on a truly nondiscriminatory basis.[5]
3. Coping jointly with the serious problems posed by clogged grievance procedures and the critical shortage of competent, experienced and acceptable neutrals in both the public and private sectors.

---

[4] As noted earlier in Chapter 9, many employers and unions have made a concerted effort along these lines. Worthy of special note in this connection are the efforts by the National Alliance of Businessmen, sparked by the personal leadership of Henry Ford II. For a graphic recent account of these efforts, see *Time*, July 20, 1970, pp. 62–68.

[5] The sobering complex of factors that contribute to making even vigorous black recruitment efforts fall short of black leaders' expectations are evaluated in detached and candid fashion by Derek C. Bok and John T. Dunlop, *Labor and the American Community* (New York: Simon and Schuster, Inc., 1970), pp. 116–37. Bok and Dunlop conclude that "it is probably correct to say that greater progress has been made in securing equal opportunity in employment than in any other field of American life" (*ibid.*, p. 136). It is tragically ironic when we find the eminent black authority on economic development, Sir W. Arthur Lewis, concluding that "the trade unions are the black man's greatest enemy in the United States" [*The New York Times Magazine*, May 11, 1969, as quoted in Abraham L. Gitlow, "The Trade Union Prospect in the Coming Decade," *Labor Law Journal*, XXI (March, 1970), p. 148]. Although the facts do not support Sir Arthur's scathing indictment, his conclusion should give pause to any union or union leader who thinks enough has been done in this critical problem area.

4. Negotiating specially tailored provisions for handling complex problems related to plant removals and closings and the job dislocations caused by technological change.
5. Establishing rigorous programs to develop line supervisors and local union officials trained to exercise full discretion in grievance disposition instead of passing the decisional buck up the line.
6. Development of special education awareness programs for supervisors, employees and local union leaders related to explaining public impatience with strikes, slowdowns, wildcats, featherbedding and similar phenomena that continue to give collective bargaining a poor image in laymen's eyes.

Another focus of such "awareness" education should be on such matters as:

7. Improved employee self-discipline in terms of honoring both the spirit and letter of contract requirements on job performance standards, reduction of absenteeism or unexcused absences, regular use of grievance procedure, elimination of discriminatory attitudes or conduct in relation to race or sex in particular and so forth.
8. Improved supervisory understanding of the role of unionism and the multiple pressures operating upon local and international union leaders.
9. Joint concern for avoiding use of economic force by greater stress on bargaining out rational, viable solutions to all disputed matters and then jointly determining to assert and maintain the primacy—in fact, the supremacy—of the collective agreement for its duration.
10. Jointly striving to improve the understanding of the community as to what can properly be expected from collective bargaining and what problems are not suitable for resolution by collective bargaining.

POSITIVE COLLECTIVE BARGAINING: A REVISED STATEMENT

In both previous editions I outlined the essential ingredients for a *positive, affirmative* collective bargaining relationship.

The 1951 statement was retained with only minor editorial changes in 1959. In the present restatement, most of the components of positive collective bargaining remain the same as in 1951 and 1959. However, the many changes in labor relations since 1959 have added some new dimensions. A fresh statement is thus required.

The summary review of the unfinished business of collective bargaining demonstrates that the challenge facing management and union practitioners of collective bargaining is perhaps more formidable than ever before. Fortunately, the ability to meet this challenge is greater than ever before. The 1970s will be a stern proving ground for constructive evolution in both public and private sector bargaining.

Answering the challenge most effectively, in my judgment, requires firm joint understanding and acceptance by management, union and the represented employees of certain basic concepts set forth below:

1. Collective bargaining henceforth must be viewed as a process with a trilateral and not strictly bilateral perspective. Conscious effort must be devoted to adapting private decision-making to the goals and purposes of public policy. The freedom of discretion desired and needed by employers and unions can only be preserved through successful efforts to devetail negotiated policies with governmental goals in such matters as:

   a. absorbing disadvantaged persons into the work force, as discussed in Chapter 9;
   b. making economic packages consistent with price stability and real wage maintenance, as discussed in Chapter 11;
   c. gearing negotiated health and welfare plans into a national system of prepaid medical care and health insurance;
   d. adapting negotiated income maintenance plans to national unemployment insurance programs and adapting negotiated retirement plans to federal old-age insurance programs, as noted in Chapter 12;
   e. ensuring consistency between negotiated antidiscrimination provisions and state and federal policies in this field;
   f. revising working rules and seniority practices to make effective use of federal payments for on-the-job training of new employees.

These are representative illustrations of how private decision-making can be consciously geared to governmental policy for the long-run benefit of the community as a whole.

2. Developing the recommended trilateral focus will require some basic changes in how most employers and unions think of their roles in the collective bargaining process. In conventional bargaining management frequently assumes a defensive posture, reacting to the union initiative at contract renegotiation time. The trilateral orientation calls for much more than acting and reacting. Joint committees are needed for study and action on long-range employer and union goals. Future manpower needs and future economic objectives must be anticipated. Both parties can then be better prepared to negotiate necessary changes in the contract in line with the findings of joint committees.

Most employers will need to rethink their customary stance on managerial prerogatives and take a more flexible view on the scope of collective bargaining. Management will be assuming more initiative in advancing proposals of its own. It will not be waiting to react defensively to whatever the union may demand. By the same token, union leaders may be expected to think more imaginatively about *their* roles than they have been accustomed to doing. One example of what I have in mind would be to discard the stereotyped charge of "bargaining backward" whenever management proposes a change in job mix or job assignments in favor of giving such proposals careful consideration *on their merits*. The labor relations scene can no longer tolerate obstructionism for the sake of obstructionism. The Sheet Metal Workers' rejection of the national railroad settlement, which their representatives and those of three other unions had agreed upon, is a case in point.[6]

3. The trilateral orientation also calls for changed management and union thinking on usage of neutrals in both negotiation and administration of contracts. Specifically, the proposed joint long-range planning committee could include one or more neutrals as part of its staffing. An important role for the neutral would be to serve as representative of the public or community viewpoint whenever employer and union representatives were formulating private policy with public policy implications. Use of neutrals in this way requires complete rethinking of everybody's role on the management and union side of the bargaining table. The results *could be* impressive.

The use of neutrals in contract administration would require few departures from current thinking. The principal goal would be greater progress toward optimal use of grievance arbitration as suggested in Chapter 7. Neutrals utilized in the planning and contract negotiation phases could also be used for private mediation of future terms disputes. This might reduce still further the resort to economic force for resolving "interests" disputes. The potential of *voluntarily adopted* final and binding arbitration on future terms issues should be considered seriously by the parties in key bargaining relationships. Such unquestioned friends of the collective bargaining process as Arvid Anderson and Jack Stieber are taking a more receptive view of future terms arbitration. Stieber observes that many employers and unions are re-examining their attitudes.[7]

4. Finally, if collective bargaining is to stress the positive approach, there must be genuine belief in the expanding potential of the bargaining process. This requires ungrudging acceptance of the union by management and recognition by the union of certain management imperatives, such as the need to increase productivity and lower unit labor costs wherever possible. Such a focus on expanding collective bargaining horizons must be accompanied by a realization that collective bargaining is not a panacea for all of society's ills. The main effort will continue to be on the improved utilization of collective bargaining as an instrument for maintaining at the micro-economic level a functional balance between the requirements of stability and accommodation to the dynamics of technological and social

---

[6] It is not my intention to single out railroad unionism as such. However, the railroad industry does appear to have more than its share of cases of negative bargaining.

[7] See Jack Stieber's paper in the 1970 National Academy of Arbitrators *Proceedings* volume, edited by Gerald A. Somers and published by the Bureau of National Affairs, Inc., Washington, D.C.

change. Nevertheless, there needs to be an increased appreciation of the need to utilize collective bargaining in *new joint ventures*.

Positive collective bargaining calls for a high order of rationality, intelligence and social vision on the part of all concerned with the bargaining process, *including the employees themselves*.[8] Nothing proposed in this section can work well if there is a failure to reach out to the bargaining unit employees in such a way as to make each one of them appreciate and support what is contemplated by management and union leadership. The special orientation needed for "regular" employees in programs to assimilate disadvantaged persons illustrates the magnitude of the educational task confronting those who seek to achieve positive collective bargaining as here described.

The Future of Collective Bargaining

Achieving positive collective bargaining will not be easy for anyone. Some of the suggested specifics will be neither possible nor necessary for many small employers and union locals. However, the proposed trilateral focus *can* be used by all who bargain collectively. The degree of implementation can be geared to the abilities of the particular employer-union relationship. The major bargaining "empires" such as steel, automobiles, railroading and the like can and should adopt the full range of trilateralism. Only in this fashion can the full potential and *guaranteed continued privacy* of collective bargaining be assured. There is nothing sacred about collective bargaining as a process. It will not endure forever in its conventional stance. Continued viability depends on continued adaptation to social and economic needs. The real threat of public collectivization can be met effectively only by more imaginative and responsible use of the full range of current private discretion. The future of collective bargaining as an institutional mechanism for private decision-making on wages, hours and other conditions of employment depends on how well the bargainers face up to the challenges analyzed in earlier chapters and how successfully they meet the demanding goals of positive bargaining suggested here in conclusion.

Success is by no means certain, but the situation does not justify a resigned acceptance of a takeover by the public leviathan. *What is needed is a realistic recognition of the community of interest on many vital points between private*

---

[8] When referring to new joint ventures to involve the employees themselves, I am forcibly reminded of how little has been done in the United States with the union-management cooperation plan discussed in Chapter 11. Providing for such plans through collective bargaining might serve to fire the imagination of many younger workers who claim to be "turned off" both by the employer and union "establishments." The individual worker's sense of participation and involvement could be increased without in any way detracting from the basic objectives of collective bargaining as a process.

needs and public policy. Determined action by negotiators along the lines suggested in the preceding pages can produce a more effective "mix" of private discretion and public policy than we have witnessed so far. The ability to act courageously and imaginatively is present. Today's negotiators and contract administrators are far better informed and more "professional" than their predecessors of ten or twenty years ago. They have succeeded already in overcoming some previously troublesome problems of conventional bargaining. There is no reason to suppose that they cannot move beyond conventional policies and toward the kind of joint forward progress required by positive collective bargaining and the needs of the community at large.

Collective bargaining remains the most valid institutional approach for strengthening the essential components of our private enterprise system while at the same time enhancing the dignity and freedom of the individual worker in our society. Assuming that we wish to strengthen the role of the individual through a democratized system of labor relations in both the private and governmental sectors, the energy and imagination of all concerned will be needed to effectuate the conversion from conventional to positive bargaining. The alternatives to such an effort are not pleasant to contemplate.

NAME INDEX

SUBJECT INDEX

H

Health and welfare bargaining, 319, 325-27 (*See also* Economic package bargaining):
federalizing health care, 319
rising cost problem, 326
trends in, 327
typical package, 318, 325
Holidays with pay, 332-33
"Hot cargo" clauses, 62
Hourly rate problems (*See* Day work problems)
Hughes Tool doctrine, 72 (*See also* Public policy)

I

Incentive wage payments (*See* Wage determination under Collective bargaining)
Income security plans, 328-30 (*See also* Economic package bargaining)
Industrial conflict, 191-214 (*See also* Future terms disputes, Government employee bargaining, Public policy)
Industrial jurisprudence, 215-49 (*See also* Job security problems)
definition of, 6-7
disciplinary cases, 218-28
job security and, 217
seniority as illustration of, 228-36
standards, single or double?, 226
Inflation (*See* National economic policy)
"Inflation alerts" (*See* National economic policy)
Inter-union raiding, futility of, 35-36

J

"Jawboning" (*See* National economic policy)
Job evaluation (*See* Wage determination under Collective bargaining)
Job security problems, 9-10, 215-49 (*See also* Industrial jurisprudence)
automation, a special form of technological change, 244
disadvantaged workers, special procedures for, 222-27
discipline and discharge issues, 218-22
industrial jurisprudence, elements of, 217-18
premium pay provisions as related to, 241-42
racial discrimination issues, 226-27
subcontracting, impact on job opportunities, 239-41

technological change, adjusting to, 236-39
work rules, revision of, 242-44
Joint study committees, 113-14, 126

L

Laissez faire unionization, 46-49

M

Mallinckrodt doctrine on craft severance, 33-35
Management functions (*See* Management rights)
Management rights:
administrative initiative in exercise of, 110-12
alternative theories of, 104-10
consultation and joint study committees, 112-14
controversy over, 101-14
scope of bargaining and, 102-4
union role as challenger to, 112
Management rights clauses, pros and cons, 108
Meat packing:
interplant transfer policy in, 234-35
job security issues in, 10
pattern bargaining in, 18
Model bargainers, characteristics of, 22-23
Multi-employer bargaining, 37-46 (*See also* Bargaining units)
case against, 42-44
case for, 41-42
empirical evidence on, 37-40

N

National economic policy and collective bargaining, 290-315:
collective bargaining policies consistent with, 295-99
goals of, 291
"inflation alerts," 307
"jawboning," 304-5
productivity gains bargaining, 302-3
proposed annual conference, 305-7
"public interest" bargaining, 298-99
union-management cooperation plans as aid to, 299-303
wage-price guideposts, 307-14
AFL-CIO opposition to, 310-12
impact of, 312-13
reasons for failure of, 308-12
resurrection of?, 313-14